THE CONSTITUTION OF THE ENVIRONMENTAL EMERGENCY

This book argues that environmental issues constitute an ongoing emergency for the purpose of theorising the relationship between law, legality and environmental governance. Like emergencies, environmental issues possess two salient epistemic features: the inability to know in advance which issues contain the possibility of catastrophe and the inability to know in advance what to do in response to a catastrophe. These features undermine the assumption that law can be equated with predetermined legal rules set out by the legislature and enforced by the courts. By developing a framework based on the concept of the environmental emergency, the book reveals and critiques the assumptions about law contained in existing accounts of environmental law. It then offers a theory of the rule of law that requires public officials to publicly justify their decisions on the basis of core common law constitutional principles, namely reasonableness and fairness.

The book draws out connections between common law constitutionalism and theories of deliberative democracy in order to develop an account of how the administrative state can be governed by a democratic conception of the rule of law, taking into account the special challenges posed by environmental issues. The crux of this account is that it respects and enables the autonomy of individuals, understood as rational and self-determining agents, and their capacity to actively participate in environmental governance. By requiring public officials to publicly justify their decisions in terms that those subject to the law can understand and reasonably accept, this deliberative-democratic and common law constitutional account allows citizens to obey or contest the law. It thereby enables their participation in the project of articulating and re-articulating core constitutional principles.

The book elaborates how the requirement of public justification enables a deeper, more coherent understanding of how creative institutional design and environmental principles such as precaution and sustainable development enable the maintenance of the rule of law in light of the ongoing environmental emergency. It argues, moreover, that this theory of the rule of law provides a promising foundation for meaningful constitutional environmental rights adjudication. Through an examination of several Canadian examples of controversial natural resource and energy regulation contexts, this book envisions an environmental jurisprudence that is deliberative, reasoned and always mindful of our vulnerability to catastrophic environmental harm.

The Constitution of the Environmental Emergency

Jocelyn Stacey

• HART •
OXFORD • LONDON • NEW YORK • NEW DELHI • SYDNEY

HART PUBLISHING

Bloomsbury Publishing Plc

Kemp House, Chawley Park, Cumnor Hill, Oxford, OX2 9PH, UK

First published in Great Britain 2018

A catalogue record for this book is available from the British Library.

Library of Congress Cataloging-in-Publication data

Names: Stacey, Jocelyn, author.

Title: The constitution of the environmental emergency / Jocelyn Stacey.

Description: Portland, Oregon : Hart Publishing, 2018. | Includes bibliographical references and index.

Identifiers: LCCN 2017054353 (print) | LCCN 2017055292 (ebook) | ISBN 9781509920280 (Epub) | ISBN 9781509920273 (hardback : alk. paper)

Subjects: LCSH: Environmental law. | Law—Philosophy. | Environmental protection. | Environmental disasters. | Disasters—Risk assessment.

Classification: LCC K3585 (ebook) | LCC K3585 .S865 2018 (print) | DDC 344.04/6—dc23

LC record available at https://lccn.loc.gov/2017054353

ISBN: HB: 978-1-50992-027-3
ePDF: 978-1-50992-029-7
ePub: 978-1-50992-028-0

Typeset by Compuscript Ltd, Shannon
Printed and bound in Great Britain by TJ International Ltd, Padstow, Cornwall

To find out more about our authors and books visit www.hartpublishing.co.uk. Here you will find extracts, author information, details of forthcoming events and the option to sign up for our newsletters.

Acknowledgements

This book is the product of my doctoral studies at the McGill Faculty of Law. I am tremendously fortunate to have had Evan Fox-Decent as my supervisor, who encouraged me to think much bigger than I ever would have thought possible. I benefited greatly from having two extremely dedicated committee members and mentors, Shauna Van Praagh and Hoi Kong. Thanks to Hoi in particular for his patience and guidance as I worked through the arguments in chapters three and five. The arguments in the book have also benefited from thorough feedback from the additional members of my thesis examining committee: Elizabeth Fisher, Jaye Ellis, Sara Seck and Johanne Poirier. Thanks to Sara Seck for her specific suggestion that I look into the Ontario wind turbine disputes, which ultimately led to chapter seven of this monograph. The ideas formulated in the thesis have been informed by many helpful conversations with members of the McGill Faculty of Law, my colleagues in the McGill doctor of civil law programme (in particular, Kate Glover, Dia Dabby, Bethany Hastie and Francis Lord), and more recently, my wonderful colleagues at the Allard School of Law. Thanks to my colleagues Margot Young and Mary Liston for their helpful feedback on chapter eight and to the excellent research assistance of Allard Law JD students Alexandra Catchpole, Robert Jones and Nicole Chan.

I benefited from feedback from audiences at the McGill Faculty of Law, Yale Law School, Australia National University College of Law, Centre for Deliberative Democracy and Global Governance, and the University of British Columbia Allard School of Law. As some of the arguments contained in this book are now published in the *Osgoode Hall Law Journal*, I would also like to acknowledge the comments and critiques offered by its external reviewers.

The research for this book was funded by a SSHRC Joseph Bombardier Canada Graduate Scholarship, the McGill Faculty of Law, and the Allard Prize Faculty Fund. Earlier versions of the arguments in this monograph have been published as 'The Environmental Emergency and the Legality of Discretion in Environmental Law' (2016) 52 *Osgoode Hall Law Journal* 983 and 'The Promise of the Rule of (Environmental) Law' (2016) 53 *Osgoode Hall Law Journal* 681. Some ideas explored in chapter six can be found in 'The Environmental, Democratic and Rule-of-Law Implications of Harper's Environmental Assessment Legacy' (2016) 21 *Review of Constitutional Studies* 165. The clarity of these arguments has been much improved by the careful eye of Lisa Gourd. Many thanks to her and the team at Hart Publishing for helping this monograph through its final stages.

Finally, to Ross and Cathy Stacey, thanks for your love and support right from the beginning. To Alice Woolley, thank you for encouraging me to pursue academia. I cannot imagine having taken this path were it not for your timely intervention during my LLB. I reserve my biggest thanks for Matthew Mitchell for your unwavering support. This book is for Harriet and Frederick in the hopes that you may inherit a world that is more reasoned, compassionate and ecologically sustainable than the one we currently inhabit.

Table of Contents

List of Acronyms

CEAA	Canadian Environmental Assessment Act
EBR	Environmental Bill of Rights (Ontario)
EPA	Environmental Protection Act (Ontario)
FPB	Forest Practices Board (British Columbia)
FRPA	Forest and Range Practices Act (British Columbia)
FSC	Forest Stewardship Council
GBRA	Great Bear Rainforest Agreement (British Columbia)
NEB	National Energy Board
NEBA	National Energy Board Act
REA	Renewable Energy Approval (Ontario)

Table of Legislation and Cases

Foreign Legislation

International Agreements

Jurisprudence

Foreign & International Jurisprudence

Tribunal Jurisprudence

Introduction

ENVIRONMENTAL LAW IS a vibrant, challenging and burgeoning field. It develops alongside rapidly evolving environmental science, spirited environmentalism and in response to the many pressing environmental problems we face today. Flip through the pages of any journal of environmental law and you will find countless ideas of how environmental law can be reformed to better secure environmental protection and myriad accounts of the ways in which past and current environmental laws have fallen and continue to fall short. What you are less likely to find, however, is sustained attention to the ways in which environmental issues strain some of our most basic assumptions about law.

This book distinguishes itself from most environmental law scholarship in that it does not attempt to solve any particular environmental problem. Rather, it articulates a theory of how the exercise of public authority can be governed by a democratic conception of the rule of law, elaborated, as it needs to be, for the special challenges posed by environmental issues. Environmental issues are in many ways an ideal perspective from which to revisit our assumptions about democracy, law, and the rule of law. One scholar has described environmental law as 'hot law' because 'the agreed frames, legal and otherwise, for how we understand and act in the world are in a constant state of flux and contestation'.[1] Environmental issues are complex in almost every way—scientifically, politically and disciplinarily. They challenge fundamental assumptions about what it means to be governed by law, which typically transpires through general, relatively stable rules enacted in advance by the legislature and interpreted by the courts. In other words, the complexity of environmental issues presents a fundamental problem for understanding how law can both constitute and constrain the state's regulative authority over the environment.

This book argues that the best way to understand the challenge that environmental issues pose for law is through the lens of an ongoing emergency. Like emergencies, environmental issues require decisions to be taken under conditions of deep uncertainty where the possibility of a catastrophe cannot be reliably eliminated in advance. We can thus glean important theoretical insights from legal theory on conventional emergencies to develop a better

[1] E Fisher, 'Environmental Law as "Hot" Law' (2013) 25 *Journal of Environmental Law* 347, 347–48. See also A Philippopoulos-Mihalopoulos, 'Looking for the Space between Law and Ecology' in A Philippopoulos-Mihalopoulos (ed), *Law and Ecology: New Environmental Foundations* (London, Routledge, 2011) 1 (on the radical potential of environmental law).

understanding of the relationship between law and environmental issues. The central challenge of emergencies is succinctly captured in the work of controversial Nazi legal theorist, Carl Schmitt. Schmitt argued that the unforeseeable, existential threat—the exception or emergency—necessitates unconstrained executive discretion. He argued, in other words, that the emergency cannot be governed by law. We will see that Schmitt's challenge and its potential responses provide the framework for understanding and responding to the challenge that environmental issues pose for law.

The book elaborates a concept of the 'environmental emergency': the idea that all environmental issues contain the constitutive features of an emergency. We will see these features arise from the complex, adaptive nature of ecological systems, which makes it impossible to reliably eliminate in advance the possibility of an environmental catastrophe. Conceiving of environmental issues as an emergency has several rationales. First, it reflects the internal orientation of the field of environmental law. Much of environmental law is aimed at curbing our worst excesses and abuses of the environment, staving off a true disaster. Environmentalism, a driving force of environmental law reform, is also preoccupied with forecasts of the next imminent environmental disaster. This book taps into this deep sense that environmental issues present a distinctive, potentially existential challenge, and it inquires into the implications of this challenge for law. Second, focusing on the possibility of the worst-case scenario—the unforeseen, existential threat—allows us to develop a comprehensive theory of the rule of law. The concept of the environmental emergency reveals how law can both constitute and constrain the exercise of public authority at all times and for all issues, even in the event of an environmental catastrophe. The environmental catastrophe (eg, extreme weather, crop failure, epidemic) is a necessary feature of the concept of the environmental emergency. But this is distinct from the argument that all environmental issues confront us as an ongoing emergency, which justifies the theory of the rule of law elaborated and defended within this book. Finally, we will see that the concept of the environmental emergency provides a useful framework or outline for the book, by building on existing theoretical work on national security emergencies. The emergency framework allows us to dip into a variety of ongoing conversations in environmental law for the purpose of showing how a self-consciously theoretical approach to environmental law has the potential to reorient these conversations toward why environmental law (as opposed to governance, politics, economics, etc) is something worth having in the first place.

In this book, I defend and elaborate an understanding of the rule of law as a collective requirement on all institutions of government to publicly justify decisions on the basis of core common law principles. I build on the work of Lon Fuller, David Dyzenhaus and others who argue that what makes law law—that is, what gives law its authority—is its compliance with the rule of law. This authority derives from the fact that the rule of law respects the autonomy of individuals, understood as rational and self-determining agents, who are capable of actively participating in shaping their public institutions. An ongoing requirement of public justification enables individuals to reason with the law; it facilitates and empowers active participation by those subject to the law. The public-justification conception of the rule of law obliges public decision-makers to justify their decisions with reasons that individuals can understand and reasonably accept. Individuals can then choose whether to obey the law or to contest it. Through this reasoning process, they are active participants in the rule-of-law project of ensuring public decisions reflect our best collective understanding of our core constitutional principles and how they can be fulfilled in any given case.

The theory presented here lies at the interface between common law constitutionalism and deliberative democracy. Common law constitutionalism holds that the common law, with its long historical evolution, reflects the deeply rooted values that are constitutive of the community. On this view, public officials must justify their decisions on the basis of core common law constitutional principles, such as reasonableness and fairness. Judges are entitled to intervene when a public decision is successfully contested on the basis that it does not reflect these principles. Theories of deliberative democracy emphasise the reason-giving demands on both citizens and officials. On this view, collective rule is legitimate when public decisions are justified by general, public-regarding reasons that those affected can reasonably accept. Others have noted this continuity between deliberative democracy and common law constitutionalism,[2] but its implications for the administrative state and environmental decision-making in particular remain to be explored. The contribution of this book is to focus squarely on this intersection, which plays out in the depths and details of environmental decision-making that simultaneously and directly engage both democratic and legal aspects of public justification. It provides a theory that explains how these environmental decisions can have both legal and democratic authority.[3]

The rule-of-law requirement of public justification provides a coherent theory from which to understand and, in many instances, reorient existing practices in environmental law. In particular, it allows us to appreciate the role of creative institutional design—even unconventional, non-adjudicative

[2] D Dyzenhaus, 'The Legitimacy of Legality' (1996) 46 *University of Toronto Law Journal* 129; H Kong, 'Election Law and Deliberative Democracy: Against Deflation' (2015) 9 *Journal of Parliamentary and Political Law* 35.

[3] The book theorises how legality can constitute 'the green state': R Eckersley, *The Green State: Rethinking Democracy and Sovereignty* (Cambridge, MA, MIT Press, 2004). It can also be understood as an exercise of administrative constitutionalism, or elaborating the norms that constitute public administration: E Fisher, *Risk Regulation and Administrative Constitutionalism* (Oxford, Hart Publishing, 2007).

institutions—in maintaining the rule of law under the conditions presented by the environmental emergency. The rule-of-law requirement of public justification allows us to refine the contours of well-known but somewhat controversial (or at least confounded) environmental principles, such as the precautionary principle and sustainable development. Moreover, we will see that these principles have an essential but unrealised role in maintaining the rule of law by modifying the requirements of the common law principles of fairness and reasonableness. Furthermore, the requirement of public justification provides guidance on how public institutions can reason adequately in light of conflicting environmental values and half-hearted legislative commitments to public justification. Finally, we will see that the public-justification conception of the rule of law provides a promising foundation for developing a meaningful constitutional environmental rights jurisprudence. While immediate law reform is not the primary objective of the book, we will see that in each of these contexts, important normative implications follow from this conception of the rule of law.

While this account of the rule of law is not necessarily tied to any particular jurisdiction, this book develops the public-justification conception in the context of Canadian environmental and administrative law. Canada presents particularly fruitful and largely unexplored terrain on which to construct a theory of environmental law based on common law constitutionalism. Canadian jurisprudence has proven fertile ground for common law constitutionalism,[4] which as we will see, provides a persuasive response to the challenge of emergencies. To date, common law constitutionalism has largely ignored the policy-dominated regulatory domain of public law. In addition, we will see that Canadian law and policy are deeply ambivalent about environmental protection. Canadian environmental law is the product of a wilderness or preservationist national identity and a natural resource exploitation reality.[5] Canada thus presents a hard case for understanding how the rule of law ought to operate in light of these deeply conflicting environmental values. In other words, environmental issues—like emergencies—can force us to re-examine the 'agreed legal frames' in both public and environmental law.

[4] MD Walters, 'The Common Law Constitution in Canada: Return of *Lex Non Scripta* as Fundamental Law' (2001) 51 *University of Toronto Law Journal* 91; D Dyzenhaus, *The Constitution of Law: Legality in a Time of Emergency* (Cambridge, Cambridge University Press, 2006); E Fox-Decent, *Sovereignty's Promise: The State as Fiduciary* (Oxford, Oxford University Press, 2011).

[5] S Wood, G Tanner and BJ Richardson, 'What Ever Happened to Canadian Environmental Law?' (2011) 37 *Ecology Law Quarter* 981, 981 and 986–87.

I. METHODOLOGY, TERMINOLOGY AND CONTEXT

The book adopts a conceptual methodology to explain what it means to govern the environment by law. It refers to this conceptual framework as the environmental emergency because it is built on the argument that environmental issues contain the constitutive features of an emergency. The environmental emergency allows us to uncover and critique existing rule-of-law assumptions in Canadian environmental law and develop an alternative account of the rule of law that takes seriously the complexity of environmental issues. The rule-of-law theory developed within this book, however, follows a tradition of democratic pragmatism.[6] Understanding the rule of law as a democratic project—ie, as an ongoing commitment to public justification—means that its content is never fixed. Public justification is essential to the process of realising, deliberating upon and re-articulating core constitutional principles. The methodology for developing this conception of the rule of law, as we will see in Part II of the book, is to draw out theoretical insight from existing institutional practices that do especially well or poorly at fostering a commitment to public justification.

The rule of law is often labelled an 'essentially contested concept' because it 'inevitably involves endless disputes about [its] proper use.'[7] Two conceptions of the rule of law are contrasted in this book. The first conception, which I refer to as the formal conception, is developed in the first three chapters. The formal conception of the rule of law emphasises the requirement of a formal allocation of distinct powers between institutions of government. The formal conception, put differently, is largely commensurate with a strong separation of powers. The second conception of the rule of law is the theory developed in the book that, at base, requires public decision-makers to publicly justify their decisions on the basis of common law constitutional principles. I refer to this as the public-justification conception, or the requirement of public justification. After chapter four, however, no such qualifying language should be necessary. The argument here is both normative and comprehensive, that is, the public-justification conception of the rule of law developed and advocated for in Part II can and should operate for all issues at all times.

[6] I borrow this term from JS Dryzek, *The Politics of the Earth: Environmental Discourses*, 3rd edn (Oxford, Oxford University Press, 2013) 99. By pragmatism, I mean the philosophical pragmatism of Charles Peirce and John Dewey.

[7] WB Gallie, 'Essentially Contested Concepts' (1955) 56 *Proceedings of the Aristotelian Society* 167, 169; J Waldron, 'Is the Rule of Law an Essentially Contested Concept (in Florida)?' (2004) 21 *Law and Philosophy* 137.

Environmental law also suffers from somewhat of an identity crisis. The environment is all around us. Humans are part of it, and virtually every public decision has some effect on the environment, whether intended or not. Many have therefore advocated an expansive understanding of environmental law that requires rooting out the unsustainable practices 'embedded in every aspect of economic and political life'.[8] The conventional understanding of environmental law, in contrast, tends to focus on regulating specific human activities that have direct effects on environmental and human health: eg, air and water pollution laws, endangered species protection, the regulation of natural resource development. Since the rule-of-law theory developed here is comprehensive, nothing important turns on this distinction. As will become clear, the focus of the book is on conventional environmental law and, in particular, on the conflicts between natural resource exploitation and environmental protection. While the specific case studies are essential for my methodology, the systemic features of all environmental issues are what justify approaching these issues as an ongoing emergency. By this I mean the features of complexity and the ever-present possibility of an environmental catastrophe. After making this argument in chapter one, I will refer to these features simply as complexity as opposed to uncertainty, risk or some other descriptor. As we will see, complexity best captures the kind of uncertainty we face when regulating the environment, and it is this complexity that constitutes the environmental emergency.

Before moving to the outline of the book, it is worth situating the theoretical argument in its socio-political context. This requires that I identify and respond to two principal objections to the central argument that environmental issues are best understood as an ongoing emergency. The first objection is that, at least in many liberal Western democracies, most environmental issues have not sparked the overzealous state action that characterises many conventional emergency responses. For example, in Canada, Australia and the United States, state action on perceived environmental and national security threats have starkly diverged. Counter-terror measures have proliferated, whereas state action on pressing environmental issues, such as climate change, has stagnated or regressed.[9] This seems to suggest that the problem in the environmental context is not the inability of

[8] M M'Gonigle and P Ramsey, 'Greening Environmental Law: From Sectoral Reform to Systemic Re-Formation' (2004) 14 *Journal of Environmental Law and Practice* 333, 340. See also J Holder, 'New Age: Rediscovering Natural Law' (2000) 53 *Current Legal Problems* 151, 167.

[9] There is a wealth of (largely American) legal research that examines the reasons for widespread lethargy in response to chronic environmental issues: hypothesising and documenting the collective action problem, discounting future harm, cognitive decision-making biases. For one such example specific to this point, see: CR Sunstein, 'On the Divergent American Reactions to Terrorism and Climate Change' (2007) 107 *Columbia Law Review* 503.

law to constrain political power as it is in the national security emergency context. In this respect, many environmentalists and environmental law scholars might long for the kind of preventive state action that has emerged post-9/11.[10]

I agree with this general observation. What this perspective misses, however, is the fact that environmental issues and emergencies present the same core challenge for law. As we will see in chapter one, it is the combination of epistemic features possessed by both emergencies and environmental issues that pose particular challenges for the rule of law. Moreover, it is important to note that while environmental issues are frequently exacerbated by a lack of political will, they do not exist in a complete legal void. In Canada, the provinces, territories and federal Parliament have elected to govern the environment through law. The argument of this book is that this is a meaningful commitment, one that entails much more extensive and nuanced legal obligations than the enactment of a symbolic or perhaps equivocal statute.

The second objection might call into question the value of presenting a unifying theory across either environmental law or public law. As I have just noted, environmental law is potentially all-encompassing, and it contains 'hot problems' that resist unified frameworks.[11] Narrowing the field to public environmental law offers little help. The Canadian administrative state, for example, is comprised of an intricate network of public decision-making bodies including Cabinet, Ministers, appeals tribunals and quasi-judicial regulatory bodies, which issue and review recommendations, regulations, licences, exemptions and approvals covering an enormous range of activities that impact the environment. Perhaps, as prominent public law scholars have argued, we should view our legal system as pluralistic, where statutes are permitted to 'lead a life of their own', independent of the homogenising tendencies of the common law.[12]

The unified theory of public environmental law presented here is both defensible and valuable. It is defensible in that it does not purport to offer a blanket approach to addressing any or all environmental issues. Rather, it focuses on understanding the conditions under which the state can be said to act with legal authority when it regulates the environment. I argue that public environmental decisions will have legal authority when they are

[10] J Stacey, 'Preventive Justice, the Precautionary Principle and the Rule of Law' in T Tulich et al (eds), *Regulating Preventive Justice* (New York, Routledge, 2017) 23.

[11] Fisher, 'Environmental Law' (above n 1) 354–55 (also observing that environmental law scholarship has yet to yield such a framework).

[12] HW Arthurs, 'Rethinking Administrative Law: A Slightly Dicey Business' (1979) 17 *Osgoode Hall Law Journal* 1, 22. See also S Coyle and K Morrow, *The Philosophical Foundations of Environmental Law: Property, Rights and Nature* (Oxford, Hart Publishing, 2004) 199–200 (arguing that the dominant view of environmental law is as a haphazard collection of legislative responses that does not contain the deeper conception of responsibility that they trace back through the history of common law property rights).

publicly justified on the basis of core constitutional principles. As we will see in chapters six and seven, these principles operate at a high level of generality, but they are not abstract; they are sensitive to particular decision-making contexts. In addition to being defensible, a coherent theory of environmental law is also valuable to the discipline. Despite the interconnectedness of environmental issues in the real world, the field of environmental law is marginalised from other areas of public law and increasingly fragmented.[13] This means that systemic flaws or weaknesses in environmental decision-making may be overlooked. For example, we will see in chapter two that the outcomes of judicial review of a wide range of environmental decisions can be explained by a common set of rule-of-law assumptions held by the courts and environmental advocates. Striving for a unified theory of environmental law allows us to focus on the core challenges of environmental issues to better understand the limits and potential of existing public law theory.

In the tradition of democratic pragmatism, the theory developed in this book is grounded in the institutional practices of environmental law. The book focuses on three detailed environmental contexts: forest law in British Columbia, the assessment of inter-provincial oil pipelines and wind turbine development. The first context spans a number of chapters, beginning with the specific circumstances of an unprecedented mountain pine beetle epidemic and moving through the broader legal and institutional architecture of forest governance in British Columbia. The extended focus on British Columbia forestry may seem technical or parochial for those unfamiliar with Canadian geographical and political landscapes. Canada is home to vast expanses of forest (paralleled only by the equally vast Canadian arctic). This image of expansive and untrammelled forest looms large in the Canadian wilderness psyche. Protecting some of this forest, in particular the old-growth coastal rainforest on Vancouver Island, led to the infamous 'War in the Woods', one of the largest acts of civil disobedience in Canadian history, which saw over 800 protesters arrested in 1993.[14] These iconic protests on Canada's west coast have had an enduring effect on environmental policy in the country to this day.[15] The subsequent examples of pipeline

[13] L Heinzerling, 'The Environment' in P Cane and M Tushnet (eds), *The Oxford Handbook of Legal Studies* (Oxford, Oxford University Press, 2003) 703–4; Coyle and Morrow, *Philosophical Foundations* (above n 12); E Fisher et al, 'Maturity and Methodology: Starting a Debate about Environmental Law Scholarship' (2009) 21 *Journal of Environmental Law* 213, 221 and 231.

[14] DJ Salazar and DK Alper (eds), *Sustaining the Forests of the Pacific Coast: Forging Truces in the War in the Woods* (Vancouver, University of British Columbia Press, 2014) (for nuanced perspectives on the various interests and alliances at play in west coast forest policy).

[15] See ch 3 below on the forestry governance mechanisms that resulted from these protests and ch 6 below on pipeline approvals that are currently poised to instigate acts of civil disobedience of a similar or greater magnitude.

and wind turbine development are each contained in their own chapters. These two examples highlight the contemporary challenge of reshaping the Canadian resource economy to more sustainable energy sources. While the details of these examples are distinctively Canadian, the legal issues and theory embedded within them are not. These examples raise perennial environmental law issues such as the appropriate role of judicial review, regulatory instrument choice, institutional design and the interpretation of the precautionary principle, all of which are examined in the chapters that follow.

II. OUTLINE OF THE BOOK

This book is divided into two parts. In brief, Part I establishes the concept of the environmental emergency and demonstrates its utility in unpacking rule-of-law assumptions implicit within existing approaches to environmental law. Part II turns to the rule-of-law theory of public justification and its elaboration in the environmental context.

Chapter one makes the case for approaching environmental law from the perspective of an emergency. This chapter is grounded in current ecological theory, which posits that ecosystems are complex, adaptive systems, and in risk sociology, which emphasises the inherent limits of predicting the catastrophic potential of human action. Together, these literatures reveal that environmental issues possess the constitutive features of an emergency: an inability to know in advance which issues contain the possibility of a catastrophe and an inability to know in advance what to do in response to such an unforeseen event. Having made the argument that environmental issues are best approached as an ongoing emergency, the chapter then sets out Schmitt's challenge: ie, the challenge to show that emergencies can be governed by law. I canvass two potential responses to this challenge—the extra-legal approach and an accommodation approach—which provide a background framework for understanding the arguments in the two chapters that follow. Chapter one concludes by arguing that both of these responses assume a formal conception of the rule of law that is incapable of answering Schmitt's challenge.

Chapters two and three argue that the emergency framework provides a novel critique of existing approaches to environmental law. In chapter two, I argue that the dominant position in Canadian environmental law scholarship—the environmental reform position—does not face up to the emergency features inherent in environmental issues. It therefore mistakenly advocates for a formal conception of the rule of law. Much like the accommodation approach explored in the emergency literature, the environmental reform position can offer only a façade of legality to environmental decisions, an appearance of legality that does not meaningfully constrain the exercise of administrative discretion. The chapter argues that this façade can be usefully understood in terms of legal black holes and grey holes. It illustrates how adherence to the formal conception of the rule of law has created these black and grey holes throughout Canadian environmental law.

Chapter three takes up the burgeoning literature on environmental governance. It argues that the literature correctly diagnoses the epistemic challenges of environmental issues. But because it assumes a formal conception of the rule of law, it rejects the rule of law as irrelevant to complex environmental decision-making. Much like the extra-legal approach, environmental governance proponents treat the rule of law as a luxury that we cannot afford. Instead, commentators evaluate environmental governance on the basis of an assortment of criteria: typically effectiveness, transparency, participation and accountability. And while these criteria may be important components of any conception of the rule of law, they are at best only components. This chapter argues that subsuming law within a broader paradigm of governance risks eclipsing what is distinctive about law—the fact that it respects individuals as rational agents capable of actively participating in their own system of governance. Environmental governance risks abandoning the language needed to explain fully the strengths and weaknesses of novel forms of environmental governance.

Part II of the book turns from critique to the elaboration of a democratic theory of the rule of law that responds to the environmental emergency; this is the rule-of-law theory of public justification. Chapter four introduces the contours of the theory, which forms the basis of the remainder of the book. The chapter draws out the public-justification conception of the rule of law from existing Canadian administrative law jurisprudence and argues that it responds to Schmitt's challenge by offering an account of law that both constitutes and constrains public authority. The public-justification conception requires public officials to publicly justify their exercises of authority on the basis of core common law principles, such as fairness and reasonableness. The chapter argues that the requirement of public justification lies at the interface of common law constitutionalism and theories of deliberative democracy. It argues that both theoretical traditions share an understanding of the individual as a responsible agent, capable of actively participating in the ongoing project of democratic governance under the rule of law. The requirement of public justification both protects and enables this agency through the requirement of reason-giving, a requirement informed by the common law and deliberative-democratic requirements explored in subsequent chapters.

Chapter five takes up the first of these specific requirements: creative institutional design. The crux of this chapter is that in emergency contexts (including the environmental emergency), creative institutional design will be necessary to maintain the rule of law. The chapter offers the example of the British Columbia Forest Practices Board, a hybrid institution that approximates, in unconventional ways, the requirements of public justification across a range of environmental decisions. The chapter then draws on insights from democratic experimentalism, a branch of deliberative democracy, to show how public justification can be maintained even in complex regulatory contexts that cannot fit easily into adjudicative models of review.

The focus of chapter six is then on the specific common law principles of reasonableness and fairness. Relying on Canada's National Energy Board as an example of multifaceted institutional failure, it argues that the conventional articulation of common law principles is inadequate for the environmental context. To respect the status of the legal subject as a responsible agent in the context of environmental decision-making, reasonableness and fairness must be informed by key environmental principles, namely the precautionary principle and sustainable development. It argues that a deliberative-democratic interpretation of precaution and sustainable development has the effect of modifying general common law requirements of fairness and reasonableness in order to preserve the distinctive relationship between legal subject and lawmaker. In doing so, these core environmental principles demand of the National Energy Board a process and decisions that are justified on the basis that they attend to the interests of those affected by its decisions.

Chapter seven builds directly on the analysis in chapter six of the principle of reasonableness. Chapter seven allows us to understand how a public decision-maker can reason adequately in a challenging environmental context that engages multiple, competing environmental considerations. The context for the chapter is controversial industrial wind turbine development in Ontario. This controversy has led to a robust body of tribunal jurisprudence that considers the potential harms to human and environmental health that result from wind energy. The chapter argues that the Tribunal reasons adequately about these harms when it offers a cogent justification of its decision on the basis of the relevant statutory considerations, interpreted consistently with a common law backdrop protective of individual agency. We will see that in many instances, the Tribunal reasons adequately even though its public-justification role in protecting individual agency remains implicit. We will also see, however, that by explicitly grounding its reasoning in the public-justification conception, the Tribunal is in a position to resist submitting to the apparent 'plain meaning' of its governing statute, which threatens individual agency by purporting to preclude the operation of the precautionary principle.

Finally, in chapter eight, the emergency framework returns to the fore in order to help develop the relationship between the public-justification conception of the rule of law and a constitutional right to a healthy environment. We will see that prominent academic proposals in Canada for a Charter right to a healthy environment have neglected the need for a theory of law that is facilitative of a robust constitutional environmental rights jurisprudence. It attends to the method of constitutional rights adjudication in Canada and reveals how the formal conception of the rule of law implicitly operates to undermine environment-related claims under existing provisions of the Charter of Rights and Freedoms. It argues for an understanding of constitutional law as 'administrative law writ large',[16] in which a written bill of environmental rights solidifies and strengthens the common law requirement of public justification.

The concept of the environmental emergency informs the overarching framework of the book's analysis. At the same time, the possibility of an actual environmental catastrophe is omnipresent, stressing our enduring vulnerability to environmental harm. Early chapters canvass a disaster in the forestry context and its legal and regulatory responses. Chapter six, on pipelines, addresses the possibility of a known but as yet unrealised disaster, namely a major marine oil spill. Chapter seven, on wind turbine development, merges both preventive and response dimensions of disaster.

In sum, the book develops a constitution of the environmental emergency. I mean 'constitution' in two senses of the term. First, the chapters of this book construct a concept of the environmental emergency with its own three-part internal constitution. The book's argument is part conceptual, part critical and part theory construction. But the term 'constitution' also signifies the fact that the theory developed in this book posits that the rule of law is constitutive of law itself. In other words, the book explains why having environmental law is something worth having. The assumption underlying most environmental law scholarship to date is that environmental law is the most powerful tool for protecting the environment. The account offered here shows that environmental law is not only that. Environmental law, in the sense defended in this book, makes the agency of individuals—their capacity for reason and self-determination—internal to the project of environmental governance. It empowers individuals to participate actively in the ongoing commitment to ensuring that environmental decisions reflect our best understanding of core constitutional principles. When public officials appeal to the legality of their decisions—eg, 'the statute permits me to convert this pristine lake into a toxic tailings pond'—this comes with its own kind of legitimacy.[17] The challenge, therefore, is to understand the rule of law as something meaningful. A rule-of-law theory of public justification answers this challenge.

[16] This idea originates with South African public law scholar Etienne Mureinik: D Dyzenhaus, 'Law as Justification: Etienne Mureinik's Conception of Legal Culture' (1998) 14 *South African Journal on Human Rights* 11, 31–32.

[17] Dyzenhaus, 'The Legitimacy of Legality' (above n 2). This is central to ecofeminist perspectives on environmental law. See, eg, EL Hughes, 'Fishwives and Other Tails: Ecofeminism and Environmental Law' (1995) 8 *Canadian Journal of Women and the Law* 502. Ch 2 below covers numerous examples in which an administrative decision-maker has appealed only to the scope of delegated discretion to justify making an environmentally harmful decision.

Part I

The Environmental Emergency

1

The Concept of the Environmental Emergency

> In October 1970, Canada faced its worst internal security crisis, when cells of the violent separatist group, *Le Front de Libération du Québec* (FLQ) kidnapped the British Trade Commissioner ... and kidnapped and later murdered the Quebec Minister of Labour. ... Faced with this mushrooming crisis, Canada acted swiftly and forcefully with no regard for civil liberties. Invoking the War Measures Act under a putative, and unproven, apprehended insurrection, the federal government placed Quebec under what amounted to a state of martial law.[1]

> After riding thermals for 190 miles from British Columbia, the insects fell like rain out of the sky. Farmers heard them ping on the roofs of metal barns. Hungry and fatigued, the beetles quickly hit more than 300,000 lodgepole trees. ... On each tree, they produced enough off-spring to attack another ten. Hardly a newspaper carried the story. It was, after all, just a story about trees.[2]

THIS CHAPTER ARGUES that we should approach environmental law from the perspective of an ongoing emergency. As the chapter explains, the systemic features of environmental issues give rise to the constitutive features of an emergency such that we should view all of environmental law from the perspective of the emergency. In this sense, the use of the phrase 'environmental emergency' is more conceptual than literal. Some environmental events—hurricanes, earthquakes, oil spills, etc—are emergencies in a conventional sense; I will refer to these as disasters or catastrophes. They are an essential part of the broader concept of the environmental emergency that is elaborated and defended here; but they are only a part. As we will see, the environmental emergency applies to all environmental issues: dramatic and urgent, chronic and serious, and seemingly benign. This is because the complex, adaptive nature of all environmental issues precludes reliably predicting which particular environmental issues or policy decisions contain the possibility of catastrophe, and it also precludes knowing in advance how we ought to respond once the possibility

[1] R Whitaker, 'Keeping Up with the Neighbours? Canadian Responses to 9/11 in Historical and Comparative Context' (2003) 41 *Osgoode Hall Law Journal* 241, 249.

[2] A Nikiforuk, *Empire of the Beetle* (Vancouver, Greystone Books, 2011) 74.

of a catastrophe becomes apparent. These two epistemic features are what constitute the environmental emergency, and it is this framing that allows us to productively unpack conventional assumptions about law and legality in the environmental context in Part I of this book.

The connection between emergencies and environmental issues is not necessarily obvious. As the chapter epigraphs above suggest, conventional emergencies are dramatic and sudden events that temporarily displace any semblance of normalcy. In contrast, most environmental issues are persistent challenges that we address through everyday administrative law channels such as regulation-making and licensing. This chapter argues, however, that this distinction is more apparent than real. From a legal perspective, the challenge of both environmental issues and conventional emergencies is that we cannot reliably anticipate an extreme event and therefore cannot know in advance how to respond. Consequently, the emergency undermines any conception of the rule of law that equates law with pre-existing rules. It reveals the inevitability and necessity of executive discretion.

This chapter has three objectives. First, it introduces Carl Schmitt's emergency challenge and how conventional responses to this challenge fail to show that emergencies can be governed by law. Its second objective is to argue that this challenge extends to all environmental issues because they too possess the constituent features of emergencies. Third, the chapter outlines the conception of law that underlies Schmitt's challenge.

These objectives unfold in three sections. The first section introduces the challenge that emergencies pose for law. This challenge was articulated by controversial Nazi legal scholar Carl Schmitt, who argued that unforeseeable, extreme threats cannot be governed by law. Section I below argues that environmental issues constitute emergencies because they contain the unforeseeable possibility of a catastrophe. The complex, adaptive nature of ecological systems means that it is impossible to fully anticipate the effects of our actions on the environment. The nature of the problem and our understanding of it are constantly evolving. Surprises—sometimes catastrophic surprises—are therefore inevitable. The fact that we cannot always know in advance which issues contain the possibility of catastrophe means that we must approach all environmental issues from the perspective of the emergency.

The second section of the chapter takes up two possible responses to Schmitt's challenge, and they provide a framework for the remainder of Part I of the book. We will see that Schmitt assumes a formal conception of the rule of law; that is, he equates law with relatively determinative legislated rules. For those who adhere to the formal conception of the rule of law, there are only two possible responses to the emergency: resort to extra-legal measures or attempt to accommodate emergencies within legal order by relaxing ordinary rule-of-law requirements. We will see that both approaches rest on the assumption that we can create and maintain dual legal orders (one for ordinary times and another for crises). But the very fact that emergencies cannot be anticipated undermines this attempt to create and confine a separate emergency order. Moreover, the attempt to accommodate the emergency within legal order risks proliferating legal black and grey holes, which give only the appearance and not the reality of legal constraint. These responses to Schmitt's challenge only help bolster Schmitt's claim that the emergency cannot be governed by law.

The third section below argues that Schmitt's challenge extends to the entire administrative state. The emergency, as Schmitt noted, poses a glaring problem for the formal conception because it reveals the necessity of unconstrained discretion. But broad legislative grants of power to the executive are characteristic of the modern administrative state. The exercise of both exceptional and everyday discretionary powers poses the same problem for the formal conception of the rule of law: the problem of discretion. By explicating this connection between the formal conception of the rule of law and discretion, we will then be in a position to subject environmental issues, understood as an ongoing emergency, to Schmitt's challenge in chapters two and three.

I. THE ENVIRONMENTAL EMERGENCY

The concept of the environmental emergency arises from the complex, adaptive nature of environmental issues. In this section we will see that the emergency is any unforeseeable, extreme event that cannot be anticipated through *ex ante* legal norms. I argue that serious environmental issues constitute emergencies because they have catastrophic potential, but due to their complexity, it is impossible to know in advance the precise details of the catastrophic threat. After introducing Schmitt's challenge, this section turns to ecology and risk literatures to argue that environmental issues have the definitional features of emergencies. The example of an unprecedented insect epidemic provides context for this analysis.

A. Schmittian Emergencies

Emergencies have long posed a problem for political and legal theorists. Emergencies strain our commitment to the rule of law. The sudden and extreme nature of emergencies demands urgent action. Crises cause us to rally around the flag, which motivates the government to take whatever measures are necessary to bring the emergency to an end. Often these exceptional measures violate or curtail constitutional commitments to basic civil liberties and ordinary due process.[3] The historical record suggests that legislatures and courts do not present significant constraints on executive emergency action. Legislatures may delegate broad emergency powers to the executive in advance,[4] and courts tend to defer to the executive because they are reluctant to interfere with the sensitive and high-stakes issues that pertain to an emergency response.[5] In short, emergencies appear to demand exceptional executive action, that is, action determined by necessity and unconstrained by law.

Schmitt offered a theoretical account of this historical pattern. His argument was simple but powerful. The emergency, according to Schmitt, cannot be governed by law. Schmitt described the emergency as the unforeseeable, existential threat that cannot be anticipated in law.[6] Since the emergency is unexpected, it cannot be defined through *ex ante* legal rules, and because its severity demands an urgent response, it is impossible to respond through the ordinary legislative process.[7] Because the emergency cannot be regulated through legislated rules, Schmitt maintained that the best that can be done is to indicate who gets to decide that such an emergency exists and what to do in response.[8] For Schmitt, only the sovereign (or the modern-day executive) could fulfil this role. Schmitt argued that in the event of a truly existential threat, the sovereign may even need to suspend legal order altogether.[9] Any attempt to prescribe how the sovereign must respond to the emergency is undermined by the fact that the emergency cannot be predicted in advance and therefore may require the violation of pre-existing rules. The fact that the sovereign is so empowered reveals that he or she is in the position to respond most expeditiously to serious though not existential threats.[10] In the face of an unforeseeable and extreme emergency, Schmitt argued, the sovereign can do whatever is necessary to bring the crisis to an end. Executive discretion, on this view, cannot be constrained by law.

Schmitt's is an extreme position that comes with disturbing political baggage. He was a Nazi insider, whose conception of law and critique

[3] O Gross and FN Aolain, *Law in Times of Crisis* (New York, Cambridge University Press, 2006) 64.

[4] For example, War Measures Act, RSC 1970, c W-2 [repealed]; Emergencies Act, RSC 1985, c 22 (4th Supp); Emergency Management Act, SC 2007, c 15.

[5] Gross and Aolain, *Law in Times of Crisis* (above n 3) 77–78.

[6] C Schmitt, *Political Theology*, George Schwab (trans) (Cambridge, Massachusetts Institute of Technology Press, 1985) 6.

[7] Ibid, 6–7.

[8] Ibid, 5. Conversely, the emergency reveals who in fact the sovereign is (ibid, 6 and 13).

[9] Ibid, 12.

[10] Posner and Vermeule take up this point in EA Posner and A Vermeule, *The Executive Unbound* (Oxford, Oxford University Press, 2010) 32–33. Their work is considered in more detail below in section III.

of liberalism was consistent with the atrocities of Nazi fascism.[11] Yet his work cannot be confined to the political and historical context in which it was written. Schmitt's work rose again in prominence in the wake of the 9/11 terrorist attacks. His theory seemed to offer an explanation for the sweeping executive action taken by the United States in response to the perceived national security crisis. The President declared a state of emergency and authorised indefinite detention and 'advanced interrogation tactics' at Guantanamo Bay, as well as warrantless spying, all initially through unilateral executive action.[12] In addition, Congress delegated to the President sweeping authority to use 'all necessary and appropriate force' against terrorism.[13] As we shall later see, the United States Supreme Court was, at least initially, extremely deferential to emergency actions that deviated from ordinary constitutional requirements. The challenge for legal scholars writing about national security after 9/11 was to show that the American emergency response was not, as Schmitt would have claimed, inevitable. They sought to show that Schmitt was wrong in his assumptions about law and its ability to constrain emergency power.[14]

Schmitt's challenge—the challenge to show that emergencies can be governed by law—is the backdrop against which the contemporary emergency powers debates take place.[15] It is a challenge that is appropriately said to cast 'a dark shadow'[16] over legal and political emergency theories. Schmitt's is a challenge of the first order. There is no point in debating the appropriateness of particular legal measures in times of crisis if Schmitt was correct that emergency powers are inevitably unconstrained by law. Schmitt's challenge, then, lies at the core of the legal theoretical debate over emergencies. It arises from the fact that emergencies contain two epistemic features: a

[11] WE Scheuerman, *Between the Norm and the Exception* (Cambridge, MIT Press, 1994) 23–24; D Dyzenhaus, *Legality and Legitimacy: Carl Schmitt, Hans Kelsen and Hermann Heller in Weimar* (Oxford, Clarendon Press, 1997) 98–101.

[12] K Roach, *The 9/11 Effect: Comparative Counter-Terrorism* (Cambridge, Cambridge University Press, 2011) 4. These actions were subsequently ratified through legislation.

[13] Authorization for the Use of Military Force (AUMF), Pub L No 107-40, 115 Stat 224 (2001) (US).

[14] B Ackerman, 'The Emergency Constitution' (2004) 113 *Yale Law Journal* 1029; S Levinson, 'Constitutional Norms in a State of Permanent Emergency' (2005) 40 *Georgia Law Review* 699; D Dyzenhaus, *The Constitution of Law: Legality in a Time of Emergency* (Cambridge, Cambridge University Press, 2006) 34–35, 40.

[15] G Agamben, *State of Exception*, K Attell (trans) (Chicago, University of Chicago Press, 2005); Gross and Aolain, *Law in Times of Crisis* (above n 3) 163; T Poole, 'Constitutional Exceptionalism and the Common Law' (2009) 7 *International Journal of Constitutional Law* 247, 248; K Cedervall Lauta, *Disaster Law* (Abingdon, Routledge, 2015) 51–52. Furthermore, the basic problem that emergencies pose for law can be traced back to John Locke, *Two Treatises of Government* (London, 1764) ss 159–60. Oren Gross offers a nice overview of how a core understanding of the emergency permeates political and legal theory: O Gross, 'Chaos and Rules: Should Responses to Violent Crises Always Be Constitutional?' (2003) 112 *Yale Law Journal* 1011.

[16] Gross and Aolain, *Law in Times of Crisis* (above n 3) 162.

lack of *ex ante* knowledge about the specific events that may produce an emergency, and a lack of *ex ante* knowledge about how to respond to such an unforeseen event. These features can arise when the state faces a political or national security threat—as Schmitt claimed—but, as we will see, these features inhere in environmental issues as well.

B. The Environmental Emergency

The argument that environmental issues confront us as an ongoing emergency builds on two sets of literatures: the ecological theory of complex adaptive systems and risk sociology. In this section we see that, together, these literatures illuminate the epistemic features of emergencies inherent within environmental issues: the inability to reliably anticipate extreme events and, accordingly, the inability to adequately plan in advance our specific emergency responses. The environmental emergency arises, in short, from the *complexity* of relationships intertwined within environmental problems: a complexity so dense that it can occlude the possibility of an environmental disaster.

Environmental issues arise from the complex interactions of relationships within ecosystems (including human social relationships, which are themselves embedded in the ecological system). Complex, adaptive theory describes the behaviour of these systems. The 'complexity' of complex adaptive systems arises from the sheer number of relationships and processes that make up an ecosystem (eg, predator–prey relationships, management decisions) as well as the ways in which these relationships change over both space and time.[17] Change, ecologists note, does not happen consistently. Rather, it is characterised by periods of slowness that are punctuated by episodes of rapid change. The 'adaptiveness' in complex, adaptive theory describes the ways in which relationships within ecosystems fluctuate in response to random events. Contrary to past ecological thinking, which understood nature as 'in balance', complex adaptive theory observes that ecological processes fluctuate between different states.[18]

British Columbia's vast interior forests provide context for understanding complex, adaptive theory. The province's forests have experienced an unprecedented, decades-long insect epidemic. The mountain pine beetle has decimated the lodgepole pine population across the province.[19] At times the

[17] CS Holling and LH Gunderson, 'Resilience and Adaptive Cycles' in LH Gunderson and CS Holling (eds), *Panarchy: Understanding Transformations in Human and Natural Systems* (Washington, DC, Island Press, 2002) 26.

[18] Ibid, 26 and 33–49.

[19] British Columbia Ministry of Forests, Lands and Natural Resources, 'A History of the Battle Against the Mountain Pine Beetle, 2000 to 2012' (2012), www.worldcat.org/title/history-of-the-battle-against-the-mountain-pine-beetle-2000-to-2012/oclc/812919832, 3.

beetles travelled in such density that they could be seen as a light drizzle on weather radar and, as illustrated in the epigraph to this chapter, 'fell like rain out of the sky'.[20] The mountain pine beetle now covers an unprecedented range, extending well into the neighbouring province of Alberta. Moreover, having overrun its historic host, the beetle has begun to attack new tree species for the first time, making the entire pan-Canadian boreal forest susceptible to attack.[21] The epidemic will wreak havoc on the British Columbia forest industry, the province's primary natural resource industry. It has killed vast areas of forest in the interior of British Columbia, turning the landscape red, then grey as the attacked trees die. In addition to the economic consequences,[22] the dead forests left by the epidemic increase the province's susceptibility to extreme wildfire.[23]

Mountain pine beetle outbreaks are a regular occurrence in forests dominated by lodgepole pine.[24] Indeed, the relationship between lodgepole pine and beetle is a classic example of an adaptive ecological cycle in which a forest ecosystem is stable for a relatively long period of time and then is massively disrupted by a pest outbreak.[25] However, the scale of the present epidemic was not anticipated by decision-makers.[26] Though we now know that the epidemic was driven by the combination of fire suppression[27]

[20] Nikiforuk, *Empire of the Beetle* (above n 2) 74.

[21] B Parfitt, 'Battling the Beetle: Taking Action to Restore British Columbia's Interior Forests' (Canadian Centre for Policy Alternatives, 2005) 16.

[22] Approximately half of all lodgepole pine will be unavailable to harvest in the 10–50-year harvesting timeframe: J Pousette and C Hawkins, 'An Assessment of Critical Assumptions Supporting the Timber Supply Modelling for Mountain-Pine-Beetle-Induced Allowable Annual Cut Uplift in the Prince George Timber Supply Area' (2006) 7 BC *Journal of Ecosystems and Management* 93, 94; H Nelson, 'Does A Crisis Matter? Forest Policy Responses to the Mountain Pine Beetle Epidemic in British Columbia' (2007) 55 *Canadian Journal of Agricultural Economics* 459, 463.

[23] British Columbia Ministry of Forest, Lands and Natural Resources (Wildfire Management Branch), 'Discussion Paper: Proactive Wildfire Threat Reduction' (2014), docs.openinfo.gov.bc.ca/d63519414a_response_package_fnr-2014-00274.pdf.

[24] Forest Practices Board, 'Evaluating Mountain Pine Beetle Management in British Columbia' (Victoria Forest Practices Board, 2004) 9.

[25] CS Holling, 'Resilience and Stability of Ecological Systems' (1973) 4 *Annual Review of Ecology and Systematics* 1.

[26] The unexpectedness of this epidemic in part arises from the fact that forest management decisions were not initially being made with respect to lodgepole pine, which only received commercial interest in the 1970s. The beetle epidemic was therefore a byproduct of the increase in mature lodgepole pine, which itself was a byproduct of forest management decisions with different focuses: RJ Whitehead, L Safranyik and TL Shore, 'Preventative Management' in L Safranyik and B Wilson (eds), *The Mountain Pine Beetle: A Synthesis of Biology, Management and Impacts on Lodgepole Pine* (Pacific Forestry Centre, 2006) 136. Nor was this kind of epidemic contemplated by industry. No forestry company had a management plan or lease provision accounting for beetle outbreaks: Nikiforuk, *Empire of the Beetle* (above n 2) 52.

[27] Fire suppression tripled the area covered by mature lodgepole pine: K McGarrity and G Hoberg, 'The Beetle Challenge: An Overview of the Mountain Pine Beetle Epidemic and its Implications' (Forest Policy Resources, University of British Columbia, 2005) 4.

and climate change,[28] the complexity of ecological relationships makes it extremely difficult (if not impossible) to know in advance how disparate forest management decisions may impact the beetle's long-term population dynamics, let alone predict how those decisions might intersect with climate change.

The mountain pine beetle illustrates a second characteristic of complex, adaptive theory. Extreme events—such as massive epidemics, large hurricanes or major oil spills—occur in these systems with surprising frequency.[29] In a complex system, there is no 'average' size of event. Most oil spills will likely be small, but the probability distribution of oil spill size does not follow a normal bell curve distribution. The possibility of an extreme event cannot be discounted in advance.[30] The mountain pine beetle is an example of that extreme event: a beetle epidemic so severe that it could not have been predicted by looking at the historical record of mountain pine beetle outbreaks or indeed at any prior insect outbreak in Canada.[31]

A second body of literature, the sociology of risk, offers additional insight into how we predict and manage our vulnerability to extreme environmental events. Risk sociology emphasises the fact that our ability to alter our environment through science and technology has far outstripped our ability to predict and control the consequences of human actions. This literature directs our attention to the catastrophic potential of many decisions that impact the environment. Most notably, Ulrich Beck has argued that catastrophic risk is a permanent feature in contemporary society.[32] Beck's work on the risk society highlights the distinctive characteristics of risks that arise from industrial society: namely, their potential for systematic and irreversible harm, the invisibility of risk (until it is too late), the dependence upon but also inadequacy of science and technical discourses for understanding risk, and the need to avoid and manage catastrophe as a central means of reallocating power and authority in society.[33] Moreover, Beck has

[28] Historically, mountain pine beetle populations were kept in check by very cold weather—typically -35° Celsius for several days—which kills the beetle larvae: BC Ministry of Forests, 'A History of the Battle' (above n 19) 2. This type of weather event has not occurred in the British Columbia interior since the winter of 1995/96 (2). Above average summer temperatures have exacerbated the problem by stressing the trees and making them more susceptible to attack.

[29] DA Farber, 'Probabilities Behaving Badly: Complexity Theory and Environmental Uncertainty' (2003) 37 *UC Davis Law Review* 145, 153–54.

[30] Ibid. See also NN Taleb, *The Black Swan*, 2nd edn (New York, Random House, 2010) 26–37.

[31] B Wilson, 'An Overview of the Mountain Pine Beetle Initiative' in TL Shore, JE Brooks and JE Stone (eds), *Mountain Pine Beetle Symposium: Challenges and Solutions* (Kelowna, Natural Resources Canada, 2003) 3 (noting that by 2002, a full decade before its peak, the epidemic already rivaled any forest pest in recorded North American history).

[32] U Beck, *Risk Society: Towards a New Modernity*, Mark Ritter (tr) (London, Sage Publications, 1992) 21–22 and 24.

[33] Ibid, 22–24.

argued, catastrophe is not simply an avoidable error; rather it is the global, implicit and unavoidable byproduct of industrialisation.[34]

Risk sociologists offer up a litany of examples in which we have failed to predict catastrophe.[35] This literature stresses humility.[36] It canvasses the limitations inherent to any one disciplinary discourse.[37] As Daniel Bodansky has argued, 'many of today's most serious problems were unanticipated and would probably not have been prevented even if regulators had chosen the cautious approach.'[38] Indeed, this seems to have been the case with the mountain pine beetle epidemic, with its ongoing dynamics defying expert prediction:

> [T]he pine beetle did everything the experts said it couldn't do: it flew over mountains, it invaded northern forests, it attacked spruce trees, and it wiped out pine plantations not much thicker in diameter than baseball bats.[39]

Risk sociologists argue that there will inevitably be questions about future harm that go unasked or that are unanswerable within practical and institutional constraints of scientific research, technological production and their regulation. The challenge, according to Sheila Jasanoff, is to supplement the expansive range of expert tools of prediction with 'technologies of humility', which 'make apparent the possibility of unforeseen consequences'.[40]

[34] Ibid, 21.

[35] To name a few environmental examples that feature prominently in this literature: the Bhopal chemical plant disaster, the chronic effects of DDT, the deterioration of the ozone layer, nuclear meltdowns. Recent Canadian examples include the Mount Polley tailings pond disaster (see Independent Expert Engineering Investigation and Review Panel, 'Report on Mount Polley Tailings Storage Facility Breach' (Government of British Columbia, 2015), www.mountpolleyreviewpanel.ca/final-report); the documented sex-skewed birth ratio in Canada's Chemical Valley (see D Scott, 'Confronting Chronic Pollution: A Socio-legal Analysis of Risk and Precaution' (2008) 46 *Osgoode Hall Law Journal* 293); and the Walkerton water contamination tragedy (see DR O'Connor, 'Report of the Walkerton Inquiry' (Ontario Ministry of the Attorney General, 2002), www.archives.gov.on.ca/en/e_records/walkerton/index.html).

[36] S Jasanoff, 'Technologies of Humility: Citizen Participation in Governing Science' (2003) 41(3) *Minerva* 223, 234; B Wynne, 'Uncertainty and Environmental Learning' (1992) 2 *Global Environmental Change* 111, 114; F Fischer, 'Environmental Regulation and Risk–Benefit Analysis: From Technical to Deliberative Policy Making' in R Paehlke and D Torgerson (eds), *Managing Leviathan: Environmental Politics and the Administrative State*, 2nd edn (Peterborough, Broadview Press, 2005) 59.

[37] For an overview of kinds of uncertainty, see: Wynne, 'Uncertainty' (ibid); and E Fisher, 'Drowning by Numbers: Standard Setting in Risk Regulation and the Pursuit of Accountable Public Administration' (2000) 20(1) *Oxford Journal of Legal Studies* 109, 115–56.

[38] D Bodansky, 'Scientific Uncertainty and the Precautionary Principle' (1991) 33 *Environment: Science and Policy for Sustainable Development* 4, 43. He has observed that CFCs and DDT were subject to rigorous scientific testing but were found to be environmentally benign. The problem was not bad science but that 'scientists did not test for the right types of environmental impacts. … Extensive studies were done on the acute toxicity of DDT, but not on its chronic effects.'

[39] Nikiforuk, *Empire of the Beetle* (above n 2) 57.

[40] Jasanoff, 'Technologies of Humility' (above n 36) 240.

From these two bodies of literature we can identify three points of overlap that support the thesis that environmental issues possess the epistemic features of an emergency. First, the complexity of environmental issues, to some extent, defies prediction. This is because both our understanding of the problem and the problem itself are constantly evolving. Environmental decisions are often made in a 'no-analogue' state,[41] where past decisions are of limited usefulness because they were influenced by a host of complex interactions that have changed over time. For example, fire suppression decisions in the first half of the twentieth century were not predictive of possible effects on the mountain pine beetle in the latter half of the century because never before had these management decisions intersected with climate change. It is impossible to consistently and reliably predict in advance the specific consequences of environmental decisions. 'We are always left with best judgments, not certainties.'[42]

The uncertainty inherent within environmental decision-making certainly can be—and is—exploited by those who seek to benefit from weak (or no) regulation.[43] Acknowledging the difficulty in predicting the outcomes of environmental decisions should not be read as an endorsement of these attempts to exaggerate or manufacture uncertainty. It is certainly not the case that all environmental issues contain the possibility of a catastrophe. And in many instances it is possible to foresee the possibility of a catastrophe, although the specific details of how, when, where and why cannot be determined in advance. However, as both the literature of adaptive systems and the literature of risk sociology highlight, we have a long history of failing to anticipate serious outcomes of human action, which is in part explained by the complexity of ecological and social systems.

The second point of overlap is that both complex, adaptive theory and risk sociology emphasise that surprises—sometimes catastrophic surprises—are an inherent part of environmental decision-making. Environmental decision-making must 'embrace uncertainty and unpredictability. Surprise and structural change are inevitable in systems of people and nature.'[44]

Third, these two points of overlap take on a heightened significance in light of the overarching issue of climate change, an environmental issue of both global and existential proportions. The current trajectory of greenhouse gas emissions is projected by the end of the century to result in extreme risks

[41] A Underdal, 'Complexity and Challenges of Long-Term Environmental Governance' (2010) 20 *Global Environmental Change* 386, 388.

[42] CS Holling, 'Understanding the Complexity of Economic, Ecological, and Social Systems' (2001) 4(5) *Ecosystems* 390, 391.

[43] RE Dunlap and AM McCright, 'Climate Change Denial: Sources, Actors and Strategies' in C Lever-Tracy (ed), *Routledge Handbook of Climate Change and Society* (Abingdon, Routledge, 2010) 240, 251.

[44] Holling, 'Understanding the Complexity' (above n 42) 391.

to all biological processes on the planet.[45] While the general phenomenon of climate change is now known, along with many of its consequences—the rise of sea levels and severe heat waves that directly endanger human lives, for example[46]—most of its specific impacts remain unpredictable. For example, polar ice caps are melting at a rate that far exceeds earlier scientific predictions,[47] and ocean acidification is a byproduct of carbon dioxide absorption in the seas with potentially serious but currently unknown consequences for marine ecosystems.[48] Indeed, the greater concern arising from climate change is that we have fundamentally altered and continue to alter our ecological support systems in highly significant but unknown ways.[49] The intricate, global and unavoidable implications of climate change demand that environmental law take seriously the epistemic features of environmental issues highlighted above.

The difficulty of prediction and what this means for decision-making under conditions of uncertainty are perennial themes in environmental law and policy. Indeed, the lack of scientific certainty surrounding the possibility of an extreme event is the central concern of the precautionary principle, a core principle of international environmental law and the subject a vast academic literature in its own right.[50] While there exists extended analysis of the implications of complexity (and possible responses, such as the precautionary principle) in specific regulatory contexts, there is little systematic consideration of what this complexity means across the field of environmental law[51] and almost no consideration of the implications for our understanding of law itself, the subject of this book.[52]

We are now in a position to see that *all* environmental issues possess the constituent features of emergencies. The inability to reliably know in advance which environmental issues or policy choices contain the possibility

[45] Intergovernmental Panel on Climate Change (IPCC), 'Climate Change 2014: Impacts, Adaption, and Vulnerability, A Summary for Policymakers' (2014), www.ipcc.ch/pdf/assessment-report/ar5/wg2/ar5_wgII_spm_en.pdf, 13–14. A 4–5°C increase above preindustrial levels, the current IPCC estimate for the end of this century if emissions continue unabated.

[46] Ibid, 13.

[47] L Morello and Climate Wire, 'Polar Ice Sheets Melting Faster than Predicted', *Scientific American* (9 Mar 2011), www.scientificamerican.com/article/polar-ice-sheets-melting-faster-than-predicted/.

[48] IPCC, 'Climate Change 2014' (above n 45) 17.

[49] Ibid, 6 and 11.

[50] The precautionary principle is a subject of ch 6 below.

[51] Two noteworthy exceptions are DA Kysar, *Regulating from Nowhere: Environmental Law and the Search for Objectivity* (New Haven, Yale University Press, 2010); and E Fisher, *Risk Regulation and Administrative Constitutionalism* (Oxford, Hart Publishing, 2007).

[52] Bruce Pardy has addressed the relationship between complexity and the rule of law, albeit in a fashion that relies on an extreme form of biological determinism: B Pardy, *Ecolawgic* (Kingston, Fifth Forum Press, 2015). I have argued that his theory is incomplete and incompatible with Canadian public law: J Stacey, 'The Promise of the Rule of (Environmental) Law' (2016) 53(2) *Osgoode Hall Law Journal* 68.

of disaster and the inability to know in advance how to respond to such unforeseen events arise from the complex, adaptive nature of ecological and social systems. The challenge for environmental law, therefore, is not only acquiring and incorporating better environmental knowledge. Both ecological theory and risk sociology are clear that uncertainty will always remain. The challenge for environmental law is instead Schmitt's challenge: that is, the challenge to show that, despite this profound uncertainty, environmental issues can be governed by law.

Importantly, Schmitt's challenge extends to all environmental issues because it is not possible to 'carve out irreversible or catastrophic risks for special treatment'.[53] As we have seen, we cannot always be sure which category any given decision or issue belongs to. Moreover, the necessarily incomplete state of our knowledge requires the recognition that even gradual, low-level or chronic environmental harm may eventually reach its own tipping point, resulting in an unforeseen, extreme event. In other words, regulatory decisions that at the time of their making seem trivial or benign can in fact have irreversible environmental effects even if their full impacts do not materialise until well into the future, long past when anything can be done about it. Each environmental issue can therefore be understood as an 'emergency in miniature',[54] in which decisions must be made under conditions of uncertainty and the possibility that *this* decision will be the one that triggers the catastrophe cannot be eliminated in advance. It is our epistemic inability to distinguish benign policy choices from catastrophic ones that justifies viewing all relevant events and policies through the prism of the emergency paradigm.

II. FAILING SCHMITT'S CHALLENGE

Since environmental issues are best understood as an ongoing emergency, the next task is to understand the precise nature of the problem that all emergencies pose for law. We saw in section I that Schmitt defined the notion of the emergency and, at the same time, made specific assumptions about law. In particular, he equated law with relatively determinative rules set down in advance by the legislature.[55] I follow existing Canadian public law scholarship in referring to this as the *formal conception of the rule of law* because it hinges on a formal allocation of power between the branches

[53] Stacey, 'The Promise of the Rule of (Environmental) Law' (ibid) 22. See also Beck, *Risk Society* (above n 32) 78–79.

[54] Dyzenhaus, *The Constitution of Law* (above n 14) 60.

[55] WE Scheuerman, 'Carl Schmitt's Critique of Liberal Constitutionalism' (1996) 58 *Review of Politics* 299, 314–315; and Dyzenhaus, *The Constitution of Law* (above n 14) 61.

of government.[56] We will return to the formal conception in detail in section III, but here I observe that, for those who subscribe to a formal conception of the rule of law, there are only two responses to an emergency: either an extra-legal response or accommodation. In brief, the extra-legal approach permits public officials to act in contravention of the law in order to respond to the emergency. In contrast, under the accommodation approach, emergencies are governed by the rule of law, albeit a thinner conception of the rule of law that accepts the need for flexibility in times of crisis. I argue that both these approaches fail Schmitt's challenge: the extra-legal approach cannot confine emergency measures to times of crisis, and the accommodation approach only creates the façade, or appearance, of legality.

A. The Extra-Legal Approach to Emergency Powers

Oren Gross has offered the most comprehensive account of the extra-legal approach to understanding emergency powers.[57] Gross follows Schmitt in his open acknowledgement that emergencies cannot be governed by law. He concedes that their unforeseeable and extreme nature necessitates exceptional state action,[58] and he supports his argument with a detailed historical account of how constitutional commitments do not seem to prevent governments from taking these emergency response actions.[59] But in contrast to Schmitt, Gross argues that permitting extra-legal measures is the best hope of preserving a long-term commitment to the rule of law. Since it seems that public officials will take exceptional actions notwithstanding legal constraints, Gross argues we should permit them to do so, provided that they act openly and for the purpose of the public good.[60] Gross reasons that this keeps the rule of law intact; we do not legitimise these exceptional actions as legal. He worries that legally authorised emergency powers will normalise. Over time, legal emergency responses will seep into the ordinary

[56] M Loughlin, 'Procedural Fairness: A Study of the Crisis in Administrative Law Theory' (1978) 28 *University of Toronto Law Journal* 215; D Dyzenhaus and E Fox-Decent, 'Rethinking the Process/Substance Distinction: *Baker v Canada*' (2001) 51 *University of Toronto Law Journal* 193, 197–205; and G Cartier, 'Procedural Fairness in Legislative Functions: The End of Judicial Abstinence?' (2003) 53 *University of Toronto Law Journal* 217.

[57] Gross, 'Chaos and Rules' (above n 15). See also M Tushnet, 'Emergencies and the Idea of Constitutionalism' in M Tushnet (ed), *The Constitution in Wartime* (Durham, Duke University Press, 2005) 39; C Fatovic, *Outside the Law: Emergency and Executive Power* (Baltimore, John Hopkins University Press, 2009); NC Lazar, *States of Emergency in Liberal Democracies* (New York, Cambridge University Press, 2009); and B Honig, *Emergency Politics: Paradox, Law, Democracy* (Princeton, Princeton University Press, 2009), reviewed in D Dyzenhaus, 'Emergency, Liberalism, and the State' (2011) 9 *Perspectives on Politics* 69.

[58] Gross, 'Chaos and Rules' (above n 15) 1097.

[59] Ibid.

[60] Ibid.

legal regime and weaken ordinary rule-of-law commitments. The extra-legal approach, in contrast, has the virtue of transparency. Emergency measures, according to Gross, are seen for what they really are: extreme actions driven by necessity.[61]

In practice, an extra-legal approach means emergency powers are solely at the discretion of individual public officials. These officials must make the determination of whether an illegal action (eg, torture) is necessary. Gross argues that public officials facing such a choice will be regulated by their 'ethic of responsibility'.[62] By this, he means their desire to protect their institutions and citizens against threats and accept the consequences, whatever they may be, of their actions. Gross pins much on the uncertainty of the potential repercussions of extra-legal activity. Since public officials do not know whether the public will ratify the extra-legal action (eg, by their legislative representatives passing an Act of Indemnity) or repudiate it (eg, through criminal prosecution), he presumes overzealous extra-legality will be held in check.

The extra-legal approach hinges entirely on an assumption that emergencies are truly exceptional events that can be readily distinguished from ordinary regulatory problems faced by the state.[63] It creates a dualist regime: ie, ordinary law for ordinary times, and extra-legal actions for emergencies. The terms of Schmitt's challenge preclude the theory's defenders from identifying in advance the kinds of situations that will warrant extra-legal action. Such action is necessarily an individual determination at the discretion of public officials. Gross, for his part, offers the classic example of the ticking time-bomb scenario that might lead an official to commit torture to obtain vital information to locate and diffuse the bomb.[64] Tushnet offers the counter-example of the open-ended 'war on terror'. He warns that '[s]uspending legality during a time-limited war is one thing. Suspending it during a more or less permanent condition is quite another. The latter is the end of the rule of law itself.'[65] This lack of specificity and Tushnet's warning reveal that this is a precarious dualist order indeed.

Critics have pointed to two highly dubious assumptions on which the extra-legal approach relies. As we have seen, the extra-legal approach requires public officials to act with candour. But why would they? The prospect of

[61] Tushnet, 'Emergencies and the Idea of Constitutionalism' (above n 57) also endorses a version of the extra-legal approach: 'it is better to have emergency powers exercised in an extraconstitutional way, so that everyone understands that the actions are extraordinary, than to have the actions rationalized away as consistent with the Constitution and thereby normalized' (61).

[62] Gross, 'Chaos and Rules' (above n 15) 1108–9.

[63] Poole, 'Constitutional Exceptionalism' (above n 15) 272.

[64] Gross, 'Chaos and Rules' (above n 15) 1097–98.

[65] Tushnet, 'Emergencies and the Idea of Constitutionalism' (above n 57) 45.

potentially severe repercussions—that an official will be personally liable—would seem sufficient to drive extra-legal actions out of public sight, not into it. A second flaw is that the same influences that cause legal regulation of emergency powers to normalise would seemingly apply to extra-legal powers. Gross has documented the many ways in which exceptional powers are rationalised and eventually creep into the ordinary legal order.[66] For example, he has noted that emergency powers can become effectively permanent when a state is faced with repeated threats. In other cases, he has observed that emergency powers exercised abroad have a way of migrating across borders to be adopted at home. In other words, emergency measures can gain political currency that undermines attempts to clearly maintain a dual order. When this insight is applied to Gross' argument, it seems that once one extra-legal action is politically ratified, it is likely that public officials would be able to correctly expect that the public would ratify subsequent emergency actions as well.[67]

David Dyzenhaus has gone further by critiquing Gross' equivocation over the possible source of extra-legal powers. At times Gross has seemed to suggest that the power to act extra-legally is located within the constitutional order itself.[68] Dyzenhaus has argued that by acknowledging that officials have the *legal* power to violate the law, Gross eliminates any legal basis on which we can constrain executive discretion to prevent its conversion into an unlimited power.[69] In other words, Gross' move means there is no conceptual basis on which to make the dualist fiction real. There is no way to impose legal constraints on the exercise of discretion once we accept that it is permissible to exercise discretion in violation of the law.

B. The Accommodation Approach to Emergency Powers

These critiques of the extra-legal approach seem to have some traction. The extra-legal approach has not been the dominant response to emergency powers. Far more prevalent is the attempt to 'accommodate' emergencies within legal order.[70] The accommodation approach attempts to subject emergencies to some legal constraints, even if we have to concede that these constraints are less rigorous than in ordinary times. Dyzenhaus has

[66] Gross, 'Chaos and Rules' (above n 15) 1073–77.

[67] DH Cole, 'Judging the Next Emergency: Judicial Review and Individual Rights in Times of Crisis' (2003) 101 *Michigan Law Review* 2565, 2589; and Dyzenhaus, *The Constitution of Law* (above n 14) 52.

[68] O Gross, 'Extra-Legality and the Ethic of Political Responsibility' in VV Ramraj (ed), *Emergencies and the Limits of Legality* (Cambridge, Cambridge University Press, 2008) 97.

[69] Dyzenhaus, *The Constitution of Law* (above n 14) 52–53.

[70] EA Posner and A Vermeule, 'Accommodating Emergencies' (2003) *Stanford Law Review* 605; Gross and Aolain, *Law in Times of Crisis* (above n 3) ch 1.

attributed the accommodation approach to the 'compulsion of legality'.[71] In contrast to Gross' assumption of candour, Dyzenhaus has argued that public officials will seek to justify their actions as having legal warrant, however tenuous that warrant may be.

The paradigmatic example of the accommodation approach is the Roman constitutional dictatorship,[72] which provided for the temporary appointment of a constitutional dictator solely for the purpose of bringing an emergency to an end. The constitutional dictator enjoyed nearly unconstrained substantive decision-making power, subject only to his purpose of ending the crisis and preserving, not altering, the ordinary constitution. However, he was still subject to procedural constitutional norms.[73] The Roman constitutional dictatorship thus created a separate regime for emergency powers, one embedded within legal order but subject to distinct and diminished rule-of-law requirements.

The constitutional dictatorship is not a legal antiquity. Prominent constitutional law scholar Bruce Ackerman attempted to rekindle the constitutional dictatorship in his post-9/11 proposal for an 'Emergency Constitution'.[74] Ackerman's proposal, in fact not a constitution but a framework statute, concedes the need for exceptional Presidential powers to respond to crises such as the terrorist attacks of 9/11.[75] But Ackerman's proposal would require the President to obtain periodic legislative renewal for exceptional powers, by increasing super-legislative majorities.[76] Canada's not-so-distant War Measures Act (1970) is another example of a constitutional dictatorship of sorts.[77] It was properly enacted and constitutionally valid (at the time) legislation[78] that delegated unfettered discretion to the executive to

[71] D Dyzenhaus, 'Cycles of Legality in Emergency Times' (2007) 18 *Public Law Review* 165, 167. Dyzenhaus gives as an example Dershowitz's advocacy of torture warrants: AM Dershowitz, *Why Terrorism Works: Understanding the Threat, Responding to the Challenge* (New Haven, Yale University Press, 2002). See also WE Scheuerman, 'Survey Article: Emergency Powers and the Rule of Law After 9/11' (2006) 14 *Journal of Political Philosophy* 61, 72.

[72] J Ferejohn and P Pasquino, 'The Law of Exception: A Typology of Emergency Powers' (2004) 2 *International Journal of Constitutional Law* 210, 211: 'Modern emergencies are, to a greater or lesser extent, modeled on the ancient model of the Roman dictatorship.'

[73] C Rossiter, *Constitutional Dictatorship: Crisis Government in the Modern Democracies* (New Brunswick, Transaction Publishers, 2002) 19–25.

[74] Ackerman's proposal drew extensively on Clinton Rossiter's influential survey of emergency powers and argument for a constitutional dictatorship, again modelled on the Roman dictatorship: Ackerman, 'The Emergency Constitution' (above n 14).

[75] Ibid, 1038.

[76] Ibid, 1047.

[77] War Measures Act (above n 4).

[78] The Court upheld the exercise of powers because they were legal, that is, authorised by validly enacted legislation: *Gagnon and Vallières v The Queen* (1971), 14 CRNS 321 (Que CA). But see H Marx, 'The Apprehended Insurrection of October 1970 and the Judicial Function' (1972) 7 *University of British Columbia Law Review* 55; and JN Lyon, 'Constitutional Validity of Sections 3 and 4 of the Public Order Regulations, 1970' (1972) 18 *McGill Law*

respond to a crisis. All three examples illustrate an attempt to create a dual legal order: one set of legal rules for ordinary times and a separate set invoked in times of crisis.[79]

Dyzenhaus has argued that these emergency powers are 'legal black holes'[80]—that is, legislative attempts to create a sphere of action that is not governed by law. In other words, the legislature purports to declare in advance that any action taken under the statute is prospectively legalised.

Schmitt's work reveals that the problem with such legal black holes is that there is in fact no way to confine them. He argued that there is no way to make a dictatorship constitutional because the unforeseeable and extreme nature of the emergency means that it cannot be subject to binding legal requirements, not even requirements procedural in nature.[81] Since an emergency might even require suspension of legal order, it is impossible for law to ensure that a constitutional dictatorship remains temporary. By conceding that it is necessary to suspend the ordinary legal order in favour of a temporary dictatorship, a constitutional dictatorship implicitly concedes that it might be necessary to suspend the temporary dictatorship as well.

The same logic applies to Ackerman's 'Emergency Constitution' and to the Canadian War Measures Act. The accommodation approach, at base, thus presents the same problem as the extra-legal approach. Once we concede that the law permits us to suspend the ordinary legal order in favour of an emergency legal order, we no longer have the legal resources to ensure that the emergency legal order remains temporary and exceptional.

There is another problem with the accommodation approach, however. As the response to 9/11 in the United States and Canada demonstrates, we are not at any risk of the permanent suspension of legal order.[82] Instead, we face the more insidious problem of rapidly expanding zones of discretionary executive authority.[83] Put differently, in Canada we no longer face the prospect of the invocation of the War Measure Act, nor do we face a real prospect of its more tailored successor, the Emergencies Act (1985), playing

Journal 136 (on the Act's potential violation of the division of powers between federal and provincial governments and the ways in which the courts could have asserted a much stronger role).

[79] Gross and Aolain have offered a comprehensive account of forms of accommodation: international, constitutional, legislative levels and through judicial interpretation that relaxes ordinary rule-of-law requirements: Gross and Aolain, *Law in Times of Crisis* (above n 3) ch 1.

[80] Dyzenhaus, *The Constitution of Law* (above n 14) 3.

[81] This about-face is explored in JP McCormick, 'The Dilemma of Dictatorship: Carl Schmitt and Constitutional Emergency Powers' in D Dyzenhaus (ed), *Law as Politics: Carl Schmitt's Critique of Liberalism* (Durham, Duke University Press, 1998) 221–22.

[82] Posner and Vermeule refer to this as 'tyrannophobia': Posner and Vermeule, *The Executive Unbound* (above n 10) ch 6. See also I Zuckerman, 'One Law for War and Peace? Judicial Review and Emergency Powers between the Norm and the Exception' (2006) 13 *Constellations* 522, 528.

[83] Zuckerman (ibid) 528.

a major role in emergency response.[84] Instead, the contemporary emergency problem is reflected in the proliferation of pockets of executive discretion within ordinary statutes. In the aftermath of 9/11, the Canadian Parliament embedded terrorism-related offences within Canada's Criminal Code.[85] This means that offences related to the murky concept of terrorism are legally authorised through their placement in ordinary criminal legislation despite the difficulty of defining the concept of terrorism in advance.[86] Even more alarming is Canada's Security of Canada Information Sharing Act,[87] which further blurs the concept of 'terrorism' to allow the government to collect and share any information on 'activities that undermine the security of Canada'.[88]

This is in fact a variation of the same problem, a problem that Schmitt long ago diagnosed. He predicted that those committed to the ideal that all executive power should be subjected to the rule of law will be unable to countenance the real nature of emergencies.[89] Instead, they will attempt to pretend that executive discretion is governed by law—that is, by pre-existing statute—even when it is clear that the executive wields discretionary power. To borrow Dyzenhaus' helpful terminology, we now face the problem of multiple legal black holes *and* 'legal grey holes', which are essentially black holes in disguise. Legal black holes, recall, are attempts by the legislature to exempt the executive from rule-of-law requirements. They are 'legislative blank cheques' to the executive.[90] Legal grey holes create the appearance of legal constraint but are 'so insubstantial that they pretty well permit the government to do as it pleases'.[91] An appeals tribunal that simply rubber-stamps an executive decision is an example of a legal grey hole.[92] Schmitt's prediction suggests that those who are committed to the rule of law should be even more comfortable with legal grey holes than with black holes, because they further mask the extent to which a decision is the product of unconstrained discretion.

[84] Emergencies Act, RSC 1985, c 22 (4th Supp). It has never been invoked.

[85] Criminal Code, RSC 1985, c C-46, Part II.1.

[86] D Dyzenhaus, 'The Permanence of the Temporary: Can Emergency Powers Be Normalized?' in RJ Daniels, P Macklem and K Roach (eds), *The Security of Freedom: Essays on Canada's Anti-Terrorism Bill* (Toronto, University of Toronto Press, 2001) 21.

[87] Security of Canada Information Sharing Act, SC 2015, c 20, s 2.

[88] Public Safety Canada, 'Backgrounder: Security of Canada Information Sharing Act' (January 2015), www.canada.ca/en/news/archive/2015/01/security-canada-information-sharing-act.html. Craig Forcese and Kent Roach have argued that this is a radical departure from past anti-terror approaches and have documented the numerous ways that this broad definition can be interpreted that gives rise to considerable uncertainty about its future implementation: C Forcese and K Roach, 'Stumbling Toward Total Information Awareness: The Security of Canada Information Sharing Act' (2015) 12 *Canadian Privacy Law Review* 65.

[89] Scheuerman, 'Carl Schmitt's Critique' (above n 55) esp 306–8.

[90] Dyzenhaus, *The Constitution of Law* (above n 14) 50.

[91] Ibid, 42.

[92] Ibid, 3.

The American response to 9/11 provides an especially clear example of how Schmitt's critique can play out in practice. In 2004, the United States Supreme Court upheld the executive's authority to classify and detain US citizens as 'enemy combatants' and subject them to a distinct legal process through a system of military tribunals.[93] The plurality opinion, in line with Schmitt's prediction, deferred to the need for exceptional emergency powers but was not willing to concede that the executive operated unconstrained by law. Rather, the plurality found legal authorisation for detention in the extremely broad language of the Authorization for Use of Military Force (AUMF),[94] which states that 'the President is authorised to use all necessary and appropriate force' against terrorism.[95] While the plurality was no doubt correct that the open-ended language of 'all necessary and appropriate force' could be interpreted to include detention of enemy combatants, the legislation is far from the 'explicit congressional authorisation' that the plurality claims.[96] Justice Souter (Ginsburg J concurring) observed that the legislation

> never so much as uses the word detention, and there is no reason to think Congress might have perceived any need to augment Executive power to deal with dangerous citizens within the United States, given the well-stocked statutory arsenal of defined criminal offenses covering the gamut of actions that a citizen sympathetic to terrorists might commit.[97]

The plurality's finding that the AUMF included the authority to create a detention regime cleared the way for the conclusion that the executive also had authority to determine the procedures and therefore the rights accorded to the detainees. The Court permitted the creation of a legal grey hole, purportedly governed by the rule of law but lacking substantive due process rights accorded in ordinary cases.[98] In other words, the plurality opinion turned the rule of law into a façade of legality, which authorised actions that the executive was determined to take in any event.[99]

The accommodation approach also fails Schmitt's challenge. It results in the creation of legal black and grey holes where the exercise of emergency powers is not meaningfully governed by the rule of law. The judiciary's role is reduced to either that of timekeeper, ensuring that powers are not exercised past their expiry date, or that of the certifier of blank checks, ensuring

[93] *Hamdi v Rumsfeld*, [2004] 124 S Ct 2633 (US).

[94] Ibid, 518.

[95] AUMF (above n 13).

[96] *Hamdi* (above n 93) 517.

[97] Ibid, 548.

[98] This argument is also made by Dyzenhaus, *The Constitution of Law* (above n 14) 48–50; and Zuckerman, 'One Law for War and Peace?' (above n 82) 535–36.

[99] See Scalia J's reasons for creating a legal black hole and Thomas J's reasons for a full Schmittian argument that there is no role for the court in overseeing national security decisions.

that legislation is properly enacted. From this perspective, the courts cannot impose substantive constraints on the executive's emergency response because there are none in the legislation to enforce. Accommodating the emergency within legal order allows the executive the best of both worlds. It can exercise essentially unfettered discretion while also claiming to act in accordance with the rule of law.[100] Schmitt's position is that in an emergency, there is only a façade of legality. Executive discretion is authorised by legislation, but it does not prevent public officials from exercising discretion to achieve illiberal ends.

III. THE FORMAL CONCEPTION OF THE RULE OF LAW

We have now seen that Schmitt's argument is that the emergency reveals the necessity of executive discretion. An extra-legal approach cannot be sustained because there is no way to confine emergency powers and ensure they remain temporary and exceptional. Accommodating emergency powers within ordinary legislation is equally problematic, as it only provides a cover or façade of legality for discretionary powers. This section argues that Schmitt's challenge is not limited to exceptional emergencies. Rather, it is part of a much more fundamental and systemic critique of liberal constitutionalism, that is, the commitment to subjecting the exercise of all political power to legal authority. As I will explain, Schmitt's challenge can be reframed as the challenge that discretion poses to the formal conception of the rule of law.

Schmitt argued that the emergency fatally undermines the core tenet of liberal constitutionalism, ie, the subjection to law of all public acts.[101] Because the operation of legal order hinges on a purely discretionary decision of the sovereign, on his view, it cannot be the case that all political power is subject to legal authorisation. But Schmitt's argument is not only limited to this worst-case scenario of the existential threat. Schmitt took a narrow view of law. By equating law with legislated rules, he did not seem to allow for any kind of discretion in the application of these rules. Dyzenhaus has described Schmitt's perspective as 'a kind of naive legal positivism in which "controlled by law" means that general legal rules determine an outcome so that no human agency or judgment is required to decide what the law says'.[102] Schmitt's argument about the emergency therefore turns

[100] Dyzenhaus, *The Constitution of Law* (above n 14); Gross and Aolain, *Law in Times of Crisis* (above n 3) 63; Zuckerman, 'One Law for War and Peace?' (above n 82) 531; and Poole, 'Constitutional Exceptionalism' (above n 15) 252–58.

[101] Scheuerman, 'Carl Schmitt's Critique' (above n 55). See also Dyzenhaus, 'Emergency, Liberalism, and the State' (above n 57) 70; and Posner and Vermeule, *The Executive Unbound* (above n 10) 3.

[102] Dyzenhaus, 'Emergency, Liberalism, and the State' (above n 57) 74–75.

on an assumption about the 'extra-legal' nature of discretion. The emergency is one striking example of the exercise of discretion, but discretion exists in non-exceptional cases as well. Dyzenhaus has observed that every discretionary decision, for Schmitt, must be a 'mini state of emergency or exception'[103] because the 'official ... has to make a quasi-sovereign or legislative decision, one that is ultimately unconstrained by legal norms'.[104]

This is made particularly clear in Schmitt's work on economic emergencies. Schmitt observed that economic emergencies are also characterised by wide grants of discretionary authority to the executive comparable only to the sweeping authority granted during war or insurrection.[105] Like the national security emergency, the complex and ever-changing nature of economic problems requires 'future-oriented steering' that can be provided only by the executive.[106] Schmitt observed that legislated rules were based on past experience and could not anticipate the future economic needs of the state. Economic emergencies, then, were the link between the state of emergency and the 'growth of far-reaching discretionary executive power and the concomitant decline of elected legislatures'.[107] For Schmitt, existential threats, economic emergencies and everyday executive discretion are all points on the same continuum. In his view, they all reveal the emptiness of liberal constitutionalism, the fact that the executive wields vast and legally unconstrained power.

Contemporary American legal scholars Eric Posner and Adrian Vermeule have further drawn out these connections in their self-proclaimed 'Schmittian' account of the modern administrative state.[108] Posner and Vermeule have documented responses to recent emergencies—terrorist attacks and financial crises—and the broad delegation of everyday, non-emergency discretionary powers to expert administrative agencies. This evidence leads them to conclude that the executive is the 'center of institutional gravity'.[109] Adopting Schmitt's institutional insights, they argue that the need for fast-paced, coordinated action in response to complex and dynamic policy problems heavily favours the executive.[110] They argue the legislature

[103] Dyzenhaus, *The Constitution of Law* (above n 14) 60.

[104] Ibid.

[105] WE Scheuerman, 'The Economic State of Emergency' (2000) 21 *Cardozo Law Review* 1869, 1871.

[106] Ibid, 1887.

[107] Ibid, 1884.

[108] By this they mean legally unbounded. They argue that political constraints, elections, the party system and culture conditions offer greater constraints than law: Posner and Vermeule, *The Executive Unbound* (above n 10) 113–14. For criticism of this argument, see, eg, WE Scheuerman, 'Emergencies, Executive Power, and the Uncertain Future of US Presidential Democracy' (2012) 37 *Law and Social Inquiry* 743.

[109] Posner and Vermeule, *The Executive Unbound* (above n 10) 11.

[110] Ibid, 31–32.

and judiciary are ill-suited to make decisions under these conditions and therefore cannot effectively constrain executive action.[111]

Posner and Vermeule offer the federal Administrative Procedures Act, the heart of American administrative law, as an example of the illusory nature of legal constraints.[112] They argue that the Act is shot through with legal black and grey holes. Legal black holes are the kinds of agency action that are exempted from judicial review.[113] Legal grey holes are those standards that judges can relax when under pressure from the executive, so that executive action is not meaningfully constrained.[114] Posner and Vermeule have therefore concluded that rule-of-law constraints are 'shaky in normal times and weak or non-existent in times of crisis'.[115] The problem of the emergency, in other words, is the problem of discretion writ large.

Canadian administrative law has been strongly influenced by the work of AV Dicey,[116] who was also a committed liberal constitutionalist and thus vulnerable to Schmitt's critiques. Dicey maintained that '"[m]artial law" … is unknown to the law of England. … This is unmistakable proof of the permanent supremacy of the law under our constitution.'[117] Dicey thus rejected the dualist fiction; his conception of the rule of law made no provision for a separate emergency powers regime.[118] Instead, Dicey's conception of the rule of law was 'dualist', but in a different sense from that used above. He distinguished between the dual roles of the legislature and the judiciary. On his view, the legislature possesses a monopoly over law-making, while the judiciary possesses a monopoly over legal interpretation.[119] For Dicey,

[111] Ibid, 25–26 and 52–53. Further, according to Posner and Vermeule, to the extent that the legislature and judiciary attempt to impose these constraints, as liberal legalists would have them do, they are likely to get it wrong and undermine sound decision-making, which is defined by Posner and Vermeule as the results of cost–benefit analysis.

[112] Ibid, 93–96.

[113] For example, only 'agency action' is reviewable by the courts, which the US Supreme Court has held does not include 'programmatic decisions'. Thus, the failure of an agency to address the use of off-road vehicles in a wilderness area is not an action reviewable by the court: *Norton v Southern Utah Wilderness Alliance*, 542 US 55 (2004).

[114] For example, the 'arbitrary and capricious' standard for reviewing agency policy choices and factual findings: Posner and Vermeule, *The Executive Unbound* (above n 10) 93–96. But see EJ Criddle, 'Mending Holes in the Rule of (Administrative) Law' (2010) 104 *Northwestern University Law Review* 1271 for a critique that is consistent with the argument presented in Part Two of this book.

[115] Posner and Vermeule, *The Executive Unbound* (above n 10) 4.

[116] Dyzenhaus and Fox-Decent, 'Rethinking the Process/Substance Distinction' (above n 56); and Loughlin, 'Procedural Fairness' (above n 56).

[117] AV Dicey, *Introduction to the Study of the Law of the Constitution*, 10th edn (Toronto, Macmillan Company of Canada, 1959) 287–88. We take up Dicey's argument about emergencies in ch 4 below.

[118] Compare Ferejohn and Pasquino, 'The Law of Exception: A Typology' (above n 72) with Dyzenhaus' interpretation, which we consider below in ch 4.

[119] Dyzenhaus and Fox-Decent, 'Rethinking the Process/Substance Distinction' (above n 56) 198.

Parliamentary supremacy and the rule of law were the twin pillars of the English constitution. While Parliament has a monopoly over law-making, this power is always subject to the supervision of the courts. Dicey could therefore maintain the liberal constitutional commitment to the subjection of all political power to the rule of law.

But Dicey was also infamously hostile to the administrative state and therefore saw no distinct role for the executive.[120] The expanding administrative state threatened his vision of the constitution. Discretionary administrative decision-making, which requires weighing competing policy considerations, threatened the legislature's monopoly over law-making. And when an administrative decision-maker must interpret its authorising legislation, it threatens the judicial monopoly on interpretation. Unlike either legislative or judicial powers, Dicey understood administrative decisions as inherently arbitrary. Legislation, even by a supreme Parliament, is limited by its general and prospective nature and the supervision of the courts.[121] While the courts decide individual cases, they are constrained by the doctrine of precedent and the obligation to issue public reasons for their decisions. Dicey sought to protect the individual from the exercise of arbitrary state power by repudiating its primary source: the administrative state.

Dicey's insistence on dual constitutional monopolies and his denial of distinct executive power gives rise to a *de facto* doctrine of a strong separation of powers, even in a parliamentary system that otherwise lacks such a strong separation. In other words, Dicey can be interpreted as the source of a formal conception of the rule of law in Canada.[122] We will see how this plays out in Canadian administrative law in chapter two. But for now, it is sufficient to note that this interpretation of Dicey's theory is the same conception of the rule of law that fails Schmitt's challenge. It denies the need for exceptional discretionary powers to respond to an emergency, and it denies the need for ordinary discretionary powers in the form of the everyday administrative state. To the extent that the formal conception of the rule of law governs Canadian administrative law, we can expect that, as Posner and Vermeule have observed, it too will be riddled with legal black and grey holes.

[120] Dicey (above n 117) 188.

[121] TRS Allan, *Constitutional Justice: A Liberal Theory of the Rule of Law* (Oxford, Clarendon Press, 2001) 14–16.

[122] Dyzenhaus, *The Constitution of Law* (above n 14) 71. His is also thought of as a formal account because Dicey distinguished between the formal qualities that law must have to be law and the substantive ends the law purports to achieve: P Craig, 'Formal and Substantive Conceptions of the Rule of Law' (1997) 3 *Public Law* 467, 470–72. However, ch 4 below contests this interpretation of Dicey in a way that also blurs this line between formal (or procedural) and substantive accounts of the rule of law.

IV. CONCLUSION

This chapter has set out the framework for the analysis of environmental law that follows. It has argued that the best way to understand the problem that environmental issues pose for law is as an ongoing emergency. Environmental issues, like emergencies, contain two epistemic features: the inability to predict which issues have catastrophic potential and the inability to know in advance how to respond should a catastrophe occur. These are systemic features of environmental issues that arise from the fact that ecological systems are complex and adaptive. It is therefore not possible to predict the effects of our decisions on the environment. Indeed, it is not even possible to reliably eliminate the possibility of a catastrophe. As the mountain pine beetle epidemic illustrates, even seemingly well understood environmental issues can have catastrophic potential. This justifies approaching all of environmental law from the perspective of an ongoing emergency.

We also saw that the problem of emergencies can be framed in terms of Schmitt's challenge, the challenge to show how emergencies can be governed by law. We saw that Schmitt assumed a formal conception of the rule of law, in which the legislature is the sole source of legitimate legal norms. For those who adhere to this conception of the rule of law, there are only two possible responses to the emergency: resort to the exercise of extra-legal powers, or attempt to accommodate the emergency within legal order. These responses fail Schmitt's challenge. By conceding the need for exceptional emergency powers, we no longer have a legal basis on which to confine the use of emergency powers. In addition, accommodating emergency powers within legal order risks creating legal black and grey holes within ordinary legislation. The attempt to subject emergency powers to legal constraints only buries the discretionary nature of these powers under a façade of legality.

Finally, we saw that Schmitt's challenge is not limited to the exceptional emergency; rather, it is a broader attack on the liberal constitutional state. For Schmitt and his followers, the emergency simply brings to the surface the inadequacy of liberal constitutionalism for responding to a fast-paced world. Since legislatures cannot anticipate unforeseeable events or quickly respond to urgent or rapidly evolving problems, the best they can do is delegate broad powers to the executive. From the perspective of the formal conception of the rule of law, emergencies and discretionary administrative powers exist in legal black or grey holes. That is, they are governed by law only in the thinnest possible sense; the executive is not subject to meaningful rule-of-law constraints.

We will see in chapter four that we need not accept the terms of Schmitt's challenge. We can reject the formal conception of the rule of law. But first, we are now in a position to uncover existing assumptions in environmental law about both the nature of environmental issues and the nature of the rule of law. In other words, we can now subject existing approaches to environmental law to the terms of Schmitt's challenge.

2

Environmental Reform: The Problem of Discretion in Environmental Law

THE CONCEPT OF the environmental emergency reveals that the epistemic features of emergencies are inherent in environmental issues. The complex, adaptive nature of ecological systems means that our understanding of environmental issues and their potential regulatory solutions is necessarily limited. We cannot reliably distinguish in advance between sound policy choices and catastrophic choices, and this undermines our ability to govern environmental issues through *ex ante* legal rules. We have seen in chapter one that the environmental emergency, like all emergencies, reveals the necessity of executive discretion. This conclusion poses a key problem for those who seek to protect the environment. Just as discretionary emergency response decisions can and often do undermine civil liberties, discretionary environmental decisions can and often do undermine environmental protection.[1]

The relationship between environmental degradation and administrative discretion is the understandable concern of many environmental law scholars. Prominent Canadian commentators, for example, have argued that discretion is a fundamental and pervasive problem in Canadian environmental law and must be remedied. I call this 'the environmental reform position'. I argue that the environmental reform position has identified a symptom in environmental law (discretion) without diagnosing its underlying theoretical cause. We will see that environmental reformers are rightly concerned with discretion because Canadian environmental law is by and large governed by a formal conception of the rule of law. Discretionary environmental decisions are therefore not subject to meaningful rule-of-law constraints. However, environmental reformers have missed the deeper

[1] Much of this chapter appeared in an earlier form in J Stacey, 'The Environmental Emergency and the Legality of Discretion in Environmental Law' (2016) 52(3) *Osgoode Hall Law Journal* 983. Additional examples of legal black and grey holes in Canadian environmental law, which are introduced and analysed in section II of this chapter can be found there.

theoretical challenge. The solutions that they propose are also premised on the formal conception and therefore provide no solution at all.

The environmental reform position is a stylised account that covers a range of reform-oriented scholarship and policy proposals in Canadian environmental law. Individual reformers differ in their reasons for adopting the reform positions, and their proposals differ in the details. By grouping this literature and addressing it collectively from the perspective of the environmental emergency, we are able to tease out its assumptions about law, democracy and the nature of environmental problems. We will see that the persistence of the formal conception offers an explanation for a wide range of judicial decisions reviewing the exercise of discretionary authority over the environment. However, in failing to recognise the limits of the formal conception, environmental reformers have been complicit in the failed attempt to 'accommodate' the environmental emergency within legal order.

In the first section of the chapter, I introduce the environmental reform position. The common thread amongst environmental reformers is that administrative discretion is both a defining feature and fundamental flaw in Canada environmental law.[2] The second section argues that the emergency perspective validates the environmental reform position's concern that discretion can be exercised in an arbitrary fashion without any real chance of legal recourse. This is because the formal conception of the rule of law persists in the environmental context, and it leads judges to create legal black and grey holes. We will see that discretionary environmental decisions, such as decisions to issue regulations or licences, exist in a legal black hole. The formal conception leads judges to find these administrative decisions not justiciable, or subject to review only for their *vires*, and exempt from the common law requirement of procedural fairness. Even where the legislature has attempted to impose some, albeit minimal, substantive constraints on the exercise of discretion, judges are reluctant to give these constraints any teeth. Formalist judges, in other words, create legal grey holes. The third section of the chapter turns to the solutions offered by the environmental reform position. It argues that both proposed solutions—stricter legislated rules and independent decision-makers—are products of the formal conception of the rule of law. In other words, just like proponents of the accommodation approach in the emergency context, environmental reformers have failed Carl Schmitt's challenge.

[2] D Boyd, *Unnatural Law: Rethinking Canadian Environmental Law and Policy* (Vancouver, University of British Columbia Press, 2003) 154, 231; L Collins, 'Tort, Democracy and Environmental Governance: The Case of Non-Enforcement' (2007) 15 *Tort Law Review* 107, 111; DP Emond, '"Are We There Yet?" Reflections on the Success of the Environmental Law Movement in Ontario' (2008) 46 *Osgoode Hall Law Journal* 219, 224. For an American version of the environmental reform position, see the aptly entitled: MC Wood, '"You Can't Negotiate with a Beetle:" Environmental Law for a New Ecological Age' (2010) 50 *Natural Resources Journal* 167.

I. THE ENVIRONMENTAL REFORM POSITION

Since environmental issues are best understood as an ongoing emergency, they present the unavoidable problem of administrative discretion. However, this conclusion conflicts with the environmental reform position. While the environmental reform position is not monolithic, its core attributes are shared amongst many Canadian environmental law scholars. At base, environmental reformers object to the extent of administrative discretion that permeates Canadian environmental law. David Boyd has called environmental statutes 'paper tigers'[3] because their lofty goals are subtly but consistently undermined by discretionary loopholes through which industry receives authorisations to pollute, degrade and harm the environment.[4] A common form for Canadian environmental legislation is to set out a general ecological objective or prohibition on pollution but immediately undercut the general rule with a wide-open delegation of discretion that allows administrative decision-makers to authorise contravention of the rule.

The environmental reform position's primary concern is that this seemingly unfettered discretion is consistently exercised in a way that undermines environmental protection. Discretion allows decision-makers to favour short-term interests rather than long-term environmental protection.[5] This observation is supported by numerous theories of regulation which posit that regulated industries are able to coordinate and advance their interests within the administrative process, whereas environmental interests are underrepresented due to their diffuse and often intangible nature.[6] Further, administrative decision-makers often face both epistemic and resource constraints that require considerable cooperation from regulated parties to provide relevant information and to comply with regulation in the absence of rigorous monitoring and enforcement.[7] The significance of natural resource industries in the Canadian economy has nurtured this cosy relationship

[3] Boyd, *Unnatural Law* (ibid) 231.

[4] For some examples of the environmental reform critique of discretion, see E Walter, 'Decoding Codes of Practice: Approaches to Regulating the Ecological Impacts of Logging in British Columbia' (2005) 15 *Journal of Environmental Law and Practice* 143, 156; L Nowlan, 'CPR for Canadian Rivers: Law to Conserve, Protect, and Restore Environmental Flows in Canada' (2012) 23 *Journal of Environmental Law and Practice* 237, 257; B Pardy and A Stoehr, 'The Failed Reform of Ontario's Mining Laws' (2012) 23 *Journal of Environmental Law and Practice* 1, 6 and 13–14; and my own previous work, S Fluker and J Stacey, 'The Basics of Species at Risk Legislation in Alberta' (2012) 50 *Alberta Law Review* 95.

[5] Boyd, *Unnatural Law* (above n 2) 232, 237–38 and 263. See also the Commission for Environmental Cooperation, where parties have filed dozens of petitions on Canada's failure to enforce its environmental laws: www.cec.org.

[6] For a nice overview of these theories as well as a critique of their weaknesses and an evaluation of their empirical support, see SP Croley, 'Theories of Regulation: Incorporating the Administrative Process' (1998) 98 *Columbia Law Review* 1, 32ff.

[7] DP Emond, 'The Greening of Environmental Law' (1990) 36 *McGill Law Journal* 742, 744–45.

between industry and government,[8] which in turn fuels a deep distrust of executive discretion by environmental reformers.

Bruce Pardy has considered this relationship between environmental protection, discretion and the rule of law:

> Environmental law is one of the most extreme examples of legal disciplines in which the commitment to principles of predictability, abstraction, and separation of powers has been consistently abandoned. Without a system of generally applicable environmental rules, environmental governance becomes largely a matter of discretionary judgment calls. Discretionary decision-making means that any particular decision can be justified by social, economic, political, cultural, or aesthetic concerns of the moment, even if they have deleterious long-term effects on ecosystem function. Environmental decisions thus become political positions.[9]

From this quote we can tease apart two distinct but related concerns about discretion in environmental law.

Pardy's first concern, consistent with the sentiments outlined above, is with the correlation between discretion and environmental degradation.[10] He worries that the concentration of power over environmental decisions allows special interests to undermine the overall public interest in maintaining ecosystem function.[11] While Pardy has not framed his work in these terms, we can think of this as a classic republican concern for ensuring that political institutions protect the public good.[12] In response to this concern, Pardy has pointed to the classic republican solution—that is, dispersing political power through a strong doctrine of the separation of powers. The fact that political power is not dispersed in this way in the environmental context but rather concentrates in the form of executive discretion reveals

[8] S Wood, G Tanner and B Richardson, 'What Ever Happened to Canadian Environmental Law?' (2011) 37 *Ecology Law Quarterly* 981, 1025.

[9] B Pardy, 'Environmental Assessment and Three Ways Not to Do Environmental Law' (2010) 21 *Journal of Environmental Law and Practice* 139, 149 (footnotes omitted).

[10] See also B Pardy, 'Abstraction, Precedent, and Articulate Consistency: Making Environmental Decisions' (1998) 34 *California Western Law Review* 427, 429.

[11] Pardy, 'Environmental Assessment' (above n 9) 153. He references the risks of political tyranny and potential slippage from legislated goals in his earlier work: Pardy, 'Abstraction, Precedent, and Articulate Consistency' (ibid) 344. Collins alludes to this as well with her concern that environmental legislation that could not, without political cost, be amended or repealed can be covertly undermined through administrative decision-making: Collins, 'Tort, Democracy and Environmental Governance' (above n 2) 111.

[12] I rely on P Pettit, *Republicanism: A Theory of Freedom and Government* (Oxford, Oxford University Press, 1999); and HS Richardson, *Democratic Autonomy: Public Reasoning about the Ends of Policy* (Oxford, Oxford University Press, 2002), who both defend a contemporary version of republicanism as non-domination. Richardson has described three conceptions of non-arbitrariness (at ch 3). Pardy's work would fall under Richardson's 'objectivist' conception of non-arbitrariness because he works from the basis that there is an objective limit to the planet's life-sustaining capacity. This comes through most clearly in Pardy, 'Environmental Assessment' (above n 9) 143–44, where he argues that environmental decisions should not be altered by public input.

that we are subject to the risk of arbitrary environmental decisions. In other words, environmental decisions are arbitrary when they deviate from the public good and instead serve special interests.

In the same quote above, we can see that Pardy has also articulated a more traditional rule-of-law concern with the requirement of generality. Elsewhere, he has lamented the current state of environmental law, whereby statutes contain broad and potentially conflicting objectives to 'manage' the environment while simultaneously maintaining or promoting natural resource development.[13] He critiques the lack of generality, equality and predictability in current environmental law and argues that environmental discretion creates the problem of 'serfdom'. In other words, legal outcomes depend not on generally applicable rules but on personal status and who you know.[14] This use of 'serfdom' recalls Hayek's classic liberal account of the rule of law, which has a clear influence on Pardy's work.[15] Drawing on Hayek, Pardy argues that general, equal and certain legal rules recognise the 'right of the citizen to adapt to environmental limits set by government'.[16] Accordingly, discretionary environmental decisions interfere with an individual's ability to live her own life.

Pardy is an environmental libertarian. He therefore objects to government 'planning functions' that extensively interfere with the private sphere.[17] But both he and environmental reformers of different political persuasions would recognise a basic individual right to a healthy environment.[18] Such a right stems from the fact that 'all humans depend on healthy ecosystems for life, health and well-being.'[19] On this view, a right to a healthy environment promises to protect a sphere of private autonomy that allows individuals to lead their own lives. Discretionary environmental decisions thus risk arbitrariness because they threaten to interfere with this fundamental freedom vis-à-vis the environment.

The environmental reform position reveals that existing environmental law is potentially arbitrary in two related senses. First, it allows special interests to co-opt the decision-making process and undermine the public

[13] Pardy, 'Environmental Assessment' (above n 9) 142–43.

[14] Pardy, 'Abstraction, Precedent, and Articulate Consistency' (above n 10) 429–30.

[15] B Pardy, 'The Pardy–Ruhl Dialogue on Ecosystem Management Part V: Discretion, Complex-Adaptive Problem Solving and the Rule of Law' (2008) 25 *Pace Environmental Law Review* 341, 341.

[16] Ibid, 351; and B Pardy, 'Environmental Law and the Paradox of Ecological Citizenship: The Case for Environmental Libertarianism' (2005) 33 *Environments* 25, 30 and 34.

[17] Pardy, 'Abstraction, Precedent, and Articulate Consistency' (above n 10) 429–30.

[18] L Collins, 'An Ecologically Literate Reading of the Canadian Charter of Rights and Freedoms' (2009) 26 *Windsor Review of Legal and Social Issues* 7 (on the connection between a healthy environment and existing rights and freedoms); and D Boyd, *The Right to a Healthy Environment: Revitalizing Canada's Constitution* (Vancouver, University of British Columbia Press, 2012). These proposals are taken up in ch 8 below.

[19] Boyd, *The Right to a Healthy Environment* (ibid) 2.

good. Secondly, discretion means that environmental decisions are not taken through general and predictable legal rules. Discretion threatens the ability to live one's life free from 'ecological interference'[20] from the government and others. The environmental reform position reveals that even though discretionary environmental decisions may be authorised by a democratic legislature and formally subject to judicial review, they nonetheless pose a significant threat of arbitrariness. Current environmental law, in short, is both democratically and legally suspect.[21]

The response to the mountain pine beetle epidemic in British Columbia, however, illustrates that administrative discretion is inevitable in environmental law. The British Columbia government's emergency response was to increase dramatically the amount of timber harvested in the province to try to contain the epidemic and to harvest timber before it lost its commercial value.[22] This response was implemented through three mechanisms, all of which were exercises of administrative discretion. First, the Lieutenant Governor in Council (LGIC) promulgated an emergency Bark Beetle Regulation,[23] which allowed harvesting coordination and relaxed certain administrative requirements. The Bark Beetle Regulation delegated further unfettered discretionary authority, permitting the Minister to identify emergency management areas for mountain pine beetle treatment 'if satisfied' that a forest was attacked or under danger of attack.[24] Second, the Minister of Forests significantly lowered the amount of government royalties on beetle-killed timber in order to encourage forestry companies to prioritise the harvest of such timber. Under the Forest Act (1996), the Minister is delegated discretion to determine the 'policies and practices' for setting these royalties.[25] Third, the province's Chief Forester exercised his discretion to dramatically increase the allowable harvest in the province, well above already unsustainable levels, in order to outpace the beetles.[26]

[20] Pardy, 'The Paradox of Ecological Citizenship' (above n 16) 34.

[21] Richardson, *Democratic Autonomy* (above n 12) has labeled this problem 'bureaucratic domination', in which we are subject to the arbitrary will of administrative decision-makers. He continues (at 250–51): 'Power is arbitrary when it is not adequately controlled by a fair process of decision in which those subject to it are treated as free and equal and their fundamental rights and liberties are protected.'

[22] 95 per cent of British Columbia's forests are owned by the Crown. Forest companies gain harvesting rights by entering into tenure agreements with the government. These tenure agreements are the subject of provincial legislation and regulations that govern specific forestry practices. For a general overview, see Government of British Columbia, 'Timber Tenures in British Columbia' (2012), www.for.gov.bc.ca/ftp/hth/external/!publish/web/timber-tenures/timber-tenures-2006.pdf.

[23] Bark Beetle Regulation, BC Reg 286/2001.

[24] Ibid, 2.

[25] Forest Act, RSBC 1996, c 157, s 103.

[26] H Nelson, 'Does a Crisis Matter? Forest Policy Responses to the Mountain Pine Beetle Epidemic in British Columbia' (2007) 55 *Canadian Journal of Agricultural Economics* 459, 465. I examine the Chief Forester's role in detail below in section III.B.

These three emergency response decisions were all products of the exercise of *everyday* administrative discretion: regulation-making, individual exemptions from ordinary forestry requirements, and discretionary decisions on royalties and total harvest. These are all forms of discretion that the environmental reform position views as objectionable. Yet it is difficult to see how it could be otherwise. Even critics of the province's emergency response concede the necessity of such discretion.[27] All the decisions require sophisticated knowledge of the forest industry and moreover require continual updating across all regions of the province in response to changing environmental, economic and social conditions. Administrative discretion is necessary not only to respond immediately to an urgent environmental catastrophe—to stem the tide of a mountain pine beetle epidemic, for example—but also to ensure that each environmental decision reflects the best understanding of the invariably dynamic problem at hand.

We know from chapter one that attempts to 'accommodate' the environmental emergency within legal order will fail to impose meaningful legal constraints on the exercise of discretion. It results in the creation of legal black and grey holes. We shall now see that the formal conception persists in Canadian environmental law, validating and illuminating the root cause of the environmental reform position's concern about arbitrariness.

II. BLACK AND GREY HOLES IN CANADIAN ENVIRONMENTAL LAW

Chapter one introduced AV Dicey and attributed the formal conception of the rule of law in parliamentary systems to one interpretation of his work on the English constitution.[28] In this section, we will first see how the formal conception of the rule of law has led Diceyan judges to broker a practical, if unstable, compromise with the reality of the administrative state. We will then see that this practical and unstable compromise is the source of legal black and grey holes in environmental law. Where the legislature delegates seemingly unfettered discretion to administrative decision-makers to regulate the environment, formalist judges will be content to create legal black holes. Where the legislature has attempted to impose some substantive constraints on environmental decision-makers, formalist judges will create legal grey holes. In other words, they treat these constraints as purely formal requirements that do not effectively constrain the exercise of discretion.

[27] Even alternative proposals would have proceeded through the same discretionary regulatory mechanisms. See generally B Parfitt, 'Battling the Beetle: Taking Action to Restore British Columbia's Interior Forests' (Canadian Centre for Policy Alternatives, 2005).

[28] Recall also that I noted there is an alternative interpretation of Dicey that leads to a substantive conception of the rule of law. I examine this alternative interpretation below in ch 4.

Recall from chapter one that the formal conception of the rule of law emerges from the Diceyan notion that the judiciary and the legislature have competing monopolies. Despite Canada's robust administrative state, this formal understanding of Dicey's rule of law has been 'remarkably influential'[29] in the development of Canadian administrative law. Its long-standing influence is responsible for the complex and convoluted development of administrative law doctrine as courts struggle to reconcile their acceptance of the legitimacy of the administrative state with an account of the rule of law that is inherently hostile to it. Where the legislature deliberately delegates discretionary authority to administrative decision-makers, Diceyan (or formalist) judges attempt to preserve the formal conception of the rule of law in the face of conflicting legislative intentions. On the one hand, the legislature signals that it is administrative decision-makers, not courts, that have final decision-making authority; but on the other hand, it signals that there are limits to the power of decision-makers through the boundaries set out in the statute. Formalist judges attempts to reconcile this tension by according administrative decision-makers 'free rein within certain legal limits'.[30]

'Free rein within limits' reflects a practical compromise whereby judges will strictly patrol the boundaries of legislation[31]—or a decision-maker's jurisdiction—as well as decide other matters that fall squarely within the judiciary's traditional monopoly, such as constitutional issues or the common law.[32] But judges give decision-makers free rein over the *substance* of their decisions. In other words, formalist judges are content to create legal black holes. Issues that fall within an administrator's statutory jurisdiction are governed by the rule of law only insofar as they are authorised by validly enacted legislation.

The problem is that the formal conception reflects a pragmatic stance that judges should refrain from interfering with decisions that would traditionally fall under the legislature's law-making monopoly. Issues that look like law-making, in the sense that they involve the exercise of discretion over complex policy considerations, are off limits.[33] But we shall see that

[29] *National Corn Growers Association v Canada (Import Tribunal)*, [1990] 2 SCR 1324 at para 74, 74 DLR (4th) 449 (SCC), Wilson J. The observation that the formal conception of the rule of law persists in the environmental context is a striking conclusion because in many significant ways Canadian courts have moved away from a formal conception of the rule of law. This evolution in Canadian administrative law is key to the argument of ch 4 below.

[30] D Dyzenhaus and E Fox-Decent, 'Rethinking the Process/Substance Distinction: *Baker v Canada*' (2001) 51 *University of Toronto Law Journal* 193, 204.

[31] P Craig, *Public Law and Democracy in the United Kingdom and the United States of America* (Oxford, Clarendon Press, 1990) 22.

[32] Dyzenhaus and Fox-Decent, 'Rethinking the Process/Substance Distinction' (above n 30) 204.

[33] Ibid, 207.

this pragmatic stance lacks a principled basis on which formalist judges can justify the creation of these legal black holes.[34] It also means that where the legislature attempts to impose some minimal constraints on the exercise of discretion, formalist judges are uncomfortable giving these constraints any real meaning. In other words, formalist judges are also content to create legal grey holes, which allow the executive to claim that it acts in accordance with the rule of law, while not being subject to any effective constraints.

A. Legal Black Holes: Environmental Regulations

The environmental reform position argues that discretion in environmental law evades rule-of-law constraints. Reformers observe that courts find environmental decisions unreviewable or will accord decisions such 'extreme' deference that they are not meaningfully constrained.[35] The environmental emergency validates this observation by explaining that general, policy-laden environmental decisions attract a formal conception of the rule of law, which leads to the creation of legal black holes. Since these decisions look like law-making—and sometimes *are* a form of law-making—formalist judges do not understand these decisions to be internally governed by the rule of law. As we saw in the mountain pine beetle context, the British Columbia provincial legislature delegates significant discretionary authority to the executive to issue regulations. This means that the executive has discretion both over *whether* to issue regulations and over the *substance* of those regulations. The environmental emergency reveals that regulations issued by the executive exist in a legal black hole. This black hole manifests itself in the application of legal doctrines of justiciability, *ultra vires* and the legislative exception to the requirement of procedural fairness, all of which operate to effectively exempt regulations from meaningful judicial review.

On the failure to issue regulations, the law is very clear. The matter is not justiciable, that is, not subject to judicial review. Regulations have the force of law; they are a form of delegated legislation and thus an extension of parliamentary sovereignty. Parliament can choose to legislate (or not) over any matter. Courts have applied the same logic to delegated legislation to conclude that they cannot require the executive to issue regulations where no action has been taken.[36] But regulations cannot, in principle, be entirely

[34] Ibid, 202.

[35] Boyd, *Unnatural Law* (above n 2) 269.

[36] For example, *Canadian Council for Refugees v Canada*, 2008 FCA 229, [2009] 3 FCR 136, para 53; and JM Keyes, *Executive Legislation*, 2nd edn (Toronto, LexisNexis Canada, 2010) 529.

off-limits for formalist judges. Regulations, just like any other delegated authority, are bound by their statutory scheme, and a formalist judge must patrol those statutory boundaries. Formalist judges, then, feel a great deal of strain when faced with challenges to the legality of regulations.

The Canadian Federal Court's decision in *Friends of the Earth v Canada (Governor in Council)* brings this formalist tension to the surface.[37] The issue arose from the executive's intransigence regarding the Kyoto Protocol Implementation Act (2007). The legislation, passed by the opposition parties against the minority government, set out ostensibly binding requirements, including a requirement to issue regulations to mitigate climate change by a specific deadline, which the executive failed to do.[38] The administrative decision not to issue regulations by a statutory deadline fell squarely within the traditional law-making monopoly, which requires judicial abstinence from the formalist perspective. But the refusal to act also directly undermined the objective of the legislation and the specific language of the authorising provisions. The only way the Federal Court could make sense of this tension was to conclude that the provisions 'reflect only a permissive intent'[39]—in other words, the legislature did not intend to create legally enforceable duties.[40] This interpretation allowed the Court to keep the formal conception intact. The Court created a legal black hole by patrolling the boundaries of the legislation and simply concluded that there were none that could be legally enforced.[41]

Formalist judges will not review the substance of regulations, as evidenced by Canadian environmental law. Regulations are subject to judicial review only for their *vires*—that is, on the narrow question of whether they fall within the scope of their statutory authority.[42] *Vires* review is a direct product of the formal conception whereby the judicial role is to police the boundaries, to interpret the enabling statute to ensure that the regulation falls within its jurisdiction. The substance of regulations—their wisdom or their ability to achieve the legislative objective—is entirely off-limits to courts.

[37] *Friends of the Earth v Canada (Governor in Council)*, 2008 FC 1183, [2009] 3 FCR 201.

[38] Kyoto Protocol Implementation Act, SC 2007, c 30 ss 7–9.

[39] *Friends of the Earth v Canada* (above n 37) para 37.

[40] Ibid, para 35.

[41] Ibid, para 46: 'the Court has no role to play reviewing the reasonableness of the government's response to Canada's Kyoto commitments within the four corners of the [Act]'.

[42] The Supreme Court most recently affirmed this in *Katz Group Canada Inc v Ontario (Health and Long-Term Care)*, 2013 SCC 64, [2013] 3 SCR 810. The *Katz* decision has effectively created an exception to the normal standard of review analysis that a court would conduct to determine if it should review an administrative decision for reasonableness or correctness. For an overview of recent developments with the standard of review analysis, see P Daly, 'The Scope and Meaning of Reasonableness Review' (2015) 52 *Alberta Law Review* 799. I take up the Supreme Court of Canada's approach to reasonableness review below in chs 4 and 7.

Only if a regulation is 'irrelevant', 'extraneous' or 'completely unrelated to the statutory purpose' will a court find that the regulation is invalid.[43] Regulations, in other words, fall within a legal black hole in which they are subject to only the minimal legal constraint that they are validly enacted.

Since once validly enacted, a regulation has the force of law[44] and formalist judges will not review the content of these regulations, the environmental reform position is rightly concerned that the executive has virtually unconstrained discretion to undermine environmental protection. The purpose of environmental legislation and the specific provisions enabling regulation-making are often cast in broad terms, meaning that it would take an outrageous regulation to exceed these statutory limits and be found *ultra vires*. For example, in *Sandy Pond v Canada*,[45] the Federal Court upheld a regulation that permitted the conversion of a lake into a toxic tailings pond for untreated mining effluent. The Court reasoned that the Fisheries Act (1985) was for the 'general management' of the fisheries.[46] The Court concluded that 'Parliament legislated the provisions allowing the enactment of the Regulations in question here. ... The will of the people, with respect to legislation, can be expressed at the ballot box.'[47] In other words, so long as a regulation falls within the broad boundaries of legislation, the substance of the regulation is a law-making function that falls properly within the legislature's monopoly, not the court's.

Finally, environmental regulations are not subject to the common law requirement of procedural fairness. The doctrine of procedural fairness has consistently required judges to formally classify decisions to determine whether the duty of fairness applies.[48] While the courts have expanded the duty of fairness from decisions categorised as judicial or quasi-judicial to most administrative decisions, they have retained a category of 'legislative' decisions that are exempt from common law requirements.[49] The legislative category is a remnant of the formal conception, under which the integrity

[43] *Katz Group Canada* (ibid) para 28.

[44] Statutory Instruments Act, RSC 1985, c S-22.

[45] *Sandy Pond Alliance to Protect Canadian Waters Inc v Canada*, 2013 FC 1112, para 88.

[46] Ibid, para 70 (relying on the Supreme Court of Canada's description of the Act in *Ward v Canada (Attorney General)*, [2002] 1 SCR 569 (SCC)).

[47] *Sandy Pond Alliance* (above n 45) para 88. See also *Wildlands League v Ontario (Lieutenant Governor in Council)*, 2015 ONSC 2942, in which the Court upheld a regulation that exempts entire industries from the requirements of the Endangered Species Act. Of course, it is also true that the court's formalist approach can help protect environmentally progressive regulations from challenges by industry: *Syncrude Canada Ltd v Canada (Attorney General)*, 2016 FCA 160, paras 96–100.

[48] G Huscroft, 'From Natural Justice to Fairness: Thresholds, Content, and the Role of Judicial Review' in C Flood and L Sossin (eds), *Administrative Law in Context*, 2nd edn (Toronto, Emond Montgomery Publications, 2012) 148–49.

[49] Ibid, 156–57.

of the legislative process is maintained through judicial non-interference.[50] Judges have broadened the requirements of procedural fairness to all adjudicatory administrative decisions to preserve the integrity of the judicial process. But they have no such role for decisions of a legislative nature.[51] Since environmental decisions are often complex, 'political'[52] matters which courts implicitly understand as part of the traditional law-making monopoly, they are frequently labelled 'legislative' in nature.

The formal conception has thus resulted in a long history of judicial abstinence from supervising regulation and other policy-laden administrative functions. The problem is that the formal conception is a product of a practical compromise rather than a principled one. It singles out the 'law-making' character or appearance of the administrative decision. Regulations fall squarely within the 'law-making' category because they are functionally identical to legislation and are thus understood to be outside the proper sphere of the courts. But this overstates important distinctions between the two. Unlike the legislature, the executive has no inherent authority to make law. This means that regulations always exist within a legal framework. Formalist judges ignore the fact that the legislature has deliberately relinquished its monopoly over law-making by delegating general policymaking authority to the executive.[53]

Formalist judges frequently justify their reluctance to intervene on democratic grounds. They note that regulations are typically issued by an elected decision-maker, a Minister or Cabinet. But it is incorrect to assume, as the formal conception seems to, that this is a sufficient condition for democratic legitimacy. Legislation is democratic not only because it is enacted by elected officials but also because it is the product of deliberation and open debate by opposing parties.[54] While formal regulations are subject to some uniform requirements,[55] such as publication, procedural requirements for regulations are patchy.[56] Some regulations or delegated authority may be subject to deliberation (for example, municipal bylaws), but there are no uniform requirements that ensure regulations have democratic legitimacy. Moreover, the simple fact that a democratic legislature has authorised the

[50] G Cartier, 'Procedural Fairness in Legislative Functions: The End of Judicial Abstinence?' (2003) 53 *University of Toronto Law Journal* 217, 23.

[51] Ibid, 237.

[52] *Imperial Oil v Quebec*, 2003 SCC 58, [2003] 2 SCR 624 at para 38. See also *Canadian Society of Immigration Consultants v Canada (Citizenship and Immigration)*, 2011 FC 1435, para 113.

[53] Cartier, 'Procedural Fairness in Legislative Functions' (above n 50) 238.

[54] Ibid, 242–43.

[55] Statutory Instruments Act, n 45 (notably, the s 5 requirement of publication).

[56] A Green, 'Regulations and Rule Making: The Dilemma of Delegation' in C Flood and L Sossin (eds), *Administrative Law in Context*, 2nd edn (Toronto, Emond Montgomery Publications, 2013) 142. See also A Woolley, 'Legitimating Public Policy' (2008) 58 *University of Toronto Law Journal* 153.

exercise of discretion is true of all administrative action and is not sufficient to immunise an administrative decision from judicial oversight in any other context. By treating regulations as a part of the legislative monopoly over law-making, the formal conception of the rule of law overstates the similarities between legislation and regulations.

The persistence of the formal conception in the case of regulations presents another problem. Because the formal conception of law is a product of a practical compromise, there is no principled basis on which to distinguish the kinds of 'law-making' that attract *vires* review and those that are subject to substantive review, or to distinguish those decisions that attract a duty of procedural fairness and 'legislative' decisions that do not. While formal regulations may be easy enough to delineate, there are a variety of orders and individual decisions that courts have been unwilling to effectively review.

Under the Canadian Fisheries Act, for example, the Minister has 'absolute discretion' to issue fishing licences.[57] The Federal Court has held that individual licensing decisions are subject to substantive review for reasonableness, but a decision is unreasonable only if it is 'clearly beyond the broad purposes permitted under the Act'.[58] This includes situations of bad faith, reliance on an extraneous factor or failure to comply with a statutorily imposed procedure[59]—in other words, the Court has simply subsumed *vires* review under substantive review for reasonableness. Much like the decision in *Sandy Pond*, it would take an egregious decision for a court to conclude a licensing decision is clearly beyond the purpose of the Act.

Because the formalist position is the result of a pragmatic compromise, there is no clear dimension along which courts can determine which issues are sufficiently 'political' or 'legislative' in nature that they ought to be exempt from substantive judicial review.[60] When faced with complex policy matters, a court can revert to *vires* review, even where the decision lacks the insignia of actual law-making. Moreover, this pragmatic compromise ignores the fact that environmental decision-makers are often delegated the choice of regulatory instrument.[61] That is, a decision can be taken by way of regulation, informal policy or *ad hoc* individual decisions. The substantive content of such a decision, regardless of its form, may have ostensibly the same effect on the environment and on those who are subject to the decision, but the different regulatory forms have potentially different rule-of-law requirements.

[57] Fisheries Act, RSC 1985, c F-14 s 7.

[58] *Carpenter Fishing Corp v Canada*, [1998] 2 FC 548, 155 DLR (4th) 572, para 37, reaffirmed in *Association des crevettiers acadiens du Golfe inc v Canada (Attorney General)*, 2011 FC 305.

[59] Carpenter (ibid) para 37.

[60] Cartier, 'Procedural Fairness in Legislative Functions' (above n 50) 233.

[61] For example, the Fisheries Act (above n 57) s 35(2).

B. Legal Grey Holes: Ineffective Substantive Constraints

The formal conception of the rule of law also leads judges to create legal grey holes in instances where the legislature has imposed some minimal substantive constraints on environmental decisions. These substantive constraints are often set out as a list of factors that decision-makers must consider. These factors are converted into a legal grey hole when formalist judges construe them as an empty box-ticking exercise that does not effectively constrain the exercise of discretion.

For example, in *David Suzuki Foundation v British Columbia (Attorney General)*,[62] the David Suzuki Foundation challenged the Lieutenant Governor in Council's decision to permit the export of timber from British Columbia's northwest region. Under the Forest Act, the LGIC could grant the permit 'if satisfied' that, amongst other conditions, the timber was in surplus.[63] The Foundation argued that the surplus condition was not met and therefore the exemption was *ultra vires* the Act.[64] The British Columbia Supreme Court disagreed. It found that the phrase 'if satisfied that' conferred an 'exclusive',[65] 'complete, unfettered, subjective discretion'[66] on the LGIC to issue an exemption. The Court reasoned that the Act required only that the LGIC 'be satisfied' that the conditions were met; it did not require review to ensure there was adequate evidence of a timber surplus to support the decision. Since the order itself stated that the LGIC was satisfied as to the existence of the conditions, the Court found it was entitled to take the order at its word.[67] The Court understood its role in 'a basic jurisdictional' sense, meaning that its role was to patrol the boundaries of the legislation and not second-guess decisions taken within those bounds.[68]

Even where a court purports to conduct substantive review to determine whether a decision is reasonable, it can still create a legal grey hole. In *Sierra Club v Ontario (Ministry of Natural Resources)*,[69] the Sierra Club challenged the Minister's decision to permit the disturbance of endangered species habitat for the construction of a new bridge across the Detroit River. The legislation set out the Minister's authority in purely subjective terms, requiring that the Minister consult with 'a person who is considered by the

[62] *David Suzuki Foundation v British Columbia (Attorney General)*, 2004 BCSC 620.

[63] Forest Act (above n 25) s 128(1). At the time, there was a prohibition on the export of timber from the region. The permit was an exemption to the prohibition.

[64] *David Suzuki Foundation v BC* (above 62) para 1.

[65] Ibid, para 11.

[66] Ibid, para 12.

[67] Ibid, para 147.

[68] Ibid, para 91.

[69] *Sierra Club v Ontario (Ministry of Natural Resources)*, 2011 ONSC 4655, [2011] OJ No 4373.

Minister to be an expert … and to be independent of the person who would be authorised by the permit to engage in the activity'.[70] At issue was the fact that one expert report on which the Minister relied and which contradicted a second expert was produced by an employee of the company bidding for the project.[71] While the Court expressed reservations about the appearance of bias 'which the Minister might have been better to avoid',[72] the Court nonetheless found that the Minister complied with the Act. It did so in purely formal terms. The expert provided the Minister with a statement that declared his independence, and the Court therefore held that '[s]trictly speaking, it confirm[ed] the independence of the expert.'[73] In the Court's view, all that the Act required was 'that the Minister consult and obtain a written report'.[74] In other words, the Court created a legal grey hole. On this view, a legislative requirement to consult with independent experts before deciding whether an activity will jeopardise the survival or recovery of an endangered species is no more than a formal reporting exercise that does not receive meaningful scrutiny on review.

The Court's discomfort with its supervisory role echoed throughout the decision in *Sierra Club*. It held that the subjective language in the legislation served 'to broaden the deference the court should provide to the decision to issue the Permit'.[75] It tersely dismissed the argument that the purpose of the language was to ensure the Minister consulted the best scientific information available[76] and that the Minister's discretion was constrained by the precautionary principle.[77] The Court stated that to take a more active supervisory role would not accord the 'breadth of deference required where a public policy decision is at issue'.[78] Instead, the Court was prepared to allow the Minister the appearance of legality without actually subjecting the Minister's discretion to any meaningful legal constraints.

Indeed, it seems that only in egregious cases where decisions completely lack any evidentiary basis will the courts intervene.[79] So long as there is evidence that the decision-maker turned her mind to the relevant statutory factors—ticked the appropriate boxes—the courts will not question the basis

[70] Endangered Species Act, 2007, SO 2007, c 6 at 17(2).

[71] *Sierra Club v Ontario* (above n 69) para 64.

[72] Ibid, para 68.

[73] Ibid, para 65.

[74] Ibid, paras 72 and 90.

[75] Ibid, para 39.

[76] Ibid, paras 92–93.

[77] Ibid, para 60 (concluding that it is only one factor to be considered . Ch 5 below addresses the precautionary principle in more detail.

[78] Ibid, para 63.

[79] *Alberta Wilderness Association v Minister of Environment*, 2009 FC 710, [2009] FCJ No 876; *Environmental Defence Canada v Ministry of Fisheries and Oceans*, 2009 FC 878, [2009] FCJ No 1052.

for the decision-maker's subjective judgment.[80] Without some examination of the decision-maker's reasons for a decision, however, virtually any outcome is permissible, since environmental legislation is cast in the broadest of terms. So, for example, a controversial decision to poison wolves in order to protect an endangered caribou population may appear to fall within the range of acceptable outcomes. But if the reasons disclose that the decision was reached in order to protect the oil and gas industry—the real threat to the endangered species—then the decision no longer appears so reasonable. Indeed, allegations that a decision-maker has been driven by an improper purpose such as political lobbying[81] or, as we have seen, a potential stake in the outcome, are often skimmed over on the way to the court's conclusion that the outcome falls easily within the broad perimeters of the legislation.[82]

The formalist judge, in short, focuses on the outcome of administrative decisions and the language of statutes. So long as a decision plausibly fits within the boundaries of the statute, a formalist will find no reason to interfere. To do more—that is, to examine the reasons underlying a decision—would pull judges far away from their traditional monopoly of law interpretation.[83] This approach to judicial review validates the environmental reform position's concern that the courts are not proving an effective constraint on potentially arbitrary exercises of discretion. Instead, the adherence to the formal conception of the rule of law has resulted in legal black holes and grey holes with the appearance—not the reality—of legal constraint.

III. IMPOVERISHED ENVIRONMENTAL REFORM SOLUTIONS

This chapter has argued that the environmental emergency reveals both the necessity and desirability of discretion but that the formal conception of the rule of law is incapable of providing meaningful constraints on the exercise of that discretion. In other words, the environmental reform position is right to call our attention to the pervasive problem of discretion in Canadian

[80] *Sierra Club v Ontario* (above n 69) para 77. For an example of review that defers to literal box-ticking and the failure to insert case-specific information into a *pro forma* document, see *Animal Alliance of Canada v Ontario (Minister of Natural Resources)*, 2014 ONSC 2826.

[81] *Malcolm v Canada (Fisheries and Oceans)*, 2014 FCA 130, para 57, 76 Admin LR (5th) 179.

[82] Review is often further hampered by court's unwillingness to require decision-makers to give reasons: L Sossin, 'The Unfinished Project of *Roncarelli v Duplessis*: Justiciability, Discretion, and the Limits of the Rule of Law' (2010) 55 *McGill Law Journal* 661, 684.

[83] Indeed, they sometimes worry that it would turn the court into 'an academy of science to arbitrate conflicting scientific predictions'. See *Vancouver Island Peace Society v Canada*, 1992 3 FCR 42, para 12; and *Ontario Power Generation Inc v Greenpeace Canada*, 2015 FCA 186, para 126.

environmental law, since the courts seem committed to the formal conception, which leads judges to create legal black holes and grey holes. This section addresses the solutions proposed by the environmental reform position. The first solution, crafting less discretionary environmental legislative rules, I will address briefly. We have seen already that this proposal cannot resolve the problem given Schmitt's challenge. The second solution that follows from the environmental reform position is to delegate environmental decision-making to independent experts, such as British Columbia's Chief Forester, the senior forestry official who made the decision to increase the timber harvest in areas affected by the mountain pine beetle epidemic. While independent expert decision-makers play an unquestionably important role in Canadian environmental law, we will see that this does not offer a solution to the environmental reform position's concern. The reform position's turn to independent experts is premised on the assumption that objective expertise can offer the constraints that *ex ante* legal rules fail to provide. But this approach is dangerous because it risks burying discretion beneath layers of analysis that make it less transparent and more difficult to contest.

A. Environmental Rules

The first and most logical solution to the environmental reform position's concern over discretion is to minimise or eliminate discretion through more specific legislative rules. Boyd has claimed that '[d]iscretionary language in environmental laws and regulations should be replaced by mandatory language; three decades of experience have proven time and again that politicians and bureaucrats will exercise their discretion to the environment's detriment.'[84] Similarly, Pardy has advocated crafting an 'environmental rule' that would prohibit non-natural, permanent damage to ecosystems.[85] But for reasons already discussed, neither proposal would solve the problem of discretion. To recapitulate, it is not possible to eliminate discretionary language because it is often impossible to know in advance what actions should be taken to achieve environmental protection objectives. This is the key insight that follows from viewing the environment as an ongoing emergency.

To be clear, the emergency perspective does not provide an excuse for failing to enact rigorous environmental laws. Rather, it reflects an appreciation of the fact that our best efforts to protect the environment through legislation will necessarily involve delegating discretion to administrative

[84] Boyd, *Unnatural Law* (above n 2) 293.

[85] B Pardy, 'In Search of the Holy Grail of Environmental Law: A Rule to Solve the Problem' (2005) 1 *McGill International Journal of Sustainable Development Law and Policy* 29.

decision-makers. It is therefore misleading to suggest, as some reformers do, that mandatory legal rules provide an answer. While some first-generation environmental problems lent themselves to outright prohibitions on particularly harmful pollutants or activities, our most pressing environmental issues cannot be legislated away in such a straight-forward fashion.[86] Moreover, it is important to recall that, as argued in chapter one, some environmental issues contain the possibility of an actual environmental catastrophe. There is no *ex ante* rule that can dictate the response to an extreme, unforeseeable event. In response to both extreme events and everyday environmental issues, law and policymakers face intractable complexity.

Accepting this complexity ought to be liberating, in a sense. It means that policymakers and law reformers can get on with finding solutions rather than prolonging regulatory action as we await a more precise understanding of an ill-posed and dynamic problem.[87] When legislators are able to articulate clear legal rules, we can expect that they will be upheld in court.[88] Legislated rules do not pose a problem for the formal conception of the rule of law. But as we have seen, a conception of the rule of law that understands the legislature as the only source of legal norms is insufficient to respond to the environmental emergency.

B. Independent Expert Decision-Makers

The second solution that follows from the environmental reform position—delegating environmental decision-making authority to independent experts rather than to elected members of the executive—raises a similar problem. From the perspective of the environmental reform position, independent experts are appealing because they promise to remove politics from environmental decision-making. For example, the 2012 amendments to the Canadian Environmental Assessment Act transferred final decision-making

[86] See Wood et al, 'What Ever Happened?' (above n 8) for some success stories. How we might confront such complexity is addressed by the remainder of this book.

[87] L Heinzerling, 'Pragmatists and Environmentalists' (2000) 113 *Harvard Law Review* 1421, 1445.

[88] Good examples are the successful applications for judicial review of executive action under the federal Species at Risk Act: *Environmental Defence Canada v MFO* (above n 79); *Minister of Fisheries and Oceans v David Suzuki Foundation*, 2012 FCA 40; and *Western Canada Wilderness Committee v Canada (Minister of Fisheries and Oceans and Minister of the Environment)*, 2014 FC 148 (the court highlighted the systemic problem of the Ministries missing the statutory deadlines and granted discretionary relief on the grounds that it was necessary for the court to express its disapproval: para 92). But see J Stacey, 'The Rule-of-Law Underpinnings of Endangered Species Protection: *Minister of Fisheries and Oceans v David Suzuki Foundation*, 2012 FCA 40' (2014) 27 *Journal of Environmental Law and Practice* 57.

authority from the National Energy Board to the federal Cabinet.[89] This prompted an outcry representative of the environmental reform position. The problem, one commentator observed, is that Cabinet lacks the 'objectivity and expertise' of the Board: '[s]hifting the decision for major energy projects from the Board to Cabinet will politicise what was an otherwise independent regulatory process.'[90] As we will see, an expert decision-maker, just like Cabinet, exercises significant policymaking discretion, which cannot be eliminated through objective expertise. Simply put, delegating environmental decision-making authority to an independent expert, without more, does not respond to the environmental reform position's concern about discretion.

British Columbia's Chief Forester is an example of an independent expert decision-maker. The Chief Forester implemented one of the province's key responses to the mountain pine beetle epidemic by exercising his discretion to increase the allowable harvest in areas affected by the epidemic. The determination of the annual harvest limit is '[o]f all the decisions facing forest policymakers, probably the most critical in terms of its economic importance'.[91] The Forest Act delegates significant discretion to the Chief Forester to make this determination. It sets out procedural requirements—such as the intervals on which the determination must be made—and substantive factors 'to be considered'.[92] As we saw in the previous section, given the prominence of the formal conception of the rule of law, these requirements do not impose significant constraints on how the Chief Forester exercises this discretion.

The assumption underpinning the environmental reform position is that this discretion is less objectionable when in the hands of an independent expert. The promise of independent expert decision-makers lies in the assumption that objective expertise can provide the constraints on discretion that the legislature is unable to provide.[93] Objective expertise means

[89] For an overview of these changes, see M Doelle, 'CEAA 2012: The End of Federal EA as We Know It?' (2013) 24 *Journal of Environmental Law and Practice* 1. The National Energy Board's role in conducting environmental assessment is taken up in detail below in ch 5.

[90] Ecojustice, 'Legal Backgrounder: The National Energy Board Act 1985' (2012) www.ecojustice.ca/wp-content/uploads/2015/03/SEPT-2012_FINAL_NEBA-backgrounder.pdf.

[91] P Pearse, *Timber Rights and Forest Policy in British Columbia, Volume I* (Victoria, Government of British Columbia, 1976) 219. Since the vast majority of forested land is Crown land leased out to forestry companies on long-term tenures, the allowable harvest is one of the relatively few junctures at which the government directly influences the timber harvest.

[92] Forest Act (above n 25) s 8.

[93] For the classic statement of this position, see JM Landis, *The Administrative Process* (New Haven, Yale University Press, 1938) 25–26. See also J Willis, 'Three Approaches to Administrative Law: The Judicial, the Conceptual, and the Functional' (1935) 1 *University of Toronto Law Journal* 53, 75–81. Willis's functionalist approach emphasises expediency and the role of expertise, though he does not disavow the necessity of administrative discretion.

that the decision-maker is not exercising discretion in any real sense. Rather, an independent decision-maker is simply doing what the legislature, or indeed anyone, would do if they possessed the requisite knowledge.[94]

As we will see, these assumptions are unsound, but they have a strong footing in the history of Canadian environmental law. Indeed, the office of the Chief Forester in British Columbia was originally conceived in just these terms. The Chief Forester was to be 'a first-class, scientific man [sic], thoroughly well qualified, who has had both technical and practical training and experience'.[95] The legislature delegated a task that it could not do itself. The Chief Forester was to consolidate and synthesise the vast information on the province's forests in order to act 'in all matters affecting the forest interests in the Province'.[96]

A significant part of the Chief Forester's job was (and remains) determining the rate of harvesting that would maximise long-term timber yield. For decades, this determination was made using Hanzlik's formula, a technical calculation that appeared to require purely factual inputs—the rate of forest growth, the amount of forest mature enough to harvest, areas accessible to loggers for harvesting.[97] Accordingly, when the Chief Forester conducted the analysis, there seemed to be no allowance for discretion.[98] The decision-making authority of the Chief Forester therefore appeared consistent with the formal conception of the rule of law because the Chief Forester supposedly retained a purely instrumental and technical role in using objective expertise to carry out the democratic mandate of the legislature.

This assumption that an independent expert applies solely objective expertise contains two further assumptions. It first assumes that independent decision-makers deal only with factual matters—not political or policy judgments—and second, that these factual matters can be resolved in a way that points to one objective outcome.[99] As we have seen with the mountain

Elizabeth Fisher's 'rational-instrumental' paradigm of administrative constitutionalism was very helpful for working through this argument: E Fisher, *Risk Regulation and Administrative Constitutionalism* (Oxford, Hart Publishing, 2007).

[94] RB Stewart, 'The Reformation of American Administrative Law' (1975) 88 *Harvard Law Review* 1667, 1678; M Seidenfeld, 'The Role of Politics in a Deliberative Model of the Administrative State' (2013) 81 *George Washington Law Review* 1397, 1404.

[95] FJ Fulton, *Royal Commission of Inquiry on Timber and Forestry, 1909–1910* (Victoria, Government of British Columbia, 1910) 60, 67.

[96] Ibid, 68.

[97] L Pedersen, 'Allowable Annual Cuts in British Columbia: The Agony and the Ecstasy', Jubilee Lecture at the UBC Faculty of Forestry (20 March 2003) [copy on file with author]. Hanzlik's formula is sustained annual yield = mature timber above rotation age/rotation age + mean annual increment for immature timber.

[98] LH Dellert, 'Sustained Yield: Why Has It Failed to Achieve Sustainability?' in C Tollefson (ed), *The Wealth of Forests* (Vancouver, University of British Columbia Press, 1998) 257.

[99] Richardson, *Democratic Autonomy* (above n 12) 115; F Fischer, 'Environmental Regulation and Risk–Benefit Analysis: From Technical to Deliberative Policy Making' in R Paehlke and D Torgerson (eds), *Managing Leviathan: Environmental Politics and the Administrative State*, 2dn edn (Peterborough, Broadview Press, 2005) 63.

pine beetle example, the latter assumption that factual issues can be fully resolved so as to produce an objective and positive outcome is flatly refuted by the environmental emergency. Serious environmental issues are replete with remote and unforeseeable possibilities due to the complex and dynamic nature of ecological systems. And quite to the contrary of what the expertise model posits, there is no objective way to deal with this kind of uncertainty.[100] Estimating the likelihood of extreme events is fraught with poorly understood relationships and incomplete data, sometimes making it more an exercise of 'speculation'[101] than objective analysis. Moreover, even seemingly factual issues in determining the harvest rate, such as the rotation age—a 'critical variable'[102]—in fact turn on a host of assumptions about projected improvements in forest technologies and market conditions.[103] In short, accurate forestry inventories are necessary but not sufficient to determine the desired rate of timber harvest, since the Chief Forester will have to make discretionary judgments on a whole host of uncertain factors.

The first assumption, that independent experts deal only with factual matters, is also undermined by the Chief Forester's prominent position in directing British Columbian forest policy. In this respect, the Chief Forester's determination of the allowable annual cut is significant for what it *does not* include. Even now, long after Hanzlik's formula has faded into the background, the allowable annual cut is still dictated by a policy of maximising sustained yield. Maximum sustainable yield includes the value of timber; it does not account for the myriad other benefits that individuals receive from forests—eg, hunting, grazing, water quality regulation, biodiversity and carbon sequestration. Calls to incorporate these non-timber values into the maximum sustained yield model have gone largely unheeded,[104] evidencing the difficulty of incorporating what are inherently discretionary decisions involving incommensurable trade-offs into a technical model of decision-making premised on an assumption of objective expertise.

[100] This is the main thesis of DA Kysar, *Regulating from Nowhere: Environmental Law and the Search for Objectivity* (New Haven, Yale University Press, 2010).

[101] Pearse, *Timber Rights* (above n 91) 232.

[102] Ibid, D21. The rotation age sets the age for harvesting a forest stand to maximise forest growth and the pace of harvesting old growth forest.

[103] In the first Royal Commission on the regulation of timber harvest, three experts disagreed on the correct rotation age for coastal Douglas fir, with proposals ranging from 60 to 120 years: G Sloan, 'The Forest Resources of British Columbia: Report of the Commissioner' (Victoria, 1956) 236, 241. A recent scientific study has called into question the assumption that aging trees have slower growth rates: NL Stephenson et al, 'Rate of Tree Carbon Accumulation Increases Continuously with Tree Size' (2014) 507 *Nature* 90.

[104] Dellert, 'Sustained Yield' (above n 98). There has always been unwavering faith that better modelling techniques and more data will respond to criticism. See Pearse, *Timber Rights* (above n 91) 233. See also Forest Resources Commission, 'The Future of Our Forests' (Victoria, 1991) www.for.gov.bc.ca/hfd/pubs/Docs/Mr/Rc/Rc001/Rc001.pdf, 75.

The environmental reform position's solution to delegate environmental decisions to independent experts is no solution to the deep challenge of ensuring that environmental decisions are subject to the rule of law. Independent expert decision-makers exercise considerable discretion that cannot be adequately constrained or guided by objective expertise. This means that expert decision-makers, who are not directly democratically accountable, wield significant policymaking authority that undermines the legislature's monopoly over law-making. This purported solution therefore fails to reconcile the exercise of discretion with the formal conception of the rule of law.

Put differently, the attempt to constrain inherently discretionary decisions through nothing more than predetermined expert methodologies creates a façade in the same way that Schmitt predicts that the rule of law operates as a façade over discretionary decisions in times of emergency. Layers of technical analysis that appear to constrain a decision-maker on the substantive outcome in fact require the exercise of significant discretion over what inputs to include in the technocratic calculation.[105] Indeed, the Chief Forester's approach to determining the annual harvest was criticised on this very basis, with forestry commentators observing that '[r]egardless of which formula or model was used, from the 1950s to the 1990s, economic forces caused the annual harvest to increase, in spite of the original expectation of reductions in the harvest.'[106] Far from constraining administrative discretion, expert forest analyses were in fact capacious frameworks that allowed decision-makers to covertly succumb to industry pressure. Independent expert decision-makers therefore cannot provide a complete answer to the environmental reform position's problem with discretion.

IV. CONCLUSION

This chapter has developed several themes introduced in the first chapter. First, we saw that discretion in environmental law poses the risk of arbitrariness. This is the central concern of the environmental reform position, which illustrates that discretionary environmental decisions consistently undermine environmental protection and depart from traditional rule-of-law values such as generality and consistency. Second, we saw that

[105] Kysar, *Regulating from Nowhere* (above n 100) 72. Maximum sustainable yield is only one example of an expert methodology. Perhaps more common is the methodology of risk assessment: Fisher, *Risk Regulation and Administrative Constitutionalism* (above n 93); and Fischer, 'Environmental Regulation and Risk–Benefit Analysis' (above n 99).

[106] GF Utzig and DL Macdonald, *Citizens' Guide to Allowable Annual Cut Determinations: How to Make a Difference* (Vancouver, British Columbia Environmental Network Educational Foundation, 2000) 6.

Canadian environmental law is currently governed by a formal conception of the rule of law. Since the formal conception does not face up to the emergency nature of environmental issues, it results in the creation of legal black and grey holes in environmental law, or a façade of legality. The formal conception does not, that is, prevent arbitrary environmental decisions. In addition to this façade of legality, we saw that the formal conception creates a façade of democratic legitimacy. The formal conception treats discretionary environmental decisions as functionally equivalent to legislation. It fails to acknowledge the real democratic deficit that arises when the legislature delegates environmental decision-making authority to administrative bodies without further requirements to ensure democratic accountability. The reform solution of delegating this discretion to independent experts risks compounding this democratic deficit.

We also saw that by neglecting the ways in which the environment confronts us with the unforeseen and potentially catastrophic consequences of an emergency, environmental reformers have come to rely on a formal conception of the rule of law that is incapable of supplying rule-of-law constraints on executive decision-making. The complexity of environmental decisions means that even our best efforts to secure environmental protection through legislation will still contain discretionary authority. The challenge of environmental issues cannot be met through environmental rules. Finally, there is no objective way to resolve the complexity of environmental issues. Scientific uncertainty thus gives rise to normative uncertainty about what actions are appropriate to take. The challenge of environmental issues therefore cannot be met by delegating discretion to independent experts. Even the best expertise cannot answer the question of how we ought to proceed in the face of possible but unknown or uncertain environmental harm. Much like the accommodation approach to emergency powers, the environmental reform position fails to answer Schmitt's challenge.

3

Environmental Governance: The Problem of Law in Environmental Law

RECALL FROM CHAPTER one that for those who adhere to the formal conception of the rule of law, there are only two possible responses to an emergency: accommodating emergency powers within legal order or conceding the necessity of extra-legal measures. Accommodating the environmental emergency, as we saw in chapter two, results in the rule of law operating only as a façade for discretionary powers. In this chapter, we see that the extra-legal approach has a parallel in the environmental context, insofar as some scholars treat the rule of law as essentially irrelevant to the challenge of addressing complex environmental problems. This parallel is found in the literature on environmental governance.

The argument of this chapter is that environmental governance correctly approaches environmental issues from the emergency perspective. However, since defenders of environmental governance assume a formal conception of the rule of law, they 'side-line'[1] consideration of the rule of law in favour of alternative evaluative criteria. By side-lining the rule of law, environmental governance scholars miss and neglect the internal constitution of the kind of order produced by law. They miss, in other words, the fact that the rule of law creates a particular relationship between lawmaker and legal subject, one that respects the subject's agency and right to be free from arbitrariness. While I expound on the precise nature of this relationship in Part II of the book, for present purposes it is sufficient to observe that environmental governance scholars do not directly confront the potential for arbitrariness. By dismissing the rule of law, they lose sight of its potential for helping to articulate the strengths and concerns about particular instances of environmental governance.

[1] L McDonald, 'The Rule of Law in the "New Regulatory State"' (2004) 33 *Common Law World Review* 197.

Leading Canadian environmental law scholars have identified environmental governance as an emerging approach to environmental law.[2] Environmental governance covers an expansive body of interdisciplinary scholarship and a diversity of regulatory approaches. It is a subset of a wider new governance literature that addresses questions broadly pertaining to how to regulate. The central feature of new governance is its critique of the state and its oft-associated top-down regulatory structures as the sole or even primary site of governance. Formal sources of law—statutes and regulations—are only a small part of this broader picture of governance. As we will see, this leads proponents of environmental governance to reject the formal conception of the rule of law. The formal conception is simply not applicable to the kinds of regulatory innovation that governance scholars promote. According to defenders of environmental governance, general and static legislated norms cannot, on their own, adequately respond to complex environmental problems. Instead, these complex regulatory problems require flexibility, networked public–private relationships and novel governance institutions.

The problem, however, is that rejecting the 'formalism' of the formal conception does not mean that its underlying concerns disappear. The formal conception, in its ideal form at least, protects against arbitrary state action. In requiring impersonal and general legal rules, it respects the autonomy of the individual to conduct her own affairs. It objects to policymaking by the executive, which, as we saw in chapter two, often results in advancing short-term interests over long-term protection of the environment. To the extent that environmental governance irreparably breaks from the formal conception, it must address this deeper problem of arbitrariness. To anticipate the argument in Part II of the book, I too reject the formal conception of the rule of law, but I offer an alternative that attends to the rule-of-law concerns that much environmental governance scholarship has neglected.

Governance research, as noted, is an interdisciplinary field with both legal and non-legal scholars researching the intersections, gaps and overlap between law and governance mechanisms. Much of this research takes a self-consciously 'external' view of law, which understands law solely as an instrument to achieve other ends. Admittedly, it is unfair to critique this

[2] M Doelle and C Tollefson (eds), *Environmental Law Cases and Materials*, 2nd ed (Toronto, Carswell, 2013) 285. Tollefson et al define governance as 'arrangements for steering and coordinating the affairs of interdependent social actors based on institutionalised rule systems that depart from the traditional strong centralised model of "government" that was characteristic of many Western liberal democracies in the generation that followed the Second World War': C Tollefson, FP Gale and D Haley, *Setting the Standard: Certification, Governance and the Forest Stewardship Council* (Vancouver, University of British Columbia Press, 2008) 218.

scholarship as being inattentive to the internal constitution of law; that is simply not its aim. Yet the language of governance is occupying increasing space within environmental law discourses. As environmental law scholars attempt to make sense of environmental governance and attempt to bring it into conversation with other perspectives on environmental law, we ought to closely examine what might be lost if the language of law becomes subsumed within a broader paradigm of environmental governance.

This chapter proceeds in three parts. Section I introduces the literature on new governance. It argues that we can derive two hypotheses about environmental governance from this literature. The first hypothesis is that instances of environmental governance take seriously the complexity of environmental issues, but in doing so, they reject the formal conception of the rule of law. We will see that this hypothesis emerges from the new governance critique of conventional legal regulation, known as command-and-control regulation. The second hypothesis is that the proliferation of environmental governance is transforming the nature of law itself. This hypothesis is a product of empirical analyses that illustrate how traditional and innovative policy instruments have blended to create novel forms of regulation. Put in terms of the emergency framework, this hypothesis suggests that there is no way to confine governance measures. Like exceptional emergency measures, they appear to be normalising.

The second section of this chapter then tests these two hypotheses by examining three examples of environmental governance in the British Columbia forest context: results-based legislation, collaborative ecosystem governance and transnational forest certification. It argues that each of these examples supports the two hypotheses outlined in section I. It then examines existing literature on these three forms of governance and shows they only tangentially address the underlying rule-of-law concern of arbitrariness. Both defenders and critics evaluate instances of environmental governance on the criteria of effectiveness, participation, transparency and accountability. And while these criteria are closely related to a democratic conception of the rule of law, they are only component parts. Presented as disconnected features, these evaluative criteria do not directly confront the potential for arbitrariness in environmental governance.

Section III argues that the alternative criteria found in the governance literature are not exhaustive of the rule of law. Rather, what governance scholars have missed by jettisoning the rule of law is the distinctive relationship that law constitutes between lawmaker and legal subject that explains why governance through law is something worth having. We will see that by reclaiming a focus on this relationship, we are able to more precisely articulate the strengths—where governance attends to complexity and democratic deficiencies—and the concerns brought to light by the examples of environmental governance detailed in section II.

I. OLD AND NEW GOVERNANCE

New governance is admittedly a broad tent that does not easily lend itself to generalisation. Governance—governing but without an emphasis on *government*[3]—promises to avoid the flaws of previous regulatory approaches—eg, the perceived heavy-handedness and inefficiency of command-and-control regulation and the questionable efficacy of market-based policy instruments or self-regulation.[4] This section introduces the theory behind new governance. I argue that proponents of new governance tackle the complexity of contemporary regulatory problems. However, in doing so, they adopt a formal view of law, which they equate with command-and-control regulation. This leads proponents to dismiss the rule of law as irrelevant and posit that the nature of law itself is transforming in response to the proliferation of new governance measures.

A. The Environmental Emergency and Legal Formalism

Because of its focus on regulatory complexity, new governance theory has been remarkably influential in the field of environmental law. Environmental law scholars frequently note that first-wave environmental laws have been effective at addressing many environmental issues.[5] To be sure, Canadian environmental law does not have a glowing record on environmental protection—far from it.[6] But there is a sense that much low-hanging fruit has been picked, and the problems that remain cannot be as easily addressed through uniform legal rules that target direct and concrete sources of environmental harm.[7] For example, drinking water protection cannot

[3] RAW Rhodes, 'The New Governance: Governing Without Government' (1996) 44 *Political Studies* 652.

[4] J Braithwaite and I Ayres, *Responsive Regulation* (Oxford, Oxford University Press, 1992) 3; LM Salamon, 'The New Governance and the Tools of Public Action: An Introduction' in LM Salamon (ed), *The Tools of Government: A Guide to the New Governance* (Oxford, Oxford University Press, 2002) 15; J Freeman and DA Farber, 'Modular Environmental Regulation' (2005) *Duke Law Journal* 795, 814ff; and MS Winfield, 'Governance and the Environment in Canada From Regulatory Renaissance to "Smart Regulation"' (2007) 17 *Journal of Environmental Law and Practice* 69, 75.

[5] N Gunningham, P Grabosky and D Sinclair, *Smart Regulation: Designing Environmental Policy* (Oxford, Claredon Press, 1998) 7. See S Wood, G Tanner and BJ Richardson, 'What Ever Happened to Canadian Environmental Law?' (2011) 37 *Ecology Law Quarterly* 981 for some success stories.

[6] D Boyd, *Unnatural Law: Rethinking Canadian Environmental Law and Policy* (Vancouver, University of British Columbia Press, 2003) ch 1. See Wood et al, 'What Ever Happened to Canadian Environmental Law?' (ibid).

[7] This is echoed at the international level: Gunningham et al, *Smart Regulation* (above n 5) 7; and M Koskenniemi, 'The Fate of Public International Law: Between Technique and Politics' (2007) 70 *Modern Law Review* 1, 13.

be achieved solely by eliminating point-source pollution; it also requires broader land use reform to address issues arising from agricultural practices, groundwater aquifer depletion and invasive species.[8] Species protection demands habitat preservation in resource-valuable areas, not just hunting bans. And climate change mitigation and adaptation require coordination between public and private actors at all levels of government.

First-wave environmental laws are often associated with command-and-control regulation, typically legislation that prohibits specific causes of environmental degradation and comprehensively details what actions regulated parties must take to avoid environmental harm.[9] The Forest Practices Code,[10] the legislation that governed British Columbia forest practices at the time the mountain pine beetle epidemic began in the 1990s, is an example of command-and-control regulation. The Code specified requirements for harvesting timber on Crown land.[11] Proponents of new governance argue that command-and-control regulation is poorly suited to the kind of environmental problems we now face.[12] They characterise environmental issues as scientifically uncertain and normatively complex; such issues do not lend themselves to clear *a priori* solutions.[13] New governance advocates argue that command-and-control regulation seems to require an omniscient legislature that possesses the best, if not perfect, information about the problem and its possible regulatory solutions.[14] The assumption therefore is that the legislature is able to set out in advance the appropriate 'command' to regulated entities. As we have seen in previous chapters, the mountain pine beetle epidemic illustrates that, far from omniscient, legislators will instead

[8] P Hania, 'Climate Change and the Protection of Drinking Water in Ontario: An Opportunity to Adopt Adaptive Management?' (2011) 22 *Journal of Environmental Law and Practice* 167.

[9] I adopt the moniker 'command-and-control regulation' despite the fact that it originated as a derogatory term by its critics. The term 'command-and-control regulation' is widespread in the fields of environmental law and new governance, so much so that it is even used by those with more neutral and sometimes favourable views of this form of regulation, despite its rather unflattering expression.

[10] Forest Practices Code of British Columbia Act, RSBC 1996, c 159.

[11] E Walter, 'Decoding Codes of Practice: Approaches to Regulating the Ecological Impacts of Logging in British Columbia' (2005) 15 *Journal of Environmental Law and Practice* 143.

[12] Command-and-control regulation has been heavily criticised, particularly in the American context, where it has taken a highly prescriptive form not representative to the same extent of other jurisdictions: N Gunningham, 'Environment Law, Regulation and Governance: Shifting Architectures' (2009) 21 *Journal of Environmental Law* 179, 191. See EW Orts, 'Reflexive Environmental Law' (1995) 89 *Northwestern University Law Review* 1227, 1235–41 for an overview of this criticism.

[13] G De Burca, 'New Governance and Experimentalism: An Introduction' (2010) 2010 *Wisconsin Law Review* 227, 232.

[14] CF Sabel and WH Simon, 'Epilogue: Accountability Without Sovereignty' in G De Burca and J Scott (eds), *Law and New Governance in the EU and the US* (Oxford, Hart Publishing, 2006) 398–99; DM Trubek and LG Trubek, 'New Governance and Legal Regulation: Complementarity, Rivalry, and Transformation' (2007) 13 *Columbia Journal of European Law* 539, 542; and G Teubner and A Beckers, 'Expanding Constitutionalism' (2013) 20 *Indiana Journal of Global Legal Studies* 523, 530.

be confronted with unforeseen events, some of which have catastrophic potential.

New governance scholars further argue that, even assuming the legislature has a solid epistemic foundation on which to base its decisions, command-and-control regulation is static and uniform. In their view, static rules do not promote anything more than minimal compliance and may be difficult to alter in light of changing information.[15] Yet the environmental emergency makes clear that, in addition to their complexity, environmental issues are also dynamic—changing over time and space. Uniform rules are not well suited to environmental issues that seem to demand local modifications based on ecological context and continual revision and adaptation as problems—and our understanding of them—evolve. Moreover, the environmental emergency emphasises the fact that this dynamism can also reveal the possibility of environmental catastrophe.

Finally, governance scholars note that command-and-control regulation is a poor fit with environmental issues that frequently spill over jurisdictional boundaries.[16] This means that under command-and-control regulation, many of those who suffer environmental consequences have no opportunity to participate in making relevant decisions and have no direct political recourse when they object. New governance thus promises to improve accountability with respect to cross-border effects.[17]

Critiques of command-and-control regulation are frequently overstated. Command-and-control regulation does not exist in an ideal form. As we saw in chapter two, it necessarily contains pockets of administrative discretion that allow administrative decision-makers to respond to the changing context of the regulatory problem. Command-and-control regulation is easily caricatured, however, because it aligns so nicely with the formal conception of the rule of law.[18] In its ideal form, the legislature is the source of legal norms, the exercise of administrative discretion is minimised, and, since the legislation contains such detail, its implementation can be straightforwardly enforced by the courts.

In contrast to the command-and-control model of regulation, new governance scholars focus on 'fragmentation, interdependencies, ungovernability, and the rejection of a clear distinction between public and private'.[19]

[15] Gunningham et al, *Smart Regulation* (above n 5) 45; and Orts, 'Reflexive Environmental Law' (above n 12) 1238–39.

[16] Sabel and Simon, 'Epilogue' (above n 14) 399; and De Burca, 'New Governance and Experimentalism' (above n 13) 233 (on interdependence).

[17] Sabel and Simon, 'Epilogue' (above n 14) 399.

[18] McDonald, 'The Rule of Law in the "New Regulatory State"' (above n 1) 209 (noting the conflation of the rule of law with command and control regulation).

[19] J Black, 'Constructing and Contesting Legitimacy and Accountability in Polycentric Regulatory Regimes' (2008) 2 *Regulation & Governance* 137, 140. See also Salamon, 'The Tools of Public Action' (above n 4) 9–18; and C Tollefson, AR Zito and FP Gale, 'Symposium Overview: Conceptualizing New Governance Arrangements' (2012) 90 *Public Administration* 3, 5.

They offer up a range of policy instruments—such as public–private partnerships, negotiated rule-making/regulation-making, audited self-regulation, results-based rules, disclosure regimes and decentralised, dynamic problem-solving—that, when tailored to their specific context, promise to be more effective and efficient than any linear approach to regulation.[20] In its most decentred form, new governance would conceptualise administrative decision-making 'as a set of negotiated relationships'.[21] On this view, the state is only one actor in any given governance network.

Complexity figures prominently in new governance scholarship. Governance scholars observe that contemporary regulatory problems are more challenging than in the past. They argue that the world is changing more rapidly and is more interconnected, which results in more unintended regulatory consequences.[22] Contemporary problems seem more intractable. According to new governance scholars, under these regulatory conditions, the best we can do is put in place institutions and procedures that generate information by enlisting a diverse range of participants and institutionalising flexibility to update existing approaches in light of changing information.[23] They emphasise that complexity also creates opportunities for novel collaborations; an uncertain future destabilises historically entrenched positions.[24] By seizing on this opportunity, new governance mechanisms can respond to complexity in a way that command-and-control does not. They can reduce the range of the unforeseeable and allow decision-makers to act on early warning signs.

In their enthusiasm for regulatory innovation, some proponents of new governance openly reject traditional rule-of-law constraints.[25] They frankly acknowledge that new governance 'disrespect[s] the distinction between enforcement and enactment'.[26] They advise lawyers and legal scholars to

[20] O Lobel, 'The Renew Deal: The Fall of Regulation and the Rise of Governance in Contemporary Legal Thought' (2004) 89 *Minnesota Law Review* 342, 345.

[21] J Freeman, 'The Private Role in the Public Governance' (2000) 75 *New York University Law Review* 543, 548.

[22] Lobel, 'The Renew Deal' (above n 20) 357–59. Gunther Teubner's work on reflexive law is important to note here. Teubner's diagnosis of the problems with regulation stems from his argument that law is only one system within a complex society (others include politics, religion, the economy, science). Since each system is normatively closed—that is, operates only according to its own logic—law cannot directly influence other subsystems. Legal regulation fails because it cannot perfectly dictate the operations of another system, or the opposite—it completely colonises the other system. One need not wade too deeply in the intricacies of systems theory, however, to observe that there can be a fundamental mismatch between traditional legal regulation and complex societal problems. Indeed, much of the new governance and environmental governance scholarship that I refer to in this chapter does not adopt Teubner's perspective, although there are frequent parallels. See G Teubner, 'Substantive and Reflexive Elements in Modern Law' (1983) 17 *Law and Society Review* 239, 273–75.

[23] Lobel, 'The Renew Deal' (above n 20) Part III, generally.

[24] Ibid, 377–79.

[25] Sabel and Simon, 'Epilogue' (above n 14) 400.

[26] Ibid.

'get over it'[27] and find a way to play a constructive role in designing and implementing institutions and processes that are better tailored to respond to complex environmental issues. Even those with less forceful views concede that in the new governance context, notions of legal legitimacy 'will often be irrelevant, or at least unproductive … [and] will lead us to a dead end'.[28]

The emergency framework, however, should sound a cautionary note to any approach that is so quick to jettison the rule of law in favour of necessity. As we saw in chapter one, the extra-legal approach to emergencies was subject to both empirical and conceptual critiques, which we will now see have analogues in the environmental context.

B. The Law/Governance Distinction

Despite the forceful critique of command-and-control regulation, most governance scholars envision some role for formal law in regulating complex problems. Even those most critical of command-and-control regulation concede that it can play a necessary and complementary role in a blend of policy instruments.[29] Increasingly detailed empirical work on existing regulatory regimes shows that there is no simple trajectory from government to governance.[30] Governance scholars argue that existing legal frameworks and institutions can be reconfigured to address complex environmental problems by linking together relevant administrative bodies and private parties. Novel collaborations may become the means for developing traditional legal regulation. Or traditional regulation may impose 'default rules' to force recalcitrant stakeholders to the table in order to develop more flexible regulatory approaches.[31] Governance scholars have observed that the coexistence of formal laws and novel governance techniques has resulted in hybridisation, that is, 'institutions whose very function or role has no precise analogue in prior legal regimes'.[32]

[27] BC Karkkainen, 'Collaborative Ecosystem Governance: Scale, Complexity, and Dynamism' (2002) 21 *Virginia Environmental Law Journal* 189, 235; and McDonald, 'The Rule of Law in the "New Regulatory State"' (above n 1) 208–9.

[28] Black, 'Constructing and Contesting Legitimacy' (above n 19) 145.

[29] Gunningham et al, *Smart Regulation* (above n 5) 9; and Braithwaite and Ayres, *Responsive Regulation* (above n 4) 4.

[30] See, eg, Tollefson et al, 'Conceptualizing New Governance Arrangements' (above n 19) (and the articles cited therein); C Holley and N Gunningham, 'Natural Resources, New Governance and Legal Regulation: When Does Collaboration Work?' (2011) 24 *New Zealand Universities Law Review* 309.

[31] BC Karkkainen, 'Information-forcing Regulation and Environmental Governance' in De Burca and Scott (eds), *Law and New Governance* (above n 14) 293, 301–4.

[32] Sabel and Simon, 'Epilogue' (above n 14) 396; Trubek and Trubek, 'New Governance and Legal Regulation' (above n 14); and D Trubek and L Trubek, 'The World Turned Upside Down: Reflections on New Governance and the Transformation of Law' (2010) *Wisconsin Law Review* 719, 721–22.

It seems, then, that the appropriate question is not how to categorise 'law' and 'governance' approaches to regulation but rather what the proliferation of novel governance techniques means for the rule of law. Charles Sabel and William Simon, for example, have speculated that we might be witnessing a transformation in the meaning of law itself.[33] They suggest that we should understand law as a powerful mechanism for structuring relationships that enable problem-solving because the traditional view of law solely as a dispute-resolution and rights-protection mechanism is less useful in the face of such complex regulatory problems. On this view, both law and governance are cut from the same cloth; they are both understood as instruments for resolving complex societal issues. The problem, we know from the emergency context, is that by dismissing the relevance of the rule of law, there is no way to make it relevant again. If law is understood as nothing more than a tool of governance, it can be dispensed with at will. The appropriate questions, then, are whether such a transformation is indeed occurring, and if so, whether it adequately attends to rule-of-law concerns.

II. THREE EXAMPLES OF ENVIRONMENTAL GOVERNANCE

Much can fly under the banner of new governance. Generalisations are difficult and not always helpful; detailed examples are needed to understand the context, strengths and weaknesses of mechanisms for environmental governance. From the new governance literature, we can identify two hypotheses about environmental governance: (1) governance scholarship takes seriously the complexity of environmental issues and rejects the formal conception of the rule of law; and (2) the proliferation of governance mechanisms is having a transformative effect on how law is conceptualised within environmental scholarship.

This section tests these two hypotheses against three concrete examples from the British Columbia forestry context. The examples selected display different characteristics of environmental governance. The BC Forest and Range Practices Act (2002) is the most tentative move toward environmental governance.[34] It is results-based legislation that delegates significant autonomy to holders of forest licences in the province. The Great Bear Rainforest Agreement (2016) is an example of collaborative, ecosystem-based management in a particularly sensitive and controversial region of the province.[35]

[33] Sabel and Simon, 'Epilogue' (above n 14) 403–9. While Sabel and Simon are two who most clearly eschew the formal conception of the rule of law, we will see in ch 5 below that their theory of democratic experimentalism is wholly compatible with the alternative democratic conception of the rule of law that I develop in Part II of this book.

[34] Forest and Range Practices Act (FRPA), SBC 2002, c 69.

[35] BC Ministry of Forests, 'Great Bear Rainforest Order' [hereafter 'GBR Order'], (BC Gazette I, Vol CLVI, No 4, 2016), www.for.gov.bc.ca/tasb/slrp/plan17.html#Orders.

The Forest Stewardship Council is a transnational certification body with no formal connection to provincial forestry regulation.

This section argues that these examples support both hypotheses. First, the examples of environmental governance address the complexity of environmental problems, and in doing so, they depart in significant ways from the formal conception of the rule of law. Second, they demonstrate how mechanisms of new governance and traditional legal forms of regulation blur into one another to create novel forms of regulation. This section examines the existing academic commentary on these three examples and argues that this commentary has only indirectly addressed the rule-of-law concern for arbitrariness. Instead, existing scholarship has shifted its focus to alternative criteria of effectiveness, participation, transparency and accountability.

A. Results-Based Regulation

In the aftermath of the mountain pine beetle epidemic, the province of British Columbia enacted a radical change in its approach to regulating forest practices. The Forest and Range Practices Act (FRPA), an example of results-based regulation, replaced the Forest Practices Code, a command-and-control statute. Both statutes were enacted to regulate forest practices (eg, clear-cutting, placement and construction of logging roads, location of harvesting) in order to ensure better protection of non-timber forest values, such as biodiversity, water quality and aesthetics, while maintaining timber harvest. The previous Code was criticised as 'heavy-handed' by industry, since it imposed detailed planning requirements on companies, while its weak implementation meant that it also fell short of many of its environmental promises.[36] The FRPA was promoted as legislation that would achieve the same objectives as the Code while allowing companies flexibility over how to meet those objectives.[37] The new legislation is typically characterised as results-based regulation because it sets out regulatory objectives without prescribing how regulated parties must achieve these objectives; but it also blends these results with planning requirements. It is therefore a combination of results-based and management-based regulation.

The FRPA incorporates overarching qualitative objectives—such as protecting wildlife, the productivity and hydrological function of soils, and

[36] Walter, 'Decoding Codes of Practice' (above n 11) 156–57.

[37] The regulation sets out some mandatory practices to prohibit high-risk activities (eg, damage to stream banks and fish habitat, causing landslides), but all other practices are to be specified by the companies in their plans: Forest Planning and Practices Regulation, BC Reg 14/2004 [hereafter 'FPP Regulation'], ss 35–40.

conserving the cultural heritage resources of forests[38]—and requires that companies draft and submit 'Forest Stewardship Plans' for approval by the Minister before carrying out any forestry activities.[39] The Plans must detail 'results or strategies' that disclose how the proposed activities will be consistent with the overarching objectives of the Act.[40] The Plans are the only major regulatory requirement for licence-holders prior to harvesting timber, and the grounds on which a Plan can be rejected are very limited.[41] The Plans are open to public comment,[42] and they are subject to revision and re-approval every five years.[43] Forest companies therefore have considerable autonomy over their forest practices, in exchange for relatively modest approval and reporting requirements.

The FRPA operates through a combination of legislated requirements, regulations, orders-in-council and administrative discretion that differ only in degree from the environmental regulation we saw in chapter two. At the same time, it demonstrates a clear shift away from the state as the centre of governance and instead places much of the heavy lifting on the regulated parties. The 'command', it might be said, is for a regulated party to develop its own set of rules for how to conduct forest practices.[44] Private parties are therefore key players in the specification of public objectives and their delivery, with the Forest Stewardship Plans acting as the linkages in a network of forest governance across the province.

By stepping away from traditional command-and-control regulation, the FRPA promises, in some respects, to respond to the complexity of forest management. In principle, it harnesses the tremendous information and expertise of forest companies by allowing them to develop individualised, context-specific rules for their forest practices.[45] Plans are subject to public scrutiny, and companies are required to seek re-approval to ensure the plans reflect up-to-date knowledge, incorporate lessons learned and improve their performance.

[38] FRPA (above n 34) s 149; and FPP Regulation (ibid) ss 5–10.

[39] FRPA (above n 34) s 3.

[40] Ibid, s 5.

[41] Ibid, s 6.

[42] FPP Regulation (above n 37) ss 20–22.

[43] FRPA (above n 34) s 6.

[44] Karkkainen, 'Information-Forcing Regulation' (above n 31) 295. The FRPA comes close to what Braithwaite and Ayres have described as enforced self-regulation, which requires individual firms to generate their own rules that are then publicly ratified and both privately and publicly enforced: Braithwaite and Ayres, *Responsive Regulation* (above n 4) ch 4.

[45] C Coglianese, J Nash and T Olmstead, 'Performance-Based Regulation: Prospects and Limitations in Health, Safety and Environmental Protection' (2003) 55 *Administrative Law Review* 704, 714; C Coglianese and D Lazer, 'Management-Based Regulation: Prescribing Private Management to Achieve Public Goals' (2003) 37 *Law and Society Review* 691, 706; Gunningham et al, *Smart Regulation* (above n 5) 52; and Braithwaite and Ayres, *Responsive Regulation* (above n 4) 104–5.

Proponents of results-based regulation highlight the gains in both effectiveness and efficiency.[46] By legislating for environmental results and giving companies flexibility over the means, results-based regulation recognises that individual companies operate in different ways, which create different risks. Individualised rules developed by the companies, they argue, will be more rational in this sense.[47] Proponents maintain that results-based regulation also promotes innovation and responds more quickly to emerging threats.[48] Indeed, the FRPA was introduced as a way of stimulating innovation in forest practices that can be replicated when effective. All this means that (in principle) results-based regulation will achieve the same or better environmental results in comparison with command-and-control regulation, at less public expense.

In reality, however, the FRPA has been roundly criticised as thinly veiled deregulation that cannot, even charitably, be understood as a genuine attempt to meet the stated objectives.[49] Indeed, critics have noted that the British Columbia legislature failed to heed the warnings of regulatory scholars who argue that the effectiveness of performance- and management-based regulation depends on monitoring and enforcement capacity. The very conditions that make command-and-control regulation difficult also make it difficult to specify measurable goals and for regulators to monitor and enforce planning requirements.[50] Yet the province's move to the FRPA coincided with deep cuts to the Ministry, which reinforced critics' views that 'results-based legislation' was deregulation in disguise.

Both the defence and criticism of results-based regulation have been framed predominantly in terms of effectiveness.[51] Critics primarily try to meet proponents on their own terms by arguing that when implemented, results-based regulation frequently departs from the ideal model. Adopting this perspective, Emily Walter has written:

> The FRPA appears weakly designed from this point of view, as the outputs are vague and difficult to measure, the mechanisms for monitoring and assessing them are not well defined or resourced, and incentives for firms to ensure that stated

[46] Coglianese et al, 'Performance-Based Regulation' (ibid) 701; and Gunningham et al, *Smart Regulation* (above n 5) 15.

[47] Braithwaite and Ayres, *Responsive Regulation* (above n 4) 110.

[48] Coglianese et al, 'Performance-Based Regulation' (above n 45) 711; and Braithwaite and Ayres, *Responsive Regulation* (above n 4) 110–12.

[49] Many environmental NGOs boycotted the consultation process: British Columbia Legislative Assembly, Official Reports of Debates (Hansard), 37th Parl, 2nd Sess, Vol 10 No 3 (6 Nov 2002) 4344 (Hon de Jong).

[50] Coglianese and Lazar, 'Management-Based Regulation' (above n 45) 726.

[51] Coglianese et al, 'Performance-Based Regulation' (above n 45) 714: determining whether performance-based measures are effective requires is difficult empirical work, which currently does not exist. See also J Williams, 'The Design of Performance-Based Natural Resource Regulation: Lessons from the BC Experience' (2005) 18 *Canadian Journal of Administrative Law and Practice* 61.

environmental protection goals are met are weakened by prescribed exclusions from liability.[52]

In other words, the FRPA simply will not work.[53]

Walter has further critiqued the FRPA as an example of neoliberal ideology that is inconsistent with environmental protection.[54] She argues that the FRPA reflects the logic 'that industry must play the role of regulator and producer if it is to be globally competitive, and government's oversight role must be further reduced'.[55] Forest companies are accordingly given the pivotal role in regulation, and the perspective of the company is privileged in the evaluation of the merits and weaknesses of any given regulatory approach.[56] Intriguingly, she has suggested that the shift to environmental governance requires us to pay closer attention to the 'interconnections between structural, institutional and normative dimensions of a regulatory system ... including changing patterns of private authority'.[57] But she has not elaborated on what she means by this, nor does she suggest that the concepts of the rule of law or legality could be of any assistance in working this out.[58]

While largely framed in terms of effectiveness, distinctly rule-of-law concerns arise from this picture of the FRPA. The legislation allows private parties to effectively write, rewrite and interpret the rules without guarantees that these Forest Stewardship Plans will align with public values.[59] In practice, the Plans may be public-spirited, but existing mechanisms do not protect against the threat of arbitrariness. Public scrutiny prior to approval is minimal.[60] The FRPA further delegates the approval function to professional foresters rather than to public officials.[61] And in light of the vaguely worded legislative objectives, there seems to be no meaningful role that a court could play in ensuring they are met.[62]

[52] Walter, 'Decoding Codes of Practice' (above n 11) 178. Also noted by critics is the fact that the Act and regulations prioritise timber values over other forest values (173–74). See also West Coast Environmental Law Association, 'Cutting up the Safety Net: Environmental Deregulation in British Columbia' (2005) 22.

[53] We return to the problems with the FRPA in ch 5, section III in order to understand how it can be made consistent with the rule of law.

[54] Walter, 'Decoding Codes of Practice' (above n 11) 183–84; and S Wood, 'Environmental Management Systems and Public Authority in Canada: Rethinking Environmental Governance' (2002) 10 *Buffalo Environmental Law Journal* 129, 188.

[55] Walter, 'Decoding Codes of Practice' (above n 11) 181.

[56] Ibid, 180.

[57] Ibid, 183.

[58] Indeed, to the contrary, her only reference to 'legality' suggests that she would likely view any recourse to the rule of law with deep suspicion: ibid, 185.

[59] Sabel and Simon, 'Epilogue' (above n 14) 397–98.

[60] Forest Practices Board, 'Board Bulletin, Volume 15: Public Involvement in Forest Management Planning in BC' (Government of British Columbia, 2013) 3.

[61] FRPA (above n 34) s 16(1.01).

[62] The fact that the Act requires approval so long as the plans formally comply with the legislation and regulations would also preclude review: ibid, s 16.

B. Ecosystem-Based Management

The Great Bear Rainforest Agreement (GBRA) is a more creative experiment in environmental governance. Unlike the FRPA, it is generally regarded as an environmental governance success story.[63] The GBRA is the product of a highly contentious land use planning process for an ecologically sensitive region of British Columbian forest.[64] The region, known as the Great Bear Rainforest, was the subject of an international environmental campaign to prohibit timber harvesting in old growth forest. The region is also home to dozens of First Nations with unresolved title claims. In 2016, the Agreement was finalised, consolidated into a land use order and incorporated into legislation.[65] It covers over 6.4 million hectares of old-growth coastal rainforest, 85 per cent of which is protected and 15 per cent of which is subject to rigorous principles of ecosystem-based management. The GBRA and its Marine Plan Partnership is the largest land and marine ecosystem in the world governed by ecosystem-based management principles.[66]

The story of the GBRA is both fascinating and complex.[67] The GBRA is a product of decades of conflict followed ultimately by collaboration between government, industry, environmental groups and First Nations. For present purposes, two aspects of the GBRA are notable. First, the Agreement implements rigorous ecosystem-based management principles, the objective of which is to 'maintain … ecosystem integrity and improve … human well-being concurrently'.[68] Ecosystem-based management is a significant departure from the sustainable yield approach discussed in chapter two. Sustainable yield focuses on maximising the extraction of timber over time; in contrast, ecosystem-based management strives to 'ensure the coexistence

[63] K Price, A Roburn and A MacKinnon, 'Ecosystem-Based Management in the Great Bear Rainforest' (2009) 258 *Forest Ecology and Management* 495; M Smith and D Dobell, *Place of Power: Lessons from the Great Bear Rainforest* (Vancouver, Tides Canada Foundation, 2010); and G McGee, A Cullen and T Gunton, 'A New Model for Sustainable Development: A Case Study of the Great Bear Rainforest Regional Plan' (2010) 12 *Environment, Development and Sustainability* 745. It is referred to as the Great Bear Rainforest because it is home to the iconic Spirit Bear.

[64] M Howlett, J Rayner and C Tollefson, 'From Government to Governance in Forest Planning? Lessons from the Case of the British Columbia Great Bear Rainforest Initiative' (2009) 11 *Forest Policy and Economics* 383, 388.

[65] GBR Order (above n 35); and Great Bear Rainforest (Forest Management) Act, SBC 2016, c 16.

[66] Government of British Columbia, 'Agreement Highlights' (undated), greatbearrainforest.gov.bc.ca/tile/gbr-agreement-highlights.

[67] See Smith and Dobell, *Place of Power* (above n 63) for an overview of the Agreement itself, in addition to the backstory of how it was concluded. Howlett et al, 'From Government to Governance' (above n 64) discuss the relationship between the Agreement and formal government processes. It maps on remarkably well to Teubner and Beckers' descriptive theory of societal constitutionalism: G Teubner and A Beckers, 'Expanding Constitutionalism' (2013) 20 *Indiana Journal of Global Legal Studies* 523.

[68] GBR Order (above n 35) 2.

of [healthy], fully functioning ecosystems and human communities'.[69] The management principles include, for example, the requirement to maintain a very high percentage of old-growth forest even in managed areas. The principles reflect the spatial and temporal complexity of the ecosystem by integrating aquatic and terrestrial principles and projecting these over a long timeframe.

The second notable feature of the GBRA is its collaborative approach to decision-making. The details of ecosystem-based management were developed through multiple working groups and in ongoing collaboration with First Nations communities. Once the Agreement was finalised, this collaborative governance approach was formalised through government-to-government agreements (between the provincial government and each affected First Nation), which oversee the implementation of ecosystem-based management.[70] The goal of these government-to-government agreements is 'to prepare and implement … [land use designs and practices] that identify how the biodiversity, First Nation, wildfire and managed forest objectives of the [Great Bear Rainforest] can most effectively be addressed on the ground'.[71]

The objectives and ecosystem-based management principles set out in the GBRA and operationalised through the government-to-government agreements must be incorporated into companies' Forest Stewardship Plans, as discussed above.[72] The GBRA has committed to adaptive management, which requires continual monitoring, 'learning by doing', and provides for reviewing and amending the Order if 'ecosystem integrity is not being maintained or … human well-being is not being improved'.[73]

The GBRA has been previously analysed from the perspective of new governance theory.[74] These analyses unpack the intricate interdependence between formal policymaking mechanisms and informal network arrangements. The GBRA departs from command-and-control regulation in three

[69] Nanwakolas Council, Coastal First Nations, and BC Ministry of Forests, Lands and Natural Resource Operations BC Ministry of Forests, 'Ecosystem Based Management on BC's Central and North Coast (Great Bear Rainforest): Implementation Update Report' (July 2012), coastfunds.ca/wp-content/uploads/2016/05/EBM_Implementation-Update_report_July-31_2012-1.pdf, 5.

[70] GBR Order (above n 35) cl 5 (operationalised through 'Landscape Reserve Designs', which are an intermediate-scale strategic planning process).

[71] Government of British Columbia, 'A Framework for Landscape Reserve Design in the Great Bear Rainforest' (4 July 2016) www.for.gov.bc.ca/tasb/slrp/plan17.html#Orders [hereafter 'GBR Framework'], 3.

[72] But see critique of the FRPA above, which casts some doubt on how meaningful the effect of the land use Plans are in the context of forest practices. See also Howlett et al, 'From Government to Governance' (above n 64) 388–89.

[73] GBR Order (above n 35) preamble.

[74] Howlett et al, 'From Government to Governance' (above n 64); and K Raitio and H Saarikoski, 'Governing Old-Growth Forests: The Interdependence of Actors in Great Bear Rainforest in British Columbia' (2012) 25 *Society and Natural Resources* 900.

significant ways. First, the GBRA is not a product of top-down policy development but rather the result of complex multi-party collaboration that originated outside any formal legal framework.[75] Second, the basis of these negotiations was ecosystem-based management. As noted, these are principles and indicators that are developed in collaboration with independent scientists. They comprehensively address the range of environmental issues in the region and emphasise the need for continued monitoring, learning and adjustment. In other words, the GBRA does not set down fixed rules but rather elaborates context-sensitive, flexible principles. Third, the agreement maps onto the scale of the ecosystem and addresses problems holistically. That is, it addresses a complete set of regional issues so that, for example, ameliorating one threat to the Great Bear Rainforest does not aggravate another.

In other words, the GBRA is a dramatic shift from traditional environmental regulation: it attempts to address complexity in every aspect of its institutional design. It covers an impressive geographic scope, combines scientific expertise with collaborative decision-making with affected communities, commits to ongoing monitoring and learning, and integrates these decisions within the broader regulatory framework for forestry and land use planning in the province.

Much existing work on ecosystem governance focuses on water management, but this commentary is also relevant to the Great Bear Rainforest. This literature focuses primarily on four features of ecosystem governance: its effectiveness, participation, transparency and accountability. First, proponents argue that ecosystem governance promises to be more effective than command-and-control regulation. Its effectiveness derives from the ecologically appropriate scale of decision-making.[76] Moreover, ecosystem governance brings all 'users' of the ecosystem to the table to address harms comprehensively and enables ongoing monitoring and adjustment based on past learning and changing ecological conditions.[77] On the other hand, critics question claims that ecosystem governance is more effective than conventional regulation. They point out that ecosystem management approaches typically require considerable autonomy from formal legal frameworks to allow for genuine collaboration amongst participants. There is thus no guarantee that environmental protection will prevail.

[75] Howlett et al, 'From Government to Governance' (above n 64) 383.

[76] Karkkainen, 'Collaborative Ecosystem Governance' (above n 27) 212ff; BC Karkkainen, '"New Governance" in the Great Lakes: Has Its Time Arrived?' (2006) 2006 *Michigan State Law Review* 1249; and J Benidickson, 'The Great Lakes and the Mediterranean Sea: Ecosystem-Management and Sustainability in the Context of Economic Integration' (2004) 14 *Journal of Environmental Law and Practice* 107.

[77] Karkkainen, 'Collaborative Ecosystem Governance' (above n 27) 218–19; OM Brandes et al, 'At a Watershed: Ecological Governance and Sustainable Water Management in Canada' (POLIS Project on Ecological Governance, 2005) iv; and Freeman and Farber, 'Modular Environmental Regulation' (above n 4).

Second, proponents emphasise the participatory aspects of collaborative, ecosystem governance. For example, Oliver Brandes et al have emphasised 'the need for meaningful stakeholder participation to improve decision making and create more durable results'.[78] Because stakeholders are invested in the decision-making process, the argument goes, they will remain committed to ensuring proper implementation of those governance decisions over time. But even proponents of environmental governance concede there are challenges here.[79] 'Stakeholder participation' does not equal genuine collaboration. Tough questions thus remain about how to move beyond backroom, interest-group bargaining to a more deliberative decision-making process. Many proponents suggest that law ought to play a procedural role to enhance participation and prevent interest-group capture, but they offer no real details.[80]

Critics seize on these ambiguities. They reiterate the argument that only certain groups can be represented in the decision-making process, and it is not always clear how they are selected or whether they are representative of the general public.[81] Critics further worry that the flexibility and responsiveness of ecosystem governance, while attuned to changing environmental problems, necessarily requires an ongoing effort and commitment amongst participants. Yet this kind of attention and effort is not often sustainable over long periods of time.[82] Indeed, even one of the Agreement's negotiators observed that while the Orders and legislation 'bring a lot of certainty ... there is limited money for [ongoing monitoring]'.[83]

Third, critics highlight the trade-off between collaboration and transparency.[84] While the decision-making process may be transparent to those parties internal to the process, it may be utterly opaque to those outside. Indeed, detailed information about the actual implementation of ecosystem-based management principles to the Great Bear Rainforest is not available to the public.[85] Some proponents of environmental governance argue that formal laws—presumably, such as the FRPA—can play a residual role in ensuring basic public accountability.[86] But such a claim is unpersuasive

[78] Brandes et al (ibid) 19.

[79] Karkkainen, 'Collaborative Ecosystem Governance' (above n 27) 239.

[80] Ibid, 236; and Freeman and Farber, 'Modular Environmental Regulation' (above n 4) 895–96.

[81] Black, 'Constructing and Contesting Legitimacy' (above n 19) 143.

[82] Ibid, 1297–98.

[83] L Cole, 'The Fight for the Great Bear Rainforest: How a "War in the Woods" Led to a Landmark Agreement to Save Three Million Hectares of Rainforest on the Northwest Coast of Canada' (2017) 89(4) *Geographical Magazine* 36.

[84] M Shapiro, 'Administrative Law Unbounded: Reflections on Government and Governance' (2000) 8 *Indiana Journal of Global Legal Studies* 369, 372–73.

[85] Framework and methodology documents are publicly available and contain information on the methodology of intermediate-scale planning. However, they do not indicate that these plans will be publicly accessible: GBR Framework (above n 71).

[86] Freeman and Farber, 'Modular Environmental Regulation' (above n 4) 905.

given how far this model of environmental governance departs from the formal conception of law.[87]

Finally, ecosystem governance has attracted concerns about its accountability. These concerns stem from a 'managerial' ethos inherent to decentralised governance arrangements.[88] Critics point out that environmental management is not amenable to conventional legal control because of the argued need for expert managers to 'optimise' results on a case-by-case basis.[89] Bruce Pardy, for his part, has pointed out that, unlike judges, ecosystem 'managers' are not generally required to give reasons or adhere to precedent, and they are not subject to appeal.[90] Indeed, the GBRA explicitly endorses dynamic and fine-tuned implementation over time and place through the adoption of ecosystem-based management and adaptive management practices. While the government-to-government agreements contemplate a form of internal review for effectiveness, it is not clear that there is any meaningful role for judicial review to play.

But even if reasons were required and judicial oversight were a feature of this governance mechanism, it is not clear what a formalist conception of law could demand of these decisions. When the essence of new governance is understood as the need to break free from the unacceptable features of formal law and legal institutions, law becomes just one more expert discourse with no particular claim to the top of hierarchy.[91] The managerial features of environmental governance, then, give rise to a real risk of arbitrary decision-making, a risk that its proponents and critics have yet to sufficiently confront and reconcile.

C. Transnational Certification

Forest certification is a third example of policy innovation in British Columbia forestry, and it takes environmental governance to a transnational level.[92] Numerous forest certification programmes are represented in

[87] Shapiro, 'Administrative Law Unbounded' (above n 84); and Black, 'Constructing and Contesting Legitimacy' (above n 19) 140 and 145.

[88] Koskenniemi, 'The Fate of Public International Law' (above n 7) 13. Koskenniemi was speaking of public international law, but his observations nicely map onto environmental governance. See also B Pardy, 'The Pardy–Ruhl Dialogue on Ecosystem Management, Part V: Discretion, Complex-Adaptive Problem Solving and the Rule of Law' (2008) 25 *Pace Environmental Law Review* 341, 353.

[89] M Koskenniemi, 'Constitutionalism as Mindset: Reflections on Kantian Themes about International Law and Globalization' (2007) 8 *Theoretical Inquiries in Law* 9, 13; and Pardy, 'The Pardy–Ruhl Dialogue, Part V' (ibid) 347.

[90] Pardy, 'The Pardy–Ruhl Dialogue, Part V' (above n 88) 347.

[91] Koskenniemi, 'The Fate of Public International Law' (above n 7) 19.

[92] See also Wood, 'Environmental Management Systems and Public Authority' (above n 54) on ISO 140001 standards.

the British Columbia forest industry, but the Forest Stewardship Council (FSC) standard is renowned as 'the most rigorous in protecting environmental values'.[93] The standards developed through the FSC demonstrate a different response to the limitations of the command-and-control regulatory model: it circumvents the state altogether.

The FSC is a transnational organisation comprised of non-state actors. It develops standards for environmentally appropriate, socially beneficially and economically viable forest operations.[94] By adhering to FSC standards, forest companies gain the right to affix the FSC label to their products. This allows consumers 'to act on their environmental and social preferences'.[95] Having succeeded in their market-based campaign that led to the GBRA, British Columbian forest stakeholders turned to the FSC.[96] They developed a BC-specific FSC standard, first implemented in 2005.

Forest certification differs from the previous examples in two significant respects. First, the FSC is a transnational organisation comprised entirely of non-state members. It prohibits membership of state actors and is instead comprised of private entities, civil society groups, international organisations and interested individuals.[97] Members are allocated to one of three chambers: environment (eg, environmental groups), social (eg, labour unions) or economic (eg, forest companies). Each chamber holds one third of the vote, and a super-majority of two chambers is required to pass resolutions on FSC policy, such as changes to the standards or criteria for certification.[98] The second key difference is that both membership and adherence to the FSC standards is voluntary. Any non-governmental organisation or individual who agrees to the FSC mission can become a member.[99] And any company that adheres to FSC standards can become certified.[100] Certification is often referred to as the 'carrot' that incentivises good practices,[101] as opposed to the 'stick' of boycotts or the sanctions attached to command-and-control regulation.

The FSC contains ten guiding principles, which, like the GBRA, are based on principles of ecosystem-based management. For example, Principle 6 requires that certified organisations 'maintain, conserve and/or restore

[93] Tollefson et al, *Setting the Standard* (above n 2) 188.

[94] See the Forest Stewardship Council Statutes (2014), available online at ic.fsc.org/en/choosing-fsc/fsc-membership, esp the 'Sixth' statute on p 2.

[95] Tollefson et al, *Setting the Standard* (above n 2) 19.

[96] Ibid, 190.

[97] See the Forest Stewardship Council website: ic.fsc.org/en/choosing-fsc/fsc-membership.

[98] Tollefson et al, *Setting the Standard* (above n 2) 27–28.

[99] Ibid, 276.

[100] Where a regional standard does not exist, the certifier is free to develop or adapt the international standards to suit the local context: ibid, 32.

[101] B Cashore, 'Legitimacy and the Privatization of Environmental Governance: How Non-State Market-Driven (NSMD) Governance Systems Gain Rule-Making Authority' (2002) 15 *Governance* 503, 507.

ecosystem services and environmental values'.[102] Each guiding principle contains measurable and verifiable criteria that specify how the principle is to be achieved, such as by conducting an impact assessment prior to beginning any forestry activities.[103] Where regional standards have been developed, as is the case in British Columbia, these standards further specify the criteria to suit the local context. The British Columbia standard is unique, for example, in its requirement that harvesting practices must fall within a 'range of natural variability'.[104] Since British Columbian forests currently grow in unevenly aged stands, this requirement significantly limits clear-cut harvesting without uniformly banning its use.[105]

The FSC has attracted a huge amount of academic interest as a particularly successful example of global governance.[106] The organisation has certified nearly two hundred million hectares of forests in eighty-four countries worldwide.[107] It promises to address the complex problem of sustainable forestry at both global and regional levels by linking the central, international institution with local standard bodies.[108] The FSC takes a holistic perspective on the problem by treating environmental, social and economic concerns as interconnected. As a self-consciously deliberative body with global reach, it has the capacity to generate and aggregate a huge amount of information about the state of forest management worldwide.[109]

The FSC is also a clear break from command-and-control regulation and the formal conception of the rule of law. Errol Meidinger has described forest certification as 'a multi-centred private/public [system], which operates in a loosely coordinated and sometimes disjointed fashion'.[110] And as an example of market-based or private governance,[111] its authority seems

[102] Forest Stewardship Council, 'FSC International Standard: FSC Principles and Criteria for Forest Stewardship' (July 2015), ic.fsc.org/en/document-center/id/59.

[103] Forest Stewardship Council, 'Regional Certification Standards for British Columbia' (October 2005), ca.fsc.org/preview.bc-standard.a-829.pdf, 6.2.

[104] See, eg, FSC, 'Regional Certification Standards for BC' (ibid) 6.3 7, 6.3.8 and 6.3.10.

[105] Tollefson et al, *Setting the Standard* (above n 2) 195–96 and 206.

[106] E Meidinger, 'The Administrative Law of Global Private–Public Regulation: The Case of Forestry' (2006) 17 *European Journal of International Law* 47, 77–78 (noting the rapid proliferation of forest certification worldwide and how it is affecting forest regulation).

[107] Forest Stewardship Council, 'Facts and Figures: October 4, 2017' (2017), ic.fsc.org/en/facts-and-figures.

[108] C Overdest and J Zeitlin, 'Assembling an Experimentalist Regime: Transnational Governance Interactions in the Forest Sector' (2014) 8 *Regulation and Governance* 22.

[109] Moreover, competition between different forest certification bodies reveals strengths and weaknesses from which all organisations have learned and improved: Meidinger, 'The Administrative Law of Global Private–Public Regulation' (above n 106) 78.

[110] Ibid, 48. See also Wood, 'Environmental Management Systems and Public Authority' (above n 54) 187.

[111] Cashore, 'Legitimacy and the Privatization of Environmental Governance' (above n 101); G Auld, *Constructing Private Governance: The Rise and Evolution of Forest, Coffee, and Fisheries Certification* (New Haven, Yale University Press, 2014); and Gunningham, 'Shifting Architectures' (above n 12) 197 (referring to it as 'civil regulation')

to come from the market, not from law.[112] At the same time, however, the FSC grapples with a public problem—global sustainable forestry—and purports to represent and act in the public interest. It operates through a highly sophisticated architecture that mirrors elements of a federalist, parliamentary system.[113] Commentators have argued that the FSC has effectively created a 'global forest polity'.[114] The FSC now influences domestic forest policy in tangible ways such that it cannot be considered as isolated from state-sanctioned forest practices.[115]

Meidinger has argued that environmental certification is a novel form of administrative law because it carries out essentially the same standard-setting and licensing functions as domestic regulatory bodies.[116] Because of the networked arrangement of forest certification, however, he rejects 'simplistic source-of-law models for understanding administrative law'.[117] Instead, he evaluates forest certification on the basis of alternative criteria for evaluating domestic administration: criteria of effectiveness, accuracy and accountability.[118] He has concluded, consistent with the general tide of opinion, that the FSC is highly effective,[119] though the particularities of the forest products market raise some risks about the reliability of forest certification.[120]

When Meidinger turns to the FSC's accountability, however, he encounters some difficulty. He has argued that accountability implies a principal–agent relationship and thus encourages a focus on individual accountability relationships, 'when in fact accountability mechanisms are cumulative and interactive'.[121] The FSC must be accountable to its members, to the companies it certifies and to the general public on whose behalf it purports

[112] But see J Ellis, 'Constitutionalization of Nongovernmental Certification Programs' (2013) 20 *Indiana Journal of Global Legal Studies* 1035.

[113] Tollefson et al, *Setting the Standard* (above n 2) ch 12.

[114] Ibid, 307.

[115] Meidinger, 'The Administrative Law of Global Private–Public Regulation' (above n 106) 59.

[116] Ibid, 60. Although he does not reference it, Meidinger's research on forest certification fits into the broader literature on global administrative law. See B Kingsbury, RB Stewart and N Krisch, 'The Emergence of Global Administrative Law' (2005) 68 *Law and Contemporary Problems* 15.

[117] Meidinger, 'The Administrative Law of Global Private–Public Regulation' (above n 106) 49.

[118] Ibid, 76ff.

[119] Ibid, 78–79; and Tollefson et al, *Setting the Standard* (above n 2) (on the rigour of the BC standard). But for some caveats, see E Walter, 'From Civil Disobedience to Obedient Consumerism? Influences of Market-based Activism and Eco-certification on Forest Governance' (2003) 41 *Osgoode Hall Law Journal* 531; A Marx and D Cuypers, 'Forest Certification as a Global Environmental Governance Tool: What Is the Macro-Effectiveness of the Forest Stewardship Council?' (2010) 4 *Regulation and Governance* 408; and S Bell and A Hindmoor, 'Governance Without Government? The Case of the Forest Stewardship Council' (2012) 90 *Public Administration* 144.

[120] Meidinger, 'The Administrative Law of Global Private–Public Regulation' (above n 106) 80.

[121] Ibid, 81.

to act. But it also contains further internal networks between, eg, national or regional standards bodies, third-party certifiers, companies and local stakeholders. The difficulties of assessing multiple accountability mechanisms has led Meidinger to turn to accountability 'proxies,' which he has identified as transparency and participation.

On its face, forest certification would seem to fare well in terms of transparency. Indeed, its very purpose is to clearly identify for consumers which forest products are sustainable. But Meidinger and others have observed that certification practices can actually obscure forest practices.[122] They render a complex and political problem manageable through a set of seemingly technical compliance standards whereby auditors simply tick 'yes' or 'no'. These audits and third-party auditors can act as a buffer that prevents governments or the public from really scrutinising the nature of the problem. Nonetheless, the FSC is highly regarded in terms of its transparency and opportunities for participation.[123] Its membership is open to all who subscribe to its mission. Its policies are deliberated within and across its chambers and are subject to public notice-and-comment proceedings.[124] FSC principles and criteria require auditors to consult with local stakeholders when conducting audits and to provide reasons for their decisions.[125] All FSC decisions are publicly available online and are actively scrutinised by a variety of actors.[126]

In addition to pointing to these accountability proxies, Meidinger has attempted to make sense of the overlapping accountability mechanisms within the FSC. But ultimately, he has argued that existing accountability theories are inadequate for this task.[127] He has even suggested that

[122] Ibid, 82. See also Wood, 'Environmental Management Systems and Public Authority' (above n 54) 193–200.

[123] Tollefson et al, *Setting the Standard* (above n 2) 307. See also G Auld and LH Gulbrandsen, 'Transparency in Nonstate Certification: Consequences for Accountability and Legitimacy' (2010) 10 *Global Environmental Politics* 97.

[124] Meidinger, 'The Administrative Law of Global Private–Public Regulation' (above n 106) 67.

[125] Specified in Forest Stewardship Council, 'Stakeholder Consultation for Forest Evaluation', FSC-STD-20-006 (V3-0) (2009).

[126] Most notable is the independent NGO FSC-Watch: fsc-watch.com. See Meidinger, 'The Administrative Law of Global Private–Public Regulation' (above n 106) 78 (noting that the competitor certification bodies scrutinise and criticise each other because they are competing for business).

[127] He offers three theories: (1) a sum of regulatory components approach, which he critiques as too static to capture the dynamic interactions that take place within forest certification, (2) a normative fidelity approach, which he rejects because it does not account for the abrupt and radical changes in forestry norms (eg, recognition of Indigenous rights that was previously rejected in the field) and (3) a learning approach, which he argues has the most promise but is incomplete. See Meidinger, 'The Administrative Law of Global Private–Public Regulation' (above n 106) 84–87. I take up this learning approach—democratic experimentalism—in the following chapter. I argue that the promise of democratic experimentalism can be realised only once we situate this within an equally democratic understanding of the rule of law.

accountability might boil down to effectiveness.[128] And he has admitted that it is unclear how the various accountability mechanisms within the FSC answer to society and further its interests.[129] Meidinger is not alone in this respect. Sceptics worry that the FSC is really accountable only to its members—a voluntary group that is already united by its singular mission.[130] They note there is no independent body, no international judicial review, to which outsiders may appeal when they seek to contest a decision of the FSC.[131] In short, we are told by governance scholars that accountability is a key evaluative criterion of complex governance regimes such as the FSC, but we are left with no firm grip on what this means.

The preoccupations of FSC commentators thus track those in other areas of environmental governance. Debates over 'output legitimacy' or effectiveness are always front and centre.[132] Law is 'side-lined'. It is treated in purely instrumental terms and only discussed when it serves a primary goal of effectiveness, transparency, participation or accountability.

D. Conclusion

Collectively, these three examples evidence the difficulty in distinguishing between law and governance. The British Columbia forestry context reveals that a mix of policy instruments governs forest practices in the province. Moreover, each example combines aspects of conventional legal regulation with novel governance features such as public–private relationships in the FRPA, collaborative ecosystem governance in the GBRA and the non-state, market-based design of the FSC. Drawing on existing literature, I have highlighted the strengths of these examples—how they can attend to the complexity of forestry issues, produce scientifically-based rigorous standards and foster inclusive and meaningful participation—while also noting their potential pitfalls. At the same time, we have seen that all three examples depart significantly from the formal conception of the rule of law and thus raise the underlying rule-of-law concern of arbitrariness.

These examples of environmental governance also suggest that this abandonment of the formal conception of the rule of law has come to be replaced

[128] Ibid, 86.

[129] Ibid.

[130] Walter, 'From Civil Disobedience to Obedient Consumerism?' (above n 119) 552; and Black, 'Constructing and Contesting Legitimacy' (above n 19) 141.

[131] Walter, 'From Civil Disobedience to Obedient Consumerism?' (above n 119) 138.

[132] M Wilkinson, 'Three Conceptions of Law: Towards a Jurisprudence of Democratic Experimentalism' (2010) 2010 *Wisconsin Law Review* 673, 696; and Trubek and Trubek 'The World Turned Upside Down' (above n 32) 724 (observing a common concern amongst commentators that new governance approaches will undermine programmatic agendas).

with a crowded field of metrics—effectiveness, participation, transparency and accountability—for understanding environmental governance. We will now see that these metrics are important dimensions for understanding environmental governance. But no one metric is synonymous with the rule of law.

III. RECLAIMING THE RULE OF LAW

In section II, we saw that sceptics and supporters of environmental governance have touched on arbitrariness, but largely indirectly through the language of effectiveness, transparency, participation and accountability. These are all important features, to be sure, but they do not capture what is distinctive about law. This section argues that the evaluative criteria proffered by governance scholars miss the fact that law constitutes a particular relationship between lawmaker and legal subject, a relationship that respects the autonomy of the subject. Moreover, by missing this constitutive aspect of law, governance scholars have abandoned the language needed to articulate more precisely both the strengths and the concerns illuminated by the various examples of governance outlined above.

We have seen that effectiveness is a primary concern of governance scholars. They argue that formal legal constraints can restrict our ability to do what is necessary to respond to complex environmental problems—eg, to collaborate with relevant parties to reach a difficult decision that was not visible a priori, to allow for flexible rules that respond to a dynamic problem or to formulate a transnational set of standards that address a complex problem when states are unwilling to respond adequately. For governance scholars, formal law may be valuable, but its value is contingent on an empirical determination about whether formal legal regulation is effective.

Whether any given instance of environmental governance will in fact protect the environment is of course a vital consideration. It is also a consideration that is connected to the formal conception's underlying concern with arbitrariness. As we saw in the previous chapter, evidence of environmental degradation may be evidence of arbitrariness—evidence, that is, that decisions ostensibly made in the public's name are in fact serving special interests. But we have also seen that whether a particular instance of governance is effective is frequently contested. Initial goals might be ambiguous; monitoring and evidence of environmental improvement may be patchy or may lag well behind our efforts. Reclaiming the rule of law in this conversation reveals that the focus on effectiveness as an objective ex post evaluative criterion is too narrow. The rule-of-law concern for arbitrariness safeguards individual autonomy such that we can reason collectively about the best course of action for protecting the environment. This means that we must also examine how environmental decisions are made and what measures are in place to ensure environmental governance decisions are a product of collective, public-regarding reasoning.

Governance scholars appropriately turn to features of transparency, public participation and accountability, all of which promise to attend to the potential for arbitrariness. But again, the focus is too narrow. Accountability, for its part, is a vague term that has become 'a placeholder for multiple contemporary anxieties'.[133] The literature on accountability is vast. Julia Black has succinctly described accountability in these terms: 'To be accountable is to agree to subject oneself to relationships of external scrutiny which can have consequences.'[134] The appeal of the language of accountability in the governance literature is that it addresses a breadth of relationships that extends well beyond formal legal accountabilities (such as judicial review, or liability in tort or contract). This focus on accountability, however, raises two problems. For one, the language of accountability suggests that the relationship arises only after the fact, as a mechanism to control the exercise of political power.[135] On this view, the rule of law is broader than accountability. The rule of law is not only an *ex post* check on the exercise of power. Rather, it is there from the beginning. The rule of law is also constitutive of a particular kind of relationship between lawmaker and subject, a relationship that brings about its own kind of authority and legitimacy.[136]

Second, if we broaden the definition of accountability to include a constitutive dimension, we are left with the question of why any given accountability relationship should be authoritative. For example, Black has argued that each relationship is 'an interpretive and discursive schema through which participants in the accountability relationship make sense of their own and each other's roles, which is constitutive of their relationship and which is fundamentally shaped by it'.[137] But she has not answered the next obvious question: constitutive of what? Black stresses the fact that each accountability relationship will have its own distinct logic such that one accountability relationship cannot be readily substituted for another.[138] Thus, when multiple accountability relationships coexist—as they do in any governance institution—the decision-maker will face an accountability dilemma. Black has argued that institutions must therefore choose which accountability relationships to satisfy and which to ignore.[139]

[133] JL Mashaw, 'Accountability and Institutional Design: Some Thoughts on the Grammar of Governance' in M Dowdle (ed), *Public Accountability: Designs, Dilemmas and Experiences* (Cambridge, Cambridge University Press, 2006) 117.

[134] Black, 'Constructing and Contesting Legitimacy' (above n 19) 150.

[135] D Dyzenhaus, 'Accountability and the Concept of (Global) Administrative Law' (2009) 2009 *Acta Juridica* 3, 25.

[136] Ibid, 25–26.

[137] Black, 'Constructing and Contesting Legitimacy' (above n 19) 152.

[138] Ibid.

[139] Ibid, 150–51.

This focus on multiple and competing accountability mechanisms is characteristic of a theme ever present in the governance literature: 'There is nothing to govern ... only problems to confront and decisions to make.'[140] And as Leighton McDonald has argued, this is a highly problematic conclusion from the perspective of the rule of law. Such an observation is 'inconsistent with a belief that regulation could ever be an authoritative or legitimated response to social problems. Rather, regulation just is: we can understand it, but lose sight of it as an instrument of authoritative governance.'[141]

By refocusing on the rule of law, the existence of multiple accountabilities within complex networks of governance does not disappear. Rather, it allows us to deepen our understanding of the conditions under which some of these relationships will become authoritative. As we will see in detail in the following chapter, law derives its authority from its compliance with the rule of law, such that without the rule of law, there is no rule by law.[142] This authority arises from the fact that compliance with the rule of law respects the autonomy of those subject to the law, by treating them as rational agents capable of actively participating in their own system of governance.

When governance scholars examine the criteria of transparency and participation, they surely have this idea in mind. Transparency and participation are features that are typically necessary for individuals to be active participants in any system of governance, but they are not ends in themselves. More is not always better. There may be good reasons for a decision-maker to restrict public access to information, for example to encourage regulated parties to be more forthcoming. And scholars of deliberative democracy have puzzled over the inherent trade-off between participation and deliberation: hundreds of participants cannot effectively reason together.[143] The narrow and disconnected focus on transparency and participation may explain why governance scholars are always fuzzy on the details about what these criteria actually require.[144] In any given administrative setting, requirements of participation and transparency will need to be addressed contextually.

[140] Freeman, 'The Private Role in the Public Governance' (above n 21) 548. I've rearranged the quote slightly. The original quote is: 'In my conception, however, there are only problems to confront and decisions to make. There is nothing to govern.'

[141] McDonald, 'The Rule of Law in the "New Regulatory State"' (above n 1) 202.

[142] Dyzenhaus, 'Accountability and the Concept of (Global) Administrative Law' (above n 135) 6–7.

[143] I take up deliberative-democratic theory in more detail in Part II of this book.

[144] Black makes this point in J Black, 'Proceduralizing Regulation: Part I' (2000) 20 *Oxford Journal of Legal Studies* 597. She then goes on to argue that democratising regulation requires more precision in what we mean by 'democracy', which can lead to fairly radical implications for conventional regulation: J Black, 'Proceduralizing Regulation: Part II' (2001) 21 *Oxford Journal of Legal Studies* 33.

By abandoning the rule of law, governance scholars miss how it promises to guide this contextual analysis.

To sum up, environmental governance scholars are onto something when, to paraphrase, they suggest that environmental governance presents an inherent risk of arbitrariness that demands a structural, institutional and normative analysis. Meidinger, in particular, is onto something when he suggests that we might consider the FSC as a form of administrative law.[145] But environmental governance scholars have not taken up the challenge of showing that a democratic conception of the rule of law can govern even when our institutional arrangements take seriously the environmental emergency. This is the task of the remainder of the book.

IV. CONCLUSION

This chapter has argued that the framework of the environmental emergency allows us to expose the assumptions about environmental issues and law contained in the burgeoning literature on environmental governance. I have argued that instances of environmental governance can respond to the complexity of environmental issues through flexible planning requirements, collaborative or networked governance, or non-state certification processes. This requires, however, that environmental governance depart in significant ways from the formal conception of the rule of law. Because environmental governance scholars—supporters and critics alike—generally assume a formal conception of the rule of law, they dismiss the rule of law as irrelevant. Instead, as we have seen, they evaluate environmental governance on a set of alternative criteria. I have argued that by jettisoning the rule of law, environmental governance scholars lack the language to precisely articulate the strengths and weaknesses of novel forms of governance. By reclaiming the rule of law and its underlying concern of arbitrariness, we are able to make sense of the disconnected criteria presented in the existing literature.

Chapters two and three have argued that understanding environmental issues as an ongoing emergency provides a framework for thinking through assumptions about the promise and limits of law that are implicit in existing approaches to Canadian environmental law. We have now seen that environmental reformers and environmental governance scholars both tend to assume a formal conception of the rule of law. This leads environmental reformers to ignore the emergency nature of environmental issues and

[145] On the emerging area of global administrative law, see Kingsbury et al, 'The Emergence of Global Administrative Law' (above n 116). For a critique of how global administrative law avoids the hard question of what makes it law, see Dyzenhaus, 'Accountability and the Concept of (Global) Administrative Law' (above n 135).

advocate for a rule-of-law façade that provides no meaningful legal constraint. It leads scholars of environmental governance to dismiss the rule of law as essentially irrelevant. As I have hinted throughout this chapter, however, we are not limited to the formal conception of the rule of law. The second half of the book develops an alternative theory of the rule of law, one that responds to Carl Schmitt's challenge and can be maintained even under conditions of the environmental emergency.

Part II

Responding to the Environmental Emergency

4

The Requirement of Public Justification

HAVING ARGUED EARLIER that the existing responses to the environmental emergency fail Schmitt's challenge, this chapter now returns to legal theory on national security emergencies to introduce a coherent and defensible rule-of-law response to the environmental emergency. The objective of this chapter is to set out a democratic conception of the rule of law that can both constitute and constrain the exercise of public authority over the environment. It does this by drawing out the connections between common law constitutionalism and deliberative democracy. We will see that common law constitutionalism requires public decision-makers to publicly justify their decisions on the basis of deeply rooted common law principles. Similarly, theories of deliberative democracy share a central commitment to collective rule through the giving and receiving of acceptable reasons. These two theoretical traditions share an understanding of the individual as a responsible agent who is capable of actively engaging in the ongoing project of democratic governance under the rule of law. Public officials respect individuals' rational and self-determining capacity through the requirement of reason-giving.

This theory draws heavily on the work of Lon Fuller and his insight that what makes law *law* is its compliance with the requirements of the rule of law. On this view, the rule of law gives rise to a reciprocal relationship between legal subject and state. Law is not, as Fuller put it, 'a one-way projection of authority' from lawmaker to legal subject, a command that the subject must obey or risk sanction.[1] Rather, by complying with the rule of law, public officials respect the capacity of individuals as rational and autonomous agents. This compliance is what gives law its authority; it creates a reciprocal obligation on the part of individuals to obey the law.[2]

[1] LL Fuller, *The Morality of Law*, rev edn (New Haven, Yale University Press, 1969) 207.

[2] Ibid, 39 and 219–20. Fuller's claim that compliance with the rule of law includes a reciprocal obligation of obedience is controversial. For a summary of the complex debates on the duty to obey the law, see WA Edmundson, 'State of the Art: The Duty of Obey the Law' (2004) 10 *Legal Theory* 215. For present purposes, it is sufficient to accept a weaker version of Fuller's claim that in modern liberal societies, respect for individual agency requires general compliance with the rule of law.

We will see that David Dyzenhaus has argued that Fuller's insight about the rule of law is best expressed as a requirement of public justification, which requires that public decision-makers offer reasons for their decisions that reflect core common law principles, such as fairness and reasonableness. The challenge, then, is showing how decisions made in response to complex and constantly evolving environmental issues can meet this requirement of public justification.

Importantly, this understanding of law also implies a second reciprocal relationship, one between democracy and law. From this perspective, the rule of law is a vital part of ongoing public deliberation about core constitutional commitments. When public deliberations are transformed into law, their form *as law* enables further and more specific participation through the contestation of the content of those deliberations. Through contestation, legal subjects are able to ensure that decisions are publicly justified. This practice of public justification and contestation means that the rule of law itself is central to public deliberation.[3] Every exercise of legal authority has the potential to prompt further deliberation about what our core constitutional values are and how we should achieve them. Dyzenhaus calls this the 'rule-of-law project',[4] a phrase that nicely captures the idea that a democratic society governed by the rule of law is always a work in progress that requires the ongoing commitment of its participants—both public officials and the public alike.

Understanding the rule of law as a project also has an important methodological implication. Rather than reasoning from abstract principles, for purposes of theorising we should look for real-life examples of cases or institutions that reflect rule-of-law ideals. Constitutional principles do not stand independently of the practices through which they are realised; through the requirement of public justification they are continually re-articulated and redefined. We should thus look for concrete examples that can help draw out theoretical insights about the rule of law and can be used as a platform for further interpretation and experimentation. Accordingly, this chapter begins by drawing out the requirement of public justification from existing Canadian administrative law. However, the overarching objective of this chapter is simply to introduce the contours of the public-justification conception of the rule of law, how it responds to the environmental emergency and its answer to the question of why law something is worth having in the first place. The three chapters that follow then provide the concrete examples that inform the details of this conception of law.

This chapter proceeds in two sections. The first answers Schmitt's challenge—that is, the challenge to show that emergencies can be governed

[3] See section II below.

[4] D Dyzenhaus, *The Constitution of Law: Legality in a Time of Emergency* (Cambridge, Cambridge University Press, 2006) 17.

by law. It builds on the work of David Dyzenhaus, who has argued that an alternative to the formal conception of the rule of law has emerged, albeit imperfectly, from the Supreme Court of Canada's messy administrative law jurisprudence. This alternative is a common law constitutional conception that can be traced to AV Dicey's understanding of the rule of law and how it operates in times of crisis. Dicey's common law constitutionalism and its repeated resurfacing in Canadian judicial review provide the kernel of a response to the environmental emergency. They reveal a public-justification conception of the rule of law, a conception in which public officials are required to publicly justify their decisions on the basis of core common law principles.

The second section of the chapter sketches the theoretical contours of the requirement of public justification and how it answers the question of why law is something worth having in the first place. It argues that the requirement of public justification is constitutive of a particular kind of relationship between lawmaker and legal subject. This relationship respects the agency of the legal subject, understood as her rational and self-determining capacity. The requirement of public justification protects the subject from arbitrary public decisions and, in doing so, makes her agency—her participation—internal to the rule of law itself. Moreover, this section argues that this conception of the rule of law is inherently democratic. It is of a piece with deliberative democracy, whereby law is both a product of democratic deliberation and a process for engaging in further deliberation. The public-justification conception thus has the potential (which will be explored further in subsequent chapters) to ensure that environmental decisions taken in the depths of complex regulatory regimes can have both democratic and legal authority.

I. RESPONDING TO SCHMITT'S CHALLENGE

Chapter one introduced the formal conception of the rule of law as a basic Diceyan conception, which, as we saw, made no provision for exceptional emergency powers or the administrative state. Dicey sets out two constitutional principles: parliamentary supremacy and the supremacy of the rule of law.[5] While Dicey saw these two supremacies working in concert, he was clear that if there is a conflict between the two, Parliament will win.[6] From these basic premises, it is only a small step to conclude that, on his view, the

[5] AV Dicey, *An Introduction to the Study of the Law of the Constitution*, 10th edn (Toronto, MacMillan, 1959) 407.

[6] Ibid, 39–40; and TRS Allan, *Constitutional Justice: A Liberal Theory of the Rule of Law* (Oxford, Clarendon Press, 2001) 13.

legislature is the only legitimate source of legal norms.[7] We can think of this as the 'orthodox Diceyan' account of the rule of law,[8] which is the basis of the formal conception that has persisted in Canadian administrative law. This is the position, as we have seen, that leads to the creation of legal black and grey holes in Canadian environmental law.

Following on the methodology set out in the introduction of the chapter, this section begins with an analysis of Canadian administrative law doctrine to show that an alternative account of the rule of law has emerged in Supreme Court jurisprudence. I argue that the Court has departed from a formal conception of the rule of law and has articulated, albeit inconsistently and imperfectly, a requirement that public officials publicly justify their decisions on the basis of core common law principles. We will then see that this alternative conception responds to Schmitt's challenge because it can be sustained during emergencies, including the environmental emergency.

A. Public Justification in Canadian Administrative Law

Notwithstanding the pervasive legal black and grey holes in Canadian environmental law, the Supreme Court of Canada has made significant strides away from a formal conception of the rule of law. The break from the formal conception is usually marked by the watershed Supreme Court decisions in *CUPE*[9] and *Nicholson*[10] in 1979, and it continues to this day as the judiciary seeks to reconceive its own role in relation to a legitimate administrative state. Together, *CUPE* and *Nicholson* signal the Court's recognition that administrative decision-makers 'can make rational decisions about the law' and therefore 'judges must not assume that the courts should have the last word about what the law is.'[11] But the cases also tell judges that they should intervene when administrative decision-makers 'fail to live up to the standards which in principle make their decisions rational.'[12] *Nicholson* extends the requirements of procedural fairness beyond judicial or quasi-judicial administrative decisions. However, this extension requires judges to acknowledge that rational procedures are not only those that look

[7] Dyzenhaus, *The Constitution of Law* (above n 4) 71.

[8] MD Walters, 'Dicey on Writing the Law of the Constitution' (2012) 32 *Oxford Journal of Legal Studies* 21, 22; and Allan, *Constitutional Justice* (above n 6) 13. Compare the orthodox interpretation with the substantive interpretation of Dicey offered by Walters, Allan and that of Dyzenhaus that follows later in this section.

[9] *CUPE v NB Liquor Corporation*, [1979] 2 SCR 227, 97 DLR (3d) 417 (SCC).

[10] *Nicholson v Haldimand-Norfolk Regional Police Commissioners*, [1979] 1 SCR 311, 88 DLR (3d) 671 (SCC).

[11] Dyzenhaus, *The Constitution of Law* (above n 4) 127.

[12] Ibid.

like judicial procedures but rather procedures that are appropriate to their administrative context.[13]

The theory behind the two earlier decisions merged in the Supreme Court's 1999 decision in *Baker*,[14] in which the majority endorsed an understanding of deference as respect. In *Baker*, the issue concerned a Minister's refusal to exempt from deportation Mavis Baker, who had illegally overstayed in Canada. The legislation and regulations delegated seemingly unfettered discretion to the Minister to grant an exemption 'if satisfied' that relief should be granted on humanitarian and compassionate grounds. For the Court, however, this language did not mean that the Minister operated in a legal grey hole. Rather, the Court found that the Minister's 'discretion must be exercised with the boundaries imposed in the statute, the principles of the rule of law, the principles of administrative law, the fundamental values of Canadian society, and the principles of the *Charter*'.[15]

To determine whether discretion was exercised in accordance with these fundamental principles, the Court had to impose a requirement to give reasons.[16] Under this concept of the rule of law, decision-makers are owed deference not simply because of their institutional expertise or because they have complied with the formal requirements of their enabling statute. Rather, they are owed deference when their decisions are demonstrably justified. This is Dyzenhaus' notion of deference as respect, ie, the idea that deference 'requires not submission but a respectful attention to the reasons offered or which could be offered in support of a decision'.[17] On this view, administrative discretion is not an illegitimate space uncontrolled by law but rather legitimate and worthy of judicial respect when exercised in a manner that reflects the fundamental legal principles such as those set out in *Baker*.

The Court's reasons in *Baker* reflect a requirement of public justification. Core common law principles form the constitutional backdrop of administrative decision-making, and decision-makers are obligated to show that their decisions reflect these principles. Reason-giving is essential to this conception of the rule of law because it is by offering public reasons that decision-makers discharge their duty of justification.[18] Reasons ensure that

[13] Ibid.

[14] *Baker v Canada (Minister of Citizenship and Immigration)*, [1999] 2 SCR 817, 1 Imm LR (3d) 1 (pinpoints to SCR) (SCC).

[15] Ibid, para 56.

[16] Ibid, para 43. A much earlier precursor to *Baker* was Justice Rand's much discussed reasoning in *Roncarelli v Duplessis*, [1959] SCR 121 (SCC), which also espouses a version of common law constitutionalism.

[17] *Baker* (above n 14) para 60, quoting D Dyzenhaus, 'The Politics of Deference: Judicial Review and Democracy' in M Taggart (ed), *The Province of Administrative Law* (Oxford, Hart Publishing, 1997) 286.

[18] Dyzenhaus, *The Constitution of Law* (above n 4) 139.

an individual knows that she or he has not been treated arbitrarily by the state, but they also ensure that the institutions of government can hold one another to account when they fall short in their commitment to the rule of law. Judicial review is one way to ensure that administrative decision-makers meet their requirement of public justification. But judicial review also requires that judges defer—that is, not substitute their own views—when a decision is justified on the basis of core constitutional principles.[19]

Deference as respect and the coexisting duty to give reasons are a sharp contrast to the formal conception of the rule of law, which, as we saw in chapters two and three, requires the courts to defend their monopoly over statutory interpretation and abstain from interfering with the exercise of administrative discretion. Deferring to a Minister's interpretation of a statute, even if it is a reasoned interpretation, would be tantamount to judicial abdication for a formalist judge. Similarly, it would be challenging for a formalist judge to assume a supervisory role over the exercise of Ministerial discretion, as in *Baker*. The understanding of the rule of law as public justification, espoused in *Baker*, blurs these lines. It requires the assumption that all public institutions are engaged in a collective rule-of-law project of ensuring that public decisions are made on the basis of core common law values.

The Supreme Court of Canada's commitment to the requirement of public justification has been imperfect.[20] As we have seen in the environmental context, the formal conception still persists. Even in the immigration context, the Court has retreated from the majority's decision in *Baker*. In both *Suresh*,[21] a post-9/11 national security decision, and later *Khosa*,[22] the Supreme Court stated that the Court's role was only to ensure that the Minister considered the correct factors and that 'the courts should not reweigh them.'[23] In other words, the Court retreated to a formal understanding of its role. So long as the Minister ticked the appropriate boxes and formally met the explicit statutory criteria, the Court would refuse to evaluate the Minister's exercise of discretion.[24] The Minister had free rein

[19] Ibid, 147.

[20] MD Walters, 'Respecting Deference as Respect: Rights, Reasonableness and Proportionality in Canadian Administrative Law' in H Wilberg and M Elliott (eds), *The Scope and Intensity of Substantive Review: Traversing Taggart's Rainbow* (Oxford, Hart Publishing, 2015) 417 (arguing that, despite the Court's endorsement of deference as respect, it does not practice its underlying theory); E Fox-Decent, *Sovereignty's Promise: The State as Fiduciary* (Oxford, Oxford University Press, 2011) 29 (offering the explanation for this half-hearted commitment that common law constitutionalism lacks a legal basis for the 'free floating' principle of fairness).

[21] *Suresh v Canada (Minister of Citizenship and Immigration)*, 2002 SCC 1, [2002] 1 SCR 3.

[22] *Canada (Minister of Citizenship & Immigration) v Khosa*, 2009 SCC 12, [2009] SCR 339.

[23] *Suresh* (above n 21) para 41; and *Canada v Khosa* (ibid) para 61.

[24] Fox-Decent, *Sovereignty's Promise* (above n 20) 228–29 internal endnotes.

over how to account for these factors. Moreover, there was no suggestion in either decision that the non-statutory, common law constitutional principles identified by the majority in *Baker* ought to play any role in guiding the exercise of discretion.[25]

The Court's important 2008 decision in *Dunsmuir*,[26] an attempt to set straight the principles of administrative law, itself reflected conflicting conceptions of the rule of law.[27] The majority reasserted its monopoly over some formal categories of decisions—constitutional questions[28] and true questions of *vires*,[29] for example. But it still urged courts to take a contextual approach to determining the appropriate standard of review[30] and reiterated that in cases where deference was owed, a court's role was to ensure 'the existence of justification, transparency and intelligibility within the decision-making process'.[31] The majority recommitted itself to the notion of deference as respect.[32] Since *Dunsmuir* and the subsequent decision in *Khosa*, the Supreme Court's formalistic inclinations have again, in some respects, waned.[33] The Court has deferred to administrative decision-makers on issues that fell squarely within traditional judicial strongholds, including constitutional questions,[34] the application of the common law doctrine of estoppel[35] and the breach of a statutory deadline, which would have conventionally been labelled a true question of *vires*.[36] Indeed, the Court has suggested that the concept of a true question of *vires*, the very basis on which a formalist judge justifies judicial review, may be a fiction after all[37]—signalling a rejection of the formal conception of the rule of law.

Moreover, the Court has since restated its position in *Baker* that there is no such thing as unfettered discretion.[38] It is noteworthy that this clear

[25] Ibid.

[26] *Dunsmuir v New Brunswick (Board of Management)*, 2008 SCC 9, [2008] 1 SCR 190.

[27] M Lewans, 'Deference and Reasonableness Since Dunsmuir' (2012) 38 *Queen's Law Journal* 59, 74.

[28] *Dunsmuir* (above n 26) para 58.

[29] Ibid, para 59.

[30] Ibid, para 64.

[31] Ibid, para 47.

[32] Ibid, para 48.

[33] J Stacey and A Woolley, 'Can Pragmatism Function in Administrative Law?' (2016) 74 *Supreme Court Law Review* (2d) 211 (on how Justice Rothstein's administrative law jurisprudence tracks, in unexpected ways, Dyzenhaus' notion of deference as respect).

[34] *Doré v Barreau du Québec*, 2012 SCC 12, [2012] 1 SCR 395. See more recently *Loyola High School v Quebec (Attorney General)*, 2015 SCC 12.

[35] *Nor-Man Regional Health Authority v Manitoba Association of Health Care Professionals*, 2011 SCC 59, [2011] 3 SCR 616.

[36] *Alberta (Information and Privacy Commissioner) v Alberta Teachers' Association*, 2011 SCC 61, [2011] 3 SCR 654 (pinpoints to SCC). See also *Halifax (Regional Municipality) v Nova Scotia (Human Rights Commission)*, 2012 SCC 10, [2012] 1 SCR 364 (where the SCC again distanced itself from the concept of a jurisdictional question)

[37] *Alberta v Teachers' Association* (ibid) para 34.

[38] *Catalyst Paper Corp v North Cowichan (District)*, 2012 SCC 2, [2012] 1 SCR 5.

statement occurred with respect to a municipal bylaw—delegated legislation issued by a democratically elected decision-maker. A unanimous Supreme Court found that this decision was subject to the supervision of the courts because '[t]he fact that wide deference is owed to municipal councils does not mean they have *carte blanche*.'[39] Indeed, the Court observed that the 'attempt to maintain a clear line between policy and legality has not prevailed'.[40] The Court reasserted its supervisory role to ensure that in enacting delegated legislation, a municipality adheres to both procedural and substantive requirements of legality.[41] The Court held that while a municipal council is not required to give reasons when exercising its legislative function, its reasons could be found in 'the debate, deliberations and the statements of policy that give rise to the bylaw'.[42]

It is therefore possible to trace a line through the Supreme Court of Canada's administrative law jurisprudence that leads to a rule-of-law requirement of public justification, albeit one that is sometimes imperfectly expressed. This line of jurisprudence has emerged in the wake of the Court's rejection of the formal conception, and it traverses various administrative contexts. Indeed, this recognition of the requirement of public justification includes discretionary, policy-laden executive action, such as municipal bylaws, that fall well outside the traditional judicial monopoly. Promisingly, these are the very features of environmental decisions that often cause judges to retreat to the formal conception of the rule of law. The upshot of this line of judicial authority is that the very fact that the legislature governs *by* law—eg, delegating authority to a municipality—gives rise to the rule *of* law, understood as the requirement of public justification.

B. Public Justification During Emergencies

Interestingly, Dyzenhaus has argued that this concept of public justification can be traced to Dicey's account of emergency powers. Dyzenhaus argues that Dicey's unwillingness to address discretionary executive powers prevented Dicey from seeing that his very own account contains the kernels of a rule-of-law response to the administrative state.

[39] Ibid, para 24.

[40] Ibid, para 14.

[41] Ibid, para. 16. Remarkably, the Court seems to impose a requirement of procedural fairness without addressing the category of 'legislative functions.'

[42] Ibid, para 29. See also DJ Mullan, 'Judicial Review of Executive Decision-making: Evolving Concepts of Responsibility' (1993) 19 *Queen's Law Journal* 137 (suggesting that the assumption of courts, that the executive was worthy of respect and tribunals were viewed with suspicion, might be backwards).

Dicey addressed the use of Habeas Corpus Suspension Acts in times of crisis, statutes which deny those charged with a crime the right to compel a trial or their release.[43] At first glance, a Suspension Act might appear to be a classic example of a legal black hole because it suspends constitutional rights during emergencies. But Dicey argued that it does not suspend rights; rather, it defers access to certain remedies so long as the Act is in force.[44] Dicey based this argument on the fact that an Act of Indemnity will almost always follow a Suspension Act, which demonstrates that but for the Act of Indemnity, officials would be found guilty of unlawful acts taken while the Suspension Act was in place.[45]

What is key to Dicey's account is that the two Acts do not come together and therefore do not legalise executive action in advance. An Act of Indemnity is still a legislative act and is therefore, according to Dicey, 'very different from the proclamation of martial law'.[46] The fact that it is a legislative act means that actions taken purportedly under the Act of Indemnity will be subject to review by the courts.[47] Although the effect of the Act is to immunise public officials for their emergency response actions, whether any specific action is in fact covered by the legislation can always be challenged in the courts. Even a wide delegation of power by Parliament, such as an Act of Indemnity, is subject to interpretation by judges who are influenced, Dicey stated, 'by the general spirit of the common law'.[48] Judges will, in other words, interpret the Act of Indemnity against the backdrop of core common law principles to ensure that the indemnified acts were taken in good faith and were not recklessly cruel.[49] Put differently, the discussion of the Suspension Act and Act of Indemnity is not simply about the timing of the two. Rather, as Dyzenhaus has stated, it 'opens up the conceptual space for prospective legislative responses to states of emergency which give officials authority to act … but which require that … they justify to an independent tribunal their decisions as both necessary and made in good faith'.[50]

For Dyzenhaus, then, Dicey's constitutionalism demonstrates that rule *by* law implies rule *of* law because the implementation of legislation is put

[43] Dicey, *An Introduction* (above n 5) 229.
[44] Ibid, 230.
[45] Ibid, 232.
[46] Ibid, 237.
[47] Ibid, 413. Recall that a black hole says in advance that whatever the executive does is legal: Dyzenhaus, *The Constitution of Law* (above n 4) 202.
[48] Dicey, *An Introduction* (above n 5) 413.
[49] Dyzenhaus, *The Constitution of Law* (above n 4) 203. Of course, this depends on the specific language of the statute. Were a statute to specify that it covered even recklessly cruel acts and acts otherwise taken in bad faith, then we would have a legal black hole.
[50] Ibid, 204.

under the supervision of the courts, whose job it is to maintain the rule of law. Even during an emergency, public officials are subject to a requirement of public justification. That is, they must justify the actions taken under the Suspension Act before the 'ordinary court', which is guided by the 'general spirit of the common law' in order to benefit from the protection of the Act of Indemnity.[51] Dyzenhaus has argued that Dicey's account contains three essential features: review before an independent body (for Dicey, this would have been the court), that the body has access to the information upon which the executive based its justification, and that the state bears the burden of showing that the decision was justified.[52]

Dyzenhaus argues that Dicey's account opens up the possibility of creative institutional design. Creative design is necessary because, as Dyzenhaus has charted, judges have a disappointing history of losing their 'rule-of-law nerve' in times of crisis, meaning that they seem unable to uphold this requirement of public justification.[53] Moreover, the executive often has legitimate claims to national security privilege, and national security issues raise complex and politically sensitive issues that courts do not necessarily have the expertise to assess.[54]

From the perspective of the public-justification conception of the rule of law, the separation of powers, like any institutional design, is useful only to the extent that it enables the realisation of foundational constitutional principles.[55] This, Dyzenhaus has argued, allows the requirement of public justification to be fulfilled even in times of crisis when robust judicial scrutiny is not possible.[56] For example, Dyzenhaus has pointed to a special immigration appeals tribunal in the United Kingdom in charge of reviewing deportation decisions that but for sensitive information pertaining to national security would be reviewed by the courts.[57] The tribunal has expertise in national security, immigration and law, and has special powers to allow government claims of secrecy to be tested in closed proceedings.[58]

[51] Dicey summarises this argument in Dicey, *An Introduction* (above n 5) 412–14. See also Walters, 'Dicey on Writing' (above n 8) 35: 'Dicey's three propositions on the rule of law are, as strict rules, descriptively false and normatively problematic, but as general principles they may be, even today, both factually true and morally compelling.'

[52] Dyzenhaus, *The Constitution of Law* (above n 4) 204–5.

[53] Eg, *Suresh* (above n 21) and *Canada v Khosa* (above n 22). Dyzenhaus, *The Constitution of Law* (above n 4) discusses prominent UK wartime decisions. See also J Jowell, 'The Democratic Necessity of Administrative Justice' (2006) *Acta Juridica* 13, 21: 'Above all, courts should be willing to challenge bare assertions.'

[54] Dyzenhaus, *The Constitution of Law* (above n 4) 219.

[55] D Dyzenhaus, 'Constituting the Rule of Law: Fundamental Values in Administrative Law' (2002) 27 *Queen's Law Journal* 445, 451.

[56] Dyzenhaus, *The Constitution of Law* (above n 4) 174–90.

[57] Special Immigration Appeals Commission Act 1997, 1997 c 68 (UK).

[58] Dyzenhaus, *The Constitution of Law* (above n 4) 163.

The procedures are far from perfect,[59] but on their face, they reflect a commitment to public justification. The tribunal ensures that the executive's deportation decisions are justified, and in turn the court ensures that the tribunal's decisions are justified.[60] The court must also justify its decision on the basis of fundamental common law principles.[61] Thus, judicial review need not be conceived of as an all-or-nothing endeavour whereby judges are torn between blindly deferring to the executive or second-guessing and intruding on national security decisions. Rather, it can be understood as a more nuanced role whereby the courts ensure that other institutions of government are maintaining their commitment to the rule of law,[62] understood as a requirement to publicly justify decisions on the basis of core constitutional principles.

Dyzenhaus' articulation of common law constitutionalism offers a full response to Schmitt's challenge, which was set out in chapter one. Dyzenhaus does not admit the exception. Discretionary emergency powers are subject to the requirement of public justification. Even the decision to abandon ordinary constitutional requirements to respond to an emergency is subject to the requirement of public justification. On this view, the rule of law is constitutive of law itself. If the decision cannot be publicly justified, it does not have a claim to be 'law'. Dyzenhaus has conceded that there is no way to prevent a determined parliament from creating a legal black hole through unequivocal, express language. But the answer to Schmitt's challenge in such a case is that the failure to abide by the rule of law calls into question the claim to legal authority: ie, the legal black hole may be formally valid, but it will have a dubious claim to authority.[63] The court's role in this instance is that of meteorologist, 'alerting the commonwealth to the storm clouds on the horizon when the rule of law which secures the fabric of civil society is put under strain'.[64]

The public-justification conception has significant implications for environmental law. It requires first that all public environmental decisions are reasoned; second, that the reasons are directed to those affected by the

[59] *Secretary of State for the Home Department v MB* [2007] QB 415. Sullivan J, overturned by the Court of Appeal, described the special advocates procedure as creating a 'thin veneer of legality'. Numerous lawyers acting as special advocates and representing the claimant's interests in the closed proceedings have quit because of the inadequacy of the process: C Dyer, 'Terror QC: More Will Quit Special Court', *Guardian* (20 December 2004), www.theguardian.com/politics/2004/dec/20/terrorism.humanrights.

[60] Dyzenhaus, *The Constitution of Law* (above n 4) 178. Though Dyzenhaus has made clear that his is an aspirational account, since the role of judicial review that he describes is one that judges tend to struggle with.

[61] Dyzenhaus, 'Constituting the Rule of Law' (above n 55) 501–2.

[62] See also L Sossin, 'The Unfinished Project of *Roncarelli v Duplessis*: Justiciability, Discretion, and the Limits of the Rule of Law' (2010) 55 *McGill Law Journal* 661, 687.

[63] Dyzenhaus, *The Constitution of Law* (above n 4) 204.

[64] Ibid, 12.

decision; and third, that the reasons reflect core constitutional principles. The chapters that follow pick up on these threads. They elaborate how the commitment to public justification can be realised through creative institutional design tailored to the features of the environmental emergency, how core common law principles must be interpreted in light of relevant environmental principles, and the necessary orientation of public reasons that interpret and administer a statutory scheme that balances competing environmental considerations.

For present purposes, it is sufficient to note the that these facets of public justification in environmental law are all connected to the essential components of the response to Schmitt's challenge introduced in this section above. As we have seen, the requirement of public justification has been recognised in Canada's administrative law jurisprudence as arising from the ordinary application of the common law. Its common law origin means that the requirement of public justification cannot be suspended through the declaration of a state of emergency or modified through an 'emergency constitution'. *Public justification is constitutive of law itself* and thus operates at all times and in all contexts. Should a legislature decide to unequivocally remove or abridge the requirement of public justification through legislation, it chooses to do so without the benefit of claiming that it acts with legal authority.

II. PUBLIC JUSTIFICATION: A DEMOCRATIC CONCEPTION OF THE RULE OF LAW

As is clear from the preceding analysis, the public-justification conception of the rule of law is fundamentally concerned with the maintenance of certain core legal principles. This is in stark contrast to the formal conception of the rule of law, which in its strongest, Schmittian form, seems to assume that it is possible and desirable for a legal system to be comprised solely of determinate legal rules. As we will see over the following chapters, the core common law principles served by the requirement of public justification are, in contrast, sufficiently context-sensitive to be maintained under the conditions of the environmental emergency, while still guiding and constraining public decision-making in concrete and meaningful ways. The objective of this section of the chapter is to sketch out the normative backdrop of the requirement of public justification and to establish that it constitutes a special relationship between lawmaker and legal subject, a relationship that protects and enhances the agency of the subject and makes his participation internal to the rule of law. We will see that the requirement of public justification rests comfortably at the interface of common law constitutionalism and deliberative democracy. Accordingly, it has the potential to respond to the environmental emergency—that is, it can explain how complex environmental decisions can nonetheless possess both democratic and legal authority.

The requirement of public justification is a blend of Diceyan common law constitutionalism—whereby judges interpret legal texts 'in the general spirit of the common law'—and Fuller's idea that legal order ought to be always oriented toward the inner morality of the law.[65] As we will see, the requirement that public officials publicly justify their decisions on the basis of core common law principles captures the quality of this relationship across law-making contexts from legislating to adjudicating and administrative decision-making.

The idea that the rule of law is fundamentally about legal principles appears, at least at the surface, difficult to square with Fuller's well known work detailing the formal indicia of law. In his parable of King Rex, Fuller outlined eight features that are required to successfully make law: public, general, prospective, clear, non-contradictory and stable rules that are capable of being fulfilled and implemented congruently with the declared rule.[66] Apart from the feature of congruent implementation, his list pertains to the making of law in the form of rules.

For Fuller, what is significant, however, is that these features mean that law cannot be a simple command. A lawmaker cannot command whatever she wants. In order to make law, she can only issue commands in the *form* of law. Fuller highlighted the significance of generality, prospectivity and congruent implementation as features that cannot be understood solely in terms of their efficacy. That is, to take one example, in any given case it might be more effective for an official to issue an individualised rather than general command.[67] Fuller argued that these rule-of-law features make sense only if we understand the legal subject as capable of self-directed action.[68] The rule of law thus imposes an obligation on the lawmaker to have regard for the subject's capacity for reason and self-determination. What is important are not the formal indicia of the rule of law for their own sake but rather that they make the legal subject's capacity for agency internal to the law itself. [69] In this sense, legal subjects are also authors of the law, for their agency imposes meaningful constraints on what a lawmaker

[65] Fuller, *The Morality of Law* (above n 1) 146–47.

[66] Ibid, 33–91.

[67] Similarly, it might be more effective in pursuit of a specific end for an official to command that a subject depart from a stated rule.

[68] Fuller, *The Morality of Law* (above n 1) 210. Fuller later (219) quips, 'It would serve little purpose, for example, to attempt a juristic ordering of relations among the inmates of a lunatic asylum.'

[69] Ibid, 162. K Rundle, *Forms Liberate: Reclaiming the Jurisprudence of Lon L Fuller* (Oxford, Hart Publishing, 2012) 10, 134 (clarifying that legal subjects are subjects of law, not subjects to law).

can and cannot do. Participation of the subject (whether active or not) is thus internal to the law.

In addition to the constraint that the form of law imposes on the lawmaker, it also constitutes a particular relationship between lawmaker and subject. That relationship, as we have seen, recognises and respects the agency of the subject. But it is also constitutive of law's authority. When a lawmaker successfully makes law—that is, by taking seriously the subject's agency—this gives rise to an obligation on the part of the subject to obey.[70] Though Fuller referred to this as a 'reciprocal' obligation on the subject, he was clear that this obligation of obedience is owed not to the lawmaker but to the subject's fellow citizens.[71]

Kristen Rundle has emphasised that Fuller's conception of the rule of law recognises legal subjects as 'responsible agents' who have the capacity to reason with the law.[72] For Fuller, law properly so called has a form that its subjects can understand and conceivably obey or contest. This agency is exemplified when the legal subject challenges the implementation and enforcement of a rule before a court. The challenge requires the subject to make a reasoned claim about the proper interpretation and application of the stated rule. The legal subject's agency is respected when the court responds to this claim through reasons that reflect not 'their fancy or … crabbed literalness' but rather the 'principles of interpretation that are appropriate to their position in the whole legal order'.[73] Here Fuller pointed to the common law as the source of interpretive principles, or what Dicey would call 'the spirit of the common law'.[74] For Dicey, as with Fuller, common law principles are what orient legal interpretation, not an artificial quest for legislative intent.[75] As we will see in later chapters, two of these deeply seated common law principles are fairness and reasonableness—principles that, when realised, are how the legal subject knows she has not be treated arbitrarily by the state.

While Dicey denied any interpretive role for administrative decision-makers, Fuller seemed more open to institutional innovation for ensuring congruence between official action and declared rule.[76] What seems key is that the special relationship between subject and lawmaker is maintained, not the particular institutional configuration that makes it happen. Indeed, Fuller viewed the feature of congruence as revealing 'as no other problem

[70] Fuller, *The Morality of Law* (above n 1) 209, 219–20. See above n 2 on the complexity of this issue.

[71] Ibid, 207–8.

[72] Rundle, *Forms Liberate* (above n 69) 10.

[73] Fuller, *The Morality of Law* (above n 1) 82.

[74] Dicey, *An Introduction* (above n 5) 413–14.

[75] Fuller, *The Morality of Law* (above n 1) 83–34; and Dicey, *An Introduction* (above n 5) 413–14.

[76] Fuller, *The Morality of Law* (above n 1) 81–82.

can, the cooperative nature of the task of maintaining legality'.[77] Building on this insight, Dyzenhaus has extended Fuller's two-way relationship outward from legislative rules to the more complex inner workings of the administrative state. This extension is expressed, as we have seen, as the requirement of public justification. Publicly justifying administrative decisions is how these decisions maintain the participatory element inherent in Fuller's desiderata. Reasons are how the legal subject knows she has not been treated arbitrarily. They reveal whether the decision-maker took the subject's interests seriously in reaching the decision and enable the subject's further participation by creating the possibility of meaningful review.[78] The rule of law, understood as public justification, thus carries with it an obligation on all public officials to make decisions in a form that respects the subject's rational capacity to engage with the law.

The requirement of public justification is of a piece with the core attributes of a deliberative democracy. According to Amy Gutmann, a deliberative democracy is 'a distinctive kind of democracy, a system of popular rule that encourages citizens to deliberate over political decisions'.[79] In its ideal form, a deliberative democracy results in 'reasoned agreement among free and equal citizens'.[80] Public decisions reached in this manner are argued to be the most 'justifiable form of political power because [persuasion] is the most consistent with respecting the autonomy of persons, their capacity for self-government'.[81] The idea of responsible agency underpins deliberative-democratic theory: 'To deliberate with another is to understand the other as a self-authoring source of reasons and claims.'[82] Respecting individuals as responsible agents requires a system of governance that protects and facilitates this agency—that is, a system in which public institutions and decisions are justified by reasons that individuals cannot reasonably reject.[83]

[77] Ibid, 91.

[78] D Dyzenhaus, 'Accountability and the Concept of (Global) Administrative Law' (2009) 2009 *Acta Juridica* 3, 14.

[79] A Gutmann, 'Democracy' in R Goodin, P Pettit and T Pogge (eds), *A Companion to Contemporary Political Philosophy* (Oxford, Blackwell Publishing, 2007) 528.

[80] J Cohen, 'Deliberation and Democratic Legitimacy' in J Bonham and W Rehg (eds), *Deliberative Democracy: Essays on Reason and Politics* (Cambridge, MA, MIT Press, 1997) 73; and J Habermas, *Between Facts and Norms*, W Rehg (trans) (Cambridge, MA, MIT Press, 1996) 226–27.

[81] Gutmann, 'Democracy' (above n 79) 527. Whether deliberative democracy has an epistemic justification as well is the subject of much debate in the literature. See D Estlund, *Democratic Authority: A Philosophical Framework* (Princeton, Princeton University Press, 2008); H Landemore, *Democratic Reason: Politics, Collective Intelligence, and the Rule of the Many* (Princeton, Princeton University Press, 2013) chs 4 and 5.

[82] J Parkinson and J Mansbridge, *Deliberative Systems: Deliberative Democracy at the Large Scale* (Cambridge, Cambridge University Press, 2012) 11.

[83] Ibid, 25; A Gutmann and D Thompson, *Why Deliberative Democracy?* (Princeton, Princeton University Press, 2004) 3; and R Forst, *The Right to Justification: Elements of a Constructivist Theory of Justice*, J Flynn (trans) (New York, Columbia University Press,

True deliberation is characterised by a number of features. First, it is distinguishable from pluralism or bargaining because participants in a deliberative democracy must articulate public-regarding reasons, ie, reasons that are oriented toward the common good and take into account the perspectives of others.[84] Sharing information and asserting opinions do not count as the dialogic and reciprocal exchange of reasons required in a deliberative democracy. Second, deliberation requires that, at least in principle, participants' views are not fixed. They are open to being persuaded by the superior reasoning of another's proposal.[85] Third, deliberation is characterised by conditions of equality. Deliberation is inclusive, public and free of both internal and external coercion.[86] Deliberative conditions are intended to allow for the 'unforced force of the better argument'.[87] Deliberative democrats argue that real-life deliberation ought to mirror, to the extent possible, these ideal conditions of deliberation.[88]

Beyond the giving of reasons, which is common to the requirement of public justification and the tenets of an ideal deliberative democracy, deliberation seems to track the core common law principles of fairness and reasonableness. Inclusive, public and uncoerced deliberation recalls the common law principle of fairness. The exchange of reasons—and not mere assertions or individual preferences—implies justification, the idea that there is a rational basis for supporting a particular proposal. This recalls the common law principle of reasonableness. Moreover, deliberative democrats, much like Fuller and Dicey, emphasise that the scope and application of these principles are to be determined contextually—that is, through actual deliberation amongst those affected by the decision.[89]

In theories of deliberative democracy, true deliberation of the variety just described is essential to establishing the democratic legitimacy of collective decisions. As Habermas has stated, 'Policies that are adopted in a manner that does not conform to the conditions for the democratic genesis of

2011) 6 (setting out criteria of generality and reciprocity). Contemporary deliberative democratic theory owes its start to Habermas, *Between Facts and Norms* (above n 80), who argued that procedures of ideal deliberation give rise to the collective judgement of the people.

[84] J Habermas, 'Habermas on Law and Democracy: Reply to Symposium Participants' (1996) 17 *Cardozo Law Review* 1477, 1484; and Cohen, 'Deliberation and Democratic Legitimacy' (above n 80) 69.

[85] Cohen, 'Deliberation and Democratic Legitimacy' (above n 80) 69 and 77; and J Elster, 'The Market and the Forum: Three Varieties of Political Theory' in Bonham and Rehg (eds), *Deliberative Democracy* (above n 80) 11.

[86] Cohen, 'Deliberation and Democratic Legitimacy' (above n 80) 74.

[87] Habermas, *Between Facts and Norms* (above n 80) 306.

[88] Cohen, 'Deliberation and Democratic Legitimacy' (above n 80) 70.

[89] Gutmann and Thompson, *Why Deliberative Democracy?* (above n 83) 100. See also Fuller, *The Morality of Law* (above n 1) 91; and TRS Allan, *The Sovereignty of Law* (Oxford, Oxford University Press, 2013) 317 (on the interpretive nature of law that is entirely dependent on real-life context).

law are merely cloaked in juridical form.'[90] Deliberation is a precondition to legitimate law-making. Similarly, Dyzenhaus has noted that a public-justification conception of the rule of law requires a 'culture of justification—a culture in which every exercise of power is expected to be justified'.[91] He has suggested that democratic deliberation is a necessary precondition to both legitimacy *and* legality.

But it is possible to take this one step further, to understand deliberative democracy and the rule of law as mutually constitutive rather than sequential.[92] Legal decisions are both the product of democratic deliberation and a site of further deliberation.[93] Law is the legitimate form of political action,[94] but the process of converting public deliberations into law also creates a 'surplus value' through its compliance with the rule of law.[95] This is because the form of law enables further participation on the part of its subjects through practices of obedience and contestation. Contestation, in particular, requires legal subjects to frame their claims in terms of reasons and moreover demands a reasoned response from decision-makers. Not only does the public-justification conception require a culture of justification, but it also cultivates and enhances that culture by making democratic deliberation internal to the rule of law itself. On this view, the rule of law enables further public deliberation about our most basic democratic and legal commitments and how best to achieve them.[96]

This means that legislators are not only political actors within a deliberative democracy who generate reasons that they hope their constituents will accept. They are also legal actors who perform a legal role by putting in motion a process of law-making whereby legal subjects are able to receive

[90] Habermas, *Between Facts and Norms* (above n 80) 429.

[91] Dyzenhaus, *The Constitution of Law* (above n 4). Dyzenhaus has attributed this notion of a culture of justification to Etienne Murienik: D Dyzenhaus, 'Law as Justification: Etienne Mureinik's Conception of Legal Culture' (1998) 14 *South African Journal on Human Rights* 11.

[92] R Levy, 'The Law of Deliberative Democracy: Seeding the Field' (2013) 12(4) *Election Law Journal* 355, 357 (distinguishing between what he calls the deliberation-law and law-deliberation relations).

[93] H Kong, 'Election Law and Deliberative Democracy: Against Deflation' (2015) 9 *Journal of Parliamentary and Political Law* 35, 41 (noting that this is an extension of deliberative democratic theory which construes law solely as a product of deliberation); and D Dyzenhaus, 'The Legitimacy of Legality' (1996) 46 *University of Toronto Law Journal* 129, 177.

[94] Recall ch 1 above and the discussion of the 'compulsion of legality' at note 71 and accompanying text. See also Habermas, *Between Facts and Norms* (above n 80) 297–98 (on the legitimating conditions for law).

[95] D Dyzenhaus, 'Preventive Justice and the Rule-of-Law Project' in A Ashworth, L Zedner and P Tomlin (eds), *Prevention and the Limits of the Criminal Law* (Oxford, Oxford University Press, 2013) 96.

[96] In this way, the public-justification conception of the rule of law bridges liberal and civic republican strands of deliberative democracy: RB Talisse, 'Deliberation' in D Estlund (ed), *The Oxford Handbook of Political Philosophy* (Oxford, Oxford University Press, 2012) 212–13.

the public justification to which they are entitled. The legal obligation of legislators, in other words, is to debate in a way that ensures that when government implements the legislation, it is capable of doing so in a manner that complies with the requirement of public justification.[97] Similarly, administrative decision-makers are not only political actors, technocrats or managers working expeditiously toward a specific policy objective. They are also legal actors and as such are always subject to a legal obligation to ensure those efforts can be publicly justified on the basis of core constitutional principles.

As should now be clear, the requirement of public justification is democratic in a fundamentally different way than the formal conception of the rule of law. The formal conception gains its democratic status through the protection of the legislative monopoly over law-making. It tries to ensure that significant policy decisions are taken by the legislature. And as we saw in Part I of the book, it fails. Significant policy decisions are made every day by administrative decision-makers, collaborative governance bodies and transnational organisations claiming to act in the public interest. Public justification requires, in contrast, reasoned public decision-making that takes seriously the perspectives of those affected. It further requires appropriate institutional channels to contest public decisions when they are not perceived as justified in this way. The legislature, as a participant in the rule-of-law project, remains a source of democratic legitimacy. But the requirement of public justification does not stop here because it imposes further obligations on all public decisions, even those taken in the depths of complex regulatory schemes.[98]

Moreover, it is worth noting that the requirement of public justification also eschews any hard-line distinction between public and private.[99] The exercise of public power—public in the Deweyan sense of addressing a problem with collective consequences[100]—must comply with the requirement of public justification in order to have legal authority. Circling back to the examples in chapter three, it is thus of no significance that in the case of the British Columbia Forest and Range Practices Act (FRPA), public policy is in substance developed by forest companies, so long as the plans comply with the requirement of public justification (which, as we will see, they

[97] D Dyzenhaus, 'Deference, Security and Human Rights' in B Goold and L Lazarus (eds), *Security and Human Rights* (Oxford, Hart Publishing, 2007) 143.

[98] HS Richardson, *Democratic Autonomy: Public Reasoning about the Ends of Policy* (Oxford, Oxford University Press, 2002) 250 (on agency deliberation as a fundamental aspect of collective rule); JL Mashaw, 'Public Reason and Administrative Legitimacy' in J Bell et al (eds), *Public Law Adjudication in Common Law Systems: Process and Substance* (Oxford, Hart Publishing, 2016) 17 (on the underappreciated democratic value of reason-giving in American administrative law).

[99] Allan, *Constitutional Justice* (above n 6) 11.

[100] J Dewey, *The Public and Its Problems* (Chicago, Swallow Press, 1954) 47.

currently do not). Similarly, the Forest Stewardship Council, the non-state transnational certification body introduced in the previous chapter, might be understood to govern through law when it complies with the rule of law requirement of public justification. Indeed, one explanation for the Forest Stewardship Council's perceived legitimacy in the absence of any direct state involvement could be the extent to which it complies with the public-justification conception of the rule of law.

III. CONCLUSION

This chapter has traced the origins of the requirement of public justification through Canadian administrative law. It has situated this conception of the rule of law within the work of Fuller, Dicey and Dyzenhaus. It has argued that the public-justification conception of the rule of law responds to Schmitt's challenge. There is no 'exception' or space outside of law because compliance with the rule of law—understood as publicly justifying decisions on the basis of core constitutional principles—is constitutive of law itself. Creative institutional design enables the maintenance of publicly-justified decisions even under the conditions of an emergency. Finally, this chapter has also directly answered the question of why law is worth having in the first place. Law implies the rule of law, which respects the agency of its subjects. It protects legal subjects from arbitrary public decisions by making their participation internal to law itself through the requirement of publicly justified decisions that sufficiently account for the legal subject's interests. It makes possible the subject's ongoing and active participation in deliberating upon and refining the content of the law.

From this introduction we can begin to appreciate that the public-justification conception is a superior conception of the rule of law rather than a second-best (if necessary) alternative to the formal conception. Public justification keeps the focus on the ultimate end of the rule of law: protecting and facilitating the rational, self-determining capacity of individuals. This encourages us to think about our public institutions as intelligent and purposive attempts to maintain or promote this end and critically evaluate the ways in which they succeed and fall short. Because the public-justification conception takes seriously the ongoing participation of individuals within these public institutions,[101] it presumes complexity in public decision-making and indeed makes this complexity internal to the rule of law. Institutions are not static entities, nor are they purely instrumental means for implementing predetermined ends. We therefore need not cling to the fiction that legal

[101] See Rundle, *Forms Liberate* (above n 69) 42 for a nice summary of Fuller's contribution on this point.

decisions proceed in a linear fashion in which the legislature sets out definitive objectives that are then mechanically implemented by administrative decision-makers. Public justification entails understandings of legal authority and legal constraint that do not falter in complex regulatory contexts.

Because core constitutional principles do not stand independently of the practices through which they are realised, the requirements of the rule of law have determinate content only in relation to the specific context of a particular case. Accordingly, what follows are three distinct, detailed examples that allow us to flesh out the content of the requirement of public justification in the environmental context. The final chapter then returns to a more conceptual analysis of the relationship between the rule of law and the adjudication of constitutional environmental rights.

5

Institutional Design: Reforming Forest Practices

THIS CHAPTER ARGUES that creative institutional design allows the public-justification conception of the rule of law to be maintained even under the conditions of the environmental emergency. As we saw in the previous chapter, the requirement of public justification responds to Carl Schmitt's challenge that emergencies cannot be governed by law. Under the public-justification conception, emergencies are not legal black or grey holes because the common law supplies the requirements of legality. Common law adjudication, however, has long been the domain of the judiciary, a position exemplified by AV Dicey's vision of common law constitutionalism. But as we also saw in the previous chapter, maintaining public justification requires a commitment to institutional innovation and cooperation under emergency conditions. For example, a special immigration appeals tribunal with expert members, modified procedures and the supervision of the courts has the potential to maintain the requirement of public justification even during national security crises.[1]

This chapter develops this theme of institutional innovation in Canadian environmental law. It argues that we must look beyond variations on judicial and quasi-judicial institutions for maintaining the rule of law in the environmental context. While specialist environmental appeals tribunals, analogous to the immigration example offered by David Dyzenhaus, are ubiquitous across Canada,[2] we will see that adjudicative review is often ill suited for overseeing the range of administrative decisions taken in the environmental context. This chapter focuses on a more creative example of institutional design. Its focus is the British Columbia Forest Practices Board, a specialised public 'watchdog' agency with a mandate and suite of powers that is unique in Canadian environment and resources law. I offer this example not as an ideal model, nor to set out a decisive blueprint for

[1] See above ch 4, section I.

[2] See, for example, JV DeMarco and PR Valdoon, *Environmental Boards and Tribunals in Canada: A Practical Guide* (Markham, LexisNexis, 2011); and M Haddock, 'Environmental Tribunals in British Columbia' (Environmental Law Centre, 2011).

reform, but rather because it shows how creative institutional design can give rise to the conditions for public justification across a range of administrative decisions.

The chapter proceeds in three sections. The first introduces the institutional dimensions of public justification. It argues that every exercise of delegated authority has three dimensions of public justification: constitutive, transitive and substantive. Exercises of delegated authority must fulfil all three facets of public justification to comply with the rule of law, and the fulfilment of these facets further implicates several requirements for institutional design. These institutional dimensions of public justification then allow us to critically examine the role of the Forest Practices Board in two contexts. Section II addresses the first context. It returns to the mountain pine beetle epidemic to examine how creative institutional design can allow for public justification in response to an actual environmental disaster. It first highlights the ways in which a traditional adjudicative body such as a court or appeals tribunal would be challenged in its role of ensuring a publicly justified emergency response. It then argues that the unique features of the Forest Practices Board ameliorate these challenges and enabled the Board to meaningfully review the government's emergency response.

Section III examines the Board's response to the dramatic regulatory change from the rule-based Forest Practices Code to the performance-based Forest and Range Practices Act (FRPA), which was first explored in chapter three. It examines, in other words, how institutional design must shift when the discretionary response to the environmental emergency is not an aberration but is endemic to the regulatory regime itself. We will see that the Forest Practices Board has been critical of the implementation of the FRPA and has offered a number of concrete suggestions for institutional reform. This section turns to a governance-focused theory of deliberative democracy to assess whether the Board's response to the FRPA can be understood as discharging its obligation of public justification. It argues that democratic experimentalist ideals help explain how public justification can be maintained even in instances of post-bureaucratic, environmental governance institutional design.

I. THE INSTITUTIONAL DIMENSIONS OF PUBLIC JUSTIFICATION

The requirement of public justification, in the abstract, appears simple. It requires every exercise of public authority to be publicly justified on the basis of core common law principles. It is also fractal, meaning that it applies in this same basic formulation to every scale of public decision, great or small. The realisation of public justification, however, is not simple. It is an aspirational conception of the rule of law that requires an ongoing commitment from all participants—public officials and the public alike.

Its realisation is further complicated by the enormous complexity of the administrative state. The tripartite institutional structure of judiciary, legislature and executive belies a matrix of administrative actors performing a variety of functions from regulation to rights adjudication and government oversight.

Dyzenhaus has argued that this complexity is often obscured by the assumption that administrative law is one body of law, when in fact it is more accurate to describe the field as a composite of three bodies of law.[3] The first he identifies as constitutive law, which is the exercise of public authority that brings the administrative body into being and delegates to it authority. In other words, constitutive law is the originating statute. Second, he delineates substantive law, or the rules and decisions made by the administrative body—eg, the permits issued by an administrative decision-maker or the decisions rendered by an appeals tribunal. The third body of law, Dyzenhaus calls procedural law, or what is most often associated with administrative law—ie, the law that governs the way that administrative bodies make their decisions. I will refer to this as 'transitive' law,[4] which reflects the fact that this is the body of law that brings the substantive law into being and is also the subject of review to ensure compliance with the rule of law.

For an administrative decision to comply with the rule of law, all three of these legal dimensions must fulfil the requirement of public justification. This means that an administrative body must be the result of a public delegation of authority (constitutive law); it must publicly justify its exercise of authority (transitive law); and its justification must disclose a reasonable interpretation of the public interest (substantive law).[5]

These three dimensions of public justification have institutional implications for a range of public bodies. Constitutive law, or the public delegation of authority, clearly implicates the legislature. The legislature is responsible for the delegation of authority but, more importantly, is responsible for setting in motion a commitment to public justification. As we will see over the next several chapters, the specific details of the constitutive law have a tremendous impact on the ability of an administrative decision-maker to fulfil the requirement of public justification. Thus, while we often think of the judiciary as the ultimate guardian of the rule of law, the legislature

[3] D Dyzenhaus, 'Accountability and the Concept of (Global) Administrative Law' (2009) 2009 *Acta Juridica* 3, 4.

[4] In a well known article, Rubin coined the description 'transitive' to refer to legislation that was directly enforceable by the courts: E Rubin, 'Law and Legislation in the Administrative State' (1989) 89 *Columbia Law Review* 369, 381. In contrast to Rubin, I use 'transitive' here to describe the requirements that bring law into being (ie, constitute its legality). My reluctance to adopt Dyzenhaus' label of 'procedural' will become clear in ch 8, which addresses the undesirable effects of the process/substance distinction in environmental rights adjudication.

[5] Dyzenhaus, 'Accountability and the Concept of (Global) Administrative Law' (above n 3) 27–28.

is in the better position to create (and innovate) a framework for public justification. Transitive law, or the actual public justification of the exercise of authority, requires an independent institution to review these exercises of authority to ensure compliance. This institution may be the courts, but it need not be. Finally, and as we will see in this chapter, substantive law implicates further institutional design requirements to enable deliberation and the generation of reasons that prevent the amorphous concept of the public interest from being hollowed out into a blank cheque for public officials.

The British Columbia forestry context illustrates these various dimensions of public justification. This book has already considered a range of forms of public authority exercised with respect to forest practices. For example, the emergency Bark Beetle Regulation (2001), issued in response to the mountain pine beetle epidemic, is an exercise of public authority.[6] Its constitutive law was the Forest Practices Code, which delegated discretionary authority to make regulations.[7] The questions for section II of this chapter are whether the substantive law (ie, the content of the regulations) revealed a defensible interpretation of the public interest and whether there is an appropriate institution that can review the regulations—and the epidemic response more generally—to ensure the response was publicly justified (transitive law). We have also seen that the performance-based FRPA gives significant freedom to forest companies to design and implement tailored forest practices. Yet all three dimensions of public justification must still exist to comply with the rule of law. The FRPA is the constitutive law, which delegates authority to forestry officials to approve Forest Stewardship Plans produced by forest companies. These Forest Stewardship Plans can be understood as the substantive law of the forest practices regime. In principle, the Plans should reveal a set of practices that reflect the public interest (otherwise they ought not to be approved). As we will see in section III, further institutional creativity is needed to ensure that these exercises of authority to approve the Plans comply with the transitive law requirement of public justification.

II. THE FOREST PRACTICES BOARD AND THE MOUNTAIN PINE BEETLE RESPONSE

The mountain pine beetle epidemic in British Columbia precipitated a controversial government response during the 1990s. The primary response strategy was to facilitate widespread logging in order to recoup as much economic revenue from the forests before the timber was destroyed by the beetle. Initially, it was also thought that strategically placed and well-timed

[6] Bark Beetle Regulation, BC Reg 286/2001.

[7] Forest Practices Code of British Columbia Act, RSBC 1996, c 159.

clear-cuts could control the spread of the beetle.[8] This required fast-tracked and highly coordinated decisions that were exempt from ordinary administrative requirements.[9] The public's response to the government's strategy was not overwhelmingly positive. In many corners, it was seen as a cash grab, a reckless move that masked the deep problems plaguing an unsustainable forestry industry.[10] Environmentalists worried about the long-term health of the forests and foregone ecological benefits of allowing an insect infestation to run its course.[11] Concerned citizens believed profit-driven forestry companies were capitalising on the relaxed administrative requirements and chaotic gold-rush conditions to harvest more desirable but unaffected tree species.[12] This controversial response proceeded through three forms of administrative action: emergency regulations, Ministerial discretion over forestry royalties and the Chief Forester's discretion to increase the total allowable harvest in the province.

This section of the chapter argues that an unconventional administrative body, the Forest Practices Board (FPB), played an important role in reviewing the government's emergency beetle response. The unique features of the FPB and the way in which it carried out its mandate demonstrate that it is possible for the response to an environmental disaster to comply with the public-justification conception of the rule of law.

A. The Limitations of Adjudication

The mountain pine beetle response was not challenged through judicial review in the courts; it was not reviewed by a quasi-judicial appeals tribunal. Indeed, the emergency response highlights a number of challenges that judicial and quasi-judicial bodies face when attempting to review environmental decisions. The first set of challenges are those that could be fixed through creative and appropriate design. As we saw in chapter two, judges are concerned about being converted into 'academies of science'.[13] Their lack of specialised expertise in environmental matters is a legitimate barrier in many instances to adequately assessing whether an environmental decision is publicly justified. As Dyzenhaus has noted, however, this challenge is

[8] H Nelson, 'Does a Crisis Matter? Forest Policy Responses to the Mountain Pine Beetle Epidemic in British Columbia' (2007) 55 *Canadian Journal of Agricultural Economics* 459.

[9] See Bark Beetle Regulation (above n 6).

[10] B Parfitt, 'Battling the Beetle: Taking Action to Restore British Columbia's Interior Forests' (Canadian Centre for Policy Alternatives, 2005).

[11] Ibid. See also L Pynn, 'Part One: In the Wake of a Plague', *Vancouver Sun* (10 Sept 2012), www.vancouversun.com/technology/Part+wake+plague/5800904/story.html.

[12] L Pynn, 'Part Four: "It Looks Like Armageddon"', *Vancouver Sun* (10 Sept 2012), www.vancouversun.com/travel/Part+Four+looks+like+Armageddon/5814799/story.html.

[13] Above ch 2, n 83.

arguably ameliorated through the creation of specialised appeals tribunals, comprised of members with appropriate expertise. Indeed, in the BC forestry context, such a tribunal exists: the Forest Appeals Commission. Its members are lawyers, professional foresters and other professionals with expertise in engineering, biology or environmental studies.[14]

Judicial review also relies on interested, motivated and well-resourced individuals to seek out review. Historically, claimants seeking review had to show a direct interest in the cause to have standing before the courts. Now claimants who lack direct standing need to meet a three-part test for public interest standing, which, while not prohibitive, is certainly not an open invitation to anyone seeking to protect a public environmental good.[15] Apart from potential legal obstacles, judicial review is also expensive and time-consuming, privileging those with the resources to bring forward a claim. In the environmental context, seeking judicial review may require making freedom-of-information requests, finding experts to assist in understanding the environmental implications of the public decision and even conducting separate scientific studies. By the time judicial review proceedings have taken place, the underlying matter may be moot. Specialised appeals tribunals again can ameliorate some of these challenges. Many tribunals are designed to improve the accessibility and efficiency of review.[16] Less formal proceedings, flexible rules of evidence and expert board members and staff who can play a more active role in assisting parties are all institutional responses to the challenges of judicial adjudication.

Importantly, however, these features rely on legislatures that are willing to commit these innovations to the constitutive law of the tribunal. For example, specialised tribunals could have broad provisions for public interest standing, reducing the need for claimants to overcome threshold tests before the institution can address the central question of whether the underlying administrative decision was publicly justified. Many existing specialised appeals tribunals, however, do not. For example, individuals who are not forest licence holders do not have direct access to the Forest Appeals Commission.[17] It does not have a public interest mandate.[18]

Other challenges arise from an inherent mismatch between environmental decision-making and adjudication as a form of dispute resolution.

[14] Forest Appeals Commission, 'FAC Tribunal Member: Qualifications' (2007), www.fac.gov.bc.ca/tribunal_members/FAC_Qualifications_2007.pdf.

[15] The Supreme Court of Canada's most recent revision to the common law test was in *Canada (Attorney General) v Downtown Eastside Sex Workers United Against Violence Society*, 2012 SCC 45, [2012] 2 SCR 524.

[16] Haddock, 'Environmental Tribunals' (above n 2) 10–11.

[17] Forest and Range Practices Act [FRPA], SBC 2002, c 69, ss 82 and 83.

[18] Haddock, 'Environmental Tribunals' (above n 2) 29.

Environmental issues are, to borrow Lon Fuller's description, 'polycentric.'[19] They are issues that

> involve many affected parties and a somewhat fluid state of affairs. ... [T]he more interacting centers there are, the more the likelihood that one of them will be affected by a change in circumstances, and ... this change will communicate itself after a complex pattern to other centers.[20]

Fuller argued that these features of polycentric issues impede, if not preclude, adjudication's essence of rationality—ie, the claimant must be capable of articulating a principle for deciding the case in her favour.[21] Fuller noted that this commitment to rationality is frequently at odds with the ability of a decision-maker to act swiftly in response to evolving issues and to deal with polycentric issues in a systemic, rather than piecemeal, principle-by-principle fashion.[22]

We have seen how these underlying concerns play out in the context of judicial review.[23] Courts worry that there is no rational principle to apply when determining, for example, the legality of polycentric regulations. When environmental decisions are challenged in either the courts or tribunals, the issue is necessarily circumscribed, whittled down to the specific interests of the party engaged by the public action. The adjudicator's role is confined by the need to resolve the dispute, often in the absence of understanding the broader regulatory context or the possible knock-on effects of the outcome in the particular case.

These challenges with adjudication do not, however, preclude effective review and therefore compliance with the rule of law. For Fuller, what is essential to adjudication is 'the affected party's participation through proofs and arguments'.[24] We saw in the previous chapter that this underlying concern for the agency of the legal subject underpins his conception of the rule of law. By expressing this underlying rule-of-law concern as the requirement of public justification, we are free to imagine the institutional possibilities that Fuller only gestured toward. For example, he observed that one problem arising from the mismatch between adjudication and polycentric problems is that 'instead of accommodating his procedures to the nature of the problem he confronts, [the arbiter] may reformulate the problem so as to make it amendable to solution through adjudicative procedures.'[25] The implication is that modified procedures or 'mixed forms of social ordering' might be

[19] LL Fuller, 'The Forms and Limits of Adjudication' (1978) *Harvard Law Review* 353, 395.
[20] Ibid, 397
[21] Ibid, 369.
[22] Ibid, 398–99.
[23] See above ch 2.
[24] Fuller, 'The Forms and Limits' (above n 19) 393.
[25] Ibid, 401.

better suited to the task.[26] Elsewhere, he suggested that in some contexts an ombudsman might be the most effective control over lawlessness.[27]

The Forest Practices Board is an example of such institutional innovation, one that responds to the many limitations of adjudication as the form of ensuring public justification in environmental law. The FPB is one part of British Columbia's response to decades of escalating controversies in the forestry industry. It is described as the province's independent forestry watchdog, tasked with a mandate of reporting to the government and the public on compliance with forestry legislation.[28] The FPB is an administrative body, in the specific sense that it does not have an adjudicative or dispute-resolving function. Rather, the FPB has 'broad powers to investigate public complaints, to oversee the audit process and to report to the public'.[29] It is what one commentator has called a 'hybrid institution'[30] because it exercises a number of different regulatory functions.

The FPB was originally constituted by the Forest Practices Code but was continued under the FRPA.[31] The legislation delegates four main powers to the Board: complaints investigations, special reports and investigations, audits, and acting as public advocate. Any individual can file a complaint or request that the FPB undertake an investigation on matters of non-compliance with forest practices requirements.[32] But the legislation also gives the Board the authority to undertake special investigations and issue special reports on its own initiative.[33] In addition, it is required by the legislation to conduct periodic audits of forest companies to ensure compliance.[34] The Board has extensive powers to compel information, summon witnesses and enter premises to carry out its investigative and reporting functions.[35] The FPB's remedial powers are limited to giving recommendations resulting from their complaint, reporting and auditing powers.[36] Finally, the FPB also plays the role of public advocate by representing the public interest before the Forest

[26] Ibid, 406.

[27] LL Fuller, *The Morality of Law*, rev edn (New Haven, Yale University Press, 1969) 82. See also R Macdonald, 'The Acoustics of Accountability: Towards Well-Tempered Tribunals' in A Sajó (ed), *Judicial Integrity* (Leiden, Martinus Nijhoff, 2004) 142 (on the role of non-adjudicative accountability mechanisms).

[28] *Northwood Inc v British Columbia (Forest Practices Board)*, 2001 BCCA, 2001 Carswell BC 389, para 8 (quoting legislative Hansard).

[29] Ibid.

[30] M Liston, 'Evolving Capacities: The BC Representative for Children and Youth as a Hybrid Model of Oversight' in L Jacobs and S Baglay (eds), *The Nature of Inquisitorial Processes in Administrative Regimes* (Aldershot, Ashgate, 2013).

[31] Forest Practices Code (above n 7); and FRPA (above n 17) s 136(1).

[32] Ibid, s 123.

[33] Ibid, ss 122 and 124.

[34] Ibid, s 122.

[35] Ibid, ss 123–25.

[36] Ibid, s 131.

Appeals Commission or in court.[37] The Board is comprised of members with forestry expertise (typically professional foresters but also biologists) and lawyers with experience in forestry regulation.[38]

The Board's investigation and reporting powers respond to the weaknesses of adjudication. Interested and concerned individuals can initiate proceedings without having to show they have standing before the Board. The Board can focus exclusively on the merits of the complaint. Relatedly, the Board can initiate proceedings on its own initiative, ensuring that important public issues can be assessed regardless of the availability of an individual claimant. The special reporting function in particular enables a more systematic approach to reviewing environmental issues because it does not depend on the particular interests and concerns of one individual or group—concerns that may narrowly focus on one issue while ignoring underlying systemic problems. The Board can respond to environmental issues based on their perceived necessity, address them holistically and monitor these issues over time. Moreover, the FPB's inquisitorial powers and expertise mean that it does not depend on the resources and technical expertise of the parties before it.

The expertise, hybrid mandate and flexible remedial power of issuing recommendations also mean that the FPB is well positioned to oversee a great range of administrative decisions. Regulations—a perennial black hole for courts—do not therefore pose the same challenge to review for a specialised oversight agency such as the FPB. The FPB is constituted as independent of government, but through its recommendation-giving power, it is part of an ongoing dialogue with government. It has the capacity therefore to take a critical but systematic and long-term perspective on the regulation of forest practices in the province.

B. Ensuring a Publicly Justified Emergency Response

The FPB is a keystone in the project of public justification in the BC forestry context. Not only does it have the capacity to ensure that the government response to the mountain pine beetle epidemic was publicly justified, but it is also subject to the obligation to publicly justify its own decisions. In performing the first function of reviewing the government's beetle response, the FPB plays an important institutional role in forming the transitive law of the original administrative decision-makers. The FPB, in other words, ensures

[37] Ibid, ss 82–83.

[38] FRPA (above n 17) s 136(2). The legislation doesn't specify 'merit'. Current members are professional foresters, but past members have been lawyers, biologists and accountants. See Forest Practices Board, 'Board Members', www.bcfpb.ca/board/board-members.

that the manner in which those emergency decisions were made fulfilled the requirement of public justification.

While the FPB does not use the phrase 'public justification' nor 'rule of law', a close examination reveals that the Board exercised two of its functions to essentially determine whether the government's mountain pine beetle response was publicly justified. First, the FPB used its special reporting function to comprehensively assess the reasonableness of the harvesting strategy adopted by the government in response to the epidemic.[39] After conducting an independent analysis of the epidemic and possible harvesting models, the FPB concluded that the government's harvesting strategy was ineffective and recommended a different strategy—harvesting attacked timber rather than green timber—which the government then adopted. The Board also relied on its special reporting powers to issue a series of reports that examined the ecological impacts of the province's mountain pine beetle response and highlighted the detrimental effects the response was having on, in particular, biodiversity conservation[40] and water quality.[41] Moreover, the Board has monitored the mountain pine beetle response over the long term and has recommended further changes to forest management policy now that efforts to salvage beetle-killed timber have dwindled.[42]

These reports demonstrate how this special reporting function allows the requirement of public justification to be maintained across a much wider range of environmental decisions than a purely adjudicative model of review. The FPB operates in a way that allows even general policy decisions—regulations and legislation—to reflect the requirements of public justification. The issues taken up by the FPB in the wake of the mountain pine beetle crisis could not have been subject to effective review by the courts; they were politically loaded and highly technical. Yet the FPB's expertise and willingness to question the government's approach provided a review mechanism for complex policy decisions that generated a government response.

The FPB exercised a second function in the context of the mountain pine beetle response. The Board responded to individual complaints about the necessity of harvesting in beetle-affected areas and about the consistency of this harvesting with publicly-developed land use objectives.[43] It investigated the use of large clear-cuts that exceeded the requirements ordinarily required

[39] Forest Practices Board, 'Evaluating Mountain Pine Beetle Management in British Columbia', FPB/SR/20 (2004).

[40] Forest Practices Board, 'Biodiversity Conservation During Salvage Logging in the Central Interior of BC', FPB/SR/35 (2009).

[41] Forest Practices Board, 'The Effect of Mountain Pine Beetle Attack and Salvage Harvesting on Streamflows', FPB/SIR/16 (2007).

[42] Forest Practices Board, 'Timber Harvesting in Beetle-Affected Areas', FPB/SR/44 (201[illegible]).

[43] Forest Practices Board, 'Balancing Community Needs and Pine Beetle Logging in the Robson Valley', FPB/IRC/78 (2002).

by legislation[44] and the alleged haphazard use of arsenic-based pesticides to control the beetle.[45] Concerned citizens and NGOs—who may not have had a significant enough stake in the matter to meet the strict 'directly affected' standing requirements of many environmental tribunals—brought all these complaints. The unrestricted nature of who can file a complaint enables the FPB to focus directly on the merits of the government policy or decision.

In reviewing these complaints, the FPB has a policy that tracks the requirement of public justification. The policy outlines questions that guide the inquiry into whether the decision is both fair and reasonable.[46] The policy suggests that the Board operates on a principle of deference. It directs the Board to determine whether the government's decision was 'consistent with sound forest practices, … achieve[d] the intent of the Forest Practices Code and was … based on an adequate assessment of available information'.[47] In addition, the FPB reviews the government's 'consideration of the potential impact of a decision on those directly affected and on the general public, as well as the need for effective and efficient administration'.[48]

By following this policy when reviewing individual complaints, the FPB develops the transitive law of the government's mountain pine beetle response by actively inquiring into whether that response was publicly justified. Indeed, the FPB investigations exposed government decisions that prioritised private concerns above sound forest practices[49] and criticised decisions that were excessively technocratic and thus undermined the public accessibility of forestry decisions.[50] Their investigations reveal that the FPB often takes an expansive view of its mandate and comments broadly on matters of public importance. For example, even when it affirmed that a permit for pesticide use was justified (as determined by a different appeals tribunal), the Board cautioned the government that scientific uncertainty about the pesticide suggested it should rely on alternate methods of beetle control.[51]

As a keystone in the requirement of public justification, the Forest Practices Board is also subject to its requirements. It must, in other words, publicly justify its own decisions on the basis of core common law principles. Accordingly, it too is subject to independent review to ensure that it has done so.

[44] Forest Practices Board, 'Approval of Large Cutblocks to Control Mountain Pine Beetle in the Robson Valley', FPB/IRC/69 (2002).

[45] Forest Practices Board, 'Nadina Beetle Treatments', FPB/IRC/99 (2004).

[46] Forest Practices Board, 'Discretionary Decisions', www.bcfpb.ca/board/policies/complaint-investigations/discretionary-decisions.

[47] Ibid.

[48] Ibid.

[49] Forest Practices Board, 'Approval of Large Cutblocks' (above n 44).

[50] Forest Practices Board, 'Nadina Beetle Treatments' (above n 45).

[51] Ibid, 7.

While there is much good news about the ability and practice of the FPB in ensuring public justification, a note of caution is warranted. Despite a policy that incorporates principles of fairness and reasonableness, the special reports on the mountain pine beetle response suggest that the Board is often preoccupied with the reasonableness of government decisions to the exclusion of any consideration of fairness or the process by which government decisions were made.[52]

The judicial perspective on the FPB is also somewhat mixed, which suggests the courts do not fully appreciate the Board's role in ensuring public justification. Early in the Board's institutional life, the British Columbia Court of Appeal, in a nice example of deference as respect, upheld the Board's generous interpretation of its auditing powers.[53] Noting that the Board is 'uniquely positioned to see what is happening on the ground' and that it is limited to giving recommendations,[54] the Court of Appeal allowed the Board a robust role in reporting on forest practices that went beyond ensuring formal compliance with the legislation. More recently, however, the British Columbia Supreme Court was content to substitute its own opinion for the FPB, despite holding that the Board was the appropriate forum for review. In *Western Canada Wilderness* (2014), the Court held that the Board was in the best position to assess the claim that the Minister of Forests must issue a protective order for the endangered Coastal Douglas Fir community.[55] Nonetheless, the Court held that the regulations delegated the Minister discretion to issue this order (or not).[56] In doing so, it gave the Minister's decision 'the stamp of legality' without requiring that the Minister publicly justify his decision. The Court was right to conclude that the Board, and not the Court, was the appropriate forum for ensuring the Minister's decision was publicly justified. But by leap-frogging the Board, the Court denied the Board's status as a participant in the rule-of-law project.[57] In such instances, the Court ought to ensure the Board's decision is publicly justified, and it cannot perform this function until the Board has an opportunity to exercise its jurisdiction.

[52] See, eg, Forest Practices Board, 'Evaluating Mountain Pine Beetle Management' (above n 39).

[53] *Northwood* (above n 28).

[54] Ibid, para 22 (adopting the lower court's reasons).

[55] *Western Canada Wilderness Committee v British Columbia (Forests, Lands and Natural Resource Operations)*, [2014] 2014 BCSC 808, 84 CELR (3d) 85, para 30.

[56] Because this was a claim for mandamus, the Court reviewed the Minister's interpretation of the regulations and upon agreeing that it conferred a discretion, did not review the exercise of that discretion: ibid, paras 73–87.

[57] For another example of leap-frogging see also *Red Mountain Residents and Property Owners Assn v British Columbia (Ministry of Forests, British Columbia Forest Service, Arrow Forest District)*, 2001 BCSC 1142, 40 CELR (NS) 117. The FPB declined to review a decision partially on the basis that judicial review had already been sought. The role of the Board is not discussed in the case.

Despite these somewhat mixed messages, the FPB provides an interesting and unique example of the kind of institutional innovation that can maintain the requirement of public justification across a range of diverse environmental decisions.[58] The creation of the FPB—and indeed the fact that it has persisted even despite dramatic changes to provincial forest regulation—can be understood as a commitment by the legislature to the public-justification conception of the rule of law.

III. THE FOREST PRACTICES BOARD AND ITS GOVERNANCE RESPONSE

The innovative design of the FPB enabled it to oversee the government's emergency response in a way that closely approximates the public-justification conception of the rule of law. The question for this section is what happens when discretion is not an aberration—as in the case of the mountain pine beetle response—but is rather the central feature of a regulatory regime, as we saw in chapter three. Here we will see that the FPB continues to play its important oversight role, despite major reforms to the regulation of forest practices in the province. The Board is a harsh but arguably constructive critic of the revised regulatory regime. The substance of its critiques, however, do not fit intuitively into the common law framework of reasonableness and fairness. It is thus necessary to return to theories of deliberative democracy to understand whether the FPB has performed its public justification role.

A. The Role of the Forest Practices Board Under the FRPA

The FPB originated under the Forest Practices Code, which set out detailed and comprehensive rules directing forest practices in the province. Under this legislation, the Board had a strict compliance mandate that included ensuring that both government and industry complied with the detailed

[58] The closest provincial analogue to the FPB was Alberta's now defunct Environmental, Monitoring, Evaluation and Reporting Agency, an independent scientific body that aimed to provide 'open and transparent access to scientific data and information on the condition of Alberta's environment', established under the Protecting Alberta's Environment Act, SA 2013, c P-26.8 [repealed]. At the federal level, Canada has a specialised Auditor General for environmental issues, the Commissioner of the Environment and Sustainable Development (Office of the Auditor General of Canada). The Commissioner issues annual reports to Parliament (www.oag-bvg.gc.ca/internet/English/parl_lp_e_901.html)and responds to individual petitions. I am not the first to suggest that an ombudsman plays a role in upholding the rule of law. See T Buck, R Kirkham and B Thompson, *The Ombudsman Enterprise and Administrative Justice* (Farnham, Ashgate, 2011) 26–28 (on its potential for upholding rule of law values, but how this is an uneasy fit with traditional theories of constitutionalism).

code. In 2002 when the legislature introduced the FRPA, which is performance-based legislation, the Board was retained, but the way it performed its watchdog function had to change. The new legislation precipitated a decrease in the number of complaints investigations and the Board's involvement in reviews and appeals[59]—understandable given the legislation's shift away from formal compliance. But over the same period the Board has increased the number of audits and special reports produced annually, suggesting that the Board has subtly redefined its role.

The FPB has become a major critic of the FRPA and its performance-based scheme. Much of its criticism has been directed at the use of Forest Stewardship Plans ('Plans'), the central regulatory requirement under the FRPA. Forest Stewardship Plans are the only type of plan required by the Act that is subject to public comment and government approval. They are required to detail the licensee's strategies and results (ie, the specific forest practices) designed to meet the performance-based objectives of the FRPA.[60] An approved Plan is a prerequisite to any timber harvesting.[61] The Plans were originally touted by the legislature as a mechanism to improve innovation, lead to effective compliance and enforcement, and allow for effective public consultation.[62] The FPB's comprehensive investigation into content and implementation of these Plans led the Board to conclude that the regulatory regime is 'truly disappointing', that the Plans are 'unacceptable' and that approvals are being issued despite non-compliance with 'required approval tests'.[63] This section highlights four critiques by the Board: effectiveness of plan commitments, conduciveness to public review and comment, the prioritising of timber harvest, and lack of resources for enforcement.

First, the Board has consistently observed that existing Plans frequently fail to contain measurable and enforceable commitments.[64] The FPB's comprehensive investigation concluded that all sampled Plans 'had significant problems with measurability or verifiability, making some results, strategies or measures difficult or impossible to enforce'.[65] Plans contained imprecise and undefined key terms; they failed to contain details on who would

[59] Trends were observed by reviewing the FPB Annual Reports between 2014 and 1996. These are general trends; inconsistencies in reporting and internal procedures for conducting, in particular, complaints investigations make it difficult to draw firm conclusions.

[60] FRPA (above n 17) s 5.

[61] Ibid, s 3.

[62] Forest Practices Board, 'Forest Stewardship Plans: Are They Meeting Expectations?' FPB/SIR/44 (2015), www.bcfpb.ca/wp-content/uploads/2016/04/SIR44-FSP-Are-They-Meeting-Expectations.pdf, 1.

[63] Ibid, i.

[64] Forest Practices Board, 'A Review of the Early Forest Stewardship Plans under FRPA', FPB/SR/28 (2006) 2; and Forest Practices Board, 'Community Watersheds: From Objectives to Results on the Ground', FPB/SIR/40 (2014) 12.

[65] Forest Practices Board, 'Forest Stewardship Plans' (above n 62) 13 (emphasis added).

carry out the commitments and when.[66] The FRPA contains only minimal requirements for the content of the Plans, requiring only that a Plan include the 'intended results and strategies' in relation to the objectives under the FRPA.[67] These results and strategies must be 'consistent' with the objectives; they need not demonstrate that they will in fact achieve these objectives.[68] But even the minimal standard of being 'consistent with' the objectives has not been fulfilled. The Board observed that most Plans 'contain results or strategies that do not demonstrate consistency with objectives'.[69] Despite these failings, Plans are nonetheless approved.[70]

Second, the FPB has criticised the Plans as inhibiting meaningful public participation. It concluded that 'some characteristics of [Plans] are not consistent with the notion that the public requires suitable information and appropriate review opportunities to provide meaningful comment.'[71] The regulatory regime requires public notice-and-comment periods, but it mandates only that the plan is made available to interested and motivated individuals who contact the individual forest company.[72] In the event that members of the public do reach out to a forest company, they are likely to find a vague Plan that does not disclose the details of how any given individual might be affected by future forest practices.[73] The Plans are not required to show where logging roads will be built or where harvesting will occur. These details are left to 'site plans', which are not subject to government approval nor to public notice-and-comment requirements.[74] The Board has further criticised the use of technical and legal language that can make it difficult for the public to understand the content of Plans.[75] Finally, it has observed that the opportunities for public review and comment are limited to the original submission of a Plan for approval; Plans are routinely extended without any opportunity for public input.[76]

Third, the Board has criticised the existing results-based objectives for prioritising timber harvest, making most of the other objectives subject

[66] Ibid, 13.

[67] FRPA (above n 17) s 5. It also includes various technical requirements, such as the requirement to list the licences that the Plan covers and the requirement to include a map of the area to which the Plan applies.

[68] Ibid.

[69] Forest Practices Board, 'Forest Stewardship Plans' (above n 62) 17.

[70] Ibid, 13 and 22.

[71] Forest Practices Board, 'Forest Stewardship Plans' (above n 62) 6. See also Forest Practices Board, 'Public Involvement in Forest Management Planning in BC', Board Bulletin, vol 15 (2013) 4–5 (noting that the adequacy of public involvement is a common theme in complaints).

[72] Forest Planning and Practices Regulation [FPPR], BC Reg 14/2004, ss 20–22.

[73] Plans typically apply to very large areas, can pertain to multiple licensees, and some land areas are subject to multiple, overlapping Plans: Forest Practices Board, 'Forest Stewardship Plans' (above n 62) 7.

[74] FRPA (above n 17) s 10; and Forest Practices Board, 'Public Involvement' (above n 71) 4.

[75] Ibid, 3; and FPB, Forest Practices Board, 'Forest Stewardship Plans' (above n 62) 8.

[76] Forest Practices Board, 'Forest Stewardship Plans' (above n 62) 8–9.

to the condition that they do not unduly reduce the amount of timber harvested from British Columbia's forests.[77] The FPB has noted that there is much interest 'for a more balanced consideration of the full range of forest resource values and the economic and ecological necessity of doing so'.[78] And the Board has stated, 'At the very least, there are likely to be areas of the province in which different values might take priority for ecological, economic, community safety or aesthetic reasons and that might require an objective that is less constrained.'[79] The Board has suggested that the government refine the objectives to allow for variation.[80] Further, the Board has observed that there is no centralised resource for viewing the entire list of results-based objectives—they are split amongst regulations and orders-in-council. Indeed, the FPB has noted that in many cases local land use planning objectives have not been converted into binding objectives under the Act.[81] The Board has recommended that 'Government should establish a single, publicly-accessible website that sets out all government objectives under FRPA.'[82]

Finally, the FPB has expressed its concern that that monitoring and enforcement of the existing regulatory scheme is currently under-resourced. The British Columbia government has committed to the 'Forest and Range Evaluation Program', a long-term programme that assesses the effectiveness of the FRPA, determines whether performance objectives are being achieved and identifies opportunities for improvement.[83] But this is labour- and cost-intensive work, and the FPB has highlighted the significant decreases in budget,[84] staff, and inspections[85] in recent years, which have imperilled rigorous analysis and raised concerns that the analysis that is occurring is not being used to improve the regulations.[86] The Board has recommended that 'Government and licensees … support a robust effectiveness evaluation program.'[87]

[77] FPPR (above n 72) ss 5–9.1.

[78] Forest Practices Board, 'A Review' (above n 64) iv (p 4 of cover letter).

[79] Ibid.

[80] Ibid.

[81] Forest Practices Board, 'Community Watersheds' (above n 64) 8.

[82] Forest Practices Board, 'A Decade in Review: Observations on Regulation of Forest and Range Practices in British Columbia', FPB/SR/46 (2014) 2.

[83] Forest and Range Evaluation Program (FREP), '3 Year Strategic Plan: April 19, 2016' (2016) www2.gov.bc.ca/assets/gov/farming-natural-resources-and-industry/forestry/frep/frep-docs/frep_3_year_strategic_plan_2016.pdf; and British Columbia Ministry of Forests, 'Forest and Range Evaluation Program Logic Model', https://www.for.gov.bc.ca/ftp/hfp/external/!publish/frep/library/FREP_Logic_Model-oct2007.pdf.

[84] Forest Practices Board, 'A Decade in Review' (above n 82) 22.

[85] Forest Practices Board, 'Monitoring Licensees' Compliance with Legislation', FPB/SIR/37 (2013).

[86] Forest Practices Board, 'Community Watersheds' (above n 64) 15–17 (observing the wide variation in the quality of professional assessments of forest practices).

[87] Forest Practices Board, 'A Decade in Review' (above n 82) 3.

The Board's reports respond to many of the concerns raised in chapter three about the FRPA's wide scope for arbitrariness. Yet the detailed language of its reports does not fit comfortably within the requirements of reasonableness and fairness as they have developed through common law adjudication. What is needed to assess whether the Board is fulfilling its public justification function is recourse to deliberative-democratic theory, in particular a governance-oriented branch of deliberative democracy known as democratic experimentalism. After introducing democratic experimentalism, I argue that the FPB's critiques of the FRPA mirror democratic experimentalist ideals to such an extent that we can understand the Board's critique as a condemnation of the government to adhere to the public-justification conception of the rule of law.

B. Democratic Experimentalism

Democratic experimentalism is a self-described 'model of institutionalised democratic deliberation that responds to the conditions of modern life'.[88] It seeks to provide a democratic framework for responding to complex regulatory problems that are not easily addressed through traditional top-down regulation. Heavily influenced by the work of Charles Peirce and John Dewey, and finding inspiration in the practices of successful and adaptive private firms, democratic experimentalists argue that post-bureaucratic regulation can provide flexibility and induce learning in a way that responds to complex and fast-changing contemporary regulatory problems, but always within a framework of democratic deliberation.[89] These successful regulatory practices are: benchmarking, simultaneous engineering and error correction.[90] Benchmarking requires regulators to continually survey existing regulatory models or approaches to identify superior approaches. Simultaneous engineering means that there are multiple regulators simultaneously implementing their own problem-solving approach. And error correction requires regulators to continuously monitor, revise and improve their regulatory approach in light of new information. Democratic experimentalists argue that the practices of benchmarking, simultaneous engineering and error correction can generate new information that provides a necessary foundation for continual public deliberation over both the means and ends of collective governance, and the relationship between the two.

88 MC Dorf and CF Sabel, 'A Constitution of Democratic Experimentalism' (1998) *Columbia Law Review* 267, 283.
89 CF Sabel and WH Simon, 'The Duty of Responsible Administration and the Problem of Police Accountability' (2016) 33 *Yale Journal on Regulation* 165, 176–77.
90 Dorf and Sabel, 'A Constitution of Democratic Experimentalism' (above n 88) 287.

In their classic account of democratic experimentalism, Michael Dorf and Charles Sabel argued that these features can be realised through a combination of extensive national oversight and significant local autonomy over problem-solving.[91] Local governance units, through rigorous citizen participation, determine the best approach to any given regulatory problem. National monitoring bodies pool information about local experimentation and provide syntheses of which regulatory approaches are working and which are not, which in turn enable local units to revise their regulatory approaches.[92]

Despite the fact that democratic experimentalists are not principally concerned with the rule of law, the ideals of democratic government to which they are committed fit hand-in-glove with the public-justification conception of the rule of law. First, democratic experimentalism requires an ongoing commitment to the practice of reason-giving. Reasons are vital to the kind of regulatory learning that democratic experimentalists imagine will put us on a better track for effective regulation. They are also vital for enabling dynamic peer review within administrative bodies and local government units, which courts and legislatures alone cannot provide.[93]

Second, the emphasis on reason-generation requires institutional changes and ongoing commitments within all major institutions of government.[94] Democratic experimentalists envision a much reduced role for the legislature whereby the legislature is responsible for identifying framework goals and delegating the necessary authority to local decision-makers to realise these goals along with the conditions that they 'publicly declare their goals and propose measures of their progress, periodically refining those measures through exchanges among themselves and with the help of correspondingly reorganised administrative agencies'.[95] Government agencies, they argue, take on the important role of monitoring these local experiments, establishing 'rolling rules', identifying leaders and laggards and providing support for building capacity within localities and private firms. In this model, agencies are not distant rule-makers but hands-on collaborators that play

[91] Ibid, 287–88 (summarising their position).

[92] They also argue that democratic experimentalism can work at the supranational level: CF Sabel and J Zeitlin, 'Learning from Difference: The New Architecture of Experimentalist Governance in the EU' (2008) 14 *European Law Journal* 271; C Overdest and J Zeitlin, 'Assembling an Experimentalist Regime: Transnational Governance Interactions in the Forest Sector' (2014) 8 *Regulation and Governance* 22 (arguing that the Forest Stewardship Council has many features of a global experimentalist institution).

[93] CF Sabel and WH Simon, 'Epilogue: Accountability Without Sovereignty' in G De Burca and J Scott (eds), *Law and New Governance in the EU and the US* (Oxford, Hart Publishing, 2006) 400.

[94] Dorf and Sabel, 'A Constitution of Democratic Experimentalism' (above n 88) 395 (noting that the problem of all-or-nothing judicial review in the US is not of the court's own making and cannot be fixed by 'doctrinal assertion alone').

[95] Ibid, 288.

a crucial role in ensuring that local decision-makers are working toward achieving legislative goals.

Democratic experimentalists outline a judicial role that is remarkably similar to that required by the public-justification conception of the rule of law. They argue that judicial review 'takes place at a metalevel'[96] because experimentalist courts do not review the actual decisions but rather the reasons decision-makers articulate for reaching these decisions and the 'respect they actually accord these reasons'.[97] Reasons must disclose a form of peer review, justifying the decision on the basis of what is implemented elsewhere. And in some circumstances, decisions might ideally be subject to actual peer review by a distinct reviewing body that stands alongside the court.[98] In this way, democratic experimentalists seek to avoid an all-or-nothing approach to judicial review that requires courts either to blindly defer or to intervene and second-guess the judgement of the administrative decision-maker.[99]

Third, much like the public-justification conception of the rule of law, democratic experimentalism sets out deceptively simple requirements that in fact demand a high level of ongoing commitment in practice. Democratic experimentalists readily concede there are no perfect examples of their ideal—it is always a work in progress. But they offer promising innovations in a range of settings from endangered species habitat protection to nuclear power regulation and community policing. The fact that these institutional experiments exist demonstrates that experimentation is possible, and it suggests that we can continue this process of experimentation and learning from prior experience.

The degree of overlap between democratic experimentalism and the public-justification conception of the rule of law suggests that democratic experimentalism offers a promising institutional framework within which the rule of law can be maintained even in the context of environmental governance.

C. Ensuring Public Justification of Forest Stewardship Plans

The FRPA tracks a democratic experimentalist framework in several ways: it provides skeletal framework legislation, empowers decentralised planning processes amongst local units (regionally-based licensees) and requires periodic public approval of the content of these plans. We can now see that these basic features are unproblematic from the perspective

[96] Ibid, 399–400 (arguing that judicial review 'moves in the direction of an express jurisprudence of excluded or impermissible reasons').

[97] Ibid, 389.

[98] Ibid, 377ff (example of peer review in the nuclear safety context) They make this point explicitly in Sabel and Simon, 'Epilogue' (above n 93).

[99] Dorf and Sabel, 'A Constitution of Democratic Experimentalism' (above n 88) 395.

of the public-justification conception of rule of law. What *is* problematic, however, are the many ways in which the FRPA and the plans fall short of the additional requirements of democratic experimentalism. By assessing the Forest Practices Board's critiques through the lens of democratic experimentalism, we can see how the FPB continues to perform a rule-of-law role even within this post-bureaucratic governance regime. The FPB's critiques can usefully be grouped in terms of the FRPA's constitutive, substantive and transitive law.

i. Constitutive Law

While the FRPA as a legislative act is a public delegation of authority, the FPB has raised several red flags about the ability of this legislation to set in motion an ongoing process of public justification. In particular, the Board has criticised the lack of opportunities created by the legislation for periodic and meaningful public participation. The limited notice-and-comment requirements of the existing scheme enable some participation—the one-time input of public concerns—but do not enable deliberation, which entails the back-and-forth giving of reasons over the content of the Plans. The legislation fails to provide a structure that allows for the ongoing—or at least periodic—deliberation and revision that is central to democratic experimentalist design. In fact, quite the opposite is true. The logical inference from the collective weight of the FPB's criticism is that the legislation actively precludes public deliberation and impedes public oversight of forest management.

Moreover, the FPB has observed that the FRPA, even as skeletal legislation, is unduly restrictive in two different ways. First, it prioritises timber harvest as an objective, a requirement that limits the scope of public deliberation. Democratic experimentalists emphasise the importance of public deliberation about both means and ends, as well as the interaction between the two. To fix one end (timber harvest) in advance constrains the range of possibilities open to consideration. The legislation impedes the local experimentation that generates constant improvement and innovation.

The FRPA is also too restrictive in that it compels the Minister to approve a Plan so long as it meets the minimal, formal requirements of the Act.[100] Again, this provision turns a requirement of democratic experimentalism on

[100] FRPA (above n 17) s16. A Plan is deemed to comply if it has been signed off on by a professional forester. Despite widespread non-compliance reported by the FPB, they are virtually never rejected. I found one appeal to the Forest Appeals Commission about a rejected amendment to a plan, where the parties settled on amended language: *Babine Forest Products Ltd v Government of British Columbia*, (2013) 2011-FOR-006(a) (Forest Appeals Commission). Also, plans have been challenged in court for failing to consult with aboriginal peoples (eg, *Klahoose First Nation v Sunshine Coast Forest District*, 2008 BCSC 1642, [2009] 1 CNLR 110).

its head. The improvement in forest practices that would result from simultaneous engineering, benchmarking and error detection can only happen if there is a credible threat of a penalty for failing to engage in these democratic experimentalist practices. To this end, democratic experimentalists encourage legislators to consider enacting a 'penalty default rule', a strict rule that would apply to regulated firms in the event they do not develop their own plans.[101] Over time, as regulators learn from prior experience, the penalty default rule can turn into a 'rolling rule' that is ratcheted up in line with industry best practices. To model this aspect of democratic experimentalism, the FRPA must create a credible threat that laggard Plans will be rejected and timber harvesting will therefore be prohibited. The current legislation effectively enshrines a reverse penalty default rule, one that encourages shirking and opportunism rather than continual improvement.

Once situated against the ideals of democratic experimentalism, we can see that the FPB's critiques not only speak to the effectiveness of the legislation but rather go to the heart of the regulatory regime's ability to fulfil the requirement of public justification. The constitutive law, in other words, is deeply flawed. The FPB's reports suggest that the FRPA ought to be understood as a legislative attempt to withdraw from the rule-of-law project of public justification.

ii. Substantive Law

The substantive law developed under the FRPA must also reflect the requirement of public justification; it must reveal a defensible interpretation of the public interest. Fortunately, the British Columbia legislature has clearly and repeatedly articulated the particular interpretation of the public interest applicable in this instance. The FRPA and its regulations deliver a set of publicly-regarding objectives: eg, protection of wildlife, visual quality, timber harvest to support a main resource industry in the province. The government further promised that the FRPA would encourage innovation in how forest companies meet these objectives, enable effective compliance and enforcement, and encourage effective public consultation.[102] Exercises of public authority under the FRPA are therefore measured against not some abstract conception of the public interest but rather the specific definition offered through the democratic process itself. Thus the question—one squarely considered and answered in the negative by the FPB—is whether those exercises of public authority in fact reflect this standard.

The particular exercises of public authority considered here are the approvals or rejections of Forest Stewardship Plans. Recall the centrality of

[101] BC Karkkainen, 'Information-Forcing Regulation and Environmental Governance' in De Burca and Scott (eds), *Law and New Governance* (above n 93) 293.

[102] Forest Practices Board, 'Forest Stewardship Plans' (above n 62) 3.

reason-giving to both public justification and democratic experimentalism. The reasons for a public decision must reveal the defensible interpretation of the public interest. But when a Plan is approved, there are no reasons in a conventional administrative law sense. The Plan forms the reasons for the decision. The FPB has reported in unequivocal terms that the contents of these Plans do not disclose a defensible interpretation of the public interest. They fall well short of the public-regarding rationale for the new regulatory regime. The Plans consistently fail to contain measurable and verifiable criteria that enable enforcement. They do not reveal how the public objectives (eg, riparian protection, wildlife protection and visual quality) are being met. They do not facilitate public participation.

Of particular significance is the legislature's claim that the FRPA would encourage innovation in forest practices. This is also a central claim of democratic experimentalism: decentralisation allows for simultaneous engineering and benchmarking—in other words, constant learning from past experience and the experience of peers. Democratic experimentalism thus has the potential to refine significantly the substantive law requirement to disclose a defensible interpretation of the public interest. Ongoing learning through peer review means that the specific content of the public interest in any given regulatory context becomes increasingly refined over time.

Democratic experimentalists argue that robust reason-giving occurs with the assistance of a centralised institution that synthesises and reports on the effectiveness of the simultaneous regulatory experiments. Yet the FPB's investigations reveal that the institutional infrastructure for information-gathering and synthesis is weak, with the capacity of the Forest and Range Evaluation Program undermined by lack of resources. A properly functioning centralised monitoring programme would produce a rolling best practices guide. And it would highlight both leaders and laggards in an effort to publicly praise and shame forest companies into doing better.

Interestingly, the flexible mandate of the FPB has allowed the Board to tentatively step into this role. The Board has documented significant problems with Plans' commitments to protecting drinking water, in particular noting that forty-one of forty-four plans investigated did not contain enough detail for the Board to conclude whether or not they were consistent with the performance objective.[103] It has offered specific examples of compliant and non-compliant language for the content of Plans.[104] And it has identified individual Plan-holders that have gone above and beyond legislative requirements to ensure public involvement in forest practices.[105] In other words, the FPB has become a significant informational resource that could

[103] Forest Practices Board, 'Community Watersheds' (above n 64) 2.

[104] Forest Practices Board, 'Forest Stewardship Plans' (above n 62).

[105] Forest Practices Board, 'Public Involvement' (above n 71) 5–6.

be and ought to be harnessed to ensure that the Forest Stewardship Plans disclose a defensible interpretation of the public interest.

iii. Transitive Law

The final rule-of-law requirement is an institutional mechanism for ensuring that each exercise of public authority is publicly justified on the basis of core common law principles such as fairness and reasonableness. The argument of this chapter is that the FPB is in many ways currently performing this function in the context of forest practices. The FPB has called into question the fairness of the process for approving Forest Stewardship Plans with its unequivocal critique of the lack of meaningful public participation in the management of public resources. The Board's observation that Plans are consistently approved and extended without meeting the basic requirements of the legislation (eg, strategies and results that are consistent with the performance-based objectives) demonstrates the unreasonableness of the exercise of approval authority.

The comprehensiveness and significance of the flaws highlighted by the FPB in carrying out this reviewing function suggest there is a great need for institutional cooperation in holding the government to account. The FPB is limited to issuing recommendations as a remedy for the flaws it detects in the management of forest practices in the province. It cannot act as a complete substitute for a reviewing institution, such as an appeals board, which could assess the legality of the approvals and intervene when an approval does not fulfil the requirement of public justification. Indeed, the FPB's work ought to facilitate this kind of adjudicative review by providing vital context, such as the extent and implications of non-compliance, that enables an adjudicative body to adequately assess claims of illegality.

Under the existing FRPA scheme, a rejected Plan can be appealed to the specialised Forest Appeals Commission, but the Commission does not have a general public interest mandate and cannot hear appeals brought by members of the general public if a Plan is perceived as weak or non-compliant.[106] The FPB, in its capacity as a public advocate, must bring these claims before the Commission on behalf of the public.[107] Alternatively, a claim might be brought for judicial review of a Plan, which has occurred when Indigenous groups have alleged that the government has not discharged its constitutional duty to consult prior to approving a Plan.[108] Only in the latter case has review of an approval been successful.

[106] Haddock, 'Environmental Tribunals' (above n 2) 29.

[107] FRPA (above n 17) s 83.

[108] See above n 100.

While tribunal or judicial review of the approval of a Plan is possible in principle, the current institutional structure is a poor fit with the requirement of public justification. Recall from the previous chapter that the requirement of public justification respects the legal subject as a responsible agent. Her participation is, in some form, internal to the rule of law. In light of the extensive failures under the FRPA to generate publicly justified forestry management decisions, it is not clear that circumscribing the public's direct access to adjudication is justifiable. The FPB as public advocate can fill gaps when there is no available or willing claimant to challenge a defective Plan, but this function ought to exist alongside public interest standing before the specialised appeals board and the courts.

IV. CONCLUSION

This chapter has argued that the FPB is an example of creative institutional design that approximates in important but unconventional ways the rule-of-law requirement of public justification. Its expertise and hybrid regulatory functions enable it to determine whether a diverse range of administrative decisions in the forestry context comply with the requirement of public justification. The chapter has further argued that democratic experimentalism, a governance-oriented strand of deliberative democracy, helps elaborate the institutional conditions that can fulfil the requirement of public justification when the delegation of broad discretionary authority is a central feature of a regulatory regime. Finally, it has argued that democratic experimentalism brings to light the FPB's continued role in maintaining the rule of law by critiquing the poor design and implementation of the FRPA.

The upshot is that we should expect creative institutional design to be an essential feature of maintaining the rule of law in the environmental context. The breadth and complexity of environmental decisions mean that courts cannot, on their own, ensure that decisions are publicly justified. Novel institutional design will require collaboration amongst institutions of government in unconventional, dynamic and perhaps surprising ways. So long as these institutions are operating on the basic premise that the others are bound by an ongoing requirement of public justification, institutional innovation should be seen as a strengthening—not a dilution—of the commitment to the rule of law.

6

Pipelines and Principles: Reasonableness and Fairness in Environmental Law

THIS CHAPTER NOW squarely addresses the two core common law principles of reasonableness and fairness and queries how these principles ought to be elaborated in the environmental context. It argues that the common law interpretations of these principles have been shaped by individualist and adjudicative dispute resolution contexts (such as public service employment and immigration decisions), which, when directly applied in the environmental context, often undermine the requirement of public justification. The chapter argues that well known environmental principles, namely the precautionary principle and sustainable development, ought to inform the interpretation of common law requirements of reasonableness and fairness. It provides a framework, in other words, for understanding how these environmental principles are an integral part of the rule-of-law project in environmental law.

The examples in this book up to now have been taken primarily from the context of an unforeseen but actual emergency related to forestry in the Canadian province of British Columbia. The challenge now is to bring lessons learned to the issue of pipeline development in North America, an environmental context in which many hope (in vain) that no emergency will arise. The key institutional actor in this regulatory setting is the Canadian National Energy Board (NEB), which assesses whether proposed interprovincial pipelines are in the public interest. As we will see, the NEB has been caught up in a wave of Parliamentary reforms that have been unabashed in their intent to undermine environmental protection in Canada. I argue that these reforms can be understood not only as an attempt to undermine environmental protection but also as an attempt to exempt pipeline approvals from the rule-of-law project. We will see that, so far, the NEB and the Federal Court of Appeal have been complicit in this creation of legal grey holes.

This chapter unpacks the variety of ways in which the NEB's process has given rise to issues of fairness and reasonableness and how conventional interpretations of these common law principles fail in this context.[1] It ultimately argues that to act with legal authority, the NEB must publicly justify its decisions on the basis of reasonableness and fairness, understood in light of sustainable development and precaution. These environmental principles are often critiqued as amorphous or ill defined. This chapter argues that deliberative-democratic theory guides defensible interpretations of the principles of sustainable development and precaution, and enables these principles to operate in a concrete manner to inform the requirement of public justification in environmental law.

The chapter contains three sections. The first introduces the four pipeline disputes, the NEB's role in the approval process and three areas of public controversy. While these controversies go to the independence, fairness and reasonableness of the NEB's assessment process, I argue that existing common law principles are insufficient. On their own, they fail to respond to the particular issues raised in the environmental context. The second section turns to the well known environmental principles of sustainable development and precaution. These principles are controversial and ambiguous, and have failed to meaningfully impact the development of Canadian environmental law. I argue that they can be understood as an attempt to maintain the distinctive relationship between legal subject and state that the public-justification conception of the rule of law makes possible. Interpreting these principles consistently with deliberative-democratic theory preserves the individual's status as a responsible agent capable of reasoning with the law. We will see that, properly understood, these environmental principles inform the common law requirements of reasonableness and fairness. The final section of the chapter returns to the NEB example. Relying on an understanding of reasonableness and fairness informed by precaution and sustainable development, it argues that the NEB has failed to publicly justify its controversial decisions. The absence of public justification provides a basis for intervention on review and, more fundamentally, means that the NEB decisions lack both legal and democratic authority.

I. THE PIPELINES, THE NEB AND THEIR PROBLEMS

With the dramatic increase in Alberta oil sands development, Canada's National Energy Board went from a relatively uninteresting technical regulatory body to a regular front-page feature of national newspapers and a centrepiece of the 2015 federal election campaign. This state of affairs has been the result of the NEB's mandate to oversee a suite of major pipeline proposals that traverse the country. These four major proposed pipelines

[1] For an early take on how procedural fairness ought to be extended to all forms of administrative decision-making but in a manner that accounts for distinctively non-adjudicative forms of decisions, see RA Macdonald, 'A Theory of Procedural Fairness' (1981) 1 *Windsor Yearbook of Access to Justice* 3.

(depicted in Figure 1) are now household names.[2] All four would carry bitumen from the Alberta oil sands and are part of an informal but transparent national energy policy to dramatically increase oil sands production.[3]

Figure 1: Major Canadian Pipeline Proposals 2016[4]

Developing the oil sands has proven controversial in large part because of its significant environmental impacts. Extracting bitumen from oil sands is

[2] TransCanada's Keystone XL project has generated the most international heat, but this has largely been in the United States with respect to the Presidential Permit required for the construction of the American portion of the pipeline. The Canadian approval of Keystone XL, granted by the NEB in 2010, passed without notice: *In the Matter of TransCanada Keystone Pipeline GP Ltd* (March 2010), OH-1-2009 (online at the NEB website, www.neb-one.gc.ca/index-eng.html).

[3] Combined, the four pipelines have the capacity to transport three million barrels of oil per day. The Premiers of the Canadian provinces released a 'Canadian Energy Strategy' that commits to expanding pipeline development and oil sands production. However, it contains no details on how this will be achieved: Council of the Federation, 'Canadian Energy Strategy' (2015).

[4] Credit for this figure goes to Matthew Mitchell.

an energy- and water-intensive process that produces approximately three times the amount of greenhouse gas emissions as conventional crude oil.[5] It results in the production of toxic tailings, which in this case are stored in tailings ponds adjacent to the Athabasca River.[6] Downstream communities worry that they are hot spots for rare forms of cancer.[7] At present, it is unclear whether established spill clean-up measures for conventional crude oil will be as effective for bitumen.[8]

Each pipeline on its own is a significant undertaking. Three pipeline proposals include the construction of port facilities to transport the bitumen by tankers to international markets.[9] Line 9 runs through Toronto and Montreal; the Trans Mountain Expansion runs through Greater Vancouver—some of the most heavily populated areas in Canada. In addition, the Northern Gateway pipeline would have traversed unceded Aboriginal territory[10] and the ecologically-sensitive Great Bear Rainforest,[11] and it would have had tankers shipping heavy crude oil through notoriously tricky navigable waters that are currently subject to a tanker moratorium.[12] After years of controversy and unfavourable court rulings, the federal government eventually 'killed' the Northern Gateway pipeline proposal.[13] The Energy

[5] Pembina Institute, 'Oil Sands Development and Climate Change: Implications for Canadians' (2006), www.pembina.org/reports/BC_oilgas06.pdf. Extraction of oil sands requires 3–4 barrels of new water for every barrel of oil produced: Natural Resources Canada, 'Oil Sands Water Management' (2015), www.nrcan.gc.ca/sites/www.nrcan.gc.ca/files/energy/pdf/oilsands-sablesbitumineux/14-0704%20Oil%20Sands%20-%20Water%20Management_e.pdf.

[6] Alberta Government, 'Lower Athabasca Region: Tailings Management Framework for the Mineable Athabasca Oil Sands' (2015), aep.alberta.ca/land/cumulative-effects/regional-planning/documents/LARP-TailingsMgtAthabascaOilsands-Mar2015.pdf.

[7] There are conflicting expert reports on this, which were summarised by CBC: CBC News, 'Study Suggests Link between Oilsands and Fort Chip Illnesses' (7 July 2014), www.cbc.ca/news/canada/edmonton/study-suggests-link-between-oilsands-and-fort-chip-illnesses-1.2698995.

[8] This became evident after the massive Enbridge spill into the Kalamazoo River. See, eg, United States Environmental Protection Agency, 'Oil Cleanup Continues on Kalamazoo River' (June 2013), https://www.epa.gov/sites/production/files/2016-06/documents/enbridge-fs-20130624.pdf (describing the need to dredge river sediment to remove submerged oil).

[9] Northern Gateway, Trans Mountain and Energy East.

[10] The Yinka Dene Alliance, a coalition of First Nations, issued a powerful statement that the Northern Gateway Pipeline would violate their Indigenous laws: Yinka Dene Alliance, 'Save the Fraser Declaration' (May 2013), savethefraser.ca/Fraser-Declaration-May2013.pdf; Yinka Dene Alliance and Save the Fraser, 'Save the Fraser Declaration: Solidarity Accord' (November 2013), savethefraser.ca/SolidarityAccord-nov2013.pdf.

[11] This is the same region that is subject to the Great Bear Rainforest Agreement. For extensive discussion on this topic, see above ch 3.

[12] R Priddle (Chair), 'Report of the Public Review Panel on the Government of Canada Moratorium on Offshore Oil and Gas Activities in the Queen Charlotte Region of British Columbia' (Ministry of Natural Resources, 2004), www.nrcan.gc.ca/sites/www.nrcan.gc.ca/files/energy/pdf/eneene/sources/offext/pdf/prpcep-eng.pdf. The current federal government has introduced a bill that would formalise this ban: Bill C-48, 'An Act respecting the regulation of vessels that transport crude oil or persistent oil to or from ports or marine installations located along British Columbia's north coast', 1st Sess, 42nd Parl.

[13] J Trudeau, 'Prime Minister Justin Trudeau's Pipeline Announcement' (Government of Canada, 30 November 2016), pm.gc.ca/eng/news/2016/11/30/prime-minister-justin-trudeaus-pipeline-announcement.

East pipeline was the longest proposed pipeline in the history of the Board,[14] running from Alberta to New Brunswick. After delays due to conflicts of interest involving members of the NEB, and changing economic conditions, the company announced in 2017 that it would no longer pursue the project.[15] Line 9 is in operation.[16] The Trans Mountain expansion has received federal and provincial support but faces litigation and vehement local opposition.[17]

These pipeline proposals have engaged a common set of institutional practices at the NEB, which regulates interprovincial and international pipelines and powerlines. In the context of the issues at hand, its primary function is to advise the Governor in Council (federal Cabinet) on whether interprovincial pipeline proposals are 'in the public convenience and necessity'[18] and whether they 'are likely to cause significant, adverse environmental effects'.[19] It has a public interest mandate, which it describes as 'promoting safety and security, environmental protection, and efficient energy infrastructure and markets in the Canadian public interest within the mandate set by Parliament'.[20]

The NEB's pipeline assessment process is governed by a combination of the National Energy Board Act 2012 (NEBA) and the Canadian Environmental Assessment Act (CEAA) 2012.[21] The process for each pipeline proposal, in broad strokes, follows the same steps.[22] The pipeline proponent submits an application for the required certificate to construct a pipeline. The Board reviews this application, determines the scope of assessment by releasing a list of issues that it will consider and opens an application period for members of the public who are interested in participating in the NEB hearing. Once the NEB has determined that the proponent's application package is complete, it issues a hearing order that details the process it

[14] National Energy Board, '2014 Annual Report to Parliament' (2015), www.neb-one.gc.ca/bts/pblctn/nnlrprt/2014/nnlrprt2014-eng.pdf, 2.

[15] TransCanada Corp, 'TransCanada Announces Termination of Energy East Pipeline and Eastern Mainline Projects' (news release, 5 Oct 2017), www.transcanada.com/en/announcements/2017-10-05-transcanada-anounces-termination-of-energy-east-pipeline-and-eastern-mainline-projects.

[16] Updates can be found on the Line 9 project-specific NEB webpage: www.neb-one.gc.ca/pplctnflng/mjrpp/ln9brvrsl/index-eng.html (last accessed 30 October 2017).

[17] Updates can be found on the Trans Mountain project-specific NEB webpage: www.neb-one.gc.ca/pplctnflng/mjrpp/trnsmntnxpnsn/index-eng.html (last accessed 30 October 2017).

[18] National Energy Board Act (NEBA), RSC 1985, c N-7, ss 2 and 52.

[19] Canadian Environmental Assessment Act 2012 (CEAA 2012), SC 2012, c 19, s 52, ss 29(1) and 31(1).

[20] National Energy Board, 'In the Matter of Enbridge Pipelines Inc' (March 2014), OH-002-2013, file A59170 [hereafter 'Line 9 Decision'], 5.

[21] CEAA 2012 (above n 19).

[22] There are two differences worth noting. First, the Line 9 approval was not subject to the CEAA, although the NEB conducted an assessment that included environment, socio-economic and land matters as well as accidents and emergency response. The NEB was the final decision-maker for the Line 9 approval; it did not require Cabinet approval. The Northern Gateway Pipeline recommendation by the NEB happened in conjunction with a Joint Review Panel (JRP), convened under the CEAA and NEBA. The terms of this JRP can be found here: www.ceaa-acee.gc.ca/050/document-eng.cfm?document=39960. Two members of the JRP were sitting NEB members; the third was appointed by the federal Minister of Environment.

will follow for assessing whether the application is in the public interest. We will see in a moment that numerous public concerns emerge from the details of this assessment process. After this process is complete, the Board issues a recommendation report to Cabinet with conditions for pipeline construction and operation that should follow in the event Cabinet decides to approve the project.

This decision-making process is mired in public controversy and legal disputes that raise questions about the fairness, reasonableness and independence of the NEB decisions. I reserve detailed analysis of these issues for section III below. In order to give some context for the elaboration of environmental principles that follows in section II, however, I first identify the issues that call into question the NEB's compliance with the requirement of public justification and the limitations in existing common law doctrine for responding to these concerns.

A. Fairness

The perceived fairness of the NEB's process has been jeopardised by amendments to the NEBA that require the NEB to prioritise efficiency and timeliness of its decision-making over fairness in carrying out its assessment. The Act also delineates two categories of persons eligible for public participation. As a result of these changes, the NEB is now assessing major pipelines without an oral hearing or oral cross-examination of the proponent's written evidence and is administering a two-step application process for determining whether interested parties have standing to participate in NEB hearings.

The lack of oral hearing is a stark departure from the NEB's past practice for pipeline proposals and from previous environmental assessments under the CEAA for major project approvals.[23] It raises questions about the ability of the NEB to fulfil its mandate of providing an expert report and recommendation to Cabinet, since public intervention is the primary mechanism for probing the proponent's information about the benefits and risks of the project. An oral hearing, however, is not generally a requirement of procedural fairness.[24] The requirements of procedural fairness have been

[23] See M Doelle, 'CEAA 2012: The End of Federal EA as We Know It?' (2013) 24 *Journal of Environmental Law and Practice* 1 for an overview of the controversial changes to federal environmental assessment.

[24] *Khan v University of Ottawa*, (1997) 34 OR (3d) 535, [1997] OJ No 2650 (Ont CA) (recognising an exception to this rule where credibility is the decisive issue because a face-to-face exchange is what allows the decision-maker to determine whether the applicant is credible. In *Black v Advisory Council for the Order of Canada*, 2013 FCA 267, 64 Admin L R (5th) 76, the Federal Court of Appeal dismissed a demand for an oral hearing. It held that the content of procedural fairness was on the low end of the spectrum because, in part, the administrative body did not have a judicial or adversarial process and only had an advisory function to the Governor in Council. In a rare case reviewing the NEB's procedure, the FCA held that the NEB was required to hold a hearing on the conditions imposed on an approved project. But the

developed with respect to the individual directly subject to state action—in this case, the pipeline proponent. In the present case, the deficiency in procedural fairness is less about the project proponent and intervenors and more about the public at large that is subject to the NEB's process and ultimately Cabinet's decision.[25] Controversial, complex and significant project approvals raise the question of whether the public has any right to procedural fairness. If so, in some instances, a public oral hearing may be the only process that can fulfil this requirement.

The NEBA and CEAA require that the National Energy Board grant standing to those 'directly affected' by the pipeline decision.[26] The NEBA also delegates the NEB discretion over whether it considers comments from those with information or expertise relevant to the decision.[27] The NEB has held that 'directly affected' excludes those with a 'mere' public interest.[28] It has also excluded interested parties on the basis that the NEB is the expert and not the person claiming to have relevant expertise or information. It is clear that the 'directly affected' language of the statute is a poor fit with the nature of environmental issues, which are complex, interconnected and potentially wide in geographic and temporal scope. At common law, however, the requirement that procedural fairness extend to those directly affected by the decision has favoured concrete and significant interests, typically property interests—a position affirmed by the NEB and upheld by the Federal Court of Appeal on review.[29] The courts have not recognised a common law right to public participation in Canadian administrative law.[30]

Court clearly stated that the NEB was 'master of its own procedure' in deciding how to hold this hearing (ie, written or oral).

[25] R Leckey, *Contextual Subjects: Family, State, and Relational Theory* (Toronto, University of Toronto Press, 2008) 224–38.

[26] NEBA (above n 18) s 55.2; and CEAA 2012 (above n 19) ss 2(2) and 15(b).

[27] NEBA (above n 18) s 55.2.

[28] National Energy Board, 'Procedural Update No 2: Ruling on Participation and Updated Timetable of Events' (22 May 2013), OH-002-2013, file A51982 [hereafter 'Line 9 Participation'], 7; National Energy Board, 'Ruling on Participation' (2 April 2014), OH-001-2014 [hereafter 'TMX Participation'], 5 (pinpoint to header page numbers) For a complete list of the interim rulings in the NEB assessment process for Trans Mountain, many of which are cited in this chapter, see National Energy Board, 'National Energy Board Report: Trans Mountain Pipeline Expansion Project' (May 2016), OH-001-2014, apps.neb-one.gc.ca/REGDOCS/File/Download/2969681, Appendix 7.

[29] National Energy Board, 'TMX Participation' (ibid) 4. Sometimes a private property interest is not even sufficient: National Energy Board, 'Line 9 Participation' (ibid) 7, upheld in *Forest Ethics Advocacy Association and Sinclair v National Energy Board*, 2014 FCA 245. See also P Craig, *Public Law and Democracy in the United Kingdom and the United States of America* (Oxford, Clarendon Press, 1990) 27.

[30] A Edgar, 'Procedural Fairness for Decisions Affecting the Public Generally: A Radical Step towards Public Consultation?' (2014) 33 *University of Tasmania Law Review* 56 (arguing in the Australian context that this is a natural extension from existing procedural fairness common law doctrine). Compare with the Administrative Procedures Act, Pub L No 79–404, 60 Stat 237 (1946) (codified as 5 USC s 553) (US) (statutory requirement for notice-and-comment prior to rule-making).

The NEB hearing process restricts public participation and is only public in the thin sense that the thousands of written documents involved in each hearing are available online. There are thus questions about whether the NEB's public interest mandate can be fulfilled by a process that eliminates oral cross-examination and guarantees participatory rights to only those with affected private property interests. Indeed, in instances of major regulatory decisions with significant long-term effects on Canadian energy policy, climate policy and long-term impacts on the communities and ecosystems through which the pipelines travel, we would expect that exclusion of the public must be explicitly justified.

B. Reasonableness

The second set of issues arising from the NEB pipeline processes pertains to the scope and adequacy of the NEB's assessment of pipeline proposals. In particular, there was significant public outcry over the Board's refusal to consider the environmental effects of upstream production and downstream use of bitumen. In particular, climate activists have criticised the Board for refusing to assess the climate impacts that inevitably result from facilitating oil sands production. Numerous potential intervenors have been denied standing on the ground that they seek to address these 'irrelevant' issues, that is, the proposed pipelines' connection with upstream and downstream uses. They have argued unsuccessfully before the NEB and the Federal Court of Appeal that the Board's narrow interpretation of its mandate and restriction on participation is both unreasonable and a violation of their Charter protection of freedom of expression[31] and right to not be deprived of life, liberty or security of the person except in accordance with the principles of fundamental justice.[32]

The NEB maintains that despite its broad discretion to determine the scope of its assessment (ie, the specific issues that inform its assessment of the public interest), the NEBA and CEAA do not confer the authority to consider upstream or downstream effects.[33] As many intervenors and

[31] National Energy Board, 'Ms Lynne M Quarmby and Others: Notices of Motion Dated 6 and 15 May 2014' (2 October 2014), Order OH-001-2014, Ruling No 34 [hereafter 'TMX Section 2 Motion'], leave to appeal denied in *Quarmby v Attorney General of Canada*, 2015 Carswell Nat 4254 (SCC). The NEB's first opportunity to hear the Charter claim was in the Trans Mountain process. However, applicants for judicial review had previously unsuccessfully argued that the NEB process violated their s 2(b) right: *Sinclair v NEB* (above n 29).

[32] National Energy Board, 'Mr LD Danny Harvey: Notice of Motion Dated 12 August 2014' (19 August 2014), OH-001-2014, Ruling No 29 [hereafter 'TMX Section 7 Ruling'].

[33] Compare NEBA (above n 18) s 52(1)(a) and CEAA 2012 (above n 19) s 19 (the definition of environmental effects includes: (a) land, water and air, including all layers of the atmosphere) with National Energy Board, 'Motions Requesting the Board Include in the List of Issues the Environmental and Socio-economic Effects Associated with Upstream Activities and Downstream Use' (23 July 2014), OH-001-2014, Ruling No 25 [hereafter 'TMX List of Issues'].

observers have argued, the Board's reasoning in this regard is a remarkable display of actively 'unimagining' the possible effects of the pipelines.[34] The need for these pipelines to ensure continued oil sands development and well-functioning energy markets are crucial components of the NEB's recommendations in favour of the pipelines.[35] Yet the interconnected and wide-ranging environmental effects of major pipeline projects suggest that it would be reasonable for the NEB to draw *some* clear line with respect to the scope of its assessment. Indeed, the Federal Court of Appeal has on two occasions upheld the NEB's interpretation of its mandate: once under NEBA, on the basis that the scope of assessment falls within a range of reasonable outcomes,[36] and once under CEAA, on the basis that the content of the assessment is subject to review only by Cabinet and not by the Court.[37] Yet in both instances, the fact that the NEB's recommendation considers the economic benefits that flow from upstream production and downstream use of oil sands while excluding the potential environmental costs remains unjustified.[38] The open-ended legislation provides no such explanation.

Participants have also argued that the NEB's consideration of a possible catastrophic oil spill has also been inadequate. They argue, for example, that with respect to the Northern Gateway Pipeline, the assessment considered only the likelihood of a spill and not the potentially severe consequences should one, however unlikely, occur.[39] In the Line 9 and Trans Mountain Expansion hearings, intervenors criticised the Board for not requiring the

[34] DN Scott, 'Situating Sarnia: "Unimagined Communities" in the New National Energy Debate' (2013) 25 *Journal of Environmental Law and Practice* 81.

[35] National Energy Board (Gateway Panel), 'Considerations: Report of the Joint Review Panel for the Enbridge Northern Gateway Pipeline, Volume 2' (2013), publications.gc.ca/collections/collection_2014/one-neb/NE23-176-2013-2-eng.pdf, 335.

[36] *Sinclair v NEB* (above n 29) para 69.

[37] *Gitxaala Nation et al v Canada (Attorney General & Minister of the Environment)*, 2016 FCA 187, paras 124–25.

[38] For two of the pipeline proposals, Trans Mountain and Energy East, the new federal government announced interim measures to assess the upstream greenhouse gas impacts of the projects, separate from the NEB's internal assessment process: Ministers J Carr and C McKenna, 'Interim Measures for Pipeline Reviews' (Environment and Climate Change Canada and Natural Resources Canada Joint Backgrounder, January 2016), www.canada.ca/en/natural-resources-canada/news/2016/01/interim-measures-for-pipeline-reviews.html. For updates on additional interim pipeline assessment measures, see also Canada's Major Projects Management Office: mpmo.gc.ca/measures/254. When the NEB Energy East panel was reconvened in 2017 to assess this pipeline, it announced that for the first time, it would consider upstream greenhouse gas emissions associated with the pipeline's products as well as how climate change law and policy would affect the viability of the project: S McCarthy, 'NEB to Assess Climate Issues in Energy East Pipeline Review' (23 Aug 2017), *Globe and Mail*, beta.theglobeandmail.com/report-on-business/industry-news/energy-and-resources/energy-east-pipeline-review-topics-to-include-impact-of-emissions/article36069855/?ref=http://www.theglobeandmail.com&.

[39] *Gitxaala Nation v Canada* (above n 37), 'Memorandum of Fact and Law of the applicant Federation of British Columbia Naturalists carrying on business as BC Nature' (22 May 2015) [copy on file with author].

proponents to develop and disclose site-specific emergency response plans.[40] When pre-existing emergency plans were available, the NEB allowed the proponent to heavily redact their contents.[41] This means that at the time of approval, the proponents' emergency response strategies had not been scrutinised by the NEB, the intervenors or the public.

The adequacy of the NEB's assessment fits uncomfortably with much judicial elaboration of the requirement of reasonableness.[42] The NEB's assessment in each case has been extensively reasoned. The very product of the assessment process is a detailed report, on the order of hundreds of pages. In carrying out this assessment task the NEB is operating squarely within its field of expertise. At the same time, however, the failure to demand further information on the consequences of an environmental disaster and on how a project proponent would respond in such a case undermines the purpose of the exercise. The current pipeline proposal hearings raise the concern that the NEB is not satisfactorily carrying out its role as an expert advisory body with respect to this central issue. As we will see in section III, the Federal Court of Appeal has adopted an especially deferential approach to reasonableness in this context.

C. Independence

The fairness and reasonableness of the National Energy Board decisions are coloured by mounting evidence that the NEB is effectively captured by industry—that is, it caters to the energy industry and does not fulfil its broader public interest mandate.[43] While there have been no systematic studies assessing possible regulatory capture, critics have pointed to the fact that the Board is comprised largely of energy experts. The Board lacks expertise in environmental assessment, spill risk and public health.[44] A repeated concern among many intervenors in the NEB hearings has been

[40] National Energy Board, 'Line 9 Decision' (above n 20) 58.

[41] National Energy Board, 'Province of British Columbia (Province) Notice of Motion Dated 5 December 2014' (15 January 2015), A 129-1 OH-001-2014, Ruling No 50, A4G5I9 [hereafter 'TMX Redaction Ruling'], 4.

[42] See, eg, *Alberta (Information and Privacy Commissioner) v Alberta Teachers' Association*, 2011 SCC 61, [2011] 3 SCR 654; and *Newfoundland and Labrador Nurses' Union v Newfoundland and Labrador*, 2011 SCC 62, [2011] 3 SCR 708, paras 12–14 (finding that it is appropriate for the Court to infer reasons that could have been offered).

[43] Canadian Broadcasting Corporation (CBC), 'National Energy Board's Impartiality over Pipeline Decisions Questioned' (5 November 2014), www.cbc.ca/news/canada/new-brunswick/national-energy-board-s-impartiality-over-pipeline-decisions-questioned-1.2824507; and M Eliesen, 'View: Energy Executive Blasts Kinder Morgan Review as "Fraudulent," Quits', *The Tyee* (3 November 2014), thetyee.ca/Blogs/TheHook/2014/11/03/VIEW-energy-exec-blasts-Kinder-Morgan-quits/.

[44] At the time of writing, only two of nineteen members have previous experience in environmental assessment. One of these members was appointed to the Energy East panel of three.

that the Board is far too willing to rely on untested information provided by the project proponent and is too quick to dismiss intervenor requests for more information.[45]

NEB panel members and the Chairperson were revealed to have met privately, outside the hearing context, with a consultant for a project proponent, leading to their recusal from the project hearing for creating a reasonable apprehension of bias.[46] Absent some obvious conduct such as this, however, it is difficult to imagine how a claim of more insidious institutional bias might be successful on judicial review. Courts have been reluctant to inquire into the operational realities of administrative decision-makers, preferring instead to examine the applicable statutory framework.[47]

Further concerns have arisen from potential interference by the executive. The NEBA grants extraordinary powers to both the Chairperson and the Minister to intervene in a hearing, for example to remove a Board member who is holding up the assessment.[48] Indeed, the legislation allows the Minister to direct the Chairperson to declare a pipeline to be in the public interest without having even completed an assessment.[49] Such a threat might seem remote but for inflammatory remarks by the Minister of Natural Resources, who on the opening day of the Northern Gateway Pipeline public hearings, declared his support for the pipeline and denounced pipeline opponents as foreign-funded, environmental ideologues.[50] These comments 'constructed a frame in which the submissions of affected communities .. were discredited in advance'.[51] Moreover, the NEB acted upon the sentiment of these comments, if not on the comments themselves. Subsequent freedom of information requests revealed that the NEB (although not sitting panel members) coordinated efforts between the Royal Canadian Mounted Police (RCMP)

[45] *Gitxaala Nation v Canada*, 'Memorandum of Fact and Law' (above n 39); Eliesen, 'View' (above n 43) (stating that of 2000 questions posed by intervenors, the NEB dismissed 95 per cent of them and did not require the company to respond. I was not able to fact-check this claim). See also above n 29, where I noted the NEB's unusual request that the company comment on who should be able to participate.

[46] National Energy Board, 'Notices of Motion from *Stratégies Énergétiques* and the *Association québécoise de lute contre la pollution atmosphérique*, and Transition Initiative Kenora (TIK)' (9 September 2016), Order OH-002-2016 Ruling No 23, file A79374.

[47] *Bell Canada v Canadian Telephone Employees Association*, 2003 SCC 36, [2003] 1 SCR 884. Discussed in L Jacobs, 'Tribunal Independence and Impartiality: Rethinking the Theory after Bell and Ocean Port Hotel—A Call for Empirical Analysis' in L Jacobs and AL Mactavish (eds), *Dialogue Between Courts and Tribunals: Essays in Administrative Law and Justice (2001–2007)* (Montreal, Les Editions Themis, 2008) 43.

[48] NEBA (above note 18) ss 6 and 52(8). Note that it further deems all evidence heard prior to change to be heard after the change.

[49] This is the combined effect of s 6 and s 52(8).

[50] 'An Open Letter from Natural Resources Minister Joe Oliver', *Globe and Mail* (9 January 2012).

[51] Scott, 'Situating Sarnia' (above n 34) 106 (speaking specifically about Indigenous communities affected by Line 9, but it applies more broadly).

and Canadian Security Intelligence Service (CSIS) to spy on the peaceful activities of environmental and aboriginal groups and further shared the information with industry.[52]

The Federal Court of Appeal held that the Minister's comments were insufficient to establish bias.[53] The Court reasoned that this decision-making context—namely, the political position of the Minister and the policy-based rather than judicial or quasi-judicial nature of the decision—demanded only that the decision-maker's mind not be closed such that representations to the contrary would be futile.[54] In the Court's view, '[t]he evidence of one Minister's comment made years before the decision at issue is insufficient to establish that the outcome of the Governor in Council's decision was predetermined.'[55]

Together, the allegations of industry capture and executive interference suggest that the NEB is not able to effectively carry out its role of providing recommendations on the public interest. Taken as a whole, it is reasonable to conclude that the NEB hearings are a something of a sham, a formal exercise in which recommendations are weighted in favour of approval and moreover precede decisions that the executive is determined to take in any event. If this is the case, then the NEB offers only a façade of legality. Its practices are not publicly justified, and moreover, its failure undermines the ability of Cabinet to discharge its rule-of-law obligation to publicly justify its final decision should it approve a pipeline.

The current institutional practices at the NEB are all consistent with the subtext of the changes to the NEB's governing legislation, which were transparent in their attempt to stack the deck in favour of pipeline approvals. But what is key to the argument that follows in this chapter is that Parliament did not do this explicitly. Rather, these legislative changes maintained a process with many of the trappings of the rule of law. Federal authority to approve an interprovincial pipeline is preconditioned by an expert advisory body conducting a public process, with a statutory mandate to consider the environmental and socio-economic effects of projects. These elements open up the possibility of maintaining the rule-of-law project, understood as the requirement of public justification. Understanding the rule of law as the requirement of public justification requires all institutions of government to resist the creation of legal grey holes. That is, unless statutory language unambiguously exempts the NEB from rule-of-law requirements, it must do its best to publicly justify its decisions within its institutional constraints.

[52] S McCarthy, 'CSIS, RCMP Monitored Activist Groups before Northern Gateway Hearings', *Globe and Mail* (21 November 2013), www.theglobeandmail.com/report-on-business/industry-news/energy-and-resources/csis-rcmp-monitored-activists-for-risk-before-enbridge-hearings/article15555935/.

[53] *Gitxaala Nation v Canada* (above n 37) para 195.

[54] Ibid, para 199.

[55] Ibid, para 200.

And where it acquiesces to the creation of a legal grey hole, the institution tasked with review is entitled to intervene.

This next section turns to the content of public justification. As we have just seen, it is not clear that the existing interpretations of the common law requirements of reasonableness and fairness attend to the realities of environmental problems. The evolution of procedural fairness at common law still reflects a focus on individual interests, typically infringements of private property rights or individual liberty. The long history of judicial abstinence from legislative issues, as we saw in chapter two, lingers in the form of reluctance on the part of judges to directly engage with the real-world operations of regulators on what are seen as policy issues. While reasonableness is a malleable concept, the uncertainty surrounding environmental effects means that virtually any decision can be reasonable in the abstract. Common law principles, however, are not fixed. They are sensitive to context. We will now see that in the environmental context, two candidate environmental principles allow us to elaborate these common law requirements.

II. IN DEFENCE OF ENVIRONMENTAL PRINCIPLES

This section introduces and defends two environmental principles: sustainable development and precaution. We will see that the requirements of these principles are subject to significant debate. Their seemingly commonsense aims—such as development within ecological limits—quickly dissolve whenever applied to specific contexts. Critics allege 'these principles tend to be malleable and vacuous, providing political and legal decision-makers with more room, not less, to craft results that they prefer.'[56] I argue that this critique is misguided because it fails to appreciate these principles as part of the rule-of-law project of public justification. Environmental principles can be understood as an attempt to safeguard the distinctive relationship between legal subject and state that the requirement of public justification makes possible, while also taking into account the challenging conditions of the environmental emergency.

Recall from chapter four that public justification constitutes a distinctive legal relationship between lawmaker and legal subject. Rule-of-law requirements presuppose the subject's status as a responsible agent, someone who is capable of understanding and obeying or contesting the law. Lawmakers demonstrate that they respect this status through the requirement of public justification, that is, by justifying their decisions on terms that legal subjects cannot reasonably reject. One of the sources of these 'terms'

[56] B Pardy, 'Environmental Assessment and Three Ways Not to Do Environmental Law' (2010) 21 *Journal of Environmental Law and Practice* 139, 148. See also CD Stone, 'Is There a Precautionary Principle?' (2001) 31 *Environmental Law Reporter* 10790.

is the common law constitution and, in particular, the principles of fairness and reasonableness. We saw that the Supreme Court of Canada's decision in *Baker* reflected this public-justification conception of the rule of law.[57] The Supreme Court held that Mavis Baker was entitled to an open process in which she had the possibility of influencing the outcome and to reasons that demonstrated she was not treated arbitrarily by the State. In other words, she was recognised as a responsible agent, capable of understanding and obeying or contesting the law.[58]

We also saw in chapter four that there is significant overlap between the requirement of public justification and theories of deliberative democracy. Both understand law-making as an essential site of public deliberation where law is both the product of public deliberation and the basis for further deliberation. Reason-giving and appropriate review mechanisms are vital components of public justification. Both are necessary for legal subjects to 'reason with' the law, to participate in ongoing deliberations about whether each case really reflects the core constitutional values of the community.

Recalling chapter four, we can distil three commonalities between the public-justification conception and theories of deliberative democracy.[59] First, they share an understanding of the individual as a responsible agent capable of engaging in the ongoing project of collective governance. Second, they share central guiding principles, such as generality, and argue that these principles should lead to specific institutional designs. And third, they share a pragmatic orientation that requires an ongoing commitment to reflection, deliberation and revision in order to better approximate the ideals of a deliberative democratic system governed by law.

I now argue that we can understand sustainable development and the precautionary principle as attempts to maintain this relationship between legal subject and state in light of profound environmental challenges. These are complex principles, and the shared features of deliberative democracy and the public-justification conception of the rule of law cannot provide definitive definitions.[60] What they can provide, however, are the contours of these environmental principles and allow us to eliminate some of their persistent and confounding interpretations. We will then see how these environmental principles interact with the common law requirements of fairness and reasonableness.

[57] *Baker v Canada (Minister of Citizenship and Immigration)*, [1999] 2 SCR 817, 1 Imm LR (3d) 1. This case is discussed above in ch 4, section I.

[58] Leckey, *Contextual Subjects* (above n 25) 215–16 (arguing that the Supreme Court had in mind a thicker account of Mavis Baker, still, as a contextually embedded legal subject).

[59] See also H Kong, "Election Law and Deliberative Democracy: Against Deflation" (2015) 9 *Journal of Parliamentary and Political Law* 35, 40–41.

[60] See A Woolley, 'Legitimating Public Policy' (2008) 58 *University of Toronto Law Journal* 153, 176–77 (defending deliberative democracy as an orienting theory capable of offering some guidance on public process, despite its vagueness and contested elements).

A. Sustainable Development

> *Sustainable development is development that meets the needs of the present without compromising the ability of future generations to meet their own needs.*[61]

Sustainable development is a concept that aims to integrate ecological limits, development and equity within all public decision-making.[62] The World Commission on Environment and Development (the Brundtland Commission, quoted above) popularised the concept. It was the first major international effort to understand the interrelationship between poverty, development and environmental degradation, and the first to recognise the need for intergenerational equity.[63] Central to sustainable development are the ideas of *needs*—the essential needs of those living in poverty—and *limits*—the physical limits of the Earth to provide for these needs over the long term.[64] The concept recognises the injustice of historical patterns of development on developing countries and on future generations that will be immensely constrained by current wasteful production and consumption practices.

Sustainable development is arguably the most influential concept in environmental law worldwide.[65] Virtually every country and every sector of social life has embraced it.[66] Sustainable development is incorporated into countless

[61] World Commission on Environment and Development (WCED), *Our Common Future* (Oxford, Oxford University Press, 1987) 43.

[62] Whether sustainable development is its own stand-alone legal principle is highly contested. Many have argued that it is far more complex than this: perhaps its own body of law (eg, M-C Cordonier Segger and A Khalfan, *Sustainable Development Law: Principles, Practices and Prospects* (Oxford, Oxford University Press, 2004)) or an 'interstitial' legal norm that modifies other primary norms (eg, V Lowe, 'Sustainable Development and Unsustainable Arguments' in A Boyle and D Freestone (eds), *International Law and Sustainable Development: Past Achievements and Future Challenges* (Oxford, Oxford University Press, 1999) 31) or a discourse (eg, JS Dryzek, *The Politics of the Earth: Environmental Discourses*, 3rd edn (Oxford, Oxford University Press, 2013) 147. Its close relationship to principles such as polluter-pays and the precautionary principle suggests that it may be more of an umbrella concept. (See DB Magraw and LD Hawke, 'Sustainable Development' in D Bodansky, J Brunnee and E Hey (eds), *The Oxford Handbook of International Environmental Law* (Oxford, Oxford University Press, 2008) 613; and C Voigt, *Sustainable Development as a Principle of International Law* (Leiden, Martinus Nijhoff Publishers, 2009) 37.) My primary concern here is how sustainable development might interact with existing common law norms in the domestic context. I recognise that this is a narrow focus, though it may have much broader implications for the development of the concept of sustainable development.

[63] WCED, *Our Common Future* (above n 61) 43.

[64] Ibid.

[65] WM Lafferty, 'The Politics of Sustainable Development: Global Norms for National Implementation' (1996) 5 *Environmental Politics* 185, 185; and S Wood, G Tanner and BJ Richardson, 'What Ever Happened to Canadian Environmental Law?' (2011) 37 *Ecology Law Quarterly* 981, 992.

[66] K Bosselmann, *The Principle of Sustainability: Transforming Law and Governance* (Aldershot, Ashgate, 2008) 1; and Voigt, *Sustainable Development* (above n 62) 3–4. Recall ch 4 above and the Forest Stewardship Council as an example of transnational sustainability governance.

international agreements[67] and pieces of domestic legislation around the world.[68] It is central to the idea of corporate social responsibility[69] and, as is often overlooked, is meant to operate at the individual level to change unsustainable patterns of consumption.[70]

The concept's potentially all-encompassing nature is both a strength and weakness. It is framed in terms that are difficult to reject. It is hard to imagine a country or corporation touting a commitment to *unsustainable* development.[71] But at the same time, the fact that it is meant to cover everything means it risks saying nothing.[72] Sustainable development has been described as 'almost infinitely variable'[73] and as an 'essentially contested concept'.[74] Academic literature roughly categorises sustainable development into 'weak' and 'strong' definitions. Weak sustainable development, as we will see, promises to integrate economic, social and environmental considerations, but without more, it endorses the status quo. Strong sustainable development has more radical potential for law and governance through its connection to ecological limits,[75] but it also fails to offer sufficient guidance to decision-makers.

Canada's Federal Sustainable Development Act is illustrative of weak sustainable development.[76] It describes sustainable development as 'based on an ecologically efficient use of natural, social and economic resources'.[77] It fails to acknowledge any possible conflict between economic, environmental and social considerations. It currently authorises a 'Plan for Responsible Resource Development' that, far from critically evaluating the sustainability of current natural resource development in the country, whole-heartedly

[67] UN General Assembly, 'Rio Declaration on Environment and Development', United Nations Conference on Environment and Development (1992), UN Doc A/CONF.151/26 (vol I); 31 ILM 874, www.un.org/documents/ga/conf151/aconf15126-1annex1.htm, Principles 1 and [illegible].

[68] See, eg, Resource Management Act 1991 (New Zealand); Sustainable Planning Act 2009 (Queensland, Australia); and Sustainability Victoria Act 2005 (Victoria, Australia). In Canada, see the Federal Sustainable Development Act (FSDA), SC 2008, c 33; the Sustainable Development Act, CCSM c S270 (Manitoba); Sustainable Development Act, (2006) CQLR c D-8.1.1 (Québec); and the Environmental Goals and Sustainable Prosperity Act, SNS 2007, c 7 (Nova Scotia). We will see that numerous statutes also include specific provisions on sustainable development.

[69] Wood et al, 'What Ever Happened to Canadian Environmental Law?' (above n 6[illegible]) 993–94.

[70] S Tirone, K Gallant and K Sykes, 'Environmental Goals and Sustainable Prosperity Act and the People of the Province: EGSPA's Social Deficit' (2012) 35 *Dalhousie Law Journal* 71

[71] Lafferty, 'The Politics of Sustainable Development' (above n 65) 185.

[72] Voigt, *Sustainable Development* (above n 62) 18.

[73] S Coyle and K Morrow, *The Philosophical Foundations of Environmental Law: Property, Rights and Nature* (Oxford, Hart Publishing, 2004) 203.

[74] Lafferty, 'The Politics of Sustainable Development' (above n 65) 186.

[75] A Ross, 'Modern Interpretations of Sustainable Development' (2009) 36 *Journal of Law and Society* 32.

[76] FSDA (above n 68).

[77] Ibid, s 5.

endorses the status quo.[78] While the Plan commits to better monitoring and enforcement, it fails to address the forward-looking aspect of sustainable development, which requires an assessment of whether the regulations and policies are themselves sustainable in the first place.[79] It demonstrates what one commentator has called a 'brownish' definition of sustainable development because it simply accentuates the environmental aspects of development decisions that the government is determined to take in any event.[80]

A common critique of weak definitions of sustainable development is that they are 'ill-suited to taking clear stances where there are tradeoffs between environmental, social and economic considerations, and to setting a few (instead of dozens of) strategic priorities for action'.[81] Critics argue that the idea that sustainable development requires decision-makers to integrate the three 'pillars' of economy, equity and environment consistently plays out in favour of economy.[82]

The response comes from defenders of strong sustainable development, who prioritise the environment pillar of sustainable development. They ground their argument in the simple reality that the Earth has finite ecological thresholds; neither its natural resources nor its ability to assimilate the byproducts of development is unlimited.[83] Defenders of the strong definition argue that integrated decision-making alone is not enough because it does not appreciate this ecological bottom line, nor the ethical obligation owed to future generations to not push the Earth's ecological capacities to the limit. On this view, sustainable development is not *ad hoc* balancing between economic, social and environmental objectives. Instead, ecological sustainability provides the 'normative core' of sustainable development such that economic prosperity and social justice can take place only above this ecological bottom line.[84]

[78] Government of Canada, 'Responsible Resource Development' (2012), www.nrcan.gc.ca/media-room/backgrounders/2012/3269.

[79] D Boyd, 'Sustainability Law: (R)Evolutionary Directions for the Future of Environmental Law' (2004) 14 *Journal of Environmental Law and Practice* 357, 364–65 (emphasising the forward-looking aspect of sustainable development); and CS Findlay, et al, 'Sustainability Lost: Comments on "Planning for a Sustainable Future: A Federal Sustainable Development Strategy for Canada"' (2010) 22 *Journal of Environmental Law and Practice* 77.

[80] JE Viñuales, 'The Rise and Fall of Sustainable Development' (2013) 22 *Review of European Community and International Environmental Law* 3, 6 and 7.

[81] Ibid, 7; and B Pardy, 'In Search of the Holy Grail of Environmental Law: A Rule to Solve the Problem' (2005) 1 *McGill International Journal of Sustainable Development Law and Policy* 29, 33 (sustainable development does not give us a clear roadmap for how to get to sustainability).

[82] Viñuales, 'The Rise and Fall' (above n 80) 6; Ross, 'Modern Interpretations' (above n 75) 35; and Wood et al, 'What Ever Happened to Canadian Environmental Law?' (above n 65) 993.

[83] Bosselmann, *The Principle of Sustainability* (above n 66) 53; Ross, 'Modern Interpretations' (above n 75) 37–38; and Voigt, *Sustainable Development* (above n 62) 38–46.

[84] Bosselmann, *The Principle of Sustainability* (above n 66) 53.

The difficulty with this latter approach to sustainable development is that there is no set of uncontroversial ecological limits that can guide decision-making. There may be broad support around some ecological thresholds—limiting global climate change to 1.5 or 2 degrees Celsius to prevent catastrophic effects, for example—but others will be unknown or fiercely contested. As argued in Part One of this book, there is no objective means for predicting these environmental limits. Added complexity arises when we attempt to determine how specific environmental decisions contribute to or undermine sustainability, which is also often far from clear.[85]

The result is that a strong definition of sustainable development seems either to require a prohibition on development in the face of ecological uncertainty (contrary to a plain reading of sustainable *development*)[86] or to dissolve into a potentially unconstrained balancing exercise. For example, the New Zealand Resource Management Act (1991) sets out a strong definition of sustainable management, to be applied to all administrative decision-making.[87] For decades, however, the definition was interpreted as allowing decision-makers to exercise their 'overall judgment'.[88] The latter raises the same concerns as weak definitions of sustainable development: there are seemingly no constraints on the *ad hoc* balancing that tends to favour continued development.

Despite these critiques of both the weak and strong definitions, we can see that sustainable development attempts to respond to features identified by the environmental emergency. It appropriately calls our attention to the fact that ecological systems have their own determinative if unpredictable processes that are not infinitely malleable. Its focus on integrated decision-making responds to the fact that we cannot reliably distinguish between benign regulatory decisions and those with the possibility of catastrophe. In addition, integration of economic, social and environmental considerations recognises the limits of any one expert discourse in understanding regulatory problems and proposing solutions. Sustainable development also highlights the fact that those affected by regulatory decisions are not

[85] Hydroelectric and nuclear energy development are good examples here because they are often promoted as remedies to climate change.

[86] Eg, *Bow Valley Naturalists Society v Canada (Minister of Canadian Heritage)*, [2001] 2 FC 461.

[87] Resource Management Act (NZ) (above n 68).

[88] These cases are discussed in Bosselmann, *The Principle of Sustainability* (above n 66) 64–66. The Supreme Court of New Zealand rejected the overall judgment approach in *Environmental Defence Society Inc v The New Zealand King Salmon Company Ltd* [2014] NZSC 38. In the Canadian context, see also W Lahey and M Doelle, 'Negotiating the Interface of Environmental and Economic Governance: Nova Scotia's Environmental Goals and Sustainable Prosperity Act' (2012) 35 *Dalhousie Law Journal* 1 (on how the strong goals of Nova Scotia Act are implemented through further planning requirements making it difficult to assess whether the goals of actual sustainability are being met).

necessarily those in the here and now. Sustainable development emphasises equity, regardless of geographic or temporal proximity to any one particular regulatory decision or project. The challenge, then, is to show that these core elements of sustainable development can meaningfully guide decision-making without attracting the problems of the strong or weak definitions.

A deliberative-democratic interpretation of sustainable development offers a way through the impasse of these competing conceptions of sustainable development. As we have just seen, both weak and strong versions of sustainable development focus on the three pillars of economy, environment and equity in decision-making. Weak sustainable development tends to sweep conflict under the rug in favour of economic interests. Strong sustainable development recognises conflict but, in the absence of objective guidance, defaults to inevitable trade-offs between economic interests and environmental protection. In short, both versions focus entirely on the proper balance and distribution of environmental and economic benefits and harms.

Deliberative-democratic principles, in contrast, encourage us to understand sustainable development as a concept that recognises individuals as responsible agents. They are not just passive recipients of environmental goods and harms but rather active participants who are entitled to justification.[89] Interpreting sustainable development in line with the deliberative-democratic ideals above, we must be prepared to reject certain reasons as impermissible because they are not, for example, reciprocal or general. Reciprocal reasons are those that are public-regarding (that is, they are not solely self-interested) and accessible to others.[90] General reasons are those that address all who are similarly affected by a decision.[91] A decision that excludes the consideration of future generations or far-away individuals who will nonetheless be impacted is not justified from this perspective. A deliberative-democratic interpretation of sustainable development pushes us, in other words, towards a radically inclusive understanding of public decision-making.[92]

The very purpose of sustainable development is to acknowledge the decisional stakes for those who are not typically represented in the decision-making process. Thus, deliberative-democratic principles require that decision-makers treat future generations and disadvantaged groups

[89] R Forst, *The Right to Justification: Elements of a Constructivist Theory of Justice*, J Flynn (trans) (New York, Columbia University Press, 2011) 200.

[90] Ibid, 6; and A Gutmann and D Thompson, *Why Deliberative Democracy?* (Princeton, Princeton University Press, 2004) 4.

[91] Forst, *The Right to Justification* (above n 89) 6.

[92] R Eckersley, *The Green State: Rethinking Democracy and Sovereignty* (Cambridge, MA, Massachusetts Institute of Technology Press, 2004) 137–38.

as 'moral constituents',[93] even if those decision-makers are not directly accountable to them in a democratic process. Indeed, deliberative democrats argue that deliberation promotes mutual respect and a greater sense of responsibility for collective decisions and their consequences.[94] A deliberative-democratic interpretation is thus consistent with the promises of environmental stewardship and intergenerational equity that sustainable development has thus far struggled to instil in the institutions tasked with its implementation.

From this perspective, sustainable development further requires institutional conditions that promote deliberation. Those institutions with a sustainable development mandate must be justified on the basis that they promote deliberation. Collaborative forums designed to bring together a broad range of issues and interests might be justified on the basis that they further public deliberation in a way that traditional hierarchical and siloed government bureaucracies cannot.[95] Decision-makers with a mandate to promote 'intergenerational solidarity'[96] might also be justified on the basis that they ensure the interests of future generations are addressed in the decision-making process. What is key in all cases is that both decisions and institutions operating under the banner of sustainable development are justified through public deliberation.

Requiring actual deliberation over sustainable development decisions avoids the dichotomy between naïve optimism and immediate trade-offs posed by the strong and weak versions above. Because deliberation seeks a 'rationally motivated consensus',[97] participants engage in a wide-ranging and genuine search for alternative 'win–win' scenarios. But it does not collapse into weak sustainable development if these do not exist. Instead, it narrows in on issues that are genuine points of conflict and permits trade-offs only as a last resort.[98]

[93] Gutmann and Thomspon, *Why Deliberative Democracy?* (above n 90) 37–38; and Forst, *The Right to Justification* (above n 89) 265.

[94] Forst, *The Right to Justification* (above n 89) 179.

[95] This point is made clearly in one of the last reports of Canada's National Round Table on The Environment and Economy (NRTEE), before it was defunded by the federal government in 2013. NRTEE was a direct response to WCED, *Our Common Future* (above n 61). It was an independent public policy advisory group that provided advice to the federal government on sustainable development policy. See National Round Table on the Environment and Public Policy Forum, 'Progress Through Process' (Ottawa, 2012).

[96] *Imperial Oil v Quebec*, 2003 SCC 58, [2003] 2 SCR 624, para 19.

[97] J Cohen, 'Deliberation and Democratic Legitimacy' in J Bonham and W Rehg (eds), *Deliberative Democracy: Essays on Reason and Politics* (Cambridge, MA, MIT Press, 1997) 75.

[98] Gutmann and Thomspon, *Why Deliberative Democracy?* (above n 90) 18; and HS Richardson, *Democratic Autonomy: Public Reasoning about the Ends of Policy* (Oxford, Oxford University Press, 2002) ch 15 (on how majority rule is a temporary closure device). *Environmental Defence Society* (above n 88), paras 130–31. For examples of this in practice, see: RB Gibson, 'Beyond the Pillars: Sustainability Assessment as a Framework for Effective Integration of Social, Economic and Ecological Considerations in Significant Decision-Making' (2006) 8 *Journal of Environmental Assessment Policy and Management* 259.

This emphasis on actual deliberation poses two potential problems, however. First, actual deliberation is unlikely to generate consensus. Where deliberation leads to decisions that are substantively unjust—that is, they rest on reasons that are not reciprocal or general—the rule-of-law project requires appropriate institutional channels for contestation.[99] Contestation enables other public institutions (conventionally, the courts on judicial review) to require these decisions to be justified. Even still, publicly justified decisions typically have dissenters. As we have seen, deliberative democrats adopt a pragmatic stance that emphasises the provisionality of deliberations. So long as future opportunities exist to revisit decisions and to seek reforms, a lack of consensus does not undermine the overall commitment to deliberative democracy.

A second possible challenge comes from the complex nature of the problems to be deliberated. Cass Sunstein, a deliberative democrat, has argued that regulatory issues are best addressed exclusively by experts through determinative methods of cost–benefit analysis.[100] Unlike at the constitutional level, where disagreement occurs over *beliefs*, he argues, regulating poses the problem of *risk*. Experts, not laypersons, according to Sunstein, are in the best position to determine the best course of action in the face of these risks. He has argued that the complexity of risk assessment exacerbates cognitive biases that lead laypersons to irrational decisions.[101] Instead, Sunstein has argued for non-deliberative decision-making techniques, namely cost–benefit analysis.[102] As we will now see, the precautionary principle responds to Sunstein's critique of a deliberative interpretation of sustainable development.

B. The Precautionary Principle

> *Where there are threats of serious or irreversible damage, lack of full scientific certainty shall not be used as a reason for postponing cost-effective measures to prevent environmental degradation.*[103]

The precautionary principle is perhaps the most familiar and the most contested principle of environmental law.[104] The principle originated in

[99] See also Forst, *The Right to Justification* (above n 89) 182.

[100] Compare CR Sunstein, *Designing Democracy: What Constitutions Do* (Oxford, Oxford University Press, 2001) and CR Sunstein, *Risk and Reason: Safety, Law, and the Environment* (Cambridge, Cambridge University Press, 2002).

[101] Sunstein is deeply pessimistic about non-expert perceptions of risk: ibid, 33–49. At 76 he writes, 'Ordinary people do not show a richer rationality.'

[102] Ibid, 106–7.

[103] UN General Assembly, 'Rio Declaration' (above n 67) Principle 15.

[104] D Bodansky, 'Deconstructing the Precautionary Principle' in DD Caron and HN Scheiber (eds), *Bringing New Law to Ocean Waters* (Leiden, Martinus Nijhoff, 2004) 381 (described as one the ten commandments of international environmental law).

German environmental policy but rose to prominence with its above articulation in the Rio Declaration on Environment and Development in 1992,[105] and it was rapidly taken up by domestic and international environmental laws in the decades that followed. The sentiment behind the principle, which is often described as 'better safe than sorry', is hard to disagree with—much like the broad understanding of sustainable development. Precaution simply represents the idea that when we are faced with potentially serious but uncertain threats, it is better to take early action to avoid such a worst-case scenario. What the principle requires of administrative decision-makers, as we will now see, is rather less clear.

The precautionary principle is well represented in Canadian environmental law. It can be found in the preambles of many federal environmental statutes and some provincial statutes, and is a substantive provision in several federal statutes.[106] These legislative statements are consistent with the Supreme Court's recognition that the precautionary principle is an emerging norm of customary international law[107] and a federal guidance framework that identifies precaution as a 'legitimate and distinctive decision-making approach within risk management'.[108] Despite this clear evidence that precaution operates as a guiding principle in Canadian environmental law, there is a widespread sense amongst legal academics that its potential has yet to be realised.[109]

The principle's disappointing track record is partially due to confusion over its ambiguous administrative requirements. I will address this confusion in a moment. But first I contend that the principle is best understood as a deliberative-democratic response to the problem posed by Sunstein. Sunstein's argument, in short, is that experts are in the best position to make determinations about environmental risk through rational and comprehensive methodologies such as risk assessment and cost–benefit analysis. In contrast to these risk methodologies, Sunstein has argued that the precautionary principle isolates particularly visible risks in the decision-making process for special treatment.[110] To take one example, the Lac-Mégantic disaster in Quebec might lead laypersons to 'over-estimate' the risks of

[105] J Peel, *The Precautionary Principle in Practice* (Annandale, Federation Press, 2005) 16.

[106] For example, CEAA 2012 (above n 19) s 4; Species at Risk Act, SC 2002, c 29, ss 38 and 41; Canadian Environmental Protection Act 1999, SC 1999, c 33, ss 2, 6(1.1) and 76.1; Pest Control Products Act, SC 2002, c 28, s 20; and Oceans Act, SC 1996, c 31, s 30.

[107] *114957 Canada Ltée (Spraytech, Société d'arrosage) v Hudson (Town)*, 2001 SCC 40, [2001] 2 SCR 241, paras 30–32; and *Castonguay Blasting Ltd v Ontario (Environment)*, 2013 SCC 52, [2013] 3 SCR 323, para 20.

[108] Privy Council Office of Canada, 'A Framework for the Application of Precaution in Science-Based Decision Making about Risk' (2003) 4.1.

[109] Eg, C Tollefson and J Thornback, 'Litigating the Precautionary Principle in Domestic Courts' (2008) 19 *Journal of Environmental Law and Practice* 33, 57.

[110] CR Sunstein, *Laws of Fear: Beyond the Precautionary Principle* (Cambridge, Cambridge University Press, 2005).

oil transport by rail.[111] According to Sunstein, the precautionary principle encourages this kind of cognitive bias and provides a justification for decision-makers to act on misplaced public fears. In contrast, Sunstein argues that proper risk assessment corrects these biases by attending to risks on all sides of the equation.[112] Once we acknowledge the full complement of risks, he argues that the principle becomes incoherent and paralysing because, taken literally, it 'forbids all courses of action, including regulation'.[113]

From a deliberative-democratic perspective, however, the objective of the precautionary principle is not to dictate any particular outcome. Rather, it is simply to highlight the inherent limits in any expert analysis of future harm.[114] Risk assessment may be able to adequately address gaps within existing scientific knowledge;[115] but as we saw in chapter one, ecosystems are complex and adaptive systems characterised by unforeseeability and indeterminacy. This kind of complexity means that there are questions that no scientific methodology can feasibly answer. There are also questions we do not yet know to ask. Put differently, the precautionary principle identifies and corrects a different cognitive bias than the one Sunstein has pointed out. Precaution ensures that 'no evidence of harm' is not treated as equivalent to 'no harm'. The precautionary principle is not, as Sunstein has argued, an (arbitrary) alternative to risk assessment. The principle addresses a fundamentally different question: what does a decision-maker do with a necessarily incomplete risk assessment in hand?[116]

Fundamentally, the precautionary principle is an attempt to understand how public decisions can be justified in the absence of a solid factual foundation.[117] This means:

> [The] principle regulates the reasons for a decision and the process by which a decision is made. … This is because regulating outcomes (beyond requiring

[111] On 6 July 2013, the breaks on a parked train failed, causing the train to speed downhill and derail in the centre of Lac-Mégantic, Quebec. The train, carrying over six million litres of bitumen, exploded, killing forty-seven people and destroying much of the town. See Transportation Safety Board of Canada, 'Lac-Mégantic Runaway Train and Derailment Investigation Summary' (2014), http://www.tsb.gc.ca/eng/rapports-reports/rail/2013/r13d0054/r13d0054-r-es.asp.

[112] Sunstein, *Laws of Fear* (above n 110) 58–59.

[113] Ibid, 26.

[114] Peel, *The Precautionary Principle* (above n 105) ch 3.

[115] For example, a scientific gap arises when we do not know whether a particular pollutant will interact with another to harm the environment. This is a gap 'within' science because it is a question we know to ask, and we may be able to approximate an answer to through known scientific methodologies.

[116] J Ellis, 'Overexploitation of a Valuable Resource? New Literature on the Precautionary Principle' (2006) 17 *European Journal of International Law* 445, 453; and Richardson, *Democratic Autonomy* (above n 98) 234ff.

[117] E Fisher, 'Review: *Laws of Fear: Beyond the Precautionary Principle*' (2006) *Modern Law Review* 288, 289.

> decision makers to pursue broad statutory goals) is logically impossible in cases of scientific uncertainty.'[118]

In practice, this translates to a central preoccupation with the relationship between expert and non-expert views of scientific uncertainty. No precautionary principle proponent is anti-science; all seek sound environmental regulation that is based on the best understanding of the problem. Defenders of the principle, instead, are concerned with scientific hubris and the 'action-orientation' of expert methodologies.[119]

A deliberative-democratic interpretation of the precautionary principle promises to open up these expert discourses to public scrutiny and input. Theories of deliberative democracy understand that expert decision-making is essential in any complex society.[120] But in a deliberative system, expert decisions must reflect deliberative principles—ie, they must be justified on the basis of reasons that those subject to the decision cannot reasonably reject. Deliberative democrats argue that the best way to ensure justified decisions is through representative and inclusive deliberative forums. These expose areas of uncertainty and encourage a broad search for agreeable alternatives rather than a narrow determination of 'acceptable risk'.[121] Kerry Whiteside has argued that

> linking precaution to deliberative democracy is intended to imply that the processes that trigger and implement precautionary measures should include regularized

[118] E Fisher and R Harding, 'The Precautionary Principle and Administrative Constitutionalism: The Development of Frameworks for Applying the Precautionary Principle' in E Fisher, J Jones and R von Schomberg (eds), *Implementing the Precautionary Principle: Perspectives and Prospects* (Cheltenham, Edward Elgar, 2006) 115.

[119] KH Whiteside, *Precautionary Politics: Principle and Practice in Confronting Environmental Risk* (Cambridge, MA, MIT Press, 2006) 126–28; and F Fischer, 'Environmental Regulation and Risk–Benefit Analysis: From Technical to Deliberative Policy Making' in R Paehlke and D Torgerson (eds), *Managing Leviathan: Environmental Politics and the Administrative State*, 2nd edn (Peterborough, Broadview Press, 2005) 67–68. See also B Wynne, 'May the Sheep Safely Graze? A Reflexive View of the Expert–Lay Knowledge Divide' in S Lash, B Szerszynski and B Wynne (eds), *Risk, Environment and Modernity: Towards a New Ecology* (London, Sage, 1998) 78 (on how the expert/layperson binary needs to be problematised).

[120] J Parkinson and J Mansbridge, *Deliberative Systems: Deliberative Democracy at the Large Scale* (Cambridge, Cambridge University Press, 2012) 14–16; Gutmann and Thompson, *Why Deliberative Democracy?* (above n 90) 5; Richardson, *Democratic Autonomy* (above n 98) 222 (specifically on administrative agency expertise). In a more general sense, a role for expertise in a deliberative democratic system has been articulated by Habermas as a two-track system, where conditions of ideal deliberation are only required for those core structures of a constitutional democracy. See J Habermas, *Between Facts and Norms* (Cambridge, MA, MIT Press, 1996) 300.

[121] Whiteside, *Precautionary Politics* (above n 119) 57; S Jasanoff, 'A Living Legacy: The Precautionary Ideal in American Law' in JA Tickner (ed), *Precaution: Environmental Science and Preventive Public Policy* (Washington, DC, Island Press, 2003) 237. See Dayna Scott for a nice analysis of precautionary decision-making in the West Nile case and how it led to a broad search for alternatives: DN Scott, 'When Precaution Points Two Ways: Confronting "West Nile Fever"' (2005) 20 *Canadian Journal of Law and Society* 27. The emphasis on public participation is consistent throughout the precautionary principle literature. See also Peel,

> forms of nonexpert citizen participation and collective judgment. The objective is to make citizen deliberation a formal part of the process, just as regulatory bodies systematically include scientific and economic advisers.[122]

A deliberative interpretation of the precautionary principle cannot dictate specific public participation procedures in the abstract nor offer any universal reasons for preferring expert to non-expert views. But what it does offer is a renewed attention to the need for decision-makers to offer reasons for their decisions. This obligation to give reasons extends to the ultimate decision in which decision-makers must highlight points of uncertainty and how these were addressed. It also extends to procedural decisions that restrict the deliberative capacity of the decision-making forum.[123] Through this obligation to justify decisions on terms which individuals can both understand and reasonably accept, precaution in principle operates to rebuild trust between expert decision-makers and those who must live with the consequences of these expert decisions.[124]

We are now in a position to dispel two common misconceptions about the precautionary principle that persist in Canadian environmental law. The first misconception is that the precautionary principle compels a decision-maker to take a specific course of action; the second equates the precautionary principle with a reversed burden of proof.

The first misconception can be addressed and dismissed quickly. The Federal Court and Federal Court of Appeal have repeatedly asserted that the precautionary principle would have a 'paralysing effect' on development.[125]

The Precautionary Principle (above n 105); Fisher and Harding, 'The Precautionary Principle and Administrative Constitutionalism' (above n 118); G Cartier, 'Le principe de précaution et la déférence judiciare en droit administratif' (2002) 43 *Les Cahiers de droit* 79; J Benidickson et al, 'Practicing Precaution and Adaptive Management: Legal, Institutional and Procedural Dimensions of Scientific Uncertainty, Final Report' (Institute of the Environment, University of Ottawa, forthcoming) F17.

[122] Whiteside, *Precautionary Politics* (above n 119) 119. Contrast this with a much narrower interpretation—that precaution should lead to greater margins of safety within expert analysis and that has nothing to do with public participation: DA Farber, 'Probabilities Behaving Badly: Complexity Theory and Environmental Uncertainty' (2003) 37 *UC Davis Law Review* 145, 168.

[123] Benidickson et al, 'Practicing Precaution and Adaptive Management' (above n 121) F21.

[124] Trust is crucial to accounts of deliberative-democratic administrative decision-making: Fischer, 'Environmental Regulation and Risk–Benefit Analysis' (above n 119) 71–72 (conflicting scientific expertise leads citizens to conduct their own socio-cultural analyses); and Mansbridge and Parkinson, *Deliberative Systems* (above n 120). See Scott, 'When Precaution Points Two Ways' (above n 121) for a positive example of trust in public decision-makers.

[125] *Canadian Parks and Wilderness Society v Canada (Minister of Canadian Heritage)*, 2003 FCA 197, [2003] FCJ 703, para 24; *Pembina Institute for Appropriate Development v Canada (Attorney General)*, 2008 FC 302, [2008] FCJ No 324, para 32; *Greenpeace Canada v Canada (Attorney General)*, 2014 FC 463, [2014] FCJ No 515, para 83 (repeating the quote, although the Court in this case actually does properly apply the precautionary principle even if reluctant to name it as such). The idea that a 'strong version' of precaution would compel the state to take action to eliminate risk persists in the precautionary principle literature more broadly. Olivier

As we have seen, this claim is not supported by the language in the Rio Declaration, by any specific statutory expressions of the principle in Canadian environmental law, or least of all, by a deliberative interpretation of the principle. As a result, the Federal Courts have failed to seriously engage with the merits of the principle and its potential for informing administrative law requirements of reasonableness and fairness.

Accepting that the principle does not operate as a prohibition on development, environmental law scholars have sought an alternative interpretation in order to give the precautionary principle 'some specific work to do'.[126] Most Canadian legal academics have settled on the idea that the principle requires a reversal of the burden of proof.[127] In their view, the principle requires that the proponents of potentially harmful activities demonstrate an absence of harm. This is supported by the substantive provisions of some environmental statutes that combine a statement of the precautionary principle with a requirement to reverse the burden of proof.[128] However, this narrow interpretation of the principle seems to confuse the precautionary principle with a specific precautionary measure.[129] It also reduces a principle

Godard has helpfully distinguished between the precautionary principle and the principle of abstention, an impossible principle promoted by some environmental advocates that requires abstaining from all activities that could cause harm: O Godard, 'The Precautionary Principle and Catastrophism on Tenterhooks: Lessons from a Constitutional Reform in France' in Fisher et al (eds), *Implementing the Precautionary Principle* (above n 118) 65–66. The principle of abstention is vociferously promoted by many environmental non-governmental organisations in international environmental campaigns, which has given this 'strong' articulation of the principle some visibility. See, eg, Earth Charter Commission, 'The Earth Charter' (2000), www.earthcharterinaction.org/content/pages/Read-the-Charter.html, Principle 6.

[126] Tollefson and Thornback, 'Litigating the Precautionary Principle' (above n 109) 34.

[127] This seems to be the default position on the precautionary principle in Canada. See ibid; DL VanderZwaag, 'The Precautionary Principle in Environmental Law and Policy: Elusive Rhetoric and First Embraces' (1998) 8 *Journal of Environmental Law and Practice* 355; L Collins, 'An Ecologically Literate Reading of the Canadian Charter of Rights and Freedoms' (2009) 26 *Windsor Review of Legal and Social Issues* 7, pt 7; Benidickson et al, 'Practicing Precaution and Adaptive Management' (above n 121); and N Chalifour, 'A (Pre) Cautionary Tale about the Kearl Oil Sands Decision: The Significance of *Pembina Institute for Appropriate Development, et al v Canada (Attorney-General)* for the Future of Environmental Assessment' (2009) 5 *McGill International Journal of Sustainable Development Law and Policy* 251. Compare with Scott, 'When Precaution Points Two Ways' (above n 121) (who does not equate the principle with the burden of proof). As the precautionary principle lends itself to a variety of interpretations across a variety of regulatory contexts, there is support for the burden of proof interpretation in the international scholarship. Fisher documents some of this support in E Fisher, *Risk Regulation and Administrative Constitutionalism* (Oxford, Hart Publishing, 2007) chs 4 and 6.

[128] Eg, Pest Control Products Act (above n 106) s 7(6); and Privy Council Office of Canada, 'A Framework for the Application of Precaution' (above n 108) 8: 'Overall, the responsibility for providing the sound scientific basis should rest with the party who is taking an action associated with a risk of serious harm.' But at the international scale, the association between burden of proof and the principle is not as well founded. See Ellis, 'Overexploitation?' (above n 116) 459.

[129] Unlike the criminal context, there is no universal burden of proof in administrative law. Statutory schemes impose a variety of different 'burdens' and 'standards' in the course of

that at its best requires a deliberative process in which decision-makers exercise 'complex judgment'[130] to a linear series of binary determinations: is there uncertainty about a threat? [Yes/no.] Can the proponent of risk rebut this assumption? [Yes/no.] And so on.[131]

A deliberative interpretation of the precautionary principle would lead to a variety of institutional arrangements, many of which would have no relationship to a juridical burden-of-proof approach. At a very basic level, the precautionary principle requires transparency about potential risks to allow the public to scrutinise and contest risk assumptions made by administrative decision-makers.[132] Formalised mechanisms of public participation, required by the principle, could include public notice-and-comment periods,[133] active intervenor status in assessment processes or negotiated regulation-making[134] or, in especially high stakes instances, perhaps even a citizens' assembly working in concert with an expert body.[135] Precaution might even require wholly separate institutions, such as public watchdogs

complex regulatory proceedings. This point is made by several academic defenders of precaution: Peel, *The Precautionary Principle* (above n 105) 155; J Jones and S Bronitt, 'The Burden and Standard of Proof in Environmental Regulation: The Precautionary Principle in an Australian Administrative Context' in Fisher et al (eds), *Implementing the Precautionary Principle* (above n 118) 137; and Fisher, *Risk Regulation and Administrative Constitutionalism* (above n 127) 44. Even in a quasi-judicial hearing such as a pipeline approval hearing, the regulator in principle is not adjudicating between adversarial parties but rather reaching a determination about the public interest after considering multifaceted factors.

130 Whiteside, *Precautionary Politics* (above n 119) 57.

131 This conflation between principle and measure has resulted in some bizarre jurisprudence in Australia, where courts rely on scientific evidence to prove scientific uncertainty. If this threshold is not met, then the courts will fall back on an inchoate notion of 'caution' as opposed to the more rigorous requirement of precaution that would result in a reversed burden of proof: *Telstra Corp Ltd v Hornsby Shire Council*, [2006] NSWLEC 285; and DE Fisher, *Australian Environmental Law: Norms, Principles and Rules*, 3rd edn (Pyrmont, Thomson Reuters, 2014) 7.60. For an interesting analysis of how *Telstra* is an attempt to reconcile two visions of administrative constitutionalism, see Fisher, *Risk Regulation and Administrative Constitutionalism* (above n 127) 154–60. In Canada, the dominant judicial approach seems to be that the precautionary principle is one factor to be considered. See, eg, *Sierra Club Canada v Ontario (Ministry of Natural Resources)*, 2011 ONSC 4655, [2011] OJ No 4373; *Lake Waseosa Ratepayers' Association v Pieper*, 2008 CLB 1707, [2008] OJ No 728 (Ont SCDC); and *Western Canada Wilderness Committee v British Columbia (Ministry of Forests, South Island Forest District)*, 2003 BCCA 403, [2003] BCJ No 1581. It is therefore understandable that Tollefson and Thornback view the *Telstra* approach as an improvement: Tollefson and Thornback, 'Litigating the Precautionary Principle' (above n 109).

132 Whiteside, *Precautionary Politics* (above n 119) 135–36. The Pest Control Products Act (above n 106) allows individuals to trigger a review of regulations and products in light of new information. The Court has interpreted this provision fairly generously: *Weir v Canada (Minister of Health)*, 2011 FC 1322.

133 D Dyzenhaus, 'Law as Justification: Etienne Mureinik's Conception of Legal Culture' (1998) 14 *South African Journal on Human Rights* 11, 35.

134 Richardson, *Democratic Autonomy* (above n 98) 220–22.

135 Cartier, 'Le principe de précaution' (above n 121) 99–100 (observing that citizen assemblies are the norm in Europe).

or auditors, that work alongside expert regulators and subject their decisions to expert peer review.[136] It is difficult to see how any of these innovations could be generated from a narrow requirement on decision-makers to reverse the burden of proof.

The deliberative interpretation of precaution is not without its own challenges. Taken seriously, a deliberative interpretation undermines defenders' attempts to limit the principle's application to issues that may have serious or irreversible impacts.[137] If the precautionary principle is best understood as an extension of deliberative democratic theory, there is no reason to limit the principle's impact to special cases. Recall that the goal of deliberative democracy is a system of governance in which free and equal citizens actively participate in decision-making processes. Furthermore, the concept of the environmental emergency emphasises our inability to reliably determine in advance which issues contain the possibility of environmental catastrophe. Indeed, the principle might be *most* beneficial in situations that do not at first glance seem to meet its threshold requirement.[138]

The answer again lies in rejecting the tendency to view the precautionary principle in black-and-white, all-or-nothing terms. The theory of the administrative state that underpins the precautionary principle—that is an administrative state governed by a democratic conception of the rule of law—is always at work. Public decision-makers must always strive to fulfil this aspiration. But when decision-makers are faced with novel issues novel risks or the foreseeable chance of a catastrophe, the precautionary principle operates to strengthen these public-justification requirements.[139] Precaution, in other words, demands more intensive procedures that enable thorough deliberation. It demands more comprehensive reasons detailing sources of uncertainty and how the decision-maker accounted for these

[136] Well-orchestrated and timely campaigns by trusted institutions might be able to preempt or mitigate polarisation on controversial topics. See Whiteside, *Precautionary Politics* (above n 119) 133 on parliamentary commissions or permanent advisory bodies fulfilling this role.

[137] This seems to be the one of the few points of consensus amongst all defenders of precaution: it only applies to specific environmental decisions. See Tollefson and Thornback, 'Litigating the Precautionary Principle' (above n 109) 55 (defending Telstra against Peel's critiques); Peel, *The Precautionary Principle* (above n 105) 221 (critiquing the using of the threshold test but retaining it in her own defence of the principle); Whiteside, *Precautionary Politics* (above n 119) 123; and Sunstein, *Laws of Fear* (above n 110) 114 (defending an 'Anti-Catastrophe Principle').

[138] See, eg, D Bodansky, 'Scientific Uncertainty and the Precautionary Principle' (1991) 33 *Environment: Science and Policy for Sustainable Development* 4, 43; and B Wynne, 'Uncertainty and Environmental Learning' (1992) 2 *Global Environmental Change* 111, 118.

[139] J-P Dupuy, 'Complexity and Uncertainty: A Prudential Approach to Nanotechnology' in Health and Consumer Protection Directorate General of the European Commission (ed), *Nanotechnologies: A Preliminary Risk Analysis on the Basis of a Workshop Organized in Brussels, 1–2 March 2004* (Brussels, European Commission, 2004) 82 (arguing that precaution reveals we are stuck in a regulatory paradox in which we are under a constant obligation to attempt to anticipate the consequences of our actions, even though it is impossible to do so).

And it demands closer scrutiny of these justifications to ensure that potentially catastrophic decisions have been made in accordance with democratic principles and the rule of law.

C. Environmental Principles and the Common Law

I have argued that the environmental principles of sustainable development and precaution should be interpreted in line with the ideals of deliberative democracy. This interpretation allows us to narrow in on some more specific requirements of these expansive principles. In particular, we have seen that deliberative-democratic theory requires that institutions tasked with sustainable development objectives must be publicly justified—that is, they must operate in a way that promotes deliberation either locally (within the institution), systemically (in other democratic institutions) or both. The deliberative interpretation of sustainable development further requires decision-makers to attend to the interests of future generations and disadvantaged groups who will be affected regardless of their geographic location. Both sustainable development and precaution require formalised mechanisms for public participation to counter expert discourses. Precaution emphasises the importance of this requirement where there is uncertainty about the threat of a catastrophe. Taken together, these requirements safeguard the autonomy of individuals—their capacity as rational and self-determining agents—even in complex decision-making contexts such as environmental decision-making.

The effect of these environmental principles therefore is to inform the common law requirements of reasonableness and fairness.[140] Sustainable development and precaution are not empty platitudes ('proceed with caution'), restatements of the status quo or additional factors for a decision-maker to take into account. Rather, they inform the requirement of public justification in environmental law, a requirement that respects legal subjects as active participants in the construction and maintenance of their system of governance. Public decisions therefore must be publicly justified on the basis that they uphold this status.

[140] For an argument that the precautionary principle is an independent element of reasonableness, even in the absence of a statutory statement of the principle, see Cartier, 'Le principe de précaution' (above n 121). Understanding environmental principles in this way helps respond to Thomas Poole's critique of Dyzenhaus' articulation of common law constitutionalism. Poole argues that common law principles are too 'soft-edged' or malleable to provide any sort of blueprint for decision-makers: T Poole, 'Constitutional Exceptionalism and the Common Law' (2009) 7 *International Journal of Constitutional Law* 247, 263–68. As we saw above in ch 4, Dyzenhaus has not claimed to offer a blueprint. Rather, he has offered core principles that are necessarily informed by their context. The normative context includes principles of sustainable development and precaution that provide a measure of sharpness to these allegedly amorphous principles.

It is not possible to offer a definitive account of either sustainable development or precaution. Both principles are invoked across a diverse and wide range of regulatory contexts. Specific statutory requirements, the nature of the particular regulatory problem, and actual deliberations amongst participants will all shape the specific requirements of these principles in any given instance. As we will see in a moment, the principles are part of the National Energy Board's regulatory framework and therefore inform its obligation of public justification.

The foregoing interpretation of sustainable development and precaution raises a prior question, however, about whether the existing institutional arrangements in Canada for assessing major pipelines could be publicly justified. It is not clear that they could be. As we will see in the next section, there are severe limitations within the existing NEB process that undermine any claim that it complies with the rule-of-law requirement of public justification. At the very least, it is easy to imagine institutional reforms that would better fulfil the deliberative ideals of sustainable development and precaution. The dramatic expansion of Alberta oil sands development facilitated by transcontinental pipelines ought to have been addressed directly rather than disjointedly and belatedly during individual pipeline proposal hearings.[141] We could imagine a comprehensive process in which the full social and ecological effects of oil sands development are assessed directly through known methods of sustainability assessment.[142] Instead of beginning with an assumption about the economic benefits of oil sands development, such an assessment might ask the prior questions of: 'How have we reached the conclusion that the tar [oil] sands create wealth? What kind of wealth? Wealth for whom?'[143] A citizens' assembly might then deliberate on the results of the assessment attending to both known and speculative sources of uncertainty. After hearing expert testimony, they might propose a range of conditions under which development would be acceptable and offer recommendations to Cabinet or the NEB that would then be responsible for giving effect to those conditions when specific projects are proposed.

This of course would require the legislature to take the lead in enabling a rigorously and publicly justified regulatory process. In certain political climates this might appear to be an exercise of wishful thinking. But these reforms draw from prior experience. Sustainability assessment and broad public participation were central to the environmental assessment

[141] I am far from the first to suggest this obvious failing in the oil sands regulatory process. See, eg, Woolley, 'Legitimating Public Policy' (above n 60) 181–82.

[142] Gibson, 'Beyond the Pillars' (above n 98).

[143] H McLeod-Kilmurray and G Smith, 'Unsustainable Development in Canada: Environmental Assessment, Cost–Benefit Analysis, and Environmental Justice in the Tar Sands' (2010) 21 *Journal of Environmental Law and Practice* 65, 67.

of the proposed Mackenzie Valley Pipeline.[144] British Columbia relied on a citizens' assembly for electoral reform;[145] a similar model was proposed for Australian climate change reform.[146] Ontario's impressive reform efforts to protect its sources of drinking water have been founded on local land-use planning that combines public deliberation and scientific expertise.[147] All of these examples come much closer to fulfilling rule-of-law aspirations than the existing regulatory scheme. The fact that they have been implemented in the past suggests that they can be implemented again and hopefully better as we learn from prior experience.

Though the existing regulatory process for approving pipelines falls far short of this ideal, understanding the rule of law as a requirement of public justification means that institutions must continue to strive to uphold the rule of law within their own institutional constraints and should be susceptible to intervention by a reviewing institution when they do not. We will now see that public justification demands much more from the NEB and the Federal Court of Appeal.

III. PUBLICLY JUSTIFYING THE PIPELINES

The NEB is governed by the CEAA, the NEBA and core common law principles of fairness and reasonableness and the requirement of independence. The CEAA explicitly directs the NEB to 'promote sustainable development in order to achieve or maintain a healthy environment and a healthy economy'[148] and dictates that it 'must exercise [its] powers in a manner that protects the environment … and appl[y] the precautionary principle'.[149] The NEB is also subject to the Federal Sustainable Development Act and, by virtue of its combined mandate to consider economic, social and environmental impacts of proposed pipelines, reflects sustainable development's

[144] Canadian Environmental Assessment Agency (CEAA), 'Joint Review Panel for the Mackenzie Gas Project' (2005), www.ceaa.gc.ca/default.asp?lang=En&xml=99CDFBEE-2F6F-49BF-99C9-38AB1FF8C281. Discussion about the desirability of this pipeline has been ongoing for a significant period. See TR Berger, 'Northern Frontier, Northern Homeland: The Report of the Mackenzie Valley Pipeline Inquiry, Vol 1' (Supply and Services Canada, 1977).

[145] ME Warren and H Pearse, *Designing Deliberative Democracy: The British Columbia Citizens' Assembly* (Cambridge, Cambridge University Press, 2008).

[146] 'PM Dumps Citizens' Assembly on Climate Change', *Australian* (7 October 2010), www.theaustralian.com.au/national-affairs/climate/pm-dumps-citizens-assembly-on-climate-change/story-e6frg6xf-1225935582575.

[147] See Ontario Government, 'Ontario Source Protection' (2014/2017), www.ontario.ca/environment-and-energy/source-protection. See also P Hania, 'Climate Change and the Protection of Drinking Water in Ontario: An Opportunity to Adopt Adaptive Management?' (2011) 22 *Journal of Environmental Law and Practice* 167.

[148] CEAA 2012 (above n 19) 4(1)(h). At s 2, the Act further adopts the language from WCED, *Our Common Future* (above n 61), not the weaker version from the FSDA (above n 68).

[149] CEAA 2012 (above n 19) s4(2).

central element of integrated decision-making.[150] The statutory provisions on sustainable development and precaution do not impose specific requirements on the NEB. This means that the deliberative-democratic interpretation of these principles should prevail. In the absence of unambiguous statutory language to the contrary, these principles operate to inform common law requirements of fairness and reasonableness that govern the NEB's assessment process. In short, for the NEB to act with legal authority, it must publicly justify its decisions on the basis of reasonableness and fairness, understood in light of sustainable development and precaution. Moreover, concerns about the NEB's independence need to be taken seriously by reviewing institutions because they directly implicate the ability of the NEB to generate fair and reasoned decisions.

At this juncture it is important to recall the central argument of chapter five that it may not be the courts that are in the best position to make some or all of these determinations. Some other form of public institution may be necessary, though for ease of reference I will refer to this reviewing body as a court, since judicial review is at present the only review mechanism available.[151]

I take up each of the issues identified in section I above that go to the fairness, reasonableness and independence of the NEB's assessment and recommendation process. This division between fairness, reasonableness and independence, however, is somewhat artificial. The fairness of the process is genuine only if it includes the possibility of influencing the substantive outcome. Moreover, procedural choices are not neutral or technical decisions but rather require justification by the decision-makers. And, particularly in complex regulatory cases, what counts as a reasonable decision will depend in large measure on the processes relied on to arrive at that determination.[152]

150 Sustainable development and precaution only feature in the Northern Gateway Pipeline JRP; they are absent in all other NEB decisions. In the JRP Report, the panel notes that sustainable development informed its approach to the design of public hearings: National Energy Board (Gateway Panel), 'Considerations, Volume 2' (above n 35) 4. The Report also states that the JRP took a precautionary approach (5). However, as becomes clear later in the Report, the JRP used the phrase 'precautionary approach' rather indiscriminately. It is most frequently used to describe how Enbridge has proposed to construct and operate the pipeline and terminal, rather than the regulatory process for evaluating Enbridge's claims. See especially 147 and 168 (referring to Enbridge's precautionary approach to reduce the likelihood of a marine spill to as low as reasonably practicable).

151 NEBA (above n 18) s 22(4). The various recommendations and decisions that result from the requirements under the NEBA and CEAA are subject either to a statutory appeal with leave of the Federal Court of Appeal or to judicial review by the Federal Court of Appeal. Canadian courts have accepted that the methodology of review is the same for both appeals and judicial review applications: *Gitxaala Nation v Canada* (above n 37) para 76; and *McLean v British Columbia (Securities Commission)*, 2013 SCC 67, [2013] 3 SCR 895.

152 Richardson, *Democratic Autonomy* (above n 98) 228: the very fact that we need experts to help make decisions means that trust cannot be fully based on their reliability. We therefore must trust the way they make decisions. See also Wynne, 'May the Sheep Safely Graze?' (above n 119) 57 (arguing that risk perception is primarily *relational*, that is, based on the perceived

This section ends with a consideration of the NEB's independence, as this provides a convenient lens through which to address two broader issues: the intensity of scrutiny by the courts, and what happens when statutory language clearly purports to exempt decision-makers from the rule-of-law project.

A. Fairness

The first section of this chapter identified two specific issues with respect to the NEB's process for assessing public proposals: denial of oral hearings and of oral cross-examination of a proponent's application, and its restrictive interpretation of the standing requirement for members of the public to participate in the assessment process. I now argue that the NEB has failed to justify these decisions by offering reasons that adequately reflect the common law principles of fairness and reasonableness.

i. Written Hearing

The first issue is whether the NEB has adequately justified its decision to hold predominantly written hearings. Recall from section I above that the 'hearing' for a pipeline approval proceeds on the basis of the proponent's detailed written application. The NEB's assessment of that application takes place through an exchange of written correspondence between the Board members, intervenors and the proponent. This written correspondence contains requests to the proponent to submit more information, conflicting evidence by intervenors and information about how interested parties will be affected by the pipeline approval. Intervenors unsuccessfully challenged the Trans Mountain Hearing Order, which denied them any opportunity to orally cross-examine the proponent on the project proposal.[153] The Hearing Order also restricted oral argument to a few days of closing argument *after* the NEB had issued its draft conditions that would apply in the event of an approval. Intervenors argued this process denied any meaningful opportunity to debate whether the pipeline should be approved in the first place. The NEB held that the process satisfied the requirements of procedural fairness. It reasoned that it was not conducting 'a criminal or civil trial' but rather

trustworthiness of the expert institutions tasked with controlling the risk); and L Heinzerling, 'Pragmatists and Environmentalists' (2000) 113 *Harvard Law Review* 1421, 1444 (emphasising the significance of the context of environmental decision-making and, in particular, whether decisions are made under conditions of trust).

[153] National Energy Board (NEB), 'Notices of Motion from Ms Robyn Allan and Ms Elizabeth May to Include Cross-Examination of Witnesses' (7 May 2014), OH-001-2014, Ruling No 14 [hereafter 'TMX Cross-Exam Ruling'].

'a process for gathering and testing evidence for the Board's preparation, as an expert tribunal, of its recommendation' of whether the proposal is in the public interest.[154]

The requirement of fairness owed by the Board, however, is not informed by the criminal or civil trial context. Instead it is informed by a deliberative-democratic interpretation of the principles of sustainable development and precaution. The Board must therefore justify its decision to withhold cross-examination on the basis that it adequately supports the deliberative capacity of the NEB and the public writ large. This flows from a purposive understanding of the Board's role, which it correctly identified in its reasons quoted above. Its dual role is to form an expert opinion on whether pipeline development is in the public interest and to support a democratically accountable decision-maker (Cabinet) in making an informed decision.

The decision to deny oral cross-examination impairs the NEB's ability to carry out this dual role, giving rise to questions about whether this decision can be justified. The lack of oral cross-examination risks undermining the deliberative capacity of the NEB in reaching its expert recommendation.[155] Intervenor scrutiny is the primary mechanism on which the NEB relies for testing the proponent's information. Board members of course exercise their own expertise, but participant input would vastly expand the range of views put to the Board. Intervenor participation would provide a significant counterweight to the fact that all the information for the project proposal has been in the proposal proponent's hands. The Board reasoned that two rounds of written information requests to the proponent is an adequate replacement to oral cross-examination. However, this claim is plainly unsupported. It does not answer to prior experience with written requests for additional information in which proponents have repeatedly failed to answer the requests.[156]

The decision to hold a written hearing also risks impairing the NEB's additional deliberative functions. The direction of the NEB's recommendation is immediately to the Cabinet, the ultimate decision-maker under the NEBA. But as we saw in the previous chapter, the direction of the reasons is also to those who are affected by the decision. The specific structure of the NEB's governing legislation is to promote democratic accountability—that is, to enable the public to hold elected officials to account for major development decisions. Put differently, the NEB's mandate is necessarily a

[154] Ibid, 4.

[155] In this sense, the expert role of the NEB is distinct from the expert evidence that is adduced by the proponent or intervenors. The NEB possesses 'evaluative expertise': Richardson, *Democratic Autonomy* (above n 98) 225. Jasanoff has focused on this kind of expertise (what she calls 'regulatory science') in S Jasanoff, *The Fifth Branch: Science Advisors as Policymakers* (Cambridge, MA, Harvard University Press, 1990) 230.

[156] See above n 45.

deliberative one in the sense that its recommendations enable further deliberation by both the Cabinet and the public about the desirability of pipeline development.

From this perspective, a written hearing is highly problematic. Important exchanges between Board members, intervenors and the project proponent are filtered through technical documents and take place largely out of public view. Where an oral hearing crystallises key issues for participants, the Board and the public, a written hearing is conducted through thousands of online documents. Any defensible justification for the elimination of oral cross-examination must therefore account for its negative impact on public deliberation.[157]

The NEB supports this decision by pointing to its legislative mandate, which prioritises timeliness over fairness.[158] The statutory constraints are real, but they do not clearly and unambiguously exclude common law requirements of procedural fairness. While the NEBA does impose a fifteen-month deadline on the NEB, it also allows the NEB to request extensions.[159] A major pipeline proposal with over four hundred intervenors and one thousand applications to participate[160] would seem an ideal instance for the Board to request such an extension. Of course, it may be denied an extension by an executive that is set on pipeline approvals. But that is beside the point. An NEB committed to public justification will fulfil its rule-of-law obligations by making it clear that the executive is choosing to act without the full benefit of the NEB's expertise and public process.

Nor do prudential considerations that typically factor into procedural decisions arise in this case. This is not a situation in which the administrative decision-maker will be faced with the prospect of conducting hundreds or thousands of individual oral hearings that would cripple the administrative process.[161] These are significant one-time approvals with effects that will extend to the public at large and well into the future. While the NEB has a broad mandate and a demanding regulatory workload, reaching a determination on whether a handful of major development projects are in the public interest is a central aspect of its mandate. As the NEB observes, it is an expert on its own process; it can surely canvass creative alternatives

[157] In the instance of Line 9, it is the only public process because this project did not require Cabinet approval. The federal Cabinet does not undertake a separate public consultation process after receiving the NEB's recommendation. CEAA 2012 (above n 19) s 31(1) and NEBA (above n 18) s 54(2) require Cabinet to issue reasons for its decision. But these reasons are typically cursory and rely exclusively on the findings in the recommendation report.

[158] NEB, 'TMX Cross-Exam Ruling' (above n 153) 4.

[159] NEBA (above n 18) s 52(7). The Minister can grant up to three months; Cabinet can grant an extension of any duration.

[160] National Energy Board, 'National Energy Board Report: Trans Mountain' (above n 28) 9.

[161] This is typically an argument against requiring oral hearings. See G Huscroft, 'From Natural Justice to Fairness: Thresholds, Content, and the Role of Judicial Review' in C Flood

for conducting oral hearings within the legislated time limits.[162] At the very least, it ought to ask which participants would actually want to intervene actively in an oral hearing, which is likely only a subset of those who apply to participate. One could imagine further grouping intervenors by issue and identifying particular contentious issues to prioritise for oral hearing.[163] Whatever procedural choices the NEB makes in this regard, their justification must be consistent with a requirement of fairness that enables deliberation by both the NEB, in forming its recommendation, and the public, in holding the ultimate decision-maker to account.

ii. Restricted Public Participation

A deliberative interpretation of sustainable development and precaution also has important implications for public participation. Pipelines, if approved, have long-term consequences. They create a literal path dependence: in the current hearings, existing pipelines are used as justification for further development.[164] They also entrench Canada's commitment to developing the controversial Alberta oil sands. Fairness, in this context, requires that the National Energy Board specifically justify shutting members of the public out of its process.

The NEBA implicates this common law requirement. It states:

> The Board shall consider the representations of any person who, in the Board's opinion, is directly affected by the granting or refusing of the application, and it may consider the representations of any person who, in its opinion, has relevant information or expertise.[165]

The NEB has interpreted this provision to restrict public participation. It has held that the 'directly affected' language of the statute evinces a legislative intention to exclude participants who have a 'general public interest'.[166] It has also rejected the 'public interest standing' test that is used for constitutional law.[167] It has stated that 'to be directly affected, the Board considers whether a person has shown a specific and detailed interest, as well as a

and L Sossin (eds), *Administrative Law in Context*, 2nd edn (Toronto, Emond Montgomery, 2012) 173.

162 Past practice for the environmental assessment of major project proposals has been to hold public hearings in the municipalities affected by the proposal. This was the format followed by the Northern Gateway Pipeline JRP.

163 The NEB already operates with process advisors that facilitate participation in the hearings. These coordinators could be utilised to restructure the hearing.

164 See, eg, National Energy Board, 'Line 9 Decision' (above n 20) 67; and National Energy Board, 'Line 9 Participation' (above n 28) 10 (on how the fact of existing pipelines should reduce administrative requirements).

165 NEBA (above n 18) s 55.2.

166 See National Energy Board, 'Line 9 Participation' (above n 28) 7.

167 Ibid, 10–11 (rejecting intervenor status for certain public interest groups).

sufficient direct project impact on the interest'.[168] On the application of the 'relevant expertise or information' standard, the NEB at times has seemed to take a generous approach by allowing parties the opportunity to provide letters of comment. But the Board has repeatedly asserted that the Board itself is the expert and possesses the relevant expertise for assessing the concerns raised by would-be participants. In other words, it relies on its own claim to technical expertise as a reason to deny standing.[169]

The Board has also held that neither section 2(b) nor section 7 of the Charter of Rights and Freedoms guarantees a public right to participation in the hearing process. The Board reasoned that its procedural decision 'revolves around a right to participate in the Board's process, not the exercise of a fundamental freedom [of speech].'[170] Jilted participants can and do express themselves in other public forums. The Board further reasoned, 'Quasi-judicial tribunals like the Board invariably establish expression-limiting rules of procedure, relevance, and decorum.'[171] The Board has denied the section 7 claim on the basis that a deprivation of life, liberty or security of the person has not been '"proven to result" from the Board's List of Issues decision or from its Ruling on Participation'.[172] The Federal Court has deferred to the Board on these matters, stating, 'Board hearings are not an open-line radio show where anyone can dial in and participate.'[173]

From the perspective of public justification, however, none of these reasons are defensible. While the 'directly affected' language may preclude a general right to public participation, it is not clear why a person must be affected differently or more severely than the 'mere' general public to count as directly affected.[174] At the very least, the NEB would have to justify its decision to import additional requirements into the statute. It is not clear this decision could be justified in light of the relevant environmental principles. In addition, a proper interpretation of sustainable development imposes positive obligations on the NEB to ensure that particular interests—those of future generations and disadvantaged groups—are represented in their process. While the NEB does undertake special efforts to include Indigenous groups,[175] it does not make a point of ensuring that its hearings are otherwise representative.

[168] National Energy Board, 'TMX Participation' (above n 28) 5.

[169] National Energy Board, 'Line 9 Participation' (above n 28) 11–12.

[170] National Energy Board, 'TMX Section 2 Motion' (above note 31) 8.

[171] Ibid, 10.

[172] National Energy Board, 'TMX Section 7 Ruling' (above n 32) 2. Failed environment-related s 7 claims are analysed in more detail below in ch 8, section II.

[173] *Sinclair v NEB* (above n 29) para 76.

[174] For a somewhat more promising line of authority, see the Alberta Court of Appeal's recent decisions: *Kelly v Alberta (Energy Resources Conservation Board)*, 2009 ABCA 349; *Kelly v Alberta (Energy Resources Conservation Board)*, 2011 ABCA 325; and *Kelly v Alberta (Energy Resources Conservation Board)*, 2012 ABCA 19.

[175] The Crown also owes a constitutional duty to consult with aboriginal peoples that is independent of the NEB's statutory authority: *Rio Tinto Alcan Inc v Carrier Sekani Tribal*

Importantly, the NEBA does not unambiguously eliminate public participation because it gives the NEB discretion to hear from those with 'relevant expertise or information'. This language could be interpreted by the NEB as statutory authority for implementing open notice-and-comment periods. And this interpretation would be justified on the basis that both sustainable development and precaution emphasise the need for inclusive and formalised public processes in environmental decision-making.[176] While the Board may not be 'an open-line radio show', it is nonetheless the only public process that precedes a major development decision.

Moreover, the Board's repeated assertion that it is the expert is not an adequate justification for excluding public applicants from participation. As we have seen, both sustainable development and precaution destabilise any claims to authoritative scientific or economic expertise. It follows that the NEB's decision to exclude certain applicants on the grounds they do not possess relevant expertise or information cannot be justified by virtue of the NEB's monopoly on expertise. It is still possible that the NEB could justify its exclusion of certain applicants in a way that is consistent with the common law requirement of fairness. But even prudential reasons are unpersuasive. At present, it seems that denying interested participants status in the hearings is proving *more* onerous than allowing a general notice-and-comment period. It requires the NEB to conduct a two-stage process for participation rather than a one-stage process that considers the applicants' comments on their merits.[177]

Notice that the requirement on the NEB to publicly justify its decisions on the basis of common law requirements means that the alleged Charter violations do not arise. On this understanding of the rule of law, there is a fundamental connection between constitutional and administrative law.[178] As David Dyzenhaus has put it, 'The Charter is not an intrusion into the Canadian legal order. Rather, it is a much more explicit and novel statement of fundamental values, so it represents continuity rather than radical change.'[179] Administrative decisions that comply with the requirement of

Council, 2010 SCC 43, [2010] 2 SCR 650. The Federal Court of Appeal found that the Crown's consultation with respect to the Northern Gateway Pipeline proposal was inadequate: *Gitxaala Nation v Canada* (above n 37).

176 On the role of notice-and-comment periods in promoting agency deliberation in the United States, see M Seidenfeld, 'The Role of Politics in a Deliberative Model of the Administrative State' (2013) 81 *George Washington Law Review* 1397. For an argument that notice-and-comment is insufficient to ensure democratic autonomy, see Richardson, *Democratic Autonomy* (above n 98) 220–21.

177 The NEB (as it is quick to note) already grants the vast majority of applications to participate, and most participants only submit a letter of comment.

178 This argument is the focus of ch 8 below.

179 D Dyzenhaus, 'Constituting the Rule of Law: Fundamental Values in Administrative Law' (2002) 27 *Queen's Law Journal* 445, 491.

public justification are those that also reflect basic rights in a constitutional democracy.[180]

B. Reasonableness

Section I above introduced two issues that implicate the reasonableness of the NEB recommendations on pipeline approvals: the Board's refusal to consider upstream and downstream environmental effects (ie, the scope of its assessment) and the adequacy of its assessment of a possible disaster. The principles of precaution and sustainable development allow us to take a purposive approach to evaluating the reasons offered by the NEB and identify the interests it must take into account when exercising its functions. The following examples show that the first task of a court is to demand reasons that demonstrate the Board itself undertook this duty of justification seriously. In the absence of such, there is no basis on which a court can defer.

i. Scope of Assessment

The NEB's justification for refusing to consider the environmental impacts of upstream production and downstream use that results from the construction of a new pipeline is that it does not have a statutory mandate to do so. The Board held that it is

> not persuaded that the effects from [oil sands] production are directly linked or necessarily incidental [to the Project]. ... the Project does not include upstream production and is not dependent on any particular upstream development. ... It is not the Board's recommendation that could directly or necessarily cause growth in oil sands development with its accompanying effects.[181]

The Board has also excluded consideration of downstream use: 'Oil, whether from Canada or from elsewhere in the world, will go to where the demand is, whether or not the Project proceeds.'[182] At the same time, however, the entire purpose of constructing these pipelines is to facilitate oil sands development and subsequent consumption.[183]

[180] See also TRS Allan, *Constitutional Justice: A Liberal Theory of the Rule of Law* (Oxford, Clarendon Press, 2001).

[181] National Energy Board, 'TMX List of Issues' (above n 33) 3.

[182] Ibid, 4.

[183] NEB (Gateway Panel), 'Considerations, Volume 2' (above n 35). NEBA (above n 18) s 52(2) specifically lists the following factors: (a) the availability of oil, gas, or any other commodity to the pipeline; (b) the existence of markets, actual or potential; (c) the economic feasibility of the pipeline; (d) the financial structure of the proponent; along with a catch-all factor '(e) any public interest that in the Board's opinion may be affected by the issuance of the certificate or the dismissal of the application'. CEAA 2012 (above n 19) s 19(1) also requires the determination of whether the project is likely to result in significant adverse environmental effects, taking into account the cumulative effects of the project.

Public justification requires that the Board offer a public-regarding reason for considering the economic benefits of oil sand development while excluding consideration of its environmental impacts. It is difficult to imagine that a permissible justification could be offered. Importantly, the 'public' that the NEB must consider is broad, since reasonableness in this context is conditioned by the principle of sustainable development. The reasons that the NEB offers must therefore address the impacts on future generations and the entire globe because the proposed pipeline further entrenches Canada's commitment to oil sands development.

Reasonableness, in other words, is highly sensitive to context. In this context, the project, the nature of the environmental problem at issue and the regulatory process itself all point in favour of a broad environmental assessment. A pipeline by its very nature is connected to other developments. It would make little sense to assess a pipeline as a disconnected entity. Some line-drawing by the Board is necessary to limit the scope of its assessment. But what is not justified is the decision to draw the line differently for considering the benefits of pipeline development than for the environmental effects. In addition, failing to consider the cumulative effects of the project and the oil sands on global climate change ignores the interconnected nature of the environmental problem. Climate change is a classic collective action problem that results from countless individual activities that on their own have a relatively small impact. Finally, the NEB's process is detailed. It is the combination of two complex regulatory processes under the NEBA and CEAA that integrate economic, environmental and social considerations. To borrow words from the Supreme Court of Canada, reviewing a decision of the NEB on a related issue, it would be 'surprising that such an elaborate review process would be created for such a limited inquiry'.[184]

The Board has further justified its decision to limit the scope of its assessment process by observing that greenhouse gas emissions from oil sands production and consumption are subject to separate regulatory processes.[185] However, this is true of *all* environmental effects of all approved developments. The Board's justification must reflect the distinctive role of the

[184] *Quebec (Attorney General) v Canada (National Energy Board)*, [1994] 1 SCR 159 at 191 (SCC). Note that the greenhouse gas emissions that the NEB considers in the pipeline assessments are those that result from valve leakage along the pipeline. This contribution to climate change is miniscule when compared to the production and consumption emissions from what is in the pipe.

[185] National Energy Board, 'TMX List of Issues' (above n 33) 3. But see *Quebec v NEB* (ibid) 194: 'The Board is the forum in which the environmental impact attributable solely to the export, that is, to the impact of the increase in power output needed to service the export contracts, will be considered. A focused assessment of these effects may be lost if subsumed in a comprehensive evaluation by the province of the environmental effects of the projects in their totality.' See also *Greenpeace v Canada AG* (above n 125) para 335.

assessment process.[186] It is the only occasion on which a determination will be made about whether the project will proceed. The Board's assessment role is to report to Cabinet and to the public on whether, taking into account the social, economic and environmental complexities of the project, an approval is in the public interest.

ii. Disaster Planning

We saw in section I above that the National Energy Board failed to consider the consequences of a major marine oil spill, assessing instead only the likelihood of such an event. We also saw that the Board has not required project proponents to produce and fully disclose site-specific emergency response plans for assessment, leaving this instead until after the projects have been approved. Yet the NEB process is the only occasion on which the Board can address the question of whether, given the chance of a disaster and the proposed response, a project is in the public interest. The adequacy of this assessment directly engages the precautionary principle.

The precautionary principle precludes the NEB from shirking from a thorough consideration of a possible catastrophe. Gaps in the analysis—such as a failure to consider the consequences of an unlikely spill—cannot, on this view, be justified. In addition, site-specific emergency plans are not derivative matters to be worked out at a later date between Board members and the pipeline proponent.[187] They are crucial factors in assessing both the likelihood and consequences of an emergency. The precautionary principle also instructs that it is not permissible for the Board to appeal solely to its own expertise in omitting these considerations. To the contrary, precaution strengthens the deliberative demands placed on the Board. Precaution requires that spill risk assessment and emergency plans are transparent and subject to public and intervenor scrutiny.[188] The Board must offer reasons for preferring one set of assumptions over another[189] and for how

[186] J Stacey, 'The Environmental, Democratic and Rule-of-Law Implications of Harper's Environmental Assessment Legacy' (2016) 21 *Review of Constitutional Studies* 165.

[187] A recent audit of the NEB revealed that the Board has a horrendous track record on overseeing emergency planning by pipeline companies: Commissioner of the Environment and Sustainable Development, '2011 December Report of the Commissioner of the Environment and Sustainable Development' (Government of Canada, 2011), www.oag-bvg.gc.ca/internet/English/parl_cesd_201112_01_e_36029.html#hd4b, 1.46ff.

[188] If Board members do not have the expertise to adequately assess the proponent's information or weigh the conflicting evidence of the proponent and intervenors, then the NEB needs to appoint an independent expert to help them do so. CEAA 2012 (above n 19) s 45 allows for a review panel to appoint an expert. NEBA (above n 18) s 10 gives the Governor in Council the authority to appoint an expert, so presumably the NEB could make a request to the GIC to do so.

[189] NEB (Gateway Panel), 'Considerations, Volume 2' (above n 35) 130 (noting the conflicting conclusions that can be draw from the studies but continuing it 'focused on the effects that

all identified sources of uncertainty factored into its conclusion. All of these reasons, moreover, must be articulated in a way that is comprehensible to the public.

Precaution also requires appropriate review mechanisms to ensure the decision-maker has adequately scrutinised scientific analyses and accounted for uncertainty. In the environmental assessment context, precaution ought to operate to enhance the 'justification, transparency and intelligibility' requirements assured by review for reasonableness.[190] This follows from the purpose of environmental assessment—that is, to provide an evidentiary base on which the public, and Cabinet which acts in its name, can rely. It also follows from a deliberative interpretation of the precautionary principle, which is squarely applicable when project proposals raise issues that 'engage the realm of highly improbable, but possibility [sic] catastrophic, events'.[191] When such concerns arise in the course of an assessment, they need to be fully aired to ensure they are put before political decision-makers (ie, Cabinet) because they require a determination of 'society's chosen level of protection against risk'.[192]

The Federal Court of Appeal, however, has refused to engage with claims that the Northern Gateway Pipeline assessment was unreasonable in light of the requirements of the CEAA, holding instead that such matters fall within the exclusive jurisdiction of federal Cabinet.[193] The Court held that only Cabinet's decision to approve the pipeline, not the assessment report, was reviewable. But it also held that Cabinet was 'entitled to a very broad margin of appreciation in making its discretionary decision upon the widest considerations of policy and public interest', suggesting that it would be highly unlikely for a court to intervene upon review.[194] Questions about the sufficiency of information provided to Cabinet were, in the Court's view, matters reserved by the legislation to Cabinet.[195] The Court offered no analysis of Cabinet's reasoning for its decision, only the conclusory statement that the decision-maker 'was entitled to assess the sufficiency of the information and recommendations it had received, balance all the considerations

were more readily measurable'); *Gitxaala Nation v Canada*, 'Memorandum of Fact and Law' (above n 39).

190 *Dunsmuir v New Brunswick (Board of Management)*, 2008 SCC 9, [2008] 1 SCR 190 2008, para 47. There is a remarkable, if only for its outlier status, Federal Court decision that reached this conclusion but was then overruled by the Federal Court of Appeal: *Greenpeace v Canada AG* (above n 125) para 272.

191 *Greenpeace v Canada AG* (above n 125) para 331.

192 Ibid. This language is from Privy Council, 'A Framework for the Application of Precaution' (above n 108).

193 *Gitxaala Nation v Canada* (above n 37) paras 124–25.

194 Ibid, paras 152 and 157.

195 Ibid, para 155.

... and come to the conclusion it did'.[196] The Court's conclusion suggests that any decision of Cabinet would be legally permissible, despite the fact that the decision is preconditioned by two detailed legislative schemes. This approach to judicial review recalls the formal conception of the rule of law; it is plainly incompatible with the public-justification conception of the rule of law.

C. Independence

We have seen that a number of flaws in the NEB's decisions require a reviewing body to intervene to demand adequate justification by the Board. However, review operates as a last resort in cases of clear intransigence on the part of the Board to participate in the rule-of-law project. The willingness of the NEB to participate in the ongoing project of public justification is itself a product of the people that make up the Board and the informal institutional norms and pressures that influence them.[197] It is predictable that a Board captured by industry or unduly influenced by a pro-pipeline executive will fail to maintain the rule-of-law project. We are thus faced with the question of what public justification requires of regulatory independence and how this issue might come before a court.

i. Regulatory Capture

As we have just seen, a deliberative interpretation of environmental principles requires close scrutiny from the courts to ensure that decisions are the result of an appropriately deliberative process and that decisions are based on permissible reasons (ie, reasons that in fact justify the decisions). This level of scrutiny is especially necessary where there are clear signals that a decision-maker's deliberative capacity is impaired. A number of factors suggest that this is the case with the NEB, for example: the Board's lack of expertise in environmental assessment or spill risk assessment; the fact that the Board has shared 'intelligence' on the peaceful activities of pipeline opponents with industry; and the Board's consistent failure to publicly justify many of its decisions, as outlined above.

The requirement of public justification requires deference to expert decision-makers, but only when deference is earned. A court committed to public justification cannot turn a blind eye to allegations of regulatory capture and limit its inquiry to the language of the statute. The actual operations of the regulator—the representativeness of the board members,

[196] Ibid, para 157.

[197] See, eg, R Macdonald, 'The Acoustics of Accountability: Towards Well-Tempered Tribunals' in A Sajó (ed), *Judicial Integrity* (Leiden, Martinus Nijhoff, 2004) 142.

whether the process included submissions by a broad range of interests and whether the Board was responsive to those interests—are all relevant when a court assesses the adequacy of the justification offered by the Board in its reasons.[198] Where capture is a plausible factor, public justification requires that the court subject the decision to more intense scrutiny. The court should be less willing to fill in the blanks of the Board's reasoning and more willing to remit the decision for reconsideration.

This is not to pretend that judicial intervention is the remedy to regulatory capture. Capture is a pernicious problem that is often detected only in the most extreme cases. Preventing regulatory capture requires a cooperative effort amongst all institutions of government where public officials approach their roles purposively.[199] Just as decades of conflict in the forestry sector resulted in the creation of a hybrid administrative body, British Columbia's forestry 'watchdog', we could imagine similar institutional innovation playing a similar role in preventing capture in the pipeline sector.[200] Judicial review cannot prevent capture, but it can serve as a spotlight on the most egregious cases. As we have seen, construing the requirements of reasonableness and fairness in light of environmental principles should make capture easier to detect. Anchoring these principles in the rule-of-requirement of public justification offers a basis for judicial intervention when problems of regulatory capture emerge.

The NEB is aware of the widespread perception that it is beholden to the energy industry. Efforts such as the Chairperson's cross-country tour[201] and the Energy East panel members' recusals have sought to restore public confidence in the Board's ability to fulfil its public interest mandate. But these efforts are palliatives. The Board has failed to recognise that its legitimacy

[198] Leckey, *Contextual Subjects* (above n 25) 237–39 (arguing that a contextual approach to judicial review can accommodate the vastly different kinds of relationships that administrative decision-makers have with individuals and the public, including requiring distance between decision-makers and the repeat players of a regulated industry).

[199] Arguably one of the most important factors here is the appointment of competent and open-minded Board members in the first place. I can't address this issue adequately here, but see Macdonald, 'The Acoustics of Accountability' (above n 197) 164; L Sossin, 'The Uneasy Relationship between Independence and Appointments in Canadian Administrative Law' in G Huscroft and M Taggart (eds), *Inside and Outside Canadian Administrative Law: Essays in Honour of David Mullan* (Toronto, University of Toronto Press, 2006) 50; and Woolley, 'Legitimating Public Policy' (above n 60) 182 (about how this requirement follows from a deliberative democratic understanding of public administration).

[200] See ch 5 above regarding the BC Forest Practices Board. However, this is not a complete answer, since it depends upon the specialised review body also retaining its independence from special interests (including now the primary decision-maker).

[201] National Energy Board, 'NEB Chair's Cross-Country Engagement begins Monday in Atlantic Canada' (Press release, 23 Jan 2015), www.neb-one.gc.ca/bts/nws/nr/2015/nr04-eng.html. Somewhat better is its new online interactive pipeline map, which improves public accessibility to oil spill and response data, but this ignores the prospective role of the NEB in helping approve these pipelines in the first place.

does not come solely from appealing to the language of its governing statute or its professional expertise. Rather, its legitimacy—both legal and democratic legitimacy—comes from institutional practices that are demonstrably justified to those who are affected by its decisions.

ii. Independence from Government

In a sense, it is somewhat surprising that the specific requirements of public justification seem to elude the NEB. The NEB after all does not bear the burden of making the final, weighty decision regarding approval or rejection of pipeline proposals; this falls to Cabinet. This raises the question of whether the NEB process is a sham, window-dressing for decisions that are fixed in advance. This possibility is heightened by the fact that the responsible Minister expressed inflammatory and threatening views about those concerned with the Northern Gateway Pipeline. These comments cannot be undone and risk undermining the NEB process. At least, however, these comments were public and contemporaneous with the NEB process. We could imagine that, were the NEB committed to the rule-of-law project, such comments would have a galvanising effect. The Board would be even more determined to foster an inclusive and deliberative process that demonstrated its independence from the executive. Such a process would not be sham even if the proposal were approved. This is because a publicly justified NEB recommendation would provide the public with the information it needs to hold the ultimate decision-maker democratically accountable.

More problematic is the fact that the NEBA specifically and unambiguously allows the Chairperson of the Board and Minister to interfere and expedite the NEB hearing process. This power to curtail the hearing process is directly at odds with the NEB's role in providing an informed recommendation on whether pipeline approval is in the public interest. The integrity of the process of public justification requires that the Chairperson and the Minister not exercise this statutory power in this way. To do so would mean there is no genuine process in place, that the approval process is a sham.

But what if the Minister were to intervene and direct the Chairperson to issue a recommendation that a pipeline is in the public interest?[202] In such a case, the action would have clear statutory authority and yet would not comply with the requirements of the public-justification conception of the rule of law. A court would have to declare that while the decision may comply with the statute, it has questionable legal authority. This is fundamental to the rule-of-law theory introduced in chapter four. Compliance with the rule of law is constitutive of legal authority. When the government exempts itself from the rule-of-law project, it loses its claim to the special kind of authority

[202] See text above associated with nn 50 and 51.

that comes from governing through law. While a court might enforce the clear language of the statute, in such a worst-case scenario, it would be doing so because the statute is valid, not because it has legal authority.[203] Put differently, the fact that the court cannot invalidate the provision of the statute does not mean it is bound to endorse its authority as law.[204] A court in such a situation can uphold the statute while also declaring that it undermines the fundamental commitment to the rule of law.

According to Dyzenhaus, the dynamic at play in common law judicial review is akin to the dynamic created by section 33 of the Charter:

> The [section 33] override does not render any of the overridable values unconstitutional. It merely gives to the legislature a limited opportunity to operate unconstitutionally, but on condition that it owns up to that fact. The override is meant to, and does, both incite and renew democratic debate about the government's decisions to govern outside the constitutional order.[205]

One could imagine the renewed democratic debate that might follow a judicial declaration that the federal government has decided to operate outside the rule of law by conducting a sham hearing for approving the construction of a controversial, interprovincial pipeline.[206] This extreme scenario brings to the surface the fundamental connection between administrative and constitutional law. The court's role in both cases is to uphold core constitutional principles and alert the public when the executive has elected to exempt itself from the rule-of-law project.

IV. CONCLUSION

This chapter has argued that the requirement of public justification imposes specific requirements on environmental decision-makers. In the environmental context, existing common law principles are inadequate to preserve the distinctive relationship between legal subject and state that the public-justification conception of the rule of law makes possible. Well-known environmental principles such as sustainable development and precaution have the potential to preserve this relationship when interpreted in light of deliberative democratic ideals. Through this line of argument, this chapter has demonstrated that administrative decisions can have both democratic and legal authority even in instances of profound environmental complexity.

[203] D Dyzenhaus, *The Constitution of Law: Legality in a Time of Emergency* (Cambridge, Cambridge University Press, 2006) 206.

[204] Ibid.

[205] Ibid, 211 (also observing that the UK Human Rights Act creates a similar dynamic).

[206] Indeed, many observers of the process have reached this conclusion on their own, even without actual Ministerial interference.

This chapter has examined how the rule of law may offer concrete guidance in the specific context of the National Energy Board's pipeline assessments. However, I have not provided definitive solutions to many of the issues raised by the NEB's assessments. Indeed, the chapter elaborates a theory of environmental law that does not conclusively reject a series of major pipeline proposals that are nothing but bad news for the environment. What it has offered instead is something more powerful: a set of questions that the NEB must answer in order to comply with the rule of law. These questions do not arise from contested claims about ecological thresholds or from the din of climate activists and environmental politics more generally. Rather, they arise from a much deeper commitment to democratic governance under the rule of law. In addition to these deep commitments, Canadian environmental law contains further specific commitments to principles of precaution and sustainable development. However underdeveloped the principles may be, or however cynical or hypocritical public officials may be when they appeal to these principles, they remain existing commitments from which we can derive concrete and rigorous legal requirements for environmental regulators. This chapter has argued that the public-justification conception of the rule of law provides a theoretical framework in which these principles play a meaningful interpretive role. They are an integral part of the rule-of-law project in environmental law, which is the project of respecting and enabling individuals as responsible agents, capable of reasoning with the law and participating in environmental governance.

7

Reasoning Adequately: Wind Turbine Risks and Benefits

THE ARGUMENT OF Part Two of the book thus far has been that public justification, at its core, requires public officials to offer reasons for their decisions. The practice of reason-giving respects the legal subject as a rational, self-determining agent, capable of reasoning with the law. More specifically, we have seen that in the environmental context, the requirement of reason-giving is informed by environmental principles such as precaution and sustainable development. These environmental principles modify or refine the content of fairness and reasonableness to ensure that those who are subject to environmental laws are respected as responsible agents.

This chapter takes this analysis one step further. It examines in detail the reasons offered by the Ontario Environmental Review Tribunal, a specialised quasi-judicial institution tasked with reviewing provincial approvals for industrial wind turbine development. In conducting this adjudicative role, the Tribunal issues comprehensive reasons for its decisions. These reasons, which engage with a confluence of environmental benefits and risks, provide a fruitful context for elaborating the public justification requirement of reasoning adequately.

This chapter argues that the Tribunal reasons adequately when its reasons are guided by relevant statutory considerations and yet remain oriented toward the legal subject's status as a responsible agent. In particular, we will see that the Tribunal is implicitly attuned to the need to respect individuals as responsible agents and their basic entitlement to publicly justified decisions that affect their interests. The Tribunal demonstrates this sensitivity in its attempts to preserve a residual role for the precautionary principle in its reasoning about wind turbine approvals. We will see, however, that the Tribunal is far too timid in its interpretation of its statute. Because its orientation toward fundamental rule-of-law principles is only ever implicit and not firmly and explicitly anchored in the requirement of public justification, it succumbs too easily to the 'plain meaning' of its governing provisions, which seemingly purport to override the application of the precautionary principle.

This chapter contains three sections. The first introduces the regulatory backdrop to industrial wind turbine development in Ontario and how and why this regime has generated significant controversy from neighbouring landowners. We will see that the result of this regulatory regime is that the Tribunal is the key institution for mediating the complex wind turbine controversies arising from the perceived lack of publicly justified approvals. In response to these controversies, the Tribunal has generated its own intricately detailed jurisprudence on wind turbine development. The next section then sets the stage for how we ought to evaluate this jurisprudence to understand whether the Tribunal is fulfilling its public justification role. This section elaborates the notion of reasonableness—or reasoning adequately—that follows from the requirement of public justification. On this view, reasonable decisions are those that offer a cogent justification of the outcome on the basis of the relevant statutory considerations, interpreted consistently with a common law backdrop that is protective of individual agency. Section III then develops the argument that the Tribunal reasons adequately when it protects the responsible agency of individuals, that is, their capacity to reason with the law. However, it fails to make explicit this fundamental role in its wind turbine reasons. In the absence of this explicit connection to public justification, the Tribunal unreasonably capitulates to the apparent plain meaning of its governing provisions, which purport to dislodge the application of the precautionary principle. Importantly, we will see that the argument that the Tribunal's interpretation is unreasonable is built on the Tribunal's own reasoning that elsewhere attends to the need to respect the legal subject's status as a responsible agent. Finally, by examining the few instances of judicial review, we will see why explicitly grounding the Tribunal's reasoning in the public-justification conception of the rule of law is necessary to prevent inappropriate judicial intervention.

I. THE CONFLUENCE OF ENVIRONMENTAL FACTORS IN WIND TURBINE DEVELOPMENT

In 2013, the Ontario government announced its long-term energy plan, which committed the province to generating approximately half its electricity from renewable energy sources by 2025.[1] Increasing electricity generation from wind power is a key pillar of this plan, and the relative contribution of wind power increased almost threefold in the first two years alone.[2] At the end

[1] Ontario Ministry of Energy, 'Ontario's Long-Term Energy Plan' (2013), www.energy.gov.on.ca/en/ltep/.

[2] From 3 per cent of total energy in 2013 (ibid) to 8.2 per cent in 2015 (Independent Electricity System Operator, 'Ontario Energy Report', Q4 2015 (Government of Ontario, 2015), www.ontarioenergyreport.ca/pdfs/5806_IESO_OntarioEnergyReportQ42016_Electricity_EN_FA.pdf).

of 2015, Ontario had over 2300 operative wind turbines and led Canada in wind energy production.[3] This growth in renewable energy proceeded hand in hand with Ontario's phasing out of coal-fired electricity generation.

Wind power is often promoted one-dimensionally as a form of clean energy, but like any development, it entails a confluence of complex environmental impacts. The potential benefits of wind energy are significant. Unlike fossil fuel combustion, it produces virtually no chemical pollutants or greenhouse gas emissions and does not require ongoing energy input to extract and process the resource.[4] But wind power comes with its own set of local concerns. Like any physical disturbance to land, wind turbine development can affect endangered species. Of particular concern are the possible impacts on migratory birds and bats through direct collisions and noise disturbance.[5] Local landowners also worry about possible health impacts associated with living near wind turbines. Sleep disturbance, nausea, headaches and anxiety are thought to result in some instances from low frequency sound and 'shadow flicker' emanating from nearby wind turbines.[6]

Many jurisdictions that have committed to ambitious renewable energy goals have sought to realise these goals in relatively short timeframes, generating considerable local opposition.[7] Ontario's process fits this trend. The government enacted significant legislative and regulatory amendments that set out a parallel, streamlined process for assessing and approving wind turbine proposals.[8] Notably, proposals are subject to modified environmental assessment requirements, not the Ontario Environmental Assessment Act (1990),[9] and modified requirements for protecting endangered species.[10] At the same time, however, this streamlined regulatory regime is set against a broader legal backdrop that contains a (provincial) statutory Environmental

[3] Canadian Wind Energy Association, 'Wind Energy in Ontario' (no date), canwea.ca/wind-energy/ontario.

[4] M McCulloch, M Raynolds and M Laurie, 'Life-Cycle Value Assessment of a Wind Turbine' (Pembina Institute, 2000), www.pembina.org/reports/windlcva.pdf.

[5] These are the subject of prominent Environmental Review Tribunal decisions, some of which are discussed below in section III. See also Ontario Ministry of Natural Resources, 'Bird and Bird Habitats: Guidelines for Wind Power Projects' (2011), dr6j45jk9xcmk.cloudfront.net/documents/2718/stdprod-071273.pdf; and Ontario Ministry of Natural Resources, 'Bats and Bat Habitats: Guidelines for Wind Power Projects' (2011), dr6j45jk9xcmk.cloudfront.net/documents/2719/stdprod-088155.pdf.

[6] Health Canada, 'Wind Turbine Noise and Health Study: Summary of Results' (2014), www.hc-sc.gc.ca/ewh-semt/noise-bruit/turbine-eoliennes/summary-resume-eng.php.

[7] P Devine-Wright, 'Public Engagement with Large-Scale Renewable Energy Technologies: Breaking the Cycle of NIMBYism' (2011) 2 *WIREs Climate Change* 19; and MA Petrova, 'NIMBYism Revisited: Public Acceptance of Wind Energy in the United States' (2013) 4 *WIREs Climate Change* 575, 586–89.

[8] The bulk of the legislative amendments can be found in the Environmental Protection Act (EPA), RSO 1990, c E19, Part V.0.1.

[9] Electricity Projects (Ontario Environmental Assessment Act 1990), O Reg 116/01, s 2(1)(d).

[10] General (Ontario Endangered Species Act 2007), O Reg 242/08, s 23.20.

Bill of Rights (1993),[11] which requires public decision-makers to consider certain environmental values, and ensures certain basic public access to information and participatory requirements. As we will see in more detail below, these legislative commitments send potentially mixed messages to the public and have enabled significant opposition to wind turbine development in the province.

Many of the public concerns about wind turbine development have been taken into account, at least at one level, through blanket provincial regulations and policies. For example, the government promulgated a regulation that prescribes minimum set-back distances from residences and maximum noise limits.[12] In *Hanna v Ontario*, concerned citizens sought judicial review of the regulation.[13] The Environmental Bill of Rights requires that the Minister 'take every reasonable step to ensure the ministry statement of environmental values is considered whenever decisions that might significantly affect the environment are made in the ministry'.[14] The statement of values includes, amongst other values, the precautionary principle and sustainability.[15] The appellants argued that there needed to be *some* evidence supporting the safety of the 550-metre set-back distance provided for in the regulation, and that the absence of any evidence meant that the regulation is 'arbitrary and fails to consider the precautionary principle'.[16]

The Court upheld the regulation. It found that the statement of environmental values was implicated in multiple ways by the province's move to renewable power generation, a move in part effectuated through the regulation.[17] The Court reasoned that the Ministry's responsibility was to consider all of these environmental values. It was not therefore appropriate for the Court to single out the precautionary principle. Significantly, the Court emphasised the role of the Environmental Review Tribunal in ensuring that the human health effects of wind turbines were sufficiently justified in each individual case. The Court reasoned:

> The Tribunal would hear relevant expert evidence and would be able to consider topography, wind patterns, make, model, size, and dBA specifications of the wind turbine, its exact location, and the location of any other proximate turbines. … The Tribunal can conduct site inspections. It has authority to appoint its own scientific experts to assist it in its endeavours.[18]

[11] Environmental Bill of Rights (EBR), SO 1993, c 28, s 11.

[12] Renewable Energy Approvals under Part V.0.1 of the Act, O Reg 359/09.

[13] *Hanna v Ontario (Attorney General)*, 2011 ONSC 609.

[14] EBR (above n 11) s 11.

[15] Ontario Ministry of the Environment and Climate Change, 'Statement of Environmental Values' (no date), www.ebr.gov.on.ca/ERS-WEB-External/content/sev.jsp?pageName=sevList&subPageName=10001.

[16] *Hanna* (above n 13) para 13.

[17] Ibid, paras 27–28.

[18] Ibid, para 29.

The conclusion in *Hanna* is defensible.[19] It reflects the fact that the regulation sets a baseline standard for industrial wind turbine development and that nothing in the regulation precludes the government from imposing more stringent conditions on a developer in any particular instance. The Court's reasoning demonstrates a nice understanding of the distinctive role of the Tribunal in ensuring the justification of individual wind turbine approvals. The environmental context of each approval and whether an approval gives rise to particular health or environmental concerns can only be adequately considered on a case-by-case basis by a body of experts. In this way, the Tribunal's role in ensuring public justification protects two sets of individual interests. It protects the individual's interest in health and a healthy environment by ensuring that the initial decision adequately accounts for these interests. It also protects the individual's interest as a responsible agent in participating in the ongoing deliberations before the Tribunal about whether the initial decision was justified in this way.

In *Hanna*, the Court concisely and prophetically identified the Tribunal as the battleground on which the wind turbine controversies have played out. The Ontario Environmental Protection Act (EPA) carves out a distinctive role for the Tribunal in adjudicating challenges to wind turbine approvals. As observed by the Court in *Hanna*, this distinctive role is a key component in the overall public justification of wind turbine development. In the span of only four years, the Tribunal issued over three dozen detailed decisions reviewing decisions to approve industrial wind turbine developments. These decisions provide a fruitful context for understanding how public decision-makers can reason adequately about environmental benefits and risks.

II. THE METHOD AND PURPOSE OF REASONABLENESS

We have seen in the previous chapters that public justification requires public officials to issue reasons for their exercises of public authority. Moreover, these reasons must provide a rational basis for the decision (ie, actually justify the outcome), and they must do so in a way that reflects core common law and statutory principles. In the case of the National Energy Board (NEB) in particular, we saw in chapter six how the principles of precaution and sustainable development operate to modify and clarify the common law requirements of reasonableness and fairness in the environmental context.

[19] It should be noted that the regulation was subject to two privative clauses, which purport to limit the court's supervisory authority to the question of whether the correct process was followed: EBR (above n 11) ss 37 and 118.

But when a public official has offered thorough reasons (unlike the NEB), how do we know whether those reasons properly reflect these statutory, common law and environmental principles? It certainly cannot be the case that any set of reasons, no matter how vacuous or disconnected from the outcome, fulfils a conception of the rule of law that respects legal subjects as responsible agents. How then do we know when a public official has reasoned adequately such that a reviewing court ought to defer? Canadian courts have puzzled over this basic question of administrative law, and as we have seen throughout the book, their decisions have yet to evince a consistent approach to determining whether administrative decisions are reasonable.[20]

Since the Supreme Court of Canada's watershed decision in *Dunsmuir* in 2008,[21] the vast majority of administrative decisions are reviewed on the basis of their reasonableness (as opposed to correctness).[22] This move has opened up the conceptual space for the courts to more fully embrace the notion of 'deference as respect' that they endorse as a central component of reasonableness review.[23] Yet the Supreme Court's understanding of reasonableness is bipolar. On the one hand, it states that 'reasonableness is concerned mostly with the existence of justification, transparency and intelligibility within the decision-making process',[24] a statement that tracks David Dyzenhaus' articulation of public justification. On the other, the Supreme Court has said that a reasonable decision is also one that 'falls within a range of possible, acceptable outcomes that are defensible in respect of the facts and law'.[25] These two branches of reasonableness pull in different directions.[26] The former implies that the courts must respectfully defer to administrative decisions that are transparent and justified by reasons. The latter implies that the courts, with their monopoly over law-interpretation, have the final say on the legislative boundaries within which decision-makers must adhere.

20 See, eg, M Lewans, 'Deference and Reasonableness Since Dunsmuir' (2012) 38 *Queen's Law Journal* 59.

21 *Dunsmuir v New Brunswick (Board of Management)*, 2008 SCC 9, [2008] 1 SCR 190.

22 There is a significant body of Canadian academic literature on post-*Dunsmuir* developments in Canadian administrative law that cannot be fully rehearsed here. For one example on this specific point, see JM Evans, 'The Triumph of Reasonableness: But How Much Does It Really Matter?' 27 *Canadian Journal of Administrative Law and Practice* 101.

23 J Stacey and A Woolley, 'Can Pragmatism Function in Administrative Law' (2016) 74 *Supreme Court Law Review* (2d) 211.

24 *Dunsmuir* (above n 21) para 47.

25 Ibid.

26 See Walters for a nice discussion of how these branches evince different underlying logics in Canadian public law: MD Walters, 'Respecting Deference as Respect: Rights, Reasonableness and Proportionality in Canadian Administrative Law' in H Wilberg and M Elliott (eds), *The Scope and Intensity of Substantive Review: Traversing Taggart's Rainbow* (Oxford, Hart Publishing, 2015) 417–19.

To fully adopt the public-justification conception of the rule of law, courts must reject the second branch of reasonableness. The idea that there is a range of acceptable outcomes presupposes that there is an uncontroversial set of boundaries that defines that range. In other words, the second branch of reasonableness rests on the tempting notion that the statute has a 'plain meaning' or that there is such thing as a clear 'legislative intention'.[27] On this view, so long as the decision falls within the range set by that plain meaning, it counts as reasonable.

The idea that there is such a thing as a 'plain meaning', however, denies the crucial role that interpretation plays in every administrative decision or act of judicial review. The meaning of a statute (ie, its range of acceptable outcomes) can never be fully understood in the abstract. The content of the law is only crystallised or elaborated when it comes in contact with the lives of those it affects.[28] Of course the statutory language plays a guiding role, but it can never be determinative. This observation is true in every context, but it follows especially clearly from the emergency perspective. The complexity of environmental decision-making means that 'unforeseen events occur to challenge our rough-and-ready preconceptions, forcing us to think harder about how best to apply the statute (and so how to understand the limits of executive power) in all the circumstances.'[29]

The practical reality that a statute does not have a 'plain meaning' means that any reasoning about a statute's meaning or content will be value-laden. And when a court upholds an administrative decision as falling within a range of reasonable outcomes, it is not mechanically enforcing the intent of the legislature. Rather, it is engaged in a normative exercise that endorses that decision as a legitimate interpretation of the law. The only question, then, is whether or not the court upholds a decision that reflects the law's overarching purpose of respecting legal subjects as responsible, autonomous agents.

Jettisoning the idea that a statute has a plain meaning redirects the court's focus away from the boundaries of a statute to the adequacy of the administrative decision-maker's interpretation of the content of the law. The reasonableness of the decision is revealed through the reasons offered and whether those reasons justify the outcome in a manner that serves statutory

[27] D Dyzenhaus, 'Dignity in Administrative Law: Judicial Deference in a Culture of Justification' (2012) 17 *Review of Constitutional Studies* 87, 104–5.

[28] Walters puts this nicely: 'Law does not exist *out there*, but rather is a product of an interpretive discourse that respects the ideas, knowledge, experience and expertise of those who are closest to the challenge of state at issue.' See Walters, 'Respecting Deference as Respect' (above n 26) 419.

[29] TRS Allan, *The Sovereignty of Law* (Oxford, Oxford University Press, 2013) 303.

principles and the fundamental interests protected by the public-justification conception of the rule of law.

We are now in a position to better understand how, on the public-justification conception of the rule of law, a court (or any reviewing institution) ought to assess the reasonableness of an administrative decision. First, a reasonable decision is one that is justified in light of the relevant statutory considerations and the fundamental interests protected by the common law. We will see, for example, that the EPA identifies particular statutory considerations—prioritisation of renewable energy development, individual interests in human health and a healthy environment. In addition, these considerations are part of a broader common law legal system that protects the individual's interest in being respected as a responsible and capable participant in public decision-making. Reasonable decisions are those that reflect these fundamental interests. Thus, the Supreme Court is right to say that reasonableness requires justification, transparency and intelligibility, but it has not gone far enough in elaborating this requirement. Clear and cogent reasons will justify a decision only when they are protective of the fundamental individual interests that underlie the public-justification conception of the rule of law.[30]

What follows from this understanding of reasoning is that any analysis of the reasonableness of an administrative decision must carefully attend to the actual reasons offered by the decision-maker. A reasonable decision will always be a context-sensitive interpretation of the law. It is therefore not defensible for a court to rely on an abstract (or context-insensitive) measure of reasonableness, such as the notion that a decision falls within the range of (predetermined) acceptable outcomes. The idea that reasons are essential to reasonableness might seem obvious but for the extensive list of examples of prominent judicial review decisions that all but ignore the reasons actually offered by the decision-makers.[31]

Finally, it is a fallacy to think that a court, or any reviewing institution, can do its job of upholding the rule of law while also avoiding 'reweighing' the factors under consideration by an administrative decision-maker.[32] Reasonableness is always an inquiry into whether the decision was justified in light of the relevant considerations, considerations derived from both the

[30] For two separate elaborations of this thinking in non-environmental contexts, see Allan, *The Sovereignty of Law* (ibid) ch 7; and E Fox-Decent, *Sovereignty's Promise: The State as Fiduciary* (Oxford, Oxford University Press, 2011) 221–25.

[31] Daly identifies five Supreme Court of Canada decisions in a two-year window in which reasonableness performs a 'rhetorical function': P Daly, 'Struggling Towards Coherence in Canadian Administrative Law? Recent Cases on Standard of Review and Reasonableness' (2016) 62 *McGill Law Journal* 527.

[32] Dyzenhaus, 'Dignity in Administrative Law' (above n 27) 109.

statutory context and common law. When an administrative decision is reasoned in this way, the court must defer. It defers not because the legislature told it to or because the decision-maker has superior but undemonstrated expertise. Rather, the court defers because it is one member of the collaborative project of public justification and the decision fulfils this requirement of legality.

It is this understanding of reasonableness that follows from the public-justification conception of the rule of law. Administrative decision-makers reason adequately when they offer cogent reasons that justify their decisions on the basis of the relevant statutory considerations, interpreted, as they need to be, consistently with a common law backdrop that is protective of individual agency. It is this understanding of reasonableness that guides our assessment of the Tribunal's controversial wind turbine jurisprudence.

III. REASONING ADEQUATELY ABOUT WIND TURBINE APPROVALS

This section builds a case for the unreasonableness of the Environmental Review Tribunal's interpretation of the statutory basis for its review of a Renewable Energy Approval (REA), or wind turbine approval.[33] It does so not based on any abstract test for reasonableness or independent environmental standard but rather from the Tribunal's own reasoning about the core statutory and common law principles that otherwise guide its approach to adjudicating wind turbine controversies. We will see that the Tribunal reluctantly capitulates to the apparent 'plain meaning' of the statute, which it views as incompatible with the precautionary principle. However, it has significant misgivings about its conclusion, and indeed, these misgivings bear out elsewhere in the Tribunal's wind turbine jurisprudence. This section argues that the Tribunal's misgivings about the non-applicability of precaution are connected to the Tribunal's implicit understanding of its role in protecting individual agency, which underpins the requirement of public justification. However, the inability of the Tribunal to precisely articulate this role means that it falls short of reasoning adequately about its statutory mandate. Finally, we shall see, its ability to explicitly connect its approach to interpreting and administering its powers with core statutory and common law principles is necessary for its decisions to withstand inappropriate judicial intervention on review.

[33] EPA (above n 8) s 145.2.1(2) (referred to as 'the statutory tests' or 'the environment test' or 'the human health test').

A. Plain Meaning and the Precautionary Principle

The EPA sets out a limited mandate for the Tribunal to review wind turbine approvals. The Act states:

> [A] person may require a hearing ... only on the grounds that engaging in the renewable energy project in accordance with the renewable energy approval will cause
>
> (a) serious harm to human health [the human health test]; or
> (b) serious and irreversible harm to plant life, animal life or the natural environment [the environment test].[34]

In addition, these two statutory tests are the only matters that can be considered by the Tribunal when conducting the hearing,[35] and the person requiring the hearing bears the onus of proving the relevant test(s) on a balance of probabilities.[36] In the first challenge to an REA,[37] the Tribunal had to interpret its mandate under these provisions. It faced the immediate problem that the statutory tests for its jurisdiction (the human health and environment tests) appeared incompatible with the precautionary principle, a principle that, as we saw in the previous chapter, plays a crucial role in ensuring public justification in the environmental context.

Recall that the precautionary principle is the notion that when there are threats of serious or irreversible damage, lack of full scientific certainty shall not be used as a reason for postponing cost-effective measures to prevent environmental degradation.[38] The principle directly responds to the complexity of environmental problems and our inability to predict with confidence the consequences of human actions on the environment. The precautionary principle enables public justification by destabilising the hegemony of expert assurances of safety and specifically requiring decision-makers to attend to the possible sources of uncertainty in their reasoning and to articulate how they have responded to this uncertainty in terms that individuals can understand and reasonably accept.

Erickson[39] concerned claims that neighbouring landowners would suffer serious harm to their health as a result of the approved wind turbine development. The appellants argued that the precautionary principle required the Tribunal to interpret the statutory tests set out in the EPA 'in a manner that

[34] Ibid, s 142.1(3).
[35] Ibid, s 145.2.1(2).
[36] Ibid, s 145.2.1(3).
[37] *Erickson v Director, Ministry of the Environment*, Nos 10-121/10-122 (Ontario Environmental Review Tribunal, 2011).
[38] See above ch 6, section II.B.
[39] *Erickson* (above n 37).

is protective and precautionary with respect to human health'.[40] They drew the Tribunal's attention to the broader regulatory context of wind turbine development, which includes an obligation on the Director to consider the precautionary principle as part of the statement of environmental values when exercising its authority to issue an REA.

The Tribunal's reasoning demonstrates that it was torn between its understanding of precaution as a fundamental guiding principle to environmental decision-making under the EPA[41] and what it took to be the plain meaning of the statutory tests. On the one hand, the Tribunal explicated the important role of the precautionary principle in Canadian and international law and highlighted the principle's role in governing decisions under the EPA.[42] Applying the precautionary principle in this context would mean that the Director's decision to grant the REA would have to account for the various sources of scientific uncertainty in a rigorous manner. The precautionary principle would strengthen the obligation on the Director to justify the REA in light of the uncertainty surrounding health and environmental impacts of industrial wind turbines. It would allow the Tribunal to intervene when the Director's decision could not be justified on this basis.

On the other hand, however, the statutory tests for the Tribunal's jurisdiction state that the only ground for review is on the question of whether the wind turbine project would cause serious harm, and further, that the appellants must bear the burden of proof in establishing that this harm would follow from the wind turbine approval. The Tribunal ultimately reasoned that the statutory test is incompatible with the precautionary principle. It found that the statutory test imposes a higher burden on the claimant—that is, a requirement to show that the approval 'will cause serious harm',[43] in contrast to the precautionary principle, which would require the claimant to show only a risk or threat of harm. The Tribunal observed that the statutory test is structured differently than the precautionary principle because the test imposes a statutory 'precondition' to the exercise of the Tribunal's discretion.[44] It noted that the statutory test 'is materially different from other more precautionary statutory tests in the EPA'.[45] The Tribunal reasoned that the precautionary principle was applicable to the exercise of authority under these different provisions of the Act, but the Tribunal could not modify what it saw as an otherwise clearly stated statutory test.

[40] Ibid, 119. Interestingly, the Director seemed to agree that the precautionary principle was applicable but that it was not met in this case because there was no evidence of risk (119–20).

[41] Ibid, 120–22.

[42] Ibid, 121.

[43] Ibid.

[44] Ibid. While the Tribunal did not say this directly, I suspect that the misconception about the precautionary principle reversing the burden of proof (discussed in the previous chapter) influenced the Tribunal's reasoning here.

[45] Ibid.

The Tribunal's interpretation is plausible. It attends to the precautionary principle and clearly articulates the principle's significance and implications. And indeed, the allure of the plain meaning of the EPA is strong in this instance. But I want to make a more ambitious argument that the Tribunal unreasonably capitulated to the apparent plain meaning of the EPA. From the perspective of public justification, a plausible interpretation is not sufficient for reasoning adequately. Rather, reasons must be properly oriented toward respecting the legal subject as a responsible agent. We will see that the Tribunal's own reasoning about how to administer the statutory tests and their remedies reveals this orientation and undermines the 'plain meaning' interpretation set out in *Erickson*.

This is an ambitious argument, in part because the Tribunal's interpretation in *Erickson* appears at first blush defensible. Under common law constitutional methodology, the legislature can displace common law principles by clear and unambiguous statutory language. It is certainly within the Ontario legislature's power to override the application of the precautionary principle in the REA context, but it must do so explicitly. However, it is not clear that the statutory tests in the EPA explicitly removed the precautionary principle. The statutory tests certainly do not do so by name. At best, the statute implies that the precautionary principle is not applicable to the statutory tests, given that it is not immediately obvious how to reconcile the precautionary principle's requirement of 'threats of harm' with the statutory tests' requirement that the appellant establish *actual* harm. Moreover, it is possible to connect the limited grounds for review to the legislature's prioritisation of renewable energy development.[46]

Yet if we accept that the precautionary principle plays an essential role in securing the rule of law in the environmental context, then we ought to tread very carefully in concluding that the legislature can displace such a fundamental principle by implication only. As we shall now see, the Tribunal had good reasons at its disposal that would have allowed it to reject the apparent 'plain meaning' of the statutory tests.

B. Precautionary Reasoning

Drawing on the Tribunal's own reasoning, this section argues that the Tribunal has articulated three good reasons for rejecting the 'plain meaning' of the EPA: (1) the plain meaning of the statutory tests renders mandatory statutory obligations unchallengeable; (2) excluding precautionary thinking risks creating a perverse regime in which the decision-makers can exploit sources of uncertainty to avoid publicly justifying their decisions; and

[46] See, eg, Green Energy Act, 2009 SO 2009, c 12, Sch A.

(3) the same reasoning for the application of the precautionary principle in the Tribunal's exercise of discretion applies to the interpretation of the statutory tests.

First, in *Erickson* itself, the Tribunal pointed to an inconsistency created by the 'plain meaning' of the statutory tests. In exercising its authority to issue an REA, the Director is bound by statute to consider the precautionary principle as part of the statement of environmental values.[47] But by precluding the application of the precautionary principle to the statutory tests, the EPA denies any remedy when the Director fails to do so (absent the additional requirement of serious harm to human health or the environment). Indeed, in *Erickson*, the Tribunal expressed concerns that the Director had inadequately carried out this duty, as it appeared that the Director 'simply paint[ed] standard measures with a precautionary brush'.[48] But nevertheless the Tribunal's interpretation of the statutory tests led it to conclude that 'no direct consequences flow from those concerns here'.[49]

When situated against the theory of public justification, the Tribunal's observation is elevated from a legislative anomaly to an attempt to exempt the Director from the rule-of-law requirement of public justification. The implication of the 'plain meaning' of the statutory tests is to impose a significant constraint on deliberation about whether each REA decision is an adequate reflection of how statutory and common law principles ought to be realised. Indeed, in this context, the relevant principles have even been explicitly and deliberately articulated under Ontario's Environmental Bill of Rights. This is not to suggest that the REAs cannot in fact be publicly justified on the basis of these principles, only instead that the 'plain meaning' of the statutory tests inhibits the ability of individuals to receive justification, which the rule of law ought to guarantee.

The Tribunal's response to the 'plain meaning' illogic has been to issue non-binding recommendations that better reflect the precautionary principle, a practice it started in *Erickson* and has repeated throughout its subsequent wind turbine jurisprudence.[50] It is a laudable attempt to use its particular environmental expertise to work within its perceived statutory constraints. But in light of the fact that the legislature did not explicitly override the application of the precautionary principle, those statutory constraints are a product of the Tribunal's own interpretive making.

The second context in which the Tribunal's own reasoning undermines its 'plain meaning' interpretation of the statutory tests is a collection of

[47] EBR (above n 11) s 11.

[48] *Erickson* (above n 37) 204–5.

[49] Ibid, 206.

[50] Ibid. See also, eg, *Lewis v Director, Ministry of the Environment*, No 14-029 (Ontario Environmental Review Tribunal, 2014) para 81 (recommending the Approval Holder not build two turbines in close proximity to a bald eagle nest until a long-term study was conducted on the effects of the remaining wind turbine farm on the eagles).

instances in which the Tribunal has been faced with key information gaps about the potential harm of a wind turbine project to an endangered species. The Tribunal's reasoning in this context demonstrates that the 'plain meaning' of the statutory tests is incompatible with the nature of environmental issues and risks creating a regime in which public decision-makers can exploit sources of uncertainty to avoid publicly justifying their decisions.

In *Alliance to Protect Prince Edward County*, appellants successfully challenged an REA on the basis that it would cause serious and irreversible harm to the endangered Blanding's turtle.[51] The appellants presented expert evidence that road infrastructure supporting the wind turbine development would lead to vehicle collisions with the threatened species and would facilitate poaching. Experts agreed that the project would cause serious harm; the contentious issue was whether the harm to the turtle population would be irreversible. However, the Tribunal did not have before it any data on the size of the Blanding's turtle population on site or in the region, and there had been no study on the current or expected increase in road traffic in the area.

Similarly, the Tribunal was confronted with an even bigger information gap with respect to the endangered redside dace in *Van Den Bosch*.[52] Historical data had identified occurrences of the declining species in the Van Den Bosch tributary, located within the project site. As recently as 2004, the Ministry had surveyed the tributary for individuals of the species (but identified no occurrences). Recent data did confirm the species' presence within the tributary's larger watershed. Yet no survey or assessment of the redside dace within the project area preceded the Director's granting of the REA, and the Director declined to attach any monitoring or follow-up conditions to the REA pertaining to the fish.

In *Hirsch*,[53] the Tribunal considered harm to the endangered little brown bat, which has experienced a ninety to ninety-give per cent population decline since 2010, largely due to the poorly understood white-nose syndrome.[54] Four previous Tribunal decisions had acknowledged the dramatic decline in the bat's population but held that the absence of population data and evidence of wind turbine harm meant that the environment test was not met.[55] However, in *Hirsch*, the Tribunal held that the

[51] *Alliance to Protect Prince Edward County (APPEC) v Ontario (Ministry of the Environment)*, [2013] OERTD No 40.

[52] *Van Den Bosch v Director, Ministry of the Environment*, No 14-007 (Ontario Environmental Review Tribunal, 2014).

[53] *Hirsch v Ontario (Ministry of the Environment and Climate Change)*, [2016] OERTD No 6.

[54] Ibid, para 125.

[55] *Lewis* (above n 50) para 92; *Fata v Director, Ministry of the Environment*, No13-145/13-146 (Ontario Environmental Review Tribunal, 2014) para 302; *APPEC* (above n 51) para 515; and *Bovaird v Director, Ministry of Environment*, No 13-070 to 13-075 (Ontario Environmental Review Tribunal, 2013) para 247.

circumstances had changed such that these gaps in understanding were no longer determinative.[56] It reasoned that the recent and ongoing precipitous decline in the bat population due to white-nose syndrome meant that 'an increase in mortality of even small numbers of Little Brown Bat constitutes a serious impact'[57] and that this harm would more likely than not cause irreversible decline to a severely stressed population.[58]

In all three decisions, the Tribunal reasoned that the absence of the key information was not determinative of the question of whether each project would cause serious and irreversible harm to the particular species in question. The Tribunal reasoned that it could not

> require an 'absolute' level of certainty with respect to the impacts of a Project. Such an approach is incompatible with the nature of biology, and our imperfect understanding of the impacts of human activity on plant life, animal life and the natural environment.[59]

The Tribunal has hence repeatedly demonstrated that it is prepared to rely on highly imperfect information to draw inferences about potential harm to these species.

Importantly for our purposes, the Tribunal's reasoning has quickly shifted from the 'nature of biology' to the nature of a regulatory scheme that can exploit these sources of uncertainty to escape publicly justifying its decisions. In each instance, the Tribunal drew attention to the fact that the information gaps are the product of an incomplete assessment of the project, an assessment that is the very purpose of requiring the proponent to obtain an REA in the first place. The Tribunal remarked that the expedited REA process made it impractical to generate specific population data in time for proper assessment and review.[60] Furthermore, in multiple instances, it has been perplexed why the government does not incorporate specific studies or monitoring conditions into the approval process.[61]

In a different context, the Tribunal has stated, 'The legal test in the EPA cannot mean that the Tribunal is unable to find serious and irreversible harm where there has not been adequate research done by the Approval Holder and Director.'[62] Herein lies a key insight into the Tribunal's understanding of its role in the approval process. The Tribunal is not prepared to allow the REA process turn into a façade of legality. It is attentive to the perversity of a regulatory regime designed to assess the possible effects of a

[56] *Hirsch* (above n 53) para 155.

[57] Ibid, para 155.

[58] Ibid, para 159.

[59] *APPEC* (above n 51) para 357.

[60] *Van Den Bosch* (above n 52) para 186.

[61] Ibid, paras 195 and 199; and *Hirsch* (above n 53) paras 135 and 138.

[62] *Bovaird* (above n 55) para 271 (speaking to a slightly different point about whether the Tribunal can refer to additional evidence that was not before the Ministry).

project but then when that assessment is done inadequately, denies a claimant the ability to challenge the decision on that very basis.

Its reasoning reflects the precautionary principle, if not in name, then in substance. The Tribunal recognises that uncertainty is endemic and that an environmental assessment will never be exhaustive, yet this does not act as a categorical bar to appellants meeting the statutory test. Rather, the Tribunal has redirected its focus to the context in which that uncertainty exists. The Tribunal is especially attentive to gaps that arise from a kind of regulatory wilful blindness or the inherent difficulty of assessing the particular ecological context (eg, obtaining hard numbers for a rare species). These gaps risk denying the appellants the public justification to which they are entitled in the first instance from the Director, and they further risk undermining the appellants' ability to actively participate in further deliberation about the adequacy of that justification before the Tribunal.

This reasoning about the administration of the statutory tests significantly erodes the Tribunal's own 'plain meaning' interpretation because it reveals the necessary role of the precautionary principle in maintaining a regime in which decisions are at least minimally justified. Without the kind of precautionary thinking that the Tribunal demonstrated in *Alliance to Protect Prince Edward County*, *Van den Bosch* and *Hirsch*, the statutory tests would be meaningless in the sense that they could virtually never be met. Moreover, the tests would have created a perverse incentive for government not to justify its decisions, because to do so would provide appellants the factual basis on which to challenge decisions before the Tribunal. Recognising the connection between the precautionary principle and the rule of law would empower the Tribunal to make explicit the necessary role of precaution in adjudicating a challenge to an REA.

Third and finally, when a statutory test has been met, the Tribunal's reasoning on its remedial authority reveals the same essential connection to its role in ensuring public justification. In the event that the Tribunal concludes that one or both of the statutory tests is met, the EPA grants the Tribunal the authority to step into the Director's shoes and revoke or amend the REA, or to order the Director to take further action.[63]

In contrast to the statutory tests, the Tribunal has held that this discretionary remedial authority must be informed by the precautionary principle. In *Alliance to Protect Prince Edward County*, the Tribunal held that the proposed wind turbine development would cause serious and irreversible harm to the endangered Blanding's turtle. This conclusion ultimately resulted in a subsequent hearing and decision on the appropriate remedy, in which the Tribunal considered whether it ought to revoke the REA or impose further conditions on the approval in the form of an impact monitoring plan.[64]

[63] EPA (above n 8) s 145.2(4).

[64] *Prince Edward County Field Naturalists v Ontario*, No 13-003 (Ontario Environmental Review Tribunal, 2016).

The Tribunal reasoned that it must exercise this discretionary authority in the public interest, informed by both the 'general and specific' purposes of the EPA.[65] It determined that the 'legislative objective of promoting renewable energy approvals … cannot be presumed to take priority over all the other factors.'[66] Further, it held:

> [As] a principle of international law incorporated into domestic law in *Spraytech* and a key principle of [the Ministry's statement of environmental values], [the precautionary principle] applies to decisions of the Director and to the Tribunal's choice of the appropriate remedy.[67]

It rejected the argument that its remedial discretion is narrowly constrained by the specific type of harm found to meet the statutory test(s).[68] The Tribunal held instead that its remedial authority is broad, and in order to reflect the public interest, it must consider relevant statutory principles—renewable energy, harm to endangered species, etc—as well as the principle of precaution.

The Tribunal has framed these interpretive conclusions as natural products of the 'modern approach to statutory interpretation'.[69] In its view, a liberal and generous interpretation of its remedial authority operates as an important counterweight to the restrictive statutory tests,[70] and it does not conflict with language elsewhere in the statute.[71] The Tribunal has bolstered this conclusion with an oddly literal observation that the EPA's purpose to protect and conserve the 'natural environment' does not specifically refer to renewable energy projects.[72]

But we are now in a position to see that the Tribunal's reasons, though framed as a free-floating act of statutory interpretation, are in fact implicitly connected to the fundamental project of public justification. The Tribunal has reasoned that its remedial discretion is inquiry into whether the general and specific purposes of the EPA, interpreted in light of the precautionary principle, are reflected in REAs and their conditions. Its remedial authority, in other words, is a direct inquiry into whether an approval was publicly justified in the first instance.

In the remedial context, appellants are respected as responsible agents, capable of fully participating in this regulatory regime. The remedial hearing, on the Tribunal's interpretation, allows for a full inquiry into whether

[65] Ibid, para 54.

[66] Ibid.

[67] Ibid, para 61. *Spraytech* refers to the Supreme Court of Canada's decision: *114957 Canada Ltée (Spraytech, Société d'arrosage) v Hudson (Town)*, 2001 SCC 40, [2001] 2 SCR 241.

[68] *Prince Edward County Field Naturalists v Ontario* (above n 64) para 64.

[69] Ibid, paras 41 and 65.

[70] *Erickson* (above n 37); *Prince Edward County Field Naturalists v Ontario* (above n 64) para 63.

[71] Ibid, para 63.

[72] Ibid, para 47.

the appellant's interests were appropriately considered in light of the statutory and common law context in the granting of the REA. The appellants are permitted to advance these claims before the Tribunal directly. And they are entitled to reasons from the Tribunal about why the REA is justified (with modified conditions), can be justified (with further directions to the Director) or cannot be justified (and so is revoked).

Despite this appropriate albeit largely implicit reasoning about the Tribunal's remedial discretion, its decisions reveal three limitations. First and most plainly, the Tribunal did not actually reason in this way when it considered the appropriate remedy in *Prince Edward County*. It did not ask, as it has said it must, whether the REA was publicly justified. Rather, it answered the much narrower question of whether the proposed conditions would be effective at preventing harm to the turtle population.[73]

The second limitation is that its interpretation of its remedial authority is question-begging. Assuming that the Tribunal is right, at least in what it says about its remedial authority (as I argue it is), then it is curious why this public justification is denied in instances when its self-imposed 'plain meaning' of the statutory test is not met. Recall that the Tribunal is entitled and indeed required to assume that all other institutions of government are committed to the rule-of-law project of public justification, including the legislature. In the absence of explicit statutory language that precludes a core legal principle—here, the precautionary principle—the Tribunal ought to assume, as it does in the remedial context, that it applies. In this way, there is no fundamental difference in the conditions for legal authority that pertain to statutory language or the exercise of discretion.[74] In every case, the question is whether, when interpreted and administered, the exercise of public authority is publicly justified in light of the relevant statutory considerations and the common law protections of individual agency.

Third, and as we explore more fully in the next section, the Tribunal's failure to explicitly connect its interpretation of its remedial authority to the underlying orientation of ensuring public justification makes its decisions vulnerable to judicial intervention upon review. Awkward statements that renewable energy projects are not encompassed by the purpose of protecting the 'environment' or 'natural environment' leap out as unprincipled potential errors, when in fact they are red herrings in the search for a consistent method for justifying major developments that contain both environmental benefits and risks.

This section has argued that the Tribunal has reasoned adequately when its reasons reveal an orientation toward preserving the status of legal

[73] Ibid, paras 133–34 (notes that, in light of its findings on mitigation measures, it need not consider any further submissions).

[74] *Baker v Canada (Minister of Citizenship and Immigration)*, [1999] 2 SCR 817, 1 Imm LR (3d) 1.

subjects as responsible agents. The Tribunal has implicitly reasoned in this way in three instances: when it identified the constraints on its ability to review the Director's consideration of the statement of environmental values, when it implicitly applied the precautionary principle to its treatment of information gaps with respect to endangered species and when it interpreted its remedial authority. Importantly, these three instances of reasoning adequately undermine the Tribunal's early conclusion that the statutory tests displace the precautionary principle. By situating the Tribunal's reasoning within the requirement of public justification, we can now see that the Tribunal unreasonably submitted to a 'plain meaning' interpretation of the statutory tests.

C. Reasoning Adequately and Earning Deference

We have seen that in the wind turbine context, the Tribunal has reasoned thoroughly, but from the perspective of the public-justification conception of the rule of law, it has not always reasoned adequately. To be clear, all of the Tribunal's reasons considered in the previous section are plausible. Indeed, in light of the Supreme Court of Canada's current bifurcated approach to reasonableness, it would be difficult for a court to find a basis on which to intervene. However, the public-justification conception of the rule of law requires more than plausible reasoning; it requires reasons that respect the responsible agency of those affected by the decisions.

This section considers the limited instances in which the courts have reviewed the Tribunal's wind turbine decisions. These decisions help us appreciate the need for the Tribunal to explicitly connect its reasons to fundamental rule-of-law principles. Even with the Tribunal's relatively timid approach to administering its powers, the courts have inappropriately intervened. Moreover, even when a court has deferred to the Tribunal's reasoning, it has done so more as a form of submission than as a respectful deference to the Tribunal as a collaborative partner in the rule-of-law project.

In *Alliance to Protect Prince Edward County*, the Tribunal held that the proposed wind turbine project would cause serious and irreversible harm to the endangered Blanding's turtle. It reached this conclusion in spite of a lack of data on the population size of the species and an absence of information about the road traffic conditions that posed the major threat to the species' survival. On judicial review, the Ontario Divisional Court held that the Tribunal's decision was unreasonable.[75] The Court stated that while it was 'not suggesting that mathematical precision was necessary regarding the population size of Blanding's turtle … there had to be some level of data

[75] *Ostrander Point GP Inc v Prince Edward County Field Naturalists*, 2014 ONSC 974.

… before a finding could be made on the issue of irreversible harm.'[76] The Court further reasoned that the Tribunal had insufficiently considered the fact that the Approval Holder was subject to mitigation conditions imposed under the Endangered Species Act. It held in conclusion that the Tribunal's decision was unreasonable and that the REA should be restored.

The Divisional Court's inappropriate decision to restore the REA demonstrates the subtlety in the method of review for reasonableness. It demonstrates the risk of reasonableness review blurring into correctness when a court does not properly attend to the fundamental principles that underlie an administrative decision. Unlike the decisions canvassed above in chapter two, this is not an instance of 'free rein within bounds'. Here, the Court attended to the reasons of the Tribunal and did so in a more robust fashion than simply checking to make sure the decision-maker had ticked the appropriate boxes. The problem is that the Court did not acknowledge in any way that it was engaged in the practice of reweighing the factors before the Tribunal. It approached its reviewing task as a de-contextualised 'treasure hunt for errors'[77] without any awareness of why these 'errors', in the actual context of the Tribunal's decision, might not have been errors at all.

The Court's application of reasonableness was misguided in two principal ways. First, by seizing on the data gaps as indicia of unreasonableness, the Divisional Court missed the underlying purpose and function of the REA regime. Unlike the Tribunal, the Court offered no sense of the implications of its decision. Yes, the Tribunal is required to reason in a way that 'allow[s] the reviewing court to understand why the Tribunal made its decision.'[78] But to demand more than this—to require the Tribunal to dismiss challenges on the basis of scientific uncertainty—is to make the Tribunal complicit in a process that denies individuals publicly justified decisions. Indeed, the Tribunal's decision was supported by reasons and evidence in this instance—the harm faced by the population was so acute and the population so vulnerable to harm that a qualitative assessment of the data supported a finding of serious and irreversible harm.[79]

Second, the Divisional Court's decision was misguided in holding the Tribunal to a much higher standard of justification than the original decision to issue the REA. This is apparent in the Court's detailed analysis of the Endangered Species Act permit, which the Court was prepared to assume

[76] Ibid, para 47.

[77] *Communications, Energy and Paperworkers Union of Canada, Local 30 v Irving Pulp and Paper Ltd*, 2013 SCC 34, [2013] 2 SCR 458, para 52 *per* Abella J.

[78] *Ostrander Point v PECFN* (above n 75) para 38 (quoting *Newfoundland and Labrador Nurses' Union v Newfoundland and Labrador (Treasury Board)*, 2011 SCC 62, [2011] 3 SCR 708, para 16.

[79] *APPEC* (above n 51) para 358. As we will see in a moment, the Court of Appeal reached this conclusion as well.

was publicly justified,[80] despite the fact that the adequacy of endangered species protection was *the* contentious issue before the Tribunal. The Court reasoned that 'the Tribunal was obliged to explain how the fact that the [Ministry] had concluded under the ESA that the Project would lead to an overall benefit to Blanding's turtle ... could mesh with its conclusion that the Project would cause irreversible harm to the same species.'[81] Yet it was not the Tribunal's role to explain the Ministry's decision on its behalf. All that was required in this instance was that the Tribunal adequately justify its decision that the Ministry's decision was *not* justified. Indeed, it did this by reasoning that its scope of analysis under the EPA was the local population (and not the entire province) and then analysing the (in)effectiveness of the proposed mitigation measures for preventing serious and irreversible harm to the vulnerable population.[82] By missing this important but subtle distinction in the Tribunal's role, the Court was prepared to let an unjustified public decision stand because of the (apparent) lack of adequate reasoning by a reviewing body. The absence of a cogent theory of the rule of law led the Court to a troubling inverted conclusion.

Fortunately, the Court of Appeal overturned the Divisional Court's problematic decision and restored the Tribunal's finding of serious and irreversible harm to the Blanding's turtle.[83] Yet the Appeal Court's reasoning similarly avoids any connection to the underlying principles served by its reviewing role, that of the Tribunal or indeed, that of the REA regulatory regime in the first instance. So while the Court of Appeal's approach to reasonableness was an improvement on the Divisional Court's, it does not instil much confidence that the courts will be willing to defer to more ambitious Tribunal decisions—for example, decisions that invoke the precautionary principle when applying the statutory tests.

Rather than justify its decision on the basis of the Tribunal's attentiveness to fundamental rule-of-law principles, the Court of Appeal deferred primarily on the basis that the Tribunal—and not the Court—was the fact-finder and assessor of expert credibility with respect to serious and irreversible harm.[84] This is no doubt correct, as far as it goes. But it suggests

[80] *Ostrander Point v PECFN* (above n 75) para 60.

[81] Ibid, para 70.

[82] *APPEC* (above n 51) para 343. One notable feature was that the developer had proposed a habitat offset area, to mitigate the harm to the turtle, but the proposed offset was existing Blanding's turtle habitat. This measure could have led the Ministry to the conclusion about the overall benefit to the species, but as the Tribunal reasoned, it could not count as an effective mitigation measure at the ecosystem scale (para 340).

[83] *Prince Edward County Field Naturalists v Ostrander Point GP Inc*, 2015 ONCA 269. Both the Divisional Court and Court of Appeal agreed that the Tribunal was required to hold a hearing on the appropriate remedy, so the matter was remitted back to the Tribunal (the subject of the *PEC* decision considered note 63).

[84] *Prince Edward County Field Naturalists v Ostrander Point GP* (ibid) paras 54–58, 61 and 66.

a form of deference as submission.[85] That is, the Court submitted to the Tribunal on the basis of its asserted or assumed expertise, not because the Tribunal reasoned in a way that earned the Court's respect (and thus deference). The Court's easy classification in this instance of the Tribunal's role as a fact-finder misses the underlying connection between the manner in which Tribunal approached this fact-finding role and the ultimate outcome of whether affected individuals were able to effectively participate in deliberations about whether the REA was publicly justified.

In short, there is nothing in the Court's reasoning that suggests it viewed the Tribunal as a collaborator in the rule-of-law project. It is this absence that reveals the need for the Tribunal to reason explicitly about core rule-of-law principles—its role in promoting public justification and for ensuring, to the extent possible, that those subject to public decisions are treated as active participants, capable of reasoning with the law. While the Court of Appeal restored the Tribunal's reasoning in this case, there is no indication that it would have been willing to do so had the Tribunal taken the bolder step of maintaining a robust role for the precautionary principle. Indeed, in the absence of the theory of public justification, such an ambitious interpretation would likely stand out as a lightning rod for inappropriate judicial intervention.

IV. CONCLUSION

This chapter has considered the contentious context of industrial wind turbine development in Ontario. Approvals for wind turbine projects are channelled through a regulatory regime that attempts to constrain the opportunities for challenging decisions that are perceived as unjustified. In this way, the legislature has fallen short of its institutional ideal. It has attempted to limit the ongoing obligation of public justification.

Nonetheless, the Environmental Review Tribunal—the battleground for these legal challenges—offers a fruitful context for understanding how, in order to be reasonable, reasons must be oriented toward fundamental rule-of-law principles even within a highly imperfect regulatory regime. This chapter has argued that reasonableness requires public officials to offer intelligible reasons that justify the outcome on the basis of the relevant statutory considerations while always reflecting the common law constitution, which is protective of legal subjects as responsible agents who are capable of reasoning with the law.

[85] D Dyzenhaus, 'The Politics of Deference: Judicial Review and Democracy' in M Taggart (ed), *The Province of Administrative Law* (Oxford, Hart Publishing, 1997) 286.

To be clear, nothing in this argument suggests that individuals who challenge REAs are entitled to the remedy they seek (which is to prevent wind turbine development). Rather, they are entitled to public justification that takes seriously the ways that their interests are affected by the public decision. We have seen that the regime here is doubly affective of their interests. The original decision to approve a development proposal implicates their interests in health and healthy environment, and the Tribunal's jurisdiction implicates their interest in being able to participate fully in the ongoing deliberations about whether the original decision adequately accounted for their interests.

The chapter has argued that when the Tribunal attends to both sets of these interests, it reasons adequately. Moreover, the instances in which the Tribunal has reasoned adequately cast a shadow across its early conclusion that its governing statutory provisions preclude the application of the precautionary principle. Anchoring the Tribunal's reasoning in the public-justification conception of the rule-of-law empowers the Tribunal to take a much more ambitious stance, one that embraces precaution as a fundamental rule-of-law principle and that resists legislative attempts to implicitly limit this principle's role in protecting individual agency in environmental decision-making.

8

The Rule of Law and the Right to a Healthy Environment

THE FOCUS OF the book thus far has been the implications of the environmental emergency framework for the province of administrative law, broadly conceived. In contrast, this chapter turns to the implications for constitutional law and, in particular, what theoretical insights the environmental emergency brings to the potential development of a Canadian Charter right to a healthy environment. Constitutional environmental rights raise a host of interesting issues that intersect with vibrant debates in legal and political theory.[1] In light of these rich debates, the argument of this chapter is modest. It marks the connection between constitutional environmental rights adjudication and the public-justification conception of the rule of law. It argues that proposals for a Charter right to a healthy environment demand a coherent theory of the rule of law, and it suggests that the public-justification conception provides a promising foundation for making such a right a meaningful one.

This chapter addresses the academic and activist momentum behind proposals for a Charter right to a healthy environment.[2] These proposals are not new; discussions about environmental rights protection in Canada predate the enactment of the Charter of Rights and Freedoms in 1982. Yet current proposals are now bolstered by subsequent decades of international experience with environmental rights, leaving Canada as an apparent laggard in domestic environmental law innovation. Proponents of a Charter right to a healthy environment argue that recognising this right in the Constitution would guarantee Canadians a minimal standard of environmental quality as well as the procedural protections (eg, public notice and

[1] For more comprehensive examinations of environmental rights in their own right, see T Hayward, *Constitutional Environmental Rights* (Oxford, Oxford University Press, 2005); and DR Boyd, *The Environmental Rights Revolution: A Global Study of Constitutions, Human Rights, and the Environment* (Vancouver, University of British Columbia Press, 2012).

[2] See, eg, the David Suzuki Foundation's Canada-wide 'Blue Dot' campaign which advocates for a Charter amendment: David Suzuki Foundation, bluedot.ca.

participatory rights) to enforce this guarantee.[3] Some proponents also argue that a Charter right could protect the environment for its own sake (eg, biodiversity or ecological integrity), independent of demonstrable impact on human individuals.[4] This chapter takes these proposals as they are; it remains agnostic on both the desirability and political feasibility of environmental rights enshrined in the Charter.

Constitutional rights proposals follow logically from the environmental reform position that was introduced and analysed above in chapter two. Recall that the primary concern of the environmental reform position is legislation that delegates sweeping discretion to the executive, allowing for environmental degradation that interferes with individual autonomy by potentially undermining life, health and well-being.[5] A constitutional right to a healthy environment would empower individuals affected in this way to make claims that their fundamental interests have been infringed and would entitle them to legal remedy should they successfully make out these claims. More than this, a constitutional environmental right would also constrain the legislature, which is subject to similar political forces as criticised by the environmental reform position. A constitutional environmental right would impose limits on the content of environmental legislation. Enshrining environmental protection in the constitution would insulate basic environmental protection from the contingencies and pressures of everyday politics.

Approaching environmental issues from the emergency perspective, however, should give us pause about the potential impact of a Charter right to a healthy environment. As Oren Gross and Fionnuala Ni Aolain have observed, constitutional rights have historically not proven an effective constraint on the state in times of crisis.[6] Should we expect that a Charter right to a healthy environment too would prove ineffective? As we will see, there is good reason to believe that it might, although the underlying reasons differ from those in the national security emergency context. As we saw in chapter 1, the primary concern of constitutional scholars writing about national security emergencies is the concentration of power with the executive and the curtailment of civil liberties. Yet constitutional environmental

[3] Constitutional environmental rights are framed in different terms: for example, a right to a 'safe', 'adequate', 'ecologically balanced' or, alternatively, 'decent' environment. They are sometimes expressed through a separate bill of environmental rights with several component parts. In light of the absence of a stand-alone environmental Charter right, this chapter refers to Canadian proposals as a 'right to a healthy environment' simply for ease of reference.

[4] Charter of Human Rights and Freedoms, CQLR c C-12, s 46.1 [hereafter 'Quebec Charter']; and Constitution of the Republic of Ecuador, arts 71 and 72.

[5] See above ch 2, section I.

[6] O Gross and FN Aolain, *Law in Times of Crisis: Emergency Powers in Theory and Practice* (Cambridge, Cambridge University Press, 2006) 7.

rights are often thought to operate in a manner that further empowers the government to address environmental problems and that constrains some individual rights and interests, such as the enjoyment of private property.[7] As a result, constitutional environmental rights tap into two deep distinctions that run through rights literature: the distinction between positive and negative rights, and the distinction between process and substance.

In this chapter, we will see that Canadian academic support for a Charter right to a healthy environment acknowledges these distinctions but treats them as antiquated or irrelevant. The problem is that current proposals for an environmental Charter lack a fully theorised understanding of the rule of law, one that connects environmental rights to the method and practice of Canadian public law more generally and rights adjudication specifically. By failing to attend to the rule of law, existing Canadian literature on this subject has not addressed the basic path determinacy[8] of common law adjudication and, in particular, the ways in which this reliance on past practice and precedent has perpetuated the process/substance and positive/negative rights dichotomies in rights adjudication in Canada. As a result, it is far from obvious that enshrining a Charter right to a healthy environment—without anything more—would have the transformative effect that its proponents hope. The public-justification conception of the rule of law, in contrast, promises a much more fruitful foundation for constitutional rights jurisprudence because it offers a coherent theory and method of common law adjudication that reconceives the two distinctions mentioned above, both of which have undermined environment-related rights claims in Canada thus far.

This chapter proceeds in three sections. Section I introduces David Boyd's leading academic proposal for a Charter right to a healthy environment. It highlights the claims that Boyd has made about what this Charter right would empower courts to do that they cannot or will not do already. Boyd has acknowledged that these claims engage the process/substance and positive/negative rights dichotomies, but he has dismissed these dichotomies as essentially irrelevant, 'theoretical' concerns. Section II then argues that Boyd has failed to sufficiently attend to the practice and method of rights adjudication in Canada. The section takes a close look at environment-related claims made under section 7 of the Charter and reveals that the process/substance and positive/negative rights distinctions are alive and well and, contrary to Boyd's conclusion, operate as significant obstacles to rights claimants. These two distinctions therefore cannot be easily dismissed as purely theoretical concerns. Section III then explains how the

[7] For a summary of the relationship between environmental catastrophe and authoritarianism, see A Dobson, *Green Political Thought*, 3rd edn (New York, Routledge, 2000) 114–16.

[8] Thanks to Mary Liston for suggesting this phrasing.

two distinctions are products of the formal conception of the rule of law and thus risk undermining robust rights protection under a prospective Charter right to a healthy environment. It then argues that, in contrast, the public-justification conception of the rule of law offers a promising foundation for constitutional rights adjudication that makes Boyd's central claims theoretically defensible and practically realisable.

I. THE CASE FOR A CHARTER RIGHT TO A HEALTHY ENVIRONMENT

Boyd has argued that Canadians ought to enjoy constitutional protection for a right to healthy environment. This right would 'ensure that everyone has access to clean air, safe water, fertile soil, and nutritious food, as well as the conservation of biological diversity and ecosystem functions'.[9] He argues that the ubiquity and severity of environmental issues have gained a recognition that demands an explicit constitutional response.[10] A Charter right to a healthy environment would reflect the severity of the environmental problems that Canadians face and moreover would reflect the fundamental values of the polity.[11]

Other environmental scholars agree that environmental rights ought to be accorded constitutional status. Tim Hayward has analogised a constitutional right to a healthy environment to fundamental constitutional protections such as freedom from torture:

> [J]ust as individuals have a right not to be subject to the kinds of harm wrought by practices of torture, unlawful detention, and so on, they may equally be thought to have a right not to be subject to comparable sorts of harm which might be wrought through practices which assail them, for instance, with toxic pollutants.[12]

Indeed, international practice lends support to these arguments.[13] Environmental rights have constitutional status in states around the world,[14] and international legal institutions recognise the importance of a right to a

[9] DR Boyd, *The Right to a Healthy Environment: Revitalizing Canada's Constitution* (Vancouver, University of British Columbia Press, 2012) 1. On the nature of environmental rights as fundamental human rights, see Hayward, *Constitutional Environmental Rights* (above n 1) 36–54; Boyd, *The Environmental Rights Revolution* (above n 1) 21; and EL Hughes and D Iyalomhe, 'Substantive Environmental Rights in Canada' (1998) 30 *Ottawa Law Review* 229.

[10] Boyd, *The Right to a Healthy Environment* (ibid) 6–10. See also Hayward, *Constitutional Environmental Rights* (above n 1) 5.

[11] Boyd, *The Right to a Healthy Environment* (above n 9) 4–6.

[12] Hayward, *Constitutional Environmental Rights* (above n 1) 149.

[13] See generally Boyd, *The Environmental Rights Revolution* (above n 1).

[14] According to Boyd, *The Right to a Healthy Environment* (above n 9) 2, 177 of 193 countries worldwide recognise a right to a healthy environment in some form.

healthy environment.[15] Québec has enacted a right to a healthy environment in its quasi-constitutional Charter of Human Rights and Freedoms.[16] But Canada has repeatedly balked at opportunities to recognise a right to healthy environment within its Charter of Rights and Freedoms.[17]

A. The Claims

A Charter right to a healthy environment is an exciting prospect for Canadian environmental law, although, as we will see, its transformative potential is unclear. Boyd has acknowledged as much but draws on international experience with environmental rights to make several lofty claims about the potential effects in Canada of a Charter right to a healthy environment. He argues that Charter recognition could bring about stimulus for stronger environmental laws, stronger implementation and enforcement of existing environmental laws, a 'safety net' that would allow courts to fill in gaps in environmental legislation, prohibition of future legislative 'rollbacks' in environmental protection, improved democratic accountability, a level playing field with social and economic rights in decision-making, environmental justice for vulnerable populations and better public education by reflecting and reinforcing Canadian environmental values.[18]

This section highlights two claims that underlie many of Boyd's asserted benefits of a Charter right to a healthy environment: that a Charter right would strengthen environmental interests as relevant considerations in legal decision-making and that it would equip judges with a novel arsenal of judicial remedies for enforcing rights protection.

First, Boyd has argued that a Charter right to a healthy environment will help to 'level the playing field' when public officials make decisions

[15] Stockholm Declaration (Declaration of the United Nations Conference on the Human Environment), 1972, UN Doc A/CONF.48/14/Rev 1, Principle 1; Aarhus Convention on Access to Information, Public Participation in Decision Making and Access to Justice in Environmental Matters, 1998, 28 ILM 515; and L Collins, 'The United Nations, Human Rights and the Environment' in A Grear and LJ Kotzé (eds), *Research Handbook on Human Rights and the Environment* (Cheltenham, Edward Elgar Publishing, 2015) 219.

[16] Quebec Charter (above n 4) s 46.1.

[17] Boyd, *The Right to a Healthy Environment* (above n 9) ch 3.

[18] Ibid, 18–19. See also J Swaigen and RE Woods, 'A Substantive Right to Environmental Quality' in J Swaigen (ed), *Environmental Rights in Canada* (Toronto, Butterworths, 1981) 195; S Theriault, 'The Food Security of the Inuit in Times of Change' (2011) 2 *Journal of Human Rights and the Environment* 136; S Paquerot, 'Environmental Concerns and the Interdependence of Human Rights: A Path to Political Responsibility?' in M Jackman and B Porter (eds), *Advancing Social Rights in Canada* (Toronto, Irwin Law, 2014) 365; K Mitchell and Z D'Onofrio, 'Environmental Injustice and Racism in Canada: The First Step is Admitting We Have a Problem' (2016) 29 *Journal of Environmental Law and Practice* 305. These all support various aspects of Boyd's claims about what a constitutional right to a healthy environment would achieve.

with environmental consequences. He has written that such a right 'could tip the balance in many regulatory, administrative, corporate, and judicial decisions, increasing the likelihood that future development will in fact be sustainable'.[19] However, the causal mechanisms for levelling the playing field are varied and underexplored in his work. His hope, in most cases, seems to be that the enshrinement of a constitutional environmental right will spur legislative commitment and innovation and improved resource allocation or prioritisation of environmental protection objectives within the executive.[20] But the fall-back in every case is that a constitutional right to a healthy environment would empower individuals and groups to seek judicial enforcement of the constitutional norm. For example, he has written:

> If Canadian governments refused to accelerate efforts to improve today's inadequate air quality, concerned individuals or communities would have recourse to the courts to seek protection of their constitutional right to a healthy environment.[21]

In each case, the court would be asked to adjudicate on whether the decision-maker—whether the legislature or an administrative decision-maker—struck the appropriate balance between protection of the constitutional right to a healthy environment and competing interests. Are Canada's air quality standards, for example, adequate to fulfil the constitutional right to a healthy environment? If not, are the limits on this right nonetheless demonstrably justified in a free and democratic society? The implication of a constitutional right to a healthy environment, in Boyd's view, is that it could lead to a 'better balance'[22] between nature and economic considerations or could counter otherwise strong statutory and common law protection of private property rights.[23]

Boyd is fuzzy on the details of how a Canadian court would engage in an inquiry about the appropriate balance between environmental and economic considerations. The existence of a constitutional right would seem to force this inquiry on judges in a way that they have thus far avoided in the administrative law context. Moreover, the nature of the inquiry—fleshing out the content of a right to a healthy environment—engages the same complex questions about ecological systems, human health and what constitutes a reasonable response to human impacts on the environment that judges

[19] Boyd, *The Right to a Healthy Environment* (above n 9) 22. See also Hayward, *Constitutional Environmental Rights* (above n 1) 8.

[20] Boyd, *The Right to a Healthy Environment* (above n 9) 148 (legislative review for Charter compliance), 150 (legislative innovation such as new enforcement agencies), 149 (improved resource allocation) and 153 (protecting progressive environmental legislation from attack by industry).

[21] Ibid, 155 and also 165–66 (on climate change mitigation).

[22] Ibid, 167.

[23] Ibid, 22–23.

have expressed much discomfort about addressing in the administrative law context.

Boyd's claim about levelling the playing field taps into deeper questions about how a court can adjudicate these matters without inappropriately substituting its own opinion on the substance of government policy. It recalls the formalist judge's perspective that the role of the courts is limited to supervising procedure and policing the clear boundaries of relevant statutes.[24] It also taps into a persistent concern that positive rights—rights that impose a positive duty on the duty-bearer—compel judges to adjudicate upon policy matters that are better left to other institutions of government.

Second, Boyd's case for a Charter right to a healthy environment relies heavily on the potential for creative and novel judicial remedies that would flow from the enactment of constitutional environmental rights. The most basic novel constitutional remedy would be the power to strike down environmental legislation that fails to comply with the right to a healthy environment.[25] Boyd is optimistic that the strike-down would be a credible threat, one that would influence governments to perform their own, pre-enactment internal reviews for Charter compliance and one that courts would follow through on in the event the government did not. The credibility of the strike-down remedy follows directly on the heels of Boyd's assumptions of judicial willingness to tackle the necessary balancing exercise in any claim of an environmental rights violation.

Boyd has suggested that the strike-down power could be further strengthened through a doctrine of non-regression.[26] Drawing on international environmental law, he and Lynda Collins have argued that non-regression could prevent 'future rollbacks that attempt to weaken environmental laws, regulations, and standards'.[27] The specific method by which a court would reach such a conclusion is not entirely clear, however. Boyd and Collins have argued that non-regression could alleviate the burden of proof on claimants by requiring only that they bring 'evidence that the impugned state action represents a reduction in environmental protection compared to its predecessor.'[28] But again they assume the willingness of courts to independently engage in this kind of causal inquiry rather than, for example, defer to government expertise.

In addition to the strike-down power, Boyd has claimed that a Charter right to a healthy environment could provide a safety net that could 'help address Canada's gaps in environmental legislation, regulations, policies,

[24] See above ch 2, section II.
[25] Constitution Act 1982, Schedule B to the Canada Act 1982 (UK), 1982, c 11, s 52.
[26] Boyd, *The Right to a Healthy Environment* (above n 9) 150–52.
[27] LM Collins and DR Boyd, 'Non-Regression and the Charter Right to a Healthy Environment' (2016) 29 *Journal of Environmental Law and Practice* 286, 293.
[28] Ibid, 303.

and implementation'.[29] He has not elaborated on the contours of this judicial power but has implied that a Charter right would allow courts to order legislators to legislate or the executive to regulate where their failure to do so violates the right to a healthy environment.[30]

Boyd has written favourably of judicial remedial innovations elsewhere. He has noted instances in which courts have made extensive remedial orders for environmental restoration, including: orders to the government to conduct environmental assessments and educational programmes; mandatory information disclosure by polluters; the development of clean-up and restoration plans; as well as the creation of an independent scientific review panel to assist the court in its oversight role.[31] He has written positively about a court retaining ongoing supervisory authority of quarterly public meetings that enable the public to question public officials on the government's progress in fulfilling the Court's order.[32]

The examples lauded by Boyd demonstrate courts compelling governments to take specific actions to restore environmental health in order to comply with their constitutional obligations. These examples implicate a key feature of so-called positive rights and thus tap into the deeper constitutional debates about the appropriateness of positive rights in a constitutional democracy. As we will see in the following sections, these debates have both theoretical and practical import for the future of environmental rights in Canada.

B. The Dichotomies

Boyd has acknowledged the fact that constitutional environmental rights implicate deeper concerns about the judicial role. He has also acknowledged that environmental rights are no panacea for the overwhelming and complex suite of environmental problems we face. Yet he is clear in his view that any reservations about the operation and desirability of a constitutional environmental right should be resolved not 'on the basis of theoretical arguments but [by] practical experience and empirical evidence'.[33] He neglects, however, the fact that Canadian practice and empirical evidence

[29] Boyd, *The Right to a Healthy Environment* (above n 9) 21.

[30] Ibid, 94 (citing foreign examples where courts ordered legislatures to enact legislation or 'influenced states to take action'). See also Boyd, *The Environmental Rights Revolution* (above n 1) 235.

[31] Boyd, *The Right to a Healthy Environment* (above n 9) 161.

[32] Ibid, 162. For a nice discussion of how ongoing judicial supervision has alternately catalysed and paralysed Indian human rights adjudication, see S Fredman, *Human Rights Transformed: Positive Rights and Positive Duties* (Oxford, Oxford University Press, 2008) 134–36.

[33] Boyd, *The Right to a Healthy Environment* (above n 9) 35.

reveal that these 'theoretical arguments' have considerable influence in how environmental rights claims are adjudicated. This section introduces two dichotomies implicated by the proposed Charter right to a healthy environment: the process/substance dichotomy and the dichotomy between positive rights and negative rights. We will see that the process/substance dichotomy has played a formative role in the conception of environmental rights but has not been the subject of the same degree of scrutiny as it has in other public law contexts. While environmental rights proponents are more in step with the broader academic debates over the positive/negative rights dichotomy, Boyd has nonetheless been too quick to declare the debate settled in favour of positive rights.

i. The Process/Substance Dichotomy and Environmental Rights Adjudication

The process/substance distinction permeates a variety of legal contexts.[34] David Dyzenhaus and Evan Fox-Decent have concisely summarised the process/substance distinction as relying on:

> a categorical difference between the outcome of a decision and the process undertaken to arrive at the decision. Thus, a substantive right is considered a right to a particular outcome or range of outcomes and is a right that cannot be generated by a procedural entitlement.[35]

Process, then, pertains to 'the fairness and efficiency of the litigation and the evidentiary process', but it can also pertain to 'the manner and means needed to access the courts, the availability of remedies, and matters relating to justiciability'.[36]

The process/substance distinction plays an ongoing role in the development of environmental law. At the international level, the United Nations has fostered a specialised body of international law on participatory rights in the environmental context.[37] These specialised participatory rights have come to play a central role in the development of environmental rights more generally and are typically cast as procedural in contrast to substantive environmental rights, which are said to guarantee some basic standard

[34] O Malcai and R Levine-Schnur, 'Which Came First, the Procedure or the Substance? Justificational Priority and the Substance–Procedure Distinction' (2014) 34 *Oxford Journal of Legal Studies* 1, 1–5; and TO Main, 'The Procedural Foundation of Substantive Law' (2010) 87 *Washington University Law Review* 801, 804–11 (on the historical origins of the distinction).

[35] D Dyzenhaus and E Fox-Decent, 'Rethinking the Process/Substance Distinction: *Baker v Canada*' (2001) 51 *University of Toronto Law Journal* 193, 195.

[36] M Liston, 'Transubstantiation in Canadian Public Law: Processing Substance and Instantiating Process' in J Bell et al (eds), *Public Law Adjudication in Common Law Systems* (Oxford, Hart Publishing, 2016) 214.

[37] Collins, 'The United Nations' (above n 15) 227.

of environmental health (the outcome). Hayward has described procedural environmental rights as 'essentially participatory rights in that they formally empower citizens to demand information relating to the environment, to participate in decision-making processes, and to apply for judicial means of redress.'[38] These three components are the central 'pillars' of the Aarhus Convention (1998),[39] an international environmental agreement that enjoys widespread support but which Canada has not signed onto.[40] This support can in part be attributed to the perception that access to information, participatory rights and access to justice are thought to be less controversial and easier to enforce than substantive environmental rights.[41]

Despite its widespread support and some noted improvements in procedural guarantees, commentary on the Aarhus Convention is not overwhelmingly positive. Scholars have observed that the agreement bifurcates process and substance.[42] The preamble of the Convention recognises that 'every person has the right to live in an environment adequate to his or her health and well-being', yet the operational provisions are only procedural. This has led commentators to situate the Aarhus Convention as part of a broader trend of 'proceduralisation' in environmental law.[43] One assumption underlying proceduralisation is that better, more informed participation will lead better environmental results. While some see the potential benefits of flexibility that come with enforcing procedures rather than substance,[44] others worry that the substantive implications of robust procedures are asserted, not proven.[45] They point to special challenges of environmental issues, such as short-term trade-offs and uncertainty about environmental

[38] Hayward, *Constitutional Environmental Rights* (above n 1) 85.

[39] United Nations Economic Commission for Europe and United Nations Environment Programme, 'Your Right to a Healthy Environment: A Simplified Guide to the Aarhus Convention on Access to Information, Public Participation in Decision-Making and Access to Justice in Environmental Matters' (July 2006), www.unece.org, 4; and M Lee and C Abbott, 'The Usual Suspects? Public Participation under the Aarhus Convention' (2003) 66 *Modern Law Review* 80, 82.

[40] For a list of parties to the Convention, see United Nations Treaty Collection, treaties.un.org/Pages/ViewDetails.aspx?src=IND&mtdsg_no=XXVII-13&chapter=27&clang=_en. See Hayward, *Constitutional Environmental Rights* (above n 1) 178, who describes it as the 'most important step yet taken towards environmental rights protection'.

[41] G Handl, 'Human Rights and Protection of the Environment' in A Eide, C Krause and A Rosas (eds), *Economic, Social and Cultural Rights: A Textbook*, 2nd edn (Dordrecht, M Nijhoff, 2001) 305; M Mason, 'Information Disclosure and Environmental Rights: The Aarhus Convention' (2010) 10 *Global Environmental Politics* 10, 17; and Hayward, *Constitutional Environmental Rights* (above n 1) 84.

[42] Mason, 'Information Disclosure' (ibid) 17; and Hayward, *Constitutional Environmental Rights* (above n 1) 180.

[43] Lee and Abbott, 'The Usual Suspects?' (above n 39) 80.

[44] See above ch 3; and J Scott, 'Flexibility, "Proceduralization" and Environmental Governance in the EU' in G de Burca and J Scott (eds), *Constitutional Change in the EU: From Uniformity to Flexibility?* (Oxford, Hart Publishing, 2000) 259.

[45] Mason, 'Information Disclosure' (above n 41) 17.

benefits, that threaten to undermine gains that might otherwise be made through better process.[46] The problem, on this view, is not necessarily the distinction between process and substance but rather the conspicuous absence of the latter.[47]

Boyd has affirmed this view, declaring, 'The debate about substantive versus procedural environmental rights has been resolved by recognition that they are both necessary and complementary.'[48] This may be true as far as it goes, but it neglects the way in the process/substance binary itself might undermine the ambitions of environmental rights.

Outside the field of environmental law, the problematic nature of the process/substance dichotomy itself is more squarely the object of scrutiny. Scholars have noted that procedural matters often have clear impacts on the substantive outcome of decisions (eg, a conclusion that a party does not have standing).[49] Procedural decisions themselves have content or substance. For example, a hearing is a process for determining the ultimate outcome, but a right to a hearing has its own content (eg, written or oral).[50] Thus, the substantive end (eg, a right to a healthy environment) must inform the form and content of process. Conversely, the rationale for procedures is that they inform and, in some manner, constrain the substantive outcome.[51] As we have seen throughout Part Two of this book, process is essential for identifying and understanding the nature of the regulatory problem and determining an appropriate response.[52] A process in which the possibility of influencing the outcome is foreclosed at the outset is a sham.[53] The inescapable conclusion is that '[s]ubstance informs process and process legitimises substance.'[54]

[46] D Shelton, 'Developing Substantive Environmental Rights' (2010) 1 *Journal of Human Rights and the Environment* 89, 91; and A Wiersema, 'A Train without Tracks: Rethinking the Place of Law and Goals in Environmental and Natural Resources Law' (2008) 38 *Environmental Law* 1239, 1298–99.

[47] See also AD Tarlock, 'Is There a There There in Environmental Law?' (2003) 19 *Journal of Land Use and Environmental Law* 213, 239–40.

[48] Boyd, *The Environmental Rights Revolution* (above n 1) 286.

[49] Liston, 'Transubstantiation in Canadian Public Law' (above n 36) 215, citing A Bickel, *The Least Dangerous Branch: The Supreme Court at the Bar of Politics* (New Haven, Yale University Press, 1986) 72.

[50] Dyzenhaus and Fox-Decent, 'Rethinking the Process/Substance Distinction' (above n 35) 195. For a detailed example, see above ch 6.

[51] L Sossin, 'The McLachlin Court and the Promise of Procedural Justice' in DA Wright and AM Dodek (eds), *Public Law at the McLachlin Court: The First Decade* (Toronto, Irwin Law, 2011); and Main, 'The Procedural Foundation' (above n 34) 819–22.

[52] A Nollkaemper, 'International Adjudication of Global Public Goods: The Intersection of Substance and Procedure' (2012) 23(3) *European Journal of International Law* 769, 781.

[53] See above ch 6, section I-C.

[54] Liston, 'Transubstantiation in Canadian Public Law' (above n 36) 220–21. See also Dyzenhaus and Fox-Decent, 'Rethinking the Process/Substance Distinction' (above n 35) 195–96; and Malcai and Levine-Schnur, 'Which Came First?' (above n 34).

Some environmental rights proponents acknowledge the interrelationship between process and substance.[55] Many promote both procedural and substantive environmental rights as complementary and essential to robust environmental protection.[56] But the distinction between procedural and substantive rights remains prevalent in the environmental rights literature, and scholars have not attended to the ways in which the distinction itself might undermine rights protection. Yet as we will see in the following section, the process/substance distinction is already influencing environmental rights adjudication in Canada.

ii. *The Positive/Negative Rights Dichotomy in Environmental Rights Enforcement*

The positive/negative rights dichotomy runs deep in the human rights literature.[57] Positive rights are rights that are said to impose affirmative duties on the state. They are largely synonymous with social, economic and cultural rights, a grouping within which a right to a healthy environment is typically situated. In contrast, negative rights are those perceived to require only forbearance by the state. Civil and political rights (eg, freedom of expression, freedom of association, freedom from torture) are classified as negative rights. The positive duties required by social, economic and cultural rights are 'generally considered to be a question of politics', calling into question their status as human rights.[58] The positive/negative dichotomy is reinforced by early international human rights agreements, which treat the two sets of rights distinctively,[59] as well as the fact that bills of rights in many Western liberal democracies only include express protection for civil and political rights.

Scholars have pointed to a variety of explanations for the half-hearted reception of positive rights as *bona fide* human rights. For example, some point to the liberal notion of freedom as non-interference as the origin of

[55] Hayward, *Constitutional Environmental Rights* (above n 1) 86; Scott, 'Flexibility' (above n 44) 273; and DR Boyd, 'Elements of an Effective Environmental Bill of Rights' (2015) 27 *Journal of Environmental Law and Practice* 201, 229ff (discussing the elements of procedural environmental rights).

[56] Boyd, 'Elements of an Effective Environmental Bill of Rights' (ibid); and Shelton, 'Developing Substantive Environmental Rights' (above n 46).

[57] For an excellent introduction to the debates surrounding social and economic rights, see Fredman, *Human Rights Transformed* (above n 32), on which this section relies.

[58] Fredman, *Human Rights Transformed* (above n 32) 1.

[59] Namely UNGA, International Covenant on Civil and Political Rights, GA res 2200A (XXI), 21 UN GAOR Supp (No 16) 52, UN Doc A/6316 (1966), 999 UNTS 171, 6 ILM 368 (1967); and UNGA, International Covenant for Economic, Social and Cultural Rights, GA res 2200A (XXI), 21 UN GAOR Supp (No 16) 49, UN Doc. A/6316 (1966), 993 UNTS 3, 6 ILM 368 (1967).

positive/negative rights dichotomy.[60] On this view, negative rights maintain the public–private divide and prevent state encroachment into private life. Positive rights, on this view, would seem to have the state interfering in the private sphere to impose a particular conception of the good.

Scepticism about the status of positive rights as rights is often expressed in the language of justiciability, the legal doctrine that delineates the appropriate role of the courts in intervening in certain issues. Positive rights sceptics highlight three related aspects of justiciability that call into question the status of positive rights.[61] First, it is said that the imposition of duties on the state entails choice (eg, is a logging ban necessary to maintain a healthy environment, or is salvage logging appropriate?) and that choice is more appropriately made by the legislature. Call this the *democratic critique*: legislatures, not unelected judges, have the democratic legitimacy to evaluate and rank the appropriate course of state action. Judicial adjudication of positive rights, on this view, pre-empts democratic deliberation about the provision of public goods and services.[62] The justiciability of positive rights also implicates the technical competence of the courts to determine social, economic and cultural matters (eg, what amounts to an adequate standard of living, a healthy environment or a right to health). Call this the *competence critique*: courts do not have the technical competence to adjudicate positive rights. Finally, positive rights are said to 'put courts in the position of overseeing large-scale bureaucratic institutions' and directing the state on how to expend its limited resources.[63] Call this the *remedial critique*. While enforcement of negative rights, the argument goes, requires the courts to declare only what the state cannot do, positive rights require the courts to enter into the business of wealth redistribution.[64]

Boyd has acknowledged that environmental rights engage all three facets of justiciability.[65] He has concluded, however, that these criticisms pose no serious barrier to the enforcement of a right to a healthy environment in Canada.[66] A Charter right to a healthy environment would be democratic, in his view, because courts 'have a legitimate supervisory role in constitutional democracies', and the Charter has democratic safeguards such as

[60] Fredman, *Human Rights Transformed* (above n 32) 1. She has also noted the influence of different political systems with positive rights being associated with communism and negative rights with capitalism.

[61] Ibid, ch 4; M Young, 'Section 7 and the Politics of Social Justice' (2005) 38 *University of British Columbia Law Review* 539, 548–57.

[62] CR Sunstein, 'Social and Economic Rights: Lessons from South Africa' (2000/2001) 11 *FORUM Constitutionnel* 123, 124.

[63] Ibid. See also Fredman, *Human Rights Transformed* (above n 32) ch 4; and Young, 'Section 7 and the Politics of Social Justice' (above n 61) 552–57.

[64] Young, 'Section 7 and the Politics of Social Justice' (above n 61) 551–52.

[65] Boyd, *The Right to a Healthy Environment* (above n 9) 28–31.

[66] Ibid, 28 and 29–30.

sections 1 and 33.[67] In response to repeated judicial assertions that courts are not academies of science, Boyd has noted that courts deal with complex facts and evidence across a variety of legal contexts.[68] Finally, he argues that doctrines of proportionality and reasonableness—as demonstrated by the South African Constitutional Court—temper the sceptic's remedial critique that positive rights compel courts to dictate the distribution of limited resources.[69]

As we will see in section III below, Boyd reaches the right conclusions about justiciability, though his conclusions are at times hard to square with the international examples of rights adjudication that he lauds elsewhere in his work.[70] And in one sense, he is quite right to dismiss the extensive and arguably outdated distinction between positive and negative rights. The tenability of the distinction between positive and negative rights has been thoroughly dismantled in the academic literature,[71] rejected by the international human rights community[72] and abandoned by other constitutional democracies.[73] Countless authors have observed how 'negative rights' impose positive obligations on the duty-bearer and require the expenditure of public funds (eg, a system for periodic elections, a functioning criminal justice system, etc). Scholars have further noted that claims of judicial incompetence are often exaggerated because the question of a right's existence and violation can be disentangled from the question of how the state might respond to the violation.[74]

Indeed, environmental rights bring into further focus the dubiousness of the distinction between positive and negative rights. Environmental rights can be framed alternately in positive terms (a right to a healthy or adequate environment) or in negative terms (freedom from state-sponsored environmental harm).[75] Some claims for environmental rights protection may impose positive obligations on the state, such as specific restoration efforts in especially degraded environments.[76] Others may require only restraint

[67] Ibid, 29.

[68] Ibid.

[69] Ibid, 30–31.

[70] Ibid, ch 4.

[71] Eg, Fredman, *Human Rights Transformed* (above n 32) ch 3; Hayward, *Constitutional Environmental Rights* (above n 1) 80–83; Sunstein, 'Social and Economic Rights' (above n 62) 124; J Waldron (ed), *'Nonsense Upon Stilts': Bentham, Burke, and Marx on the Rights of Man* (London, Methuen, 1987) 157–58; and H Shue, *Basic Rights* (Princeton, Princeton University Press, 1980).

[72] Vienna Declaration and Programme of Action: Report of the World Conference on Human Rights, Vienna, 14–25 June 1993, UN Doc A/CONF.157/23 (1993), 32 ILM 1661 (1993), I.5.

[73] M Young, 'The Other Section 7' (2013) 62 *Supreme Court Law Review* (2d) 3, 43.

[74] Young, 'Section 7 and the Politics of Social Justice' (above n 61) 553.

[75] Hayward, *Constitutional Environmental Rights* (above n 1) 78–90 (on how environmental rights are best understood as fundamental freedoms).

[76] Eg, Boyd, *The Right to a Healthy Environment* (above n 9) 160–64 (on Great Lakes restoration).

on the part of the state (eg, not issuing a permit for the discharge of toxic chemicals).

But while constitutional theory may have moved past the negative/positive rights distinction, we will see that Canadian courts have not. Boyd rightly points to decades of actual practice of environmental rights enforcement as evidence of the irrelevance of the dichotomy.[77] But he draws on the wrong practice. We will see that the positive/negative rights distinction is still alive and well in Canadian constitutional rights adjudication, and it operates in a way that will hamper the enforcement of a Charter right to a healthy environment.

II. ENVIRONMENTAL PROTECTION AND SECTION 7 ADJUDICATION

Boyd's claims about the prospects for a Charter right to a healthy environment are based first and foremost on the experience of other countries.[78] This experience, he has argued, is sufficient to dispel concerns about theoretical distinctions undermining rights protection.[79] Boyd's empirical evidence is important. As others have observed, the fraught dichotomies of positive/negative and procedural/substantive rights can be more indicative of dominant mythologies about our public institutions than of their actual functions.[80] At the same time, however, these dominant mythologies have a profound impact on the practice of rights adjudication, a practice that in common law systems embraces incrementalism and reasoning based on precedent. Indeed, Boyd himself has noticed a striking disparity in the recognition of constitutional environmental rights between common law and civil law traditions.[81] But this observation falls away when he applies the lessons from other (predominantly civil) legal systems to his case for Canadian Charter innovation.

In contrast to Boyd, this section turns to domestic rights adjudication in order to draw lessons about the potential of a Charter right to a healthy environment. In particular, it examines the adjudication of claims under section 7 of the Charter in order to assess the ongoing influence of the positive/negative and procedural/substance distinctions in Canadian law. It argues that these distinctions have played a significant role in curtailing section 7's potential outside the context of criminal law. The persistence of

77 Boyd, *The Environmental Rights Revolution* (above n 1) 286.

78 Boyd, *The Right to a Healthy Environment* (above n 9) 147.

79 Ibid, 35.

80 J Hohmann, *The Right to Housing: Law, Concepts, Possibilities* (Oxford, Hart Publishing, 2013) 235. See also Hayward, *Constitutional Environmental Rights* (above n 1) 120–22.

81 Boyd, *The Environmental Rights Revolution* (above n 1) 288.

these distinctions in Canadian Charter jurisprudence points to the importance of a coherent theory of law for the meaningful interpretation and enforcement of a Charter right to a healthy environment.

A. Section 7 of the Charter

> *Everyone has the right to life, liberty and security of the person and the right not to be deprived thereof except in accordance with the principles of fundamental justice.*[82]

Section 7 is the leading 'legal right' of the Canadian Charter of Rights and Freedoms. Section 7 doctrine, in brief, requires claimants to meet a two-stage test.[83] First, claimants must show that they experience a present harm or significant future risk of harm that infringes their life, liberty or security of the person.[84] As the Charter applies only to governmental action, contained in this first step is also the requirement that there be a 'sufficient causal connection' between state action and the alleged infringement.[85] Second, claimants must show that infringement is not in accordance with the principles of fundamental justice. Section 7 is closely connected to the rule of law, as described in this book, through its incorporation via the principles of fundamental justice of the concept of procedural fairness and of prohibitions on vague, overbroad and arbitrary laws.[86] Constitutional scholars describe section 7 in terms of two personalities: a clear and forceful presence in the criminal law context, and a promising but largely unrealised instrument for effecting social justice more broadly.[87]

Section 7 holds much potential for protecting individuals from state-caused environmental harms, and indeed, section 7 environmental jurisprudence has proliferated in Canadian courts. Claimants have argued that a variety of state actions have jeopardised their right to life, liberty or security of the person, including: permitting the increase of toxic pollutants in an area already subject to a disproportionate amount of industrial pollution;[88]

[82] Constitution Act (above n 25) s 7.

[83] *Carter v Canada (Attorney General)* 2015 SCC 5, para 55.

[84] On significant future risk of harm, see *Chaoulli v Quebec (Attorney General)*, 2005 SCC 35, [2005] 1 SCR 791, para 118.

[85] *Canada (Attorney General) v Bedford*, 2013 SCC 72, [2013] 3 SCR 1101, para 75.

[86] For a summary of the recognised principles of fundamental justice, see H Stewart, *Fundamental Justice: Section 7 of the Canadian Charter of Rights and Freedoms* (Toronto, Irwin Law, 2012).

[87] M Young, 'The Right to Life, Liberty and Security of the Person' in P Oliver, P Macklem and N Des Rosier (eds), *Oxford Handbook of the Canadian Constitution* (Oxford, Oxford University Press, 2017) 777.

[88] *Lockridge v Director, Ministry of the Environment*, 2012 ONSC 2316.

the approval of sour gas well construction near residential areas;[89] the fluoridation of municipal water;[90] and changes to nuclear energy legislation that were alleged to increase the risk of a nuclear catastrophe.[91] The largest number of environment-related section 7 claims to date have been in response to wind turbine development in Ontario, which, as we saw in the previous chapter, are said to imperil human health.[92]

While none of these section 7 claims has been successful, Canadian courts have accepted without question the application of section 7 to environment-related harms.[93] Life, liberty and security of the person are all conceptually broad enough to cover the physical health impacts and arguably the psychological impacts of living with significant toxic or environmental risk. Indeed, it would be bizarre and incoherent if the courts failed to recognise that the kinds of harms protected by section 7 can be inflicted through the environment. As we will now see, however, the development of section 7 jurisprudence has not favoured environment-related claims. The two dichotomies introduced above play a notable role in the application of section 7 and impose serious hurdles for environmental claimants.

B. The Process/Substance Dichotomy in Section 7 Jurisprudence

Environment-related claims have thus far all failed on the first stage of the section 7 analysis. It has proven insurmountable for claimants to make out the two evidentiary requirements contained in the criteria that 1) there exists a harm or significant future risk of harm, and 2) there is a sufficient causal connection between government action and the harm alleged. Courts have assured claimants that 'the evidentiary burden is not an impossible one'.[94] They rest their decisions on the failures of claimants to adduce appropriate

[89] *Graff v Alberta (Energy and Utilities Board)*, 2007 ABCA 246; *Domke v Alberta (Energy Resources Conservation Board)*, 2008 ABCA 232; and *Kelly v Alberta (Energy and Utilities Board)*, 2008 ABCA 52.

[90] *Locke v Calgary (City)*, 1993 CanLII 7226 (Alt QB); and *Millership v British Columbia & Canada (Attorney General)*, 2003 BCSC 82.

[91] *Energy Probe v Canada (Attorney General) (1994)*, 17 OR (3d) 717 (Ont SC).

[92] *Bovaird v Ontario*, [2013] OERTD No 87; *D&C Vander Zaag Farms v Ontario*, [2013] OERTD No 84; *Dixon v Ontario*, [2014] OERTD No 5; *Drennan v Ontario*, [2014] OERTD No 10; *Fairfield v Ontario*, [2014] OERTD No 71; *Fata v Ontario*, [2014] OERTD No 42; *Gillespie v Ontario*, [2014] OERTD No 72; *Kroeplin v Ontario*, [2014] OERTD No 24; *Platinum Produce Ltd v Ontario*, [2014] OERTD No 8; *Wrightman v Ontairo*, [2014] OERTD No 11; *Lambton (County) v Ontario*, [2015] OERTD No 10; *Lewis v Ontario*, 2014 Carswell Ont 15153; *Mothers against Wind Turbines v Ontario*, [2015] OERTD No 19; *Dingeldein v Ontario*, [2015] OERTD No 32; and *Gillespie v Ontario*, [2015] OERTD Case No 14-059/14-060.

[93] See, eg, *Dixon v Director, Ministry of the Environment*, 2014 ONSC 7404, paras 57–58.

[94] *Domke* (above n 89) para 29.

scientific or medical evidence to establish the causal connection between the activity and the harm (eg, wind turbine and human health impacts),[95] as well as the causal connection between the government action and the harm (eg, statutorily limited liability and nuclear safety).[96] The result is that section 7 protection against environmental harms is at present somewhat illusory. This has led leading commentators to conclude that

> [T]here is indeed no *doctrinal* problem with the application of s 7 to state-sponsored environmental harm. Instead, the primary challenge to applicants in environmental claims under s 7 is proving causation of actual or threatened harm sufficient to qualify as a deprivation of life, liberty or security of the person.[97]

The diagnosis, then, is that the problem lies with evidentiary requirements rather than the doctrinal development of section 7.[98]

However, I suggest there is a doctrinal problem with section 7 jurisprudence, one that is brought to the surface by environmental claims. This problem is the persistence of the process/substance distinction and the way it plays out through a bifurcated analysis of the harm claim and the claim that the deprivation was not in accordance with the principles of fundamental justice.[99] In successful section 7 cases, and in most contexts where a violation is alleged, the harm is self-evident or clearly evident. Proceeding with a bifurcated doctrinal analysis poses little challenge to claimants: harm and its cause can be shown independently of and prior to an analysis of the process the government used to effect the infringement. For example, incarceration is a clear deprivation of one's interest in liberty, and the state's role in sanctioning that deprivation is equally clear.

In the environmental context, however, the challenge of uncertainty means that the harm alleged and its cause are often not immediately apparent in the same way. Section 7 doctrine requires the claimant to adduce

[95] Eg, *Drennan* (above n 92) 213; and *Mothers against Wind Turbines* (above n 92) 354.

[96] *Energy Probe* (above n 91) 35.

[97] L Collins, 'An Ecologically Literate Reading of the Canadian Charter of Rights and Freedoms' (2009) 26 *Windsor Review of Legal and Social Issues* 7, 42 (emphasis added).

[98] By framing the problem as evidentiary, scholars then look for an evidentiary solution. Scholars have pointed to the potential work that the precautionary principle could do in making section 7 protection a reality for environmental claimants: Collins, 'An Ecologically Literate Reading' (ibid) 45–47; Collins, "The United Nations' (above n 15) 240; and DWL Wu, 'Embedding Environmental Rights in Section 7 of the Canadian Charter: Resolving the Tension between the Need for Precaution and the Need for Harm' (2014) 33 *National Journal of Constitutional Law* 191, 212–18. As we saw above in ch 6, however, construing the precautionary principle as an evidentiary rule is unsatisfying. It hamstrings the principle's potential and, more importantly, ignores the deeper assumptions about law that inform its interpretation and administration.

[99] To be clear, I am using process/substance here in a different sense than is typically invoked in the section 7 context. Early Charter cases and commentary frequently discussed whether the principles of fundamental justice contained substantive or only procedural guarantees (a debate that was resolved in favour of both in *Re BC Motor Vehicle Act*, [1985] 2 SCR 486 (SCC)). See Stewart, *Fundamental Justice* (above n 86) 98ff.

evidence to show on a balance of probabilities that there is a sufficient causal connection between government action and an infringement of life, liberty or security of the person. Yet the crux of many environment-related section 7 claims is that conclusions about harm cannot be disentangled from the process used to assess risks and to determine how best to proceed. Two examples illustrate this point.

In *Drennan v Ontario*, a farming family opposed to neighbouring wind turbine development argued that their right to security of the person was infringed, not only by the approved wind turbine development but also by the psychological stress of being subject to a 'fixed' regulatory process.[100] Their claim eschewed the conventional two-part framing of section 7, no doubt a response to the barriers established in environment-related section 7 precedent. But the court, challenged by these entangled claims, concluded that the case was premature. The court reasoned, 'While the alleged harm seems speculative to me, even if realised it will be temporary if the Drennans ... are successful at the end of the regulatory process.'[101] The court's conclusion avoids the specific harm alleged: the *in*security of the person caused by being subject to a regulatory process that operates to suppress dissenting views and to curtail consideration of the full range of possible though uncertain threats to human health.[102]

Similarly, in *Domke*,[103] the claimants lived in the vicinity of proposed sour gas wells, which release poisonous hydrogen sulphide fumes when drilled. They argued that the approval of the wells infringed their right to security of the person and that several aspects of the approvals process were not in accordance with principles of fundamental justice, including the restricted access to the company's information about sour gas risks and the onus on residents to negotiate with the company about the need to relocate during critical operations.[104] The Charter issue was first before the regulator (ie, the Board), which concluded:

> While it is true that the drilling and completion of a sour well could endanger the life and physical or psychological well-being were it to take place in an unsafe manner ... The Board would not approve an operation unless it was satisfied that it could be performed in a safe manner.[105]

[100] This is the same process that was the subject of ch 7 above. See *Drennan* (above n 92) paras 28–32.

[101] Ibid, para 53.

[102] See also *Lockridge* (above n 88), in which government counsel sought to exploit this bifurcation by arguing that there was no evidence of the 'synergistic effects' of pollution that are the basis of the infringement, when the claim was precisely that a cumulative effects analysis was required to comply with principles of fundamental justice.

[103] See *Domke* (above n 89); and *Highpine Oil & Gas Ltd (Re)*, [2008] AEUBD No 18.

[104] *Highpine* (ibid) para 10.

[105] Ibid, para 183.

This conclusion, which was the basis for the Alberta Court of Appeal's denial of leave,[106] was entirely question-begging. The process for determining safety, put into issue by the section 7 requirement of fundamental justice, was used to bootstrap the analysis of harm and to preclude any consideration of either the regulatory process or the interaction between the process and the harm.

A full analysis of the process/substance distinction in section 7 doctrine and its possible doctrinal responses is beyond this scope of this chapter. The point here is simply that the process/substance distinction matters. It matters because it already operates to deny environmental rights claimants recourse under existing Charter rights. Yet much of environmental law scholarship accepts and works within this existing dichotomy. For example, Collins has argued that uncertainty in environmental law has been treated as a 'procedural problem' dealt with through the allocation of the burden of proof.[107] She argues that, instead, we ought to move uncertainty across the binary and treat 'serious environmental uncertainty as a substantive violation of human rights'.[108] This is an important insight but ultimately one that accepts the viability of a distinction between substance and process. In light of the conceptual instability of the distinction, perpetuating the distinction risks undermining environmental claims. Instead, as we will see in section III, we ought to ground an environmental rights jurisprudence in a conception of the rule of law that directly confronts and reconceives this distinction.

C. The Positive/Negative Rights Dichotomy in Section 7 Jurisprudence

The challenges associated with proving harm under the existing section 7 framework mean that courts and tribunals have not yet had to resolve environment-related claims in a manner that directly implicates the positive/negative rights distinction.[109] Yet the distinction has played a notable role in how parties have framed their Charter arguments. Wind turbine opponents have framed their claims in conventional negative rights terms. For example:

> [There] has yet to be established a safe setback distance or appropriate noise level to protect human from harm to their health associated with industrial wind turbines. ... It is therefore submitted that because the legislative scheme for the creation of industrial wind turbine projects exposes the public to a risk to their health, the legislative scheme must comply with s 7 of the Charter.[110]

[106] *Domke* (above n 89) para 27.
[107] Collins, 'The United Nations' (above n 15) 241.
[108] Ibid.
[109] Cases with promising evidentiary foundations, such as *Lockridge* (above n 88) and *Kelly* (above n 89), have been resolved out of court.
[110] *Drennan* (above n 92) para 16.

Government and industry respondents have countered that the claimants were 'asserting a positive rights claim by wanting a more protective regime'.[111]

Elsewhere, concerns about justiciability have filtered into judicial reasoning in more subtle forms. In an early case implicating statutory limitations on liability for nuclear disasters, the court pointed to the trade-offs implicated by all forms of energy production, concluding that the claimants failed 'to show that there is a greater risk to the public of producing electricity by nuclear power than by alternate methods'.[112] Such reasoning recalls the democratic critique of positive rights—ie, that the legislature, not the courts, ought to make decisions involving these kinds of trade-offs. The *Domke* decision, in which the court blindly deferred to the regulator's assessment of risk, implicates the competence critique—ie, that the courts perceive themselves as insufficiently expert to adjudicate on environmental rights.[113]

The influence of the positive/negative rights distinction is evident outside of environmental law, when claimants have sought to establish social and economic rights protection under section 7. Margot Young has written:

> Canadian courts ... are puzzlingly immune to what commentators understand to be 'common sense' [the indeterminacy of the positive/negative rights distinction]. ... Judges are hesitant to explicitly recognize positive rights except in the abstract, as some sort of possible future development seemingly never realizable in the case at hand.[114]

She notes that social and economic claims under section 7 are more successful when framed as conventional negative rights. For example, in *Canada v PHS Community Service Society*, which involved the government's refusal to grant an exemption necessary for the operation of a Vancouver supervised injection site, the Supreme Court of Canada conceived of the section 7 claims as negative rights infringements.[115] It held that without the

[111] Ibid, paras 32 and 37.

[112] *Energy Probe* (above n 91) 23 and 45 (where the court considered the cost implications of insisting on greater safety requirements).

[113] *Domke* (above n 89) para 27. See also *Energy Probe* (above n 91) 27. To be sure, courts do make serious errors in the context of environmental rights. See *Dixon v Director* (above n 93) paras 82–87 and 129 (where the court misconstrued scientific causation for legal causation).

[114] Young, 'The Right to Life, Liberty and Security' (above n 87). Similarly, courts are willing to talk about the existence of environmental rights but have yet to affirm or enforce environmental rights in any specific case. For example, the Supreme Court of Canada has stated that 'individually and collectively, we are responsible for preserving the natural environment' and has acknowledged that 'the right to a safe environment' is 'a fundamental and widely shared value' in Canada: *Ontario v Canadian Pacific Ltd*, [1995] 2 SCR 1031 (SCC) para 55, endorsed again by the majority in *R v Hydro-Quebec*, [1997] 3 SCR 213 (SCC) para 124; and *114957 Canada Ltée (Spraytech, Société d'arrosage) v Hudson (Ville)*, [2001] 2 SCR 241, para 1.

[115] *Canada (Attorney General) v PHS Community Service Society*, 2011 SCC 44, paras 87 and 91–93.

exemption, criminal prohibitions threatened to impinge the liberty interests of staff, as well as the liberty and security of the person interests of the clients, by depriving them of potentially lifesaving medical care. The Court conceived of the case, in other words, in conventional criminal law terms rather than an affirmative claim to health services and, consequently, the government-issued exemption.

Similarly, the success of a section 7 challenge to a municipal bylaw prohibiting homeless people from erecting temporary shelter seemed to lie in its negative rights framing. The British Columbia Court of Appeal emphasised that the issue did not entail a positive rights claim to adequate housing, nor did it require the city 'to take any positive steps to address the issue of homelessness. The decision only require[d] the City to refrain from legislating in a manner that interferes with the s 7 rights of the homeless.'[116] By framing the issue solely in terms of negative rights, the Court was able to skirt the democratic and competence critiques. At the same time, however, the Court directly addressed and dismissed the remedial critique, observing that its decision would likely require *some* positive governmental action in response to its ruling. The necessary response, the Court reasoned, was only incidental to the Charter violation and 'could be said to be a feature of all Charter cases'.[117] Yet it was confident that the distinction could be maintained and that the need for a governmental response '[did] not involve the court in adjudicating positive rights'.[118]

These decisions evidence the contorted reasoning that judges are willing to conduct in order to maintain an unworkable distinction. While these are examples of successful and novel claims under section 7, they are hardly transformative in terms of affirming and vindicating social and economic rights in Canada. Real innovation under section 7 has been curtailed by the methodology of common law adjudication, which relies on older caselaw that is mired in these problematic dichotomies. We can speculate on how the supposed distinctions might play out in the context of a stand-alone Charter right to a healthy environment. The point here simply is that the persistence of the positive/negative rights dichotomy neglected by environmental rights proponents matters in Canadian constitutional jurisprudence. Moreover, the distinction already operates in a way that undermines the progressive potential of Charter rights that Boyd and others see in a novel Charter right to a healthy environment.

[116] *Victoria (City) v Adams*, 2009 BCCA 563, 313 DLR. (4th) 29 (BCCA) para 95. For additional prominent examples of Supreme Court of Canada jurisprudence that engages directly with the notion of positive rights, see *Gosselin v Quebec (Attorney General)*, 2002 SCC 84, [2002] 4 SCR 429; and *Chaoulli* (above n 84).

[117] *Victoria v Adams* (ibid) para 96.

[118] Ibid.

III. COMMON LAW CONSTITUTIONAL RIGHTS ADJUDICATION

Section I above argued that Boyd's prominent proposal for a Charter right to a healthy environment taps into two enduring dichotomies in constitutional theory, those between process/substance and positive/negative rights, yet Boyd treats these dichotomies as antiquated and illusory—in short, as irrelevant. I posited that Boyd has reached this conclusion because he has not sufficiently attended to the method of rights adjudication. Section II turned to the specific context of rights adjudication and examined existing attempts to locate environmental protection within section 7 of the Charter. We saw that, far from irrelevant, the two dichotomies introduced in section I are alive and well in Canadian Charter jurisprudence and currently operate as significant obstacles to both environment-related claims and claims for social and economic rights more generally under section 7.

This section connects the dots from this chapter back through to the rule-of-law argument set out earlier in this book. It first offers an explanation for the persistence of the process/substance and negative/positive rights distinctions in Canadian public law, explicating the connection between these distinctions and the formal conception of the rule of law. Once this connection is made, we will be in a position to see that the introduction of new constitutional text—ie, a Charter right to a healthy environment—will be insufficient for meaningful environmental rights protection. Specific constitutional text cannot displace judicial assumptions about the rule of law.[119] We will then return to common law constitutionalism and the public-justification conception of the rule of law. I argue that the public-justification conception of the rule of law offers a promising foundation for a jurisprudence of environmental rights in Canada because it confronts and reconceives the pervasive dichotomies that have hampered environmental rights adjudication thus far.

A. Bright Lines and the Rule of Law

Recall that the formal conception of the rule of law emphasises a formal allocation of distinct powers between institutions of government; it is premised, in other words, on a strong separation of powers. Rights instruments by their very nature put this formal allocation under strain because they require judges to engage in the kind of moral reasoning about the content of the law (as opposed to simply its application) that formalist judges think

[119] For a detailed internal analysis of the complex ways in which judges interpret constitutional text in three common law jurisdictions, see R Leckey, *Bills of Rights in the Common Law* (Cambridge, Cambridge University Press, 2015).

is properly the legislature's monopoly.[120] In other words, formalist judges approach constitutional rights adjudication not as an opportunity for deliberation but rather as a series of legal landmines that need to be contained in order to avoid inappropriate judicial encroachment on the legislature's role. As we saw in chapter two, maintaining the formal allocation of powers requires a set of doctrinal tools—eg, free rein within bounds, or patrolling the boundaries of the statute, but not the exercise of discretion. The process/substance and negative/positive rights distinctions add to the formalist's toolbox. Both distinctions operate to delineate the 'legal' from the 'political' and thus enforce a boundary between the appropriate role of the courts and that of the legislature. And as we will see, both have the potential to serve as tools for diffusing the legal landmines contained in the task of adjudicating a Charter right to a healthy environment.

Take first the process/substance distinction. As we have seen, the distinction is conceptually ambiguous but nonetheless maintained by the courts.[121] Fox-Decent has argued that the distinction keeps shut the 'Pandora's box of legality', or the idea that proper procedures are the key to the possibility of judicial scrutiny of both process *and* substance.[122] The distinction is thus a device that limits judicial supervision of the substance of public decisions. For the courts to concede openly that the process/substance distinction is unworkable in public law risks dissolving the boundary between judicial and legislative functions. By labelling issues 'substantive', courts are able to signal issues that are political and thus more appropriate for legislative resolution.[123]

Relatedly, the negative/positive rights distinction is linked to the classical liberal roots of the formal conception of law. As we saw in chapter one, the formal conception operates to keep in check state interference with individual freedom. State interference is exemplified by the state of emergency but also by the sweeping discretionary powers exercised in the modern administrative state. The negative/positive rights distinction enforces this boundary between the private and the public. Under the formal conception of the rule of law, courts can justifiably enforce negative rights because to

[120] See D Dyzenhaus, *The Constitution of Law: Legality in a Time of Emergency* (Cambridge, Cambridge University Press, 2006) 68–70 (on constitutional positivism as a compromise that formalist judges make when operating in a common law system and how the problem, as formalist judges see it, is enhanced by a bill of rights.)

[121] Even harsh critics of the distinction concede that it is not likely going anywhere: Liston, 'Transubstantiation in Canadian Public Law' (above n 36) (arguing that decisional frameworks can help mediate fraught attempts to categories public law issues as 'substance' or 'process'); and Dyzenhaus and Fox-Decent, 'Rethinking the Process/Substance Distinction' (above n 35) 196.

[122] E Fox-Decent, *Sovereignty's Promise: The State as Fiduciary* (Oxford, Oxford University Press, 2011) 189.

[123] Dyzenhaus and Fox-Decent, 'Rethinking the Process/Substance Distinction' (above n 35) 205.

do so preserves a sphere of private autonomy from encroachment by the state. The formal conception further dictates that, in contrast, in the public sphere, the legislature is the appropriate institution for making decisions about collective rule. On this view, were the courts to dissolve the positive/negative rights distinction and enforce positive rights, they would cross over the legal/political boundary and exercise functions that are properly allocated to the legislature.

We have already seen that the two distinctions are relevant to the adjudication of environmental claims under section 7 of the Charter. We can now situate them against the backdrop of the formal conception of the rule of law in order, first, to better understand how they operate in concert to thwart environmental rights enforcement and, second, to extrapolate to potential Charter adjudication of a right to a healthy environment.

As we have seen, courts have closely scrutinised the evidentiary requirements of section 7. As a process matter, adjudication of evidence is entirely appropriate from the perspective of the formal conception of the rule of law. Only if claimants can tender sufficient evidence can courts adjudicate upon their substantive rights. But here the process classification collides with the positive rights classification. While their procedural nature means evidentiary issues should be squarely within the judicial monopoly, their status as positive rights invokes the competence critique, suggesting that courts may not be technically competent to decide these evidentiary matters. If courts cannot adequately assess the scientific evidence proffered to establish harm under section 7, they will undermine environmental rights protection.[124]

We have also seen that courts have focused on the harm requirement under section 7 and have yet to engage with the principles of fundamental justice. In part, this is the result of the sequential ordering of the analysis. However, it can also be understood as a product of the two distinctions that enforce the formal conception of the rule of law. The harm component can be conceived in classical liberal terms whereby life, liberty and security of the person represent the integral components of individual autonomy. From the perspective of the formal conception of the rule of law, the courts remain within their comfort zone when determining whether the state has interfered in this private sphere.

Despite being procedural when set in contrast to life, liberty and security of the person, principles of fundamental justice very much engage positive rights concerns that courts will inappropriately meddle with the policymaking function of the legislature. This is because the principles are viewed as more indeterminate, raising concerns that the courts sit as 'super-legislator'[125] or imposes their own 'personal judgment' when elevating a

[124] Without commenting on the merits of the claim, there is some indication that this has already occurred: *Dixon v Director* (above n 93) para 129.

[125] *Re BC Motor Vehicle Act* (above n 99) 497.

principle to constitutional status.[126] The Supreme Court of Canada noted early on that principles of fundamental justice 'are to be found in the basic tenets of our legal system. They do not lie in the realm of general public policy.'[127] Over time, the Supreme Court has attempted to make more determinate the criteria for these principles. They are to be (1) legal principles (2) that enjoy sufficient consensus that they are fundamental to societal norms of justice, and (3) that can be identified with precision and applied predictably.[128] The Court has held that principles of fundamental justice directly overlap with the rule of law[129] and incorporate the common law requirements of procedural fairness.[130] But as we have seen, so long as the formal conception of the rule of law informs the content of procedural fairness, much of the administrative state remains beyond its reach.[131] And despite section 7's application to all state action, there are few examples of principles of fundamental justice strengthening these common law procedural protections outside the criminal and refugee contexts.[132]

In the environmental context, courts and tribunals have been visibly uncomfortable making the connection between the principles of fundamental justice and the regulatory state. Indeed, often the simple presence of regulation alone is accepted as evidence of Charter compliance,[133] without any of the scrutiny that courts apply to legislation in other contexts.[134] When courts recognise the need to apply well-known principles of fundamental justice, such as arbitrariness, to a regulatory scheme, they seem to lack the reasoning and language to do so. In *Drennan*, the court found the regulatory wind turbine scheme satisfied the requirement of procedural fairness because it did not contain 'unfettered discretion' and because there was no basis to suggest that the decision-makers acted in bad faith.[135] In *Millership*, the impugned bylaw authorising municipal water fluoridation was subject to a detailed, evidence-based drafting process, public debate and municipal

[126] *Millership* (above n 90) para 114.

[127] *Re BC Motor Vehicle Act* (above n 99) 503.

[128] *Canadian Foundation for Children, Youth and the Law v Canada (Attorney General)*, 2004 SCC 4, [2004] 1 SCR 76, para 8.

[129] *Re BC Motor Vehicle Act* (above n 99) 503.

[130] Stewart, *Fundamental Justice* (above n 86) ch 5; and E Fox-Decent and A Pless, 'The Charter and Administrative Law: Cross-Fertilization or Inconstancy?' in CM Flood and L Sossin (eds), *Administrative Law in Context*, 2nd edn (Toronto, Emond Montgomery, 2013) 409.

[131] See above ch 2, section II.

[132] Stewart, *Fundamental Justice* (above n 86) 285. With the notable exception being *New Brunswick (Minister of Health and Community Services) v G (J)*, [1999] 3 SCR 46.

[133] *Energy Probe* (above n 91) 26–33 (concluding that 'a review of the role of the regulator in the safe operation of nuclear reactors leaves minimal opportunity for the NLA to have any impact on safety'); and *Domke* (above n 89) paras 27 and 30.

[134] See, eg, *Canada v PHS* (above n 115); and *Canada v Bedford* (above n 85).

[135] *Drennan* (above n 92) paras 41–44.

referendum. Even still, the court could not bring itself to explicate the connection between such a rigorous regulatory process and compliance with principles of fundamental justice.[136]

Indeed, from the perspective of the formal conception of the rule of law, acknowledging that the regulatory state is subject to the meaningful application of the principles of fundamental justice would open up the Pandora's box of legality, placing courts in a position in which they second-guess the wisdom of the legislature and the executive.[137] The process/substance and negative/positive rights dichotomies inform the application of section 7 to maintain the distinction between policy and law and to protect the division of labour between the legislature and the courts. But as we have seen, judicial reluctance to engage with principles of fundamental justice is especially problematic in the environmental context. The bifurcated analysis of harm and violations of fundamental justice under section 7 ensures that the two are never considered together, denying the ways in which substance and process are conspirators in the production, detection and perception of environmental harm.

We can now see that formalist judges are equipped with a set of tools that can undermine the potential of a Charter right to a healthy environment, and we are better positioned to understand how its adjudication might play out in the Canadian context. A stand-alone Charter right to a healthy environment would require courts to develop the content of the norm 'healthy environment'. To be sure, Boyd may be right that a stand-alone Charter right could lead to a progressive-brand of formalist judging in which constitutional text is viewed as a direct attempt to move the environment across the political/legal divide and could thus be used as a toehold for robust judicial protection.[138] But this assumption is not supported by the most closely analogous existing constitutional jurisprudence in Canada, a crucial observation in a common law system in which adjudication is guided by precedent. Instead, we see that when faced with novel environment-related

[136] Ibid, para 116, stating only the conclusory: 'This is certainly not an arbitrary process' and 'it is not an infringement that occurs contrary to natural justice.'

[137] See, eg, CM Flood, '*Chaoulli*'s Legacy for the Future of Canadian Health Care Policy' (2006) 44 *Osgoode Hall Law Journal* 273 (critiquing the majority's misunderstanding of the complex field of health care policy in Canada).

[138] This is plausible. Walters has observed that different judicial ethics govern administrative and constitutional law in Canada (the functionalist and interpretivist ethics, respectively): MD Walters, 'Respecting Deference as Respect: Rights, Reasonableness and Proportionality in Canadian Administrative Law' in M Elliott and H Wilberg (eds), *The Scope and Intensity of Substantive Review: Traversing Taggart's Rainbow* (Oxford, Hart Publishing, 2015) 408 (although note that the interpretivist ethic maps onto the theory of public justification argued for here). For related arguments about treating administrative law and constitutional law adjudication differently, see, eg, M Taggart, 'Proportionality, Deference, *Wednesbury*' (2008) *New Zealand Law Review* 423; and JNE Varuhas, 'Against Unification' in Elliott and Wilberg (eds), *The Scope and Intensity of Substantive Review* (above) 91.

rights claims, judges fall back on the same set of formalist assumptions that impede meaningful judicial supervision of environmental protection in the administrative context. Moreover, as long as formalist distinctions are sustained, there is no meaningful judicial engagement with the 'common sense' notions that process and substance are mutually constitutive and that negative and positive rights are poor proxies for understanding the court's role in mediating the relationship between individual agency and the state.

Accordingly, we might then expect that the process/substance dichotomy will operate to limit judicial consideration of the substance of a right to a healthy environment. As with existing section 7 jurisprudence, evidentiary issues about state causation may take centre stage because formalist judges view these as process matters that properly fall within their monopoly. As Collins has observed, when scientific uncertainty is treated as a procedural matter, it readily undermines environmental rights protection.[139] Similarly, we might expect that formalist judges will feel more comfortable enforcing procedural environmental rights—eg, access to information and participation—than a guarantee to a basic standard of environmental health. Strict enforcement of procedural rights provides a convenient mechanism to counterbalance (or mask) any judicial retreat from the supervision of substance. Moreover, we might expect formalist judges to retreat from supervising the content of a 'healthy environment' because of assumptions about positive/negative rights. Formalist judges will be concerned that determining the content of a healthy environment is both undemocratic and outside their technical competence. As a result, they may be especially deferential to government claims that contested state measures adequately protect the environment. Indeed, in the absence of experience and expert review, it would be difficult for a court to adjudicate on, eg, whether the BC Forest and Range Practices Act (2002) is a legitimate change in regulatory strategy from the earlier Forest Practices Code, or whether it unjustifiably violates a right to a healthy environment.[140]

The result is that a Charter right to a healthy environment, in the hands of formalist judges, may simply magnify and entrench the problems already experienced in the context of administrative law. As the next section argues, the more promising foundation for the development of environmental rights lies with a conception of the rule of law that dispenses with these fraught dichotomies and explains how rights adjudication can thrive in a common law system.

[139] See discussion of Collins, 'The United Nations' (above n 15).

[140] See BC Forest and Range Practices Act, SBC 2002, c 69; and the legislation it replaced, the Forest Practices Code of British Columbia Act, RSBC 1996, c 159. For an analysis of these forestry measures, see above ch 3. Judicial deference could occur when the court considers whether there is a violation or when it considers whether that violation is justified under section 1 of the Charter.

B. The Right to Public Justification and the Right to a Healthy Environment

This section argues that the public-justification conception of the rule of law offers a promising foundation on which to build a robust constitutional environmental rights jurisprudence. While much could be written on this topic, the aim here is modest. Specifically, the section responds to Boyd's worry that 'the common-law legal system [is] an impediment to environmental sustainability' and to his query of how 'this systemic institutional weakness [can] be overcome'.[141] His worry arises from the observation that most common law systems have not recognised a stand-alone constitutional right to a healthy environment, unlike civil law systems. The response is that the foundation for a right to a healthy environment can be found in the common law constitution. Identifying, elaborating and nurturing this rule-of-law foundation allows the common law to become a strength, not a weakness, in promoting environmental sustainability.

The basic argument that has underpinned the second half of this book is that the common law, understood in its best light, contains a coherent set of legal principles that are constitutive of legal authority. These principles impose upon public decision-makers a requirement of public justification. The practice of public justification ensures that individuals affected by a decision are respected as rational, self-determining agents who are entitled to reasons that reflect their fundamental interests. The structure of public justification is thus analogous to constitutional rights adjudication in Canada. The Charter is protective of fundamental interests—in the form of constitutional rights—subject to the government's ability to justify reasonable infringements of those rights. In this way, constitutional law can be understood as 'administrative law writ large'.[142] The essence of both, on this account, is that individuals are entitled to a foundational right to public justification.[143] A right to public justification is respectful and empowering of individual agency and ensures that individuals know they have not been treated arbitrarily by the state.

As charted in this chapter, there is a basic connection between administrative and constitutional law theory and methodology. Just as the formal conception of the rule of law threatens to magnify the problems of administrative law in the constitutional context, the implications of the public-justification conception of the rule of law are magnified as well. A written

[141] Boyd, *The Environmental Rights Revolution* (above n 1) 288.

[142] D Dyzenhaus, 'Law as Justification: Etienne Mureinik's Conception of Legal Culture' (1998) 14 *South African Journal on Human Rights* 11, 31–32; and Sunstein, 'Social and Economic Rights' (above n 62) 130–31.

[143] See also R Forst, *The Right to Justification: Elements of a Constructivist Theory of Justice*, J Flynn (trans) (New York, Columbia University Press, 2011).

bill of rights strengthens and affirms what is already inherent in the common law constitution. Moreover, because this understanding of constitutional rights judging builds on past practice in common law adjudication,[144] it accounts for the basic path determinacy of common law methodology that environmental Charter rights proponents have thus far ignored.

We know now that context-sensitive interpretation is essential to common law methodology; it is thus inappropriate (indeed impossible) to detail the content of a constitutional norm, such as a right to a healthy environment, in the abstract. The content of that right must be developed incrementally, in the context of specific claims of environmental harm, and through the democratic deliberations that take place within each of the relevant public institutions. However, we are now in a position to highlight how the public-justification conception of the rule of law can play a constructive and supportive role in making Boyd's central aims realisable. Moreover, we will see that the requirement of public justification can do so in a way that avoids the dichotomies that have undermined existing environmental rights claims.

Recall from section I above Boyd's argument that a right to a healthy environment would have the effect of levelling the playing field in public decision-making. Boyd has intuited that there must be a middle ground between the idea that a constitutional environmental right acts as a trump card and the idea that environmental rights are just one of many interests to be taken into account in an act of political balancing,[145] but he has not elaborated the methodology by which this 'levelling' would take place.

The public-justification conception of law helps us understand what this legal middle ground might look like. For one, the common law requirement of public justification is largely commensurate with the so-called 'procedural' components of environmental rights. Written guarantees of access to information about environmental decision-making, participation and access to justice all serve to strengthen and inform the common law commitment to fairness in the environmental context. More importantly, however, the public-justification conception does not risk the pernicious effects of the process/substance distinction. Publicly justified decisions are those that result from a fair process.

Importantly, a fair process, on this view, is itself substantive.[146] It is a process that is respectful of the legal subject's status as a responsible agent who is a participant in the ongoing interpretive project of elaborating the constitutional norm of a 'healthy environment'. Thus, as we saw in chapter seven

[144] See above ch 4, section I.

[145] Boyd, *The Right to a Healthy Environment* (above n 9) 22–23.

[146] See, eg, M Aronson, 'The Growth of Substantive Review: The Changes, Their Causes and Their Consequences' in Bell et al (eds), *Public Law Adjudication* (above n 36) 119–20 and 122–23 (on an Australian judicial trend of increasingly substantive procedural requirements).

in the wind turbine context, even procedural matters such as evidentiary tests must be interpreted and administered consistently with the subject's capacity for reasoning with the law. Furthermore, a fair process is one that ensures the possibility of influencing the outcome. As we saw in chapter six with the National Energy Board, a predetermined outcome turns the process into a sham, and a sham process patently undermines the commitment to a conception of the rule of law that protects the individual's status as a responsible agent. Under the public-justification conception, procedural and substantive environmental rights cannot be bifurcated. The content of procedural rights is necessarily informed by the substantive end of facilitating active participation in ensuring a healthy environment.

When grounded in the requirement of public justification, a right to a healthy environment would help 'level the playing field'. It would not provide a trump card against other interests, but it would require public decision-makers to approach decisions with the appropriate rights frame in mind. Rather than engaging in an abstract act of balancing environmental and economic interests or seeking to promote overall welfare, public decision-makers would have to engage in a context-sensitive analysis of the rights claimed and whether their infringement can be justified.[147] In other words, they would have to engage in an exercise of proportionality.[148] Public decisions that are not framed in this way—ie, that fail to acknowledge the legally protected right at stake and explain why an interference with that right is justified—do not comply with the rule-of-law requirement of public justification.[149] In this way, constitutional rights adjudication is not fundamentally different from rule-of-law requirements of any exercise of public power. A constitutional right, enshrined in a written bill of rights, intensifies the burden of justification but does not change the basic obligation on public officials to demonstrate that their decisions are reflective of fundamental constitutional principles.

Recall Boyd's second principal claim, that a constitutional right to a healthy environment will equip judges with novel judicial remedies. A constitutional right would enable judges to strike down non-compliant legislation and enforce a doctrine of non-regression that would facilitate

[147] E Fox-Decent and EJ Criddle, 'Interest-Balancing vs Fiduciary Duty: Two Models for National Security Law' (2012) 13 *German Law Journal* 542–59.

[148] TRS Allan, *The Sovereignty of Law* (Oxford, Oxford University Press, 2013) 267.

[149] It is not necessary at this level of discussion to distinguish between a rights infringement and the justification of that infringement (ie, to distinguish between the enumerated Charter right and section 1). In substance, the analysis is never so clearly delineated, and the weighing of competing rights often factors into both stages of analysis: TRS Allan, 'Democracy, Legality and Proportionality' in G Huscroft, BW Miller and G Webber (eds), *Proportionality and the Rule of Law: Rights, Justification, Reasoning* (New York, Cambridge University Press, 2014) 208; D Dyzenhaus 'Proportionality and Deference in a Culture of Justification' in Huscroft et al (eds), *Proportionality and the Rule of Law* (above) 251.

a ratcheting up of environmental protection, rather than backsliding. His argument engages the familiar critiques of social and economic rights—the *democratic*, *competence* and *remedial* critiques—that have impeded the development of social and economic rights protection under section 7 of the Charter.

The public-justification conception of the rule of law explains how courts play a legitimate role in adjudicating constitutional rights, even social and economic rights which bring to the surface these three objections to judicial rights adjudication. First, as we have already seen in this half of the book, the public-justification conception is inherently democratic in at least two ways. It requires that public decision-makers justify their decisions on the basis of public-regarding reasons that those affected can reasonably accept. Public decisions therefore have a deliberative-democratic pedigree. They are not simply the result of majoritarian rule; they are the result of a process of reasoning that takes seriously the interests of those who are subject to the exercise of public authority. Moreover, the requirement of public justification enables the direct participation of affected individuals in the project of articulating and redefining the reasons for public decisions. They participate in this deliberative exercise when they contest public decisions before reviewing institutions.[150] And they participate in this deliberative exercise when those reviewing institutions demand that public decision-makers adopt more deliberative decision-making procedures. The requirement of public justification is thus compatible with the radically inclusive and deliberative democracy that green political theorists argue is necessary for furthering environmental protection and environmental justice.[151]

Under the public-justification conception of the rule of law, courts, or other reviewing institutions, do not simply substitute their own views about constitutional interpretation. Rather, they demand that legislatures and administrative decision-makers give clear and public accounts of the rights engaged by their decisions and why any infringement of those rights is justified in the circumstances. It may be the case that the complex and polycentric nature of social and economic rights means that the burden of justification is much more demanding. But rather than undermine the requirement of public justification, this fact should highlight its essentialness in a deliberative democracy.[152] Understood as part of the project of public justification,

[150] For a nice discussion of the agency-enhancing potential of rights in a related context, see Hohmann, *The Right to Housing* (above n 80) 241–42 and 248; and Forst, *The Right to Justification* (above n 143) 194–98.

[151] See, eg, R Eckersley, *The Green State: Rethinking Democracy and Sovereignty* (Cambridge, MA, MIT Press, 2004) 96 and 135–38.

[152] Fredman, *Human Rights Transformed* (above n 32) 103. See also E Mureinik, 'Beyond a Charter of Luxuries: Economic Rights in the Constitution' (1992) 8 *South African Journal on Human Rights* 464, 472–73.

rights play a crucial role in steering public decision-making away from the power politics of interest group bargaining.[153] They do so by requiring *reasoned* public decisions—that is, decisions supported by reasons that those affected can actually accept as persuasive.

The requirement of public justification is also responsive to the competence critique because it does not assume that our institutions of government are fixed. Indeed, as we have seen, public justification demands institutional creativity in the environmental context.[154] Any number of reforms might respond to concerns about judicial competence, including, as we have already seen, specialised appeals tribunals or perhaps specialised scientific amicus curiae for judicial review at higher courts.[155]

Finally, the remedial critique of positive rights loses its force when adjudication takes place against the backdrop of the public-justification conception of the rule of law. On this view, a court's remedial role is to initiate a more deliberative-democratic process, not provide the answer itself.[156] Indeed, in a detailed empirical review of the method of rights adjudication at the Supreme Court of Canada, Robert Leckey has observed a notable shift in this remedial direction. Leckey has noted that striking down legislation is only one of many nuanced remedies in the Court's constitutional toolbox.[157] Even when the Court is prepared to strike down legislation, it will often temporarily suspend its decision in order to re-engage the legislature in the process of interpreting and administering its constitutional obligations.[158]

Many difficult questions about environmental rights adjudication are unanswered and, indeed, unanswerable in the absence of constitutional text and specific claims grounded and argued in context. But it is clear that the public-justification conception of the rule of law transcends the indefensible positive/negative rights distinction in a way that nonetheless takes seriously the concerns about constitutional rights adjudication that underlie this distinction.

The result of grounding a Charter right to a healthy environment in a rule-of-law conception of public justification is likely something less potent than Boyd has in mind. The requirement of public justification would not

[153] Fredman, *Human Rights Transformed* (above n 32) 39.

[154] See above ch 5.

[155] See, eg, Hayward, *Constitutional Environmental Rights* (above n 1) 110–14; and Fredman, *Human Rights Transformed* (above n 32) ch 5 (on the particular institutional innovations in the Indian courts).

[156] Fredman, *Human Rights Transformed* (above n 32) 224–25.

[157] Leckey, *Bills of Rights* (above n 119) 96–97, 99–100 and 118. But see at 120, where he discusses the propensity of the Court to offer advice on proportionate measures, which departs from the notion that courts do not step into the legislature's role.

[158] Ibid, 103 and 158 (although he is critical of this shift in remedial practice, arguing that it dilutes individual rights protection).

permit courts to themselves set ambitious emissions targets to enforce the right to a healthy environment when the government fails to do so.[159] The requirement might make legislative 'roll-backs' in environmental protection more apparent and therefore more difficult to justify if challenged in court, but it is hard to see how a non-regression doctrine could be transplanted directly into constitutional rights adjudication in Canada.[160]

At the same time, the public-justification conception of the rule of law provides a coherent theory for constitutional environmental rights adjudication. It provides a path for distinguishing between Boyd's examples of laudably bold judges taking a stand against major development[161] or exercising extensive supervisory powers[162] and the illegitimate judicial activists that he condemns.[163] It explains Boyd's seemingly contradictory statements that in constitutional rights adjudication, judges can 'apply the principles of proportionality and reasonableness in cases that call for a careful balance'[164] while also 'tip[ping] this balance' in favour of sustainability.[165] Moreover, the public-justification conception explains—rather than asserts—how the intervention of courts in environmental decision-making is a 'legitimate supervisory role in constitutional democracies such as Canada'.[166]

IV. CONCLUSION

Novel constitutional text, despite the virtue of its constitutional status, does not come with a ready-made theory of law that facilitates its robust interpretation and enforcement. The objective of this chapter has been to show that the proposal for a Canadian Charter right to a healthy environment is in need of a supportive conception of the rule of law. It requires this rule-of-law theory because, currently, the same formalist assumptions that underpin Canadian administrative law review of environmental decisions resurface in related areas of constitutional adjudication. In the context of section 7 adjudication, the formal conception of the rule of law appears in the form of strong distinctions between process and substance, and between positive and negative rights. I have argued that these distinctions operate to undermine environment-related claims under section 7 and threaten to do so even if a stand-alone environmental right were enshrined within the Canadian Charter.

[159] Boyd, *The Right to a Healthy Environment* (above n 9) 20 (arguing that a constitutional right could provide a safety net).
[160] Ibid, 20–21 and 95.
[161] Ibid, 102.
[162] Ibid, 99.
[163] Ibid, 105–6.
[164] Ibid, 30.
[165] Ibid, 22.
[166] Ibid, 29.

The chapter has argued that the public-justification conception of the rule of law offers a more promising foundation for constitutional environmental rights jurisprudence. It draws on the idea that constitutional law ought to be understood as 'administrative law writ large'. On this view, constitutional rights adjudication is a fundamentally interpretive and collaborative democratic project in which all institutions of government share the obligation of interpreting both statutory *and* constitutional text against a rule-of-law backdrop that is protective and facilitative of individual agency. The existence of a written bill of rights, or a constitutional environmental right in particular, serves to strengthen the requirement of public justification by identifying the fundamental interests at stake in any public decision. It is this understanding of the rule of law that makes constitutional environmental rights adjudication theoretically defensible and makes its promise of greater environmental protection practically realisable in light of the conditions of the environmental emergency.

* * *

The second half of this book has introduced and begun to unpack the implications of a rule-of-law theory that follows from understanding environmental issues as an ongoing emergency. The complex, continually evolving and often pressing nature of environmental issues—just like that of conventional, political emergencies—lends itself to a concentration of power with the executive branch of government. This Part of the book has argued for a conception of the rule of law that takes seriously this complexity while also setting out the conditions under which the exercise of public power will have both democratic and legal authority. These are the conditions that follow from the requirement of public justification. Publicly justified decisions protect and facilitate the legal subject's autonomy, understood as her rational and self-determining capacity to participate actively in environmental governance.

I have defended the public-justification conception of the rule of law on the grounds that it protects individuals from arbitrary public decisions and facilitates their active participation in the project of interpreting the content of the law. I do not base my argument on any guarantee that the public-justification conception will lead to better environmental protection or help us avoid environmental catastrophe, as I do not have the empirical evidence to support this claim (and it is unlikely to be available). However, existing deliberative-democratic literature suggests that there is reason to think this conception will put us on a trajectory for improved environmental decision-making.[167] As we have seen, public justification requires

[167] See, eg, J Steele, 'Participation and Deliberation in Environmental Law: Exploring a Problem-Solving Approach' (2001) 21 *Oxford Journal of Legal Studies* 415; KH Whiteside,

institutional decision-making conditions that broaden the range of views considered; it requires decision-makers to offer responsive reasons; and it requires processes for contestation that force us to reconsider and revise our public decisions. This is a significant departure from existing institutional arrangements that tend to privilege industry involvement in administrative decision-making and to limit the opportunities for review. It is also a significant departure from the formal conception of law, which rests on unrealistic assumptions about the ability of the legislature and courts to constrain administrative powers and makes no room for the evolution of common law principles to account for the special challenges of environmental issues.

The requirement of public justification, as we have seen, lies at the interface of common law constitutionalism and deliberative democracy. It requires that public officials publicly justify their decisions on the basis of core common law principles, informed and elaborated, as they need to be, by deliberative-democratic theory so as to protect the legal subject's distinctive status in the challenging context of environmental decision-making. The conditions presented by the environmental emergency require creative institutional design to enable the public justification of complex, technical and polycentric environmental decisions. These instances of creative institutional design ought to be understood not as aberrations or departures from the rule of law but rather as more comprehensive expressions of the commitment to the public justification of a range of public decisions than often fall outside or on the margins of conventional administrative law doctrine.

We have also seen that environmental principles such as precaution and sustainable development play a unique and important role in modifying common law principles to preserve the status of the legal subject as a responsible agent in the environmental context. When interpreted in line with deliberative-democratic theory, these principles operate to broaden the range of those whose interests must be taken into account in the decision-making process, to destabilise overreliance on expert discourses and to force public decision-makers to account for their treatment of uncertainty in environmental decision-making.

Public justification demands that every exercise of public authority entails context-sensitive interpretation and administration of the law. Not only must the reasons of public officials be thorough and directed to those affected; they must reveal also an attentiveness to the status of legal subjects as responsible agents. On this view, there is no such thing as the plain meaning of a statute or a generalisable range of reasonable outcomes. Legislation

Precautionary Politics: Principle and Practice in Confronting Environmental Risk (Cambridge, MA, MIT Press, 2006) 126–32; and H Landemore, *Democratic Reason: Politics, Collective Intelligence and the Rule of the Many* (Princeton, Princeton University Press, 2013). But see also HS Richardson, *Democratic Autonomy: Public Reasoning about the Ends of Policy* (Oxford, Oxford University Press, 2002) 77–78.

is always enacted, interpreted and administered against a common law backdrop that is protective of individual agency. Publicly-justified administration is what is constitutive of legality. Moreover, this conception leads to an understanding of constitutional law as 'administrative law writ large' in which written constitutional rights serve to amplify the rule-of-law requirement of public justification.

The fact is public officials always have two options available to them.[168] They can interpret the law in a formal manner, which can lead to a vicious cycle in which the rule of law is understood as increasingly hollow in difficult cases. Alternatively, they can approach their roles purposively with the understanding that they are part of a collaborative endeavour of ensuring their decisions are publicly justified. No theory or institutional design can protect against the former option. Maintaining the rule of law, understood as public justification, is always in the hands of its participants, public officials and the public alike. The public-justification conception of the rule of law that has been elaborated in this book is an aspirational account. Nevertheless, it is both critical and constructive. It allows us to pinpoint institutions that have fallen down in their commitment to public justification and provides a basis for legal recourse, such as judicial review But it also allows us to highlight those that have done particularly well. The existence of these latter examples shows that the commitment to a democratic conception of the rule of law is achievable, if not ever perfectible.

The constitution of the environmental emergency reveals that the emergency is, in fact, the norm in environmental law. I mean this in two distinct senses. First is the very real sense in which the possibility of a disaster is inherent in environmental issues, though it is not always possible to foresee. This requires public officials to take this possibility seriously. The extent to which they do so is revealed through their commitment to public justification. The second sense is that the environmental emergency leads us to a constitution of democratic legality that is fit for all issues at all times. This democratic conception of the rule of law requires environmental law to be more deliberative, more reasoned and always mindful of our vulnerability to catastrophic environmental harm. Carl Schmitt famously said that in times of emergency, the state remains while law recedes. My aim has been to show that a democratic conception of the rule of law can answer Schmitt's challenge by unifying the means and ends of democracy through a commitment to law that can only recede if we the people let it.

[168] D Dyzenhaus, 'Cycles of Legality in Emergency Times' (2007) 18 *Public Law Review* 165.

Bibliography

Academic References

Ackerman, BA, 'The Emergency Constitution' (2004) 113 *Yale Law Journal* 1029.

Agamben, G, *State of Exception*, K Attell (trans) (Chicago, University of Chicago Press, 2005).

Allan, TRS, *Constitutional Justice: A Liberal Theory of the Rule of Law* (Oxford, Clarendon Press, 2001).

—— 'Democracy, Legality and Proportionality' in G Huscroft, BW Miller and G Webber (eds), *Proportionality and the Rule of Law: Rights, Justification, Reasoning* (New York, Cambridge University Press, 2014) 205.

—— *The Sovereignty of Law* (Oxford, Oxford University Press, 2013).

Aronson, M, 'The Growth of Substantive Review: The Changes, Their Causes and Their Consequences' in J Bell et al (eds), *Public Law Adjudication in Common Law Systems: Process and Substance* (Oxford, Hart Publishing, 2016) 113.

Arthurs, HW, 'Rethinking Administrative Law: A Slightly Dicey Business' (1979) 17 *Osgoode Hall Law Journal* 1.

Auld, G, *Constructing Private Governance: The Rise and Evolution of Forest, Coffee, and Fisheries Certification* (New Haven, Yale University Press, 2014).

Auld, G and Gulbrandsen, LH, 'Transparency in Nonstate Certification: Consequences for Accountability and Legitimacy' (2010) 10 *Global Environmental Politics* 97.

Barstow, DM and Hawke, LD, 'Sustainable Development' in D Bodansky, J Brunnee and E Hey (eds), *The Oxford Handbook of International Environmental Law* (Oxford, Oxford University Press, 2008) 613.

Beck, U, *Risk Society*, M Ritter (trans) (London, Sage Publications, 1992).

Bell, S and Hindmoor, A, 'Governance Without Government? The Case of the Forest Stewardship Council' (2012) 90 *Public Administration* 144.

Benidickson, J, 'The Great Lakes and the Mediterranean Sea: Ecosystem-Management and Sustainability in the Context of Economic Integration' (2004) 14 *Journal of Environmental Law and Practice* 107.

Benidickson J et al, *Practicing Precaution and Adaptive Management: Legal, Institutional and Procedural Dimensions of Scientific Uncertainty Final Report* (Ottawa, University of Ottawa Institute of the Environment, 2005).

Bickel, A, *The Least Dangerous Branch: The Supreme Court at the Bar of Politics* (New Haven, Yale University Press, 1986).

Black, J, 'Constructing and Contesting Legitimacy and Accountability in Polycentric Regulatory Regimes' (2008) 2 *Regulation & Governance* 137.

—— 'Proceduralizing Regulation: Part I' (2000) 20 *Oxford Journal of Legal Studies* 597.

—— 'Proceduralizing Regulation: Part II' (2001) 21 *Oxford Journal of Legal Studies* 33.

Bodansky, D, 'Deconstructing the Precautionary Principle' in DD Caron and HN Scheiber (eds), *Bringing New Law to Ocean Waters* (Leiden, Martinus Nijhoff Publishers, 2004) 381.

—— 'Scientific Uncertainty and the Precautionary Principle' (1991) 33(7) *Environment: Science and Policy for Sustainable Development* 4.

Bosselmann, K, *The Principle of Sustainability: Transforming Law and Governance* (Aldershot, Ashgate, 2008).

Boyd, D, 'Elements of an Effective Environmental Bill of Rights' (2015) 27 *Journal of Environmental Law and Practice* 201.

—— *The Environmental Rights Revolution: A Global Study of Constitutions, Human Rights, and the Environment* (Vancouver, University of British Columbia Press, 2012).

—— *The Right to A Healthy Environment: Revitalizing Canada's Constitution* (Vancouver, University of British Columbia Press, 2012).

—— 'Sustainability Law: (R)Evolutionary Directions for the Future of Environmental Law' (2004) 14 *Journal of Environmental Law and Practice* 357.

—— *Unnatural Law: Rethinking Canadian Environmental Law and Policy* (Vancouver, University of British Columbia Press, 2003).

Braithwaite, J and Ayres, I, *Responsive Regulation* (Oxford, Oxford University Press, 1992).

Brandes, OM et al, *At a Watershed: Ecological Governance and Sustainable Water Management in Canada* (Victoria, POLIS Project on Ecological Governance, 2005).

Buck, T, Kirkham, R and Thompson, B, *The Ombudsman Enterprise and Administrative Justice* (Farnham, Ashgate, 2011).

Cartier, G, 'Le principe de précaution et la déférence judiciare en droit administratif' (2002) 43 *Les Cahiers de droit* 79.

—— 'Procedural Fairness in Legislative Functions: The End of Judicial Abstinence?' (2003) 53 *University of Toronto Law Journal* 217.

Cashore, B, 'Legitimacy and the Privatization of Environmental Governance: How Non-state Market-Driven (NSMD) Governance Systems Gain Rule-Making Authority' (2002) 15 *Governance* 503.

Chalifour, N, 'A (Pre) Cautionary Tale about the Kearl Oil Sands Decision: The Significance of *Pembina Institute for Appropriate Development, et al v Canada (Attorney-General)* for the Future of Environmental Assessment' (2009) 5 *McGill International Journal Sustainable Development Law* 251.

Coglianese, C and Lazer, D, 'Management-Based Regulation: Prescribing Private Management to Achieve Public Goals' (2003) 37 *Law and Society Review* 691.

Coglianese, C, Nash, J and Olmstead, T, 'Performance-Based Regulation: Prospects and Limitations in Health, Safety and Environmental Protection' (2003) 55 *Administrative Law Review* 704.

Cohen, J, 'Deliberation and Democratic Legitimacy' in J Bonham and W Rehg (eds), *Deliberative Democracy: Essays on Reason and Politics* (Cambridge, MA, Massachusetts Institute of Technology Press, 1997) 67.

Cole, DH, 'Judging the Next Emergency: Judicial Review and Individual Rights in Times of Crisis' (2003) 101 *Michigan Law Review* 2565.

Cole, L, 'The Fight for the Great Bear Rainforest: How a "War in the Woods" Led to a Landmark Agreement to Save Three Million Hectares of Rainforest on the Northwest Coast of Canada' (2017) 89(4) *Geographical Magazine* 36.

Collins, L, 'An Ecologically Literate Reading of the Canadian Charter of Rights and Freedoms' (2009) 26 *Windsor Review of Legal and Social Issues* 7.

—— 'Tort, Democracy and Environmental Governance: The Case of Non-enforcement' (2007) 15 *Tort Law Review* 107.

—— 'The United Nations, Human Rights and the Environment' in A Grear and LJ Kotzé (eds), *Research Handbook on Human Rights and the Environment* (Cheltenham, Edward Elgar Publishing, 2015) 219.

Collins, LM and Boyd, DR, 'Non-regression and the *Charter* Right to a Healthy Environment' (2016) 29 *Journal of Environmental Law and Practice* 286.

Cordonier Segger, MC and Khalfan, A, *Sustainable Development Law: Principles, Practices, and Prospects* (Oxford, Oxford University Press, 2004).

Coyle, S and Morrow, K, *The Philosophical Foundations of Environmental Law: Property, Rights and Nature* (Oxford, Hart Publishing, 2004).

Craig, P, 'Formal and Substantive Conceptions of the Rule of Law' (1997) 3 *Public Law* 467.

—— *Public Law and Democracy in the United Kingdom and the United States of America* (Oxford, Clarendon Press, 1990).

Criddle, EJ, 'Mending Holes in the Rule of (Administrative) Law' (2010) 104 *Northwestern University Law Review* 1271.

Croley, SP, 'Theories of Regulation: Incorporating the administrative process' (1998) *Columbia Law Review* 1.

Daly, P, 'The Scope and Meaning of Reasonableness Review' (2015) 52 *Alberta Law Review* 799.

—— 'Struggling Towards Coherence in Canadian Administrative Law? Recent Cases on Standard of Review and Reasonableness' (2016) 62 *McGill Law Journal* 527.

De Burca, G, 'New Governance and Experimentalism: An Introduction' (2010) 2010 *Wisconsin Law Review* 227.

De Marco, JV and Muldoon, P, *Environmental Boards and Tribunals in Canada: A Practical Guide* (Markham, LexisNexis Canada, 2011).

Dellert, LH, 'Sustained Yield: Why Has It Failed to Achieve Sustainability?' in C Tollefson (ed), *The Wealth of Forests* (Vancouver, University of British Columbia Press, 1998) 255.

Dershowitz, AM, *Why Terrorism Works: Understanding the Threat, Responding to the Challenge* (New Haven, Yale University Press, 2002).

Devine-Wright, P, 'Public Engagement with Large-Scale Renewable Energy Technologies: Breaking the Cycle of NIMBYism' (2011) 2 *WIREs Climate Change* 19.

Dewey, J, *The Public and Its Problems* (Chicago, Swallow Press, 1954).

Dicey, AV, *An Introduction to the Study of the Law of the Constitution*, 10th edn (Toronto, MacMillan Canada, 1959).

Dobson, A, *Green Political Thought*, 3rd edn (New York, Routledge, 2000).

Doelle, M, 'CEAA 2012: The End of Federal EA as We Know It?' (2013) 24 *Journal of Environmental Law and Practice* 1.

Doelle, M and Tollefson, C (eds), *Environmental Law Cases and Materials*, 2nd edn (Toronto, Carswell, 2013).

Dorf, MC and Sabel, CF, 'A Constitution of Democratic Experimentalism' (1998) *Columbia Law Review* 267.

Dryzek, JS, *The Politics of the Earth: Environmental Discourses*, 3rd edn (Oxford, Oxford University Press, 2013).

Dunlap, RE and McCright, AM, 'Climate Change Denial: Sources, Actors and Strategies' in C Lever-Tracy (ed), *Routledge Handbook of Climate Change and Society* (Abingdon, Routledge, 2010) 240.

Dupuy, J, 'Complexity and Uncertainty: A Prudential Approach to Nanotechnology' in Health and Consumer Protection Directorate General of the European Commission (ed), *Nanotechnologies: A Preliminary Risk Analysis on the Basis of a Workshop Organized in Brussels, 1–2 March 2004* (Brussels, European Commission, 2004) 71.

Dyzenhaus, D, 'Accountability and the Concept of (Global) Administrative Law' (2009) 2009 *Acta Juridica* 3.

—— 'Constituting the Rule of Law: Fundamental Values in Administrative Law' (2002) 27 *Queen's Law Journal* 445.

—— *The Constitution of Law: Legality in a Time of Emergency* (Cambridge, Cambridge University Press, 2006).

—— 'Cycles of Legality in Emergency Times' (2007) 18 *Public Law Review* 165.

—— 'Deference, Security and Human Rights' in B Goold and L Lazarus (eds), *Security and Human Rights* (Oxford, Hart Publishing, 2007).

—— 'Dignity in Administrative Law: Judicial Deference in a Culture of Justification' (2012) 17 *Review of Constitutional Studies* 87.

—— 'Emergency, Liberalism, and the State' (2011) 9 *Perspectives on Politics* 69.

—— 'Law as Justification: Etienne Mureinik's Conception of Legal Culture' (1998) 14 *South African Journal on Human Rights* 11.

—— *Legality and Legitimacy: Carl Schmitt, Hans Kelsen and Hermann Heller in Weimar* (Oxford, Clarendon Press, 1997).

—— 'The Legitimacy of Legality' (1996) 46 *University of Toronto Law Journal* 129.

—— 'The Permanence of the Temporary: Can Emergency Powers Be Normalized?' in RJ Daniels, P Macklem and K Roach (eds), *The Security of Freedom: Essays on Canada's Anti-Terrorism Bill* (Toronto, University of Toronto Press, 2001) 21.

—— 'The Politics of Deference: Judicial Review and Democracy' in M Taggart (ed), *The Province of Administrative Law* (Oxford, Hart Publishing, 1997) 279.

—— 'Preventive Justice and the Rule-of-Law Project' in A Ashworth, L Zedner and P Tomlin (eds), *Prevention and the Limits of the Criminal Law* (Oxford, Oxford University Press, 2013).

—— 'Proportionality and Deference in a Culture of Justification' in G Huscroft, BW Miller and G Webber (eds), *Proportionality and the Rule of Law: Rights, Justification, Reasoning* (New York, Cambridge University Press, 2014) 234.

Dyzenhaus, D and Fox-Decent, E, 'Rethinking the Process/Substance Distinction: Baker v. Canada' (2001) 51 *University of Toronto Law Journal* 193.

Eckersley R, *The Green State: Rethinking Democracy and Sovereignty* (Cambridge, MA, Massachusetts Institute of Technology Press, 2004).

Edgar, A, 'Procedural Fairness for Decisions Affecting the Public Generally: A Radical Step towards Public Consultation?' (2014) 33 *University of Tasmania Law Review* 56.

Edmundson, WA, 'State of the Art: The Duty of Obey the Law' (2004) 10 *Legal Theory* 215.

Ellis, J, 'Constitutionalization of Nongovernmental Certification Programs' (2013) 20 *Indiana Journal of Global Legal Studies* 1035.

—— 'Overexploitation of a Valuable Resource? New Literature on the Precautionary Principle' (2006) 17 *European Journal of International Law* 445.

Elster, J, 'The Market and the Forum: Three Varieties of Political Theory' in J Bonham and W Rehg (eds), *Deliberative Democracy: Essays on Reason and Politics* (Cambridge, MA, Massachusetts Institute of Technology Press, 1997) 3.

Emond, DP, '"Are We There Yet?" Reflections on the Success of the Environmental Law Movement in Ontario' (2008) 46 *Osgoode Hall Law Journal* 219.

—— 'The Greening of Environmental Law' (1990) 36 *McGill Law Journal* 742.

Estlund, D, *Democratic Authority: A Philosophical Framework* (Princeton, Princeton University Press, 2008).

Evans, JM, 'The Triumph of Reasonableness: But How Much Does It Really Matter?' 27 *Canadian Journal of Administrative Law and Practice* 101.

Farber, DA, 'Probabilities Behaving Badly: Complexity Theory and Environmental Uncertainty' (2003) 37 *UC Davis Law Review* 145.

Fatovic, C, *Outside the Law: Emergency and Executive Power* (Baltimore, John Hopkins University Press, 2009).

Ferejohn, J and Pasquino, P, 'The Law of Exception: A Typology of Emergency Powers' (2004) 2 *International Journal of Constitutional Law* 210.

Findlay, CS et al, 'Sustainability Lost: Comments on "Planning for a Sustainable Future: A Federal Sustainable Development Strategy for Canada"' (2010) 22 *Journal of Environmental Law and Practice* 77.

Fischer, F, 'Environmental Regulation and Risk–Benefit Analysis: From Technical to Deliberative Policy Making' in R Paehlke and D Torgerson (eds), *Managing Leviathan: Environmental Politics and the Administrative State*, 2nd edn (Peterborough, Broadview Press, 2005) 59.

Fisher, DE, *Australian Environmental Law: Norms, Principles and Rules*, 3rd edn (Pyrmont, Thomson Reuters, 2014).

Fisher, E, 'Drowning by Numbers: Standard-Setting in Risk Regulation and the Pursuit of Accountable Public Administration' (2000) 20(1) *Oxford Journal of Legal Studies* 109.

—— 'Environmental Law as "Hot" Law' (2013) 25 *Journal of Environmental Law* 347.

—— 'Review: Laws of Fear: Beyond the Precautionary Principle' (2006) *Modern Law Review* 288.

—— *Risk Regulation and Administrative Constitutionalism* (Oxford, Hart Publishing, 2007).

Fisher, E and Harding, R, 'The Precautionary Principle and Administrative Constitutionalism: The Development of Frameworks for Applying the Precautionary Principle' in E Fisher, J Jones and R von Schomberg (eds), *Implementing the Precautionary Principle: Perspectives and Prospects* (Cheltenham, Edward Elgar, 2006) 113.

Fisher, E et al, 'Maturity and Methodology: Starting a Debate about Environmental Law Scholarship' (2009) 21 *Journal of Environmental Law* 213.

Flood, CM, '*Chaoulli*'s Legacy for the Future of Canadian Health Care Policy' (2006) 44 *Osgoode Hall Law Journal* 273.

Fluker, S and Stacey, J, 'The Basics of Species at Risk Legislation in Alberta' (2012) 50 *Alberta Law Review* 95.

Forcese, C and Roach, K, 'Stumbling Toward Total Information Awareness: The Security of Canada Information Sharing Act' (2015) 12 *Canadian Privacy Law Review* 65.

Forst, R, *The Right to Justification: Elements of a Constructivist Theory of Justice*, J Flynn (trans) (New York, Columbia University Press, 2011).

Fox-Decent, E, *Sovereignty's Promise: The State as Fiduciary* (Oxford, Oxford University Press, 2011).

Fox-Decent, E and Criddle, EJ, 'Interest-Balancing vs Fiduciary Duty: Two Models for National Security Law' (2012) 13 *German Law Journal* 542.

Fox-Decent, E and Pless, A, 'The Charter and Administrative Law: Cross-Fertilization or Inconstancy?' in CM Flood and L Sossin (eds), *Administrative Law in Context* 2nd edn (Toronto, Emond Montgomery, 2013) 407.

Fredman, S, *Human Rights Transformed: Positive Rights and Positive Duties* (Oxford, Oxford University Press, 2008).

Freeman, J, 'The Private Role in the Public Governance' (2000) 75 *New York University Law Review* 543.

Freeman, J and Farber, DA, 'Modular Environmental Regulation' (2005) *Duke Law Journal* 795.

Fuller LL, 'The Forms and Limits of Adjudication' (1978) *Harvard Law Review* 353.

—— *The Morality of Law*, rev edn (New Haven, Yale University Press, 1969).

Gallie, WB, 'Essentially Contested Concepts' (1955) 56 *Proceedings of the Aristotelian Society* 167.

Gibson, RB, 'Beyond the Pillars: Sustainability Assessment as a Framework for Effective Integration of Social, Economic and Ecological Considerations in Significant Decision-Making' (2006) 8 *Journal of Environmental Assessment Policy and Management* 259.

Godard, O, 'The Precautionary Principle and Catastrophism on Tenterhooks: Lessons from a Constitutional Reform in France' in E Fisher, J Jones and R von Schomberg (eds), *Implementing the Precautionary Principle: Perspectives and Prospects* (Cheltenham, Edward Elgar, 2006) 63.

Green, A, 'Regulations and Rule Making: The Dilemma of Delegation' in C Flood and L Sossin (eds), *Administrative Law in Context*, 2nd edn (Toronto, Emond Montgomery Publications, 2013) 125.

Gross, O, 'Chaos and Rules: Should Responses to Violent Crises Always Be Constitutional?' (2003) 112 *Yale Law Journal* 1011.

—— 'Extra-Legality and the Ethic of Political Responsibility' in VV Ramraj (ed), *Emergencies and the Limits of Legality* (Cambridge, Cambridge University Press, 2008) 60.

Gross, O and Aolain, FN, *Law in Times of Crisis* (New York, Cambridge University Press, 2006).

Gunningham, N, 'Environment Law, Regulation and Governance: Shifting Architectures' (2009) 21 *Journal of Environmental Law* 179.

Gunningham, N, Grabosky, P and Sinclair, D, *Smart Regulation: Designing Environmental Policy* (Oxford, Clarendon Press, 1998).

Gutmann, A, 'Democracy' in R Goodin, P Pettit and T Pogge (eds), *A Companion to Contemporary Political Philosophy* (Oxford, Blackwell Publishing, 2007) 521.

Gutmann, A and Thompson, D, *Why Deliberative Democracy?* (Princeton, Princeton University Press, 2004).

Habermas, J, *Between Facts and Norms*, W Rehg (trans) (Cambridge, MA, Massachusetts Institute of Technology Press, 1996).

—— 'Habermas on Law and Democracy: Reply to Symposium Participants' (1996) 17 *Cardozo Law Review* 1477.

Haddock, M, 'Environmental Tribunals in British Columbia' (University of Victoria Environmental Law Centre, 2011).

Handl, G, 'Human Rights and Protection of the Environment' in A Eide, C Krause and A Rosas (eds), *Economic, Social and Cultural Rights: A Textbook*, 2nd edn (Dordrecht, M Nijhoff, 2001) 303.

Hania, P, 'Climate Change and the Protection of Drinking Water in Ontario: An Opportunity to Adopt Adaptive Management?' (2011) 22 *Journal of Environmental Law and Practice* 167.

Hayward, T, *Constitutional Environmental Rights* (Oxford, Oxford University Press, 2005).

Heinzerling, L, 'The Environment' in P Cane and M Tushnet (eds), *The Oxford Handbook of Legal Studies* (Oxford, Oxford University Press, 2003) 701.

—— 'Pragmatists and Environmentalists' (2000) 113 *Harvard Law Review* 1421.

Hohmann, J, *The Right to Housing: Law, Concepts, Possibilities* (Oxford, Hart Publishing, 2013).

Holder, J, 'New Age: Rediscovering Natural Law' (2000) 53 *Current Legal Problems* 151.

Holley, C and Gunningham, N, 'Natural Resources, New Governance and Legal Regulation: When Does Collaboration Work?' (2011) 24 *New Zealand Universities Law Review* 309.

Holling, CS, 'Resilience and Stability of Ecological Systems' (1973) 4 *Annual Review of Ecology and Systematics* 1.

—— 'Understanding the Complexity of Economic, Ecological, and Social Systems' (2001) 4(5) *Ecosystems* 390.

Holling, CS and Gunderson, LH, 'Resilience and Adaptive Cycles' in LH Gunderson and CS Holling (eds), *Panarchy: Understanding Transformations in Human and Natural Systems* (Washington, DC, Island Press, 2002).

Honig, B, *Emergency Politics: Paradox, Law, Democracy* (Princeton, Princeton University Press, 2009).

Howlett, M, Rayner, J and Tollefson, C, 'From Government to Governance in Forest Planning? Lessons from the Case of the British Columbia Great Bear Rainforest Initiative' (2009) 11 *Forest Policy and Economics* 383.

Hughes, EL, 'Fishwives and Other Tails: Ecofeminism and Environmental Law' (1995) 8 *Canadian Journal of Women and the Law* 502.

Hughes, EL and Iyalomhe, D, 'Substantive Environmental Rights in Canada' (1998) 30 *Ottawa Law Review* 229.

Huscroft, G, 'From Natural Justice to Fairness: Thresholds, Content, and the Role of Judicial Review' in C Flood and L Sossin (eds), *Administrative Law in Context*, 2nd edn (Toronto, Emond Montgomery, 2012) 147.

Jacobs, L, 'Tribunal Independence and Impartiality: Rethinking the Theory after *Bell* and *Ocean Port Hotel* — A Call for Empirical Analysis' in L Jacobs and

AL Mactavish (eds), *Dialogue Between Courts and Tribunals: Essays in Administrative Law and Justice (2001–2007)* (Montreal, Les Editions Themis, 2008) 43.
Jasanoff, S, *The Fifth Branch: Science Advisors as Policymakers* (Cambridge, MA, Harvard University Press, 1990).
—— 'A Living Legacy: The Precautionary Ideal in American Law' in JA Tickner (ed), *Precaution: Environmental Science and Preventive Public Policy* (Washington, DC, Island Press, 2003) 227.
—— 'Technologies of Humility: Citizen Participation in Governing Science' (2003) 41(3) *Minerva* 223.
Jones, J and Bronitt, S, 'The Burden and Standard of Proof in Environmental Regulation: The Precautionary Principle in an Australian Administrative Context' in E Fisher and J Jones (eds), *Implementing the Precautionary Principle: Perspectives and Prospects* (Cheltenhem, Edward Elgar Pub, 2006) 137.
Jowell, J, 'The Democratic Necessity of Administrative Justice' (2006) *Acta Juridica* 13.
Karkkainen, BC, 'Collaborative Ecosystem Governance: Scale, Complexity, and Dynamism' (2002) 21 *Virginia Environmental Law Journal* 189.
—— 'Information-Forcing Regulation and Environmental Governance' in G De Burca and J Scott (eds), *Law and New Governance in the EU and the US* (Oxford, Hart Publishing, 2006) 293.
—— '"New Governance" in the Great Lakes: Has Its Time Arrived?' (2006) 2006 *Michigan State Law Review* 1249.
Kingsbury, B, Stewart, RB and Krisch, N, 'The Emergence of Global Administrative Law' (2005) 68 *Law and Contemporary Problems* 15.
Keyes, JM, *Executive Legislation*, 2nd edn (Toronto, LexisNexis Canada, 2010).
Kong, H, 'Election Law and Deliberative Democracy: Against Deflation' (2015) 9 *Journal of Parliamentary and Political Law* 35.
Koskenniemi, M, 'Constitutionalism as Mindset: Reflections on Kantian Themes about International Law and Globalization' (2007) 8 *Theoretical Inquiries in Law* 9.
—— 'The Fate of Public International Law: Between Technique and Politics' (2007) 70 *Modern Law Review* 1.
Kysar, DA, *Regulating from Nowhere: Environmental Law and the Search for Objectivity* (New Haven, Yale University Press, 2010).
Landemore, H, *Democratic Reason: Politics, Collective Intelligence and the Rule of the Many* (Princeton, Princeton University Press, 2013).
Lafferty, WM, 'The Politics of Sustainable Development: Global Norms for National Implementation' (1996) 5 *Environmental Politics* 185.
Lahey, W and Doelle, M, 'Negotiating the Interface of Environmental and Economic Governance: Nova Scotia's Environmental Goals and Sustainable Prosperity Act' (2012) 35 *Dalhousie Law Journal* 1.
Landis, JM, *The Administrative Process* (New Haven, Yale University Press, 1938).
Lauta, KC, *Disaster Law* (Abingdon, Routledge, 2015).
Lazar, NC, *States of Emergency in Liberal Democracies* (New York, Cambridge University Press, 2009).
Leckey, R, *Bills of Rights in the Common Law* (Cambridge, Cambridge University Press, 2015).

—— *Contextual Subjects: Family, State, and Relational Theory* (Toronto, University of Toronto Press, 2008).

Lee, MG, 'How Tribunals and Appeal Boards are Contributing to Advances in Environmental Laws' (2014) 26 *Journal of Environmental Law and Practice* 249.

Lee, M and Abbott, C, 'The Usual Suspects? Public Participation under the Aarhus Convention' (2003) 66 *Modern Law Review* 80.

Levinson, S, 'Constitutional Norms in a State of Permanent Emergency' (2005) 40 *Georgia Law Review* 699.

Levy, R, 'The Law of Deliberative Democracy: Seeding the Field' (2013) 12(4) *Election Law Journal* 355.

Lewans, M, 'Deference and Reasonableness Since Dunsmuir' (2012) 38 *Queen's Law Journal* 59.

Liston, M, 'Evolving Capacities: The BC Representative for Children and Youth as a Hybrid Model of Oversight' in L Jacobs and S Baglay (eds), *The Nature of Inquisitorial Processes in Administrative Regimes* (Aldershot, Ashgate Publishing, 2013).

Liston, M, 'Transubstantiation in Canadian Public Law: Processing Substance and Instantiating Process' in J Bell et al (eds), *Public Law Adjudication in Common Law Systems* (Oxford, Hart Publishing, 2016) 213.

Lobel, O, 'The Renew Deal: The Fall of Regulation and the Rise of Governance in Contemporary Legal Thought' (2004) 89 *Minnesota Law Review* 342.

Locke, J, *Two Treatises of Government* (London, 1764).

Loughlin, M, 'Procedural Fairness: A Study of the Crisis in Administrative Law Theory' (1978) 28 *University of Toronto Law Journal* 215.

Lowe, V, 'Sustainable Development and Unsustainable Arguments' in A Boyle and D Freestone (eds), *International Law and Sustainable Development: Past Achievements and Future Challenges* (Oxford, Oxford University Press, 1999) 19.

Lyon, JN, 'Constitutional Validity of Sections 3 and 4 of the Public Order Regulations, 1970' (1972) 18 *McGill Law Journal* 136.

M'Gonigle, M and Ramsey, P, "Greening Environmental Law: From Sectoral Reform to Systemic Re-formation' (2004) 14 *Journal of Environmental Law and Practice* 333.

Macdonald, RA, 'The Acoustics of Accountability: Towards Well-Tempered Tribunals' in A Sajó (ed), *Judicial Integrity* (Leiden, Martinus Nijhoff Publishers, 2004) 142.

—— 'A Theory of Procedural Fairness' (1981) 1 *Windsor Yearbook of Access to Justice* 3.

Main, TO, 'The Procedural Foundation of Substantive Law' (2010) 87 *Washington University Law Review* 801.

Malcai, O and Levine-Schnur, R, 'Which Came First, the Procedure or the Substance? Justificational Priority and the Substance-Procedure Distinction' (2014) 34 *Oxford Journal of Legal Studies* 1.

Marx, A and Cuypers, D, 'Forest Certification as a Global Environmental Governance Tool: What Is the Macro-effectiveness of the Forest Stewardship Council?' (2010) 4 *Regulation and Governance* 408.

Marx, H, 'The Apprehended Insurrection of October 1970 and the Judicial Function' (1972) 7 *University of British Columbia Law Review* 55.

Mashaw, JL, 'Accountability and Institutional Design: Some Thoughts on the Grammar of Governance' in M Dowdle (ed), *Public Accountability: Designs, Dilemmas and Experiences* (Cambridge, Cambridge University Press, 2006) 115.

Mason, M, 'Information Disclosure and Environmental Rights: The Aarhus Convention' (2010) 10 *Global Environmental Politics* 10.

McCormick, JP, 'The Dilemma of Dictatorship: Carl Schmitt and Constitutional Emergency Powers' in D Dyzenhaus (ed), *Law as Politics: Carl Schmitt's Critique of Liberalism* (Durham, Duke University Press, 1998) 217.

McDonald, L, 'The Rule of Law in the "New Regulatory State"' (2004) 33 *Common Law World Review* 197.

McGarrity, K and Hoberg, G, 'The Beetle Challenge: An Overview of the Mountain Pine Beetle Epidemic and Its Implications' (University of British Columbia Forest Policy Resources, 2005).

McGee, G, Cullen, A and Gunton, T, 'A New Model for Sustainable Development: A Case Study of the Great Bear Rainforest Regional Plan' (2010) 12 *Environment, Development, and Sustainability* 745.

McLeod-Kilmurray, H and Smith, G, 'Unsustainable Development in Canada: Environmental Assessment, Cost–Benefit Analysis, and Environmental Justice in the Tar Sands' (2010) 21 *Journal of Environmental Law and Practice* 65.

Meidinger, E, 'The Administrative Law of Global Private-Public Regulation: The Case of Forestry' (2006) 17 *European Journal of International Law* 47.

Mitchell, K and D'Onofrio, Z, 'Environmental Injustice and Racism in Canada: The First Step is Admitting we have a Problem' (2016) 29 *Journal of Environmental Law and Practice* 305.

Mullan, DJ, 'Judicial Review of Executive Decision-Making: Evolving Concepts of Responsibility' (1993) 19 *Queen's Law Journal* 137.

Mureinik, E, 'Beyond a Charter of Luxuries: Economic Rights in the Constitution' (1992) 8 *South African Journal on Human Rights* 464.

Nelson, H, 'Does a Crisis Matter? Forest Policy Responses to the Mountain Pine Beetle Epidemic in British Columbia' (2007) 55 *Canadian Journal of Agricultural Economics* 459.

Nikiforuk, A, *Empire of the Beetle* (Vancouver, Greystone Books, 2011).

Nollkaemper, A, 'International Adjudication of Global Public Goods: The Intersection of Substance and Procedure' (2012) 23(3) *European Journal of International Law* 769.

Nowlan, L, 'CPR for Canadian Rivers: Law to Conserve, Protect, and Restore Environmental Flows in Canada' (2012) 23 *Journal of Environmental Law and Practice* 237.

Orts, EW, 'Reflexive Environmental Law' (1995) 89 *Northwestern University Law Review* 1227.

Overdest, C and Zeitlin, J, 'Assembling an Experimentalist Regime: Transnational Governance Interactions in the Forest Sector' (2014) 8 *Regulation and Governance* 22.

Paquerot, S, 'Environmental Concerns and the Interdependence of Human Rights: A Path to Political Responsibility?' in M Jackman and B Porter (eds), *Advancing Social Rights in Canada* (Toronto, Irwin Law, 2014) 365.

Pardy, B, 'Abstraction, Precedent, and Articulate Consistency: Making Environmental Decisions' (1998) 34 *California Western Law Review* 427.

—— *Ecolawgic: The Logic of Ecosystems and the Rule of Law* (Kingston, Fifth Forum Press, 2015).

—— 'Environmental Assessment and Three Ways Not to Do Environmental Law' (2010) 21 *Journal of Environmental Law and Practice* 139.

—— 'Environmental Law and the Paradox of Ecological Citizenship: The Case for Environmental Libertarianism' (2005) 33 *Environments* 25.

—— 'The Pardy–Ruhl Dialogue on Ecosystem Management, Part V: Discretion, Complex-Adaptive Problem Solving and the Rule of Law' (2008) 25 *Pace Environmental Law Review* 341.

—— 'In Search of the Holy Grail of Environmental Law: A Rule to Solve the Problem' (2005) 1 *McGill International Journal of Sustainable Development Law and Policy* 29.

Pardy, B and Stoehr, A, 'The Failed Reform of Ontario's Mining Laws' (2012) 23 *Journal of Environmental Law* 1.

Parkinson, J and Mansbridge, J, *Deliberative Systems: Deliberative Democracy at the Large Scale* (Cambridge, Cambridge University Press, 2012).

Peel, J, *The Precautionary Principle in Practice* (Annandale, Federation Press, 2005).

Pedersen, L, 'Allowable Annual Cuts in British Columbia: The Agony and the Ecstasy', Jubilee Lecture at the University of British Columbia Faculty of Forestry (20 March 2003) [copy on file with the author].

Petrova, MA, 'NIMBYism Revisited: Public Acceptance of Wind Energy in the United States' (2013) 4 *WIREs Climate Change* 575.

Pettit, P, *Republicanism: A Theory of Freedom and Government* (Oxford, Oxford University Press, 1999).

Philippopoulos-Mihalopoulos, A, 'Looking for the Space Between Law and Ecology' in A Philippopoulos-Mihalopoulos (ed), *Law and Ecology: New Environmental Foundations* (London, Routledge, 2011) 1.

Poole, T, 'Constitutional Exceptionalism and the Common Law' (2009) 7 *International Journal of Constitutional Law* 247.

Posner, EA and Adrian, V, 'Accommodating Emergencies' (2003) *Stanford Law Review* 605.

—— *The Executive Unbound* (Oxford, Oxford University Press, 2010).

Pousette, J and Hawkins, C, 'An Assessment of Critical Assumptions Supporting the Timber Supply Modelling for Mountain-Pine-Beetle-Induced Allowable Annual Cut Uplift in the Prince George Timber Supply Area' (2006) 7 BC *Journal of Ecosystems and Management* 93.

Price, K, Roburn, A and MacKinnon, A, 'Ecosystem-Based Management in the Great Bear Rainforest' (2009) 258 *Forest Ecology and Management* 495.

Raitio, K and Saarikoski, H, 'Governing Old-Growth Forests: The Interdependence of Actors in Great Bear Rainforest in British Columbia' (2012) 25 *Society and Natural Resources: An International Journal* 900.

Rhodes, RAW, 'The New Governance: Governing without Government' (1996) 44 *Political Studies* 652.

Richardson, HS, *Democratic Autonomy: Public Reasoning About the Ends of Policy* (Oxford, Oxford University Press, 2002).

Roach, K, *The 9/11 Effect: Comparative Counter-terrorism* (Cambridge, Cambridge University Press, 2011).

Ross, A, 'Modern Interpretations of Sustainable Development' (2009) 36 *Journal of Law and Society* 32.
Rossiter, C, *Constitutional Dictatorship: Crisis Government in the Modern Democracies* (New Brunswick, Transaction Publishers, 2002).
Rubin, E, 'Law and Legislation in the Administrative State' (1989) 89 *Columbia Law Review* 369.
Rundle, K, *Forms Liberate: Reclaiming the Jurisprudence of Lon L Fuller* (Oxford, Hart Publishing, 2012).
Sabel, CF and Simon, WH, 'The Duty of Responsible Administration and the Problem of Police Accountability' (2016) 33 *Yale Journal on Regulation* 165.
—— 'Epilogue: Accountability Without Sovereignty' in G De Burca and J Scott (eds), *Law and New Governance in the EU and the US* (Oxford, Hart Publishing, 2006) 395.
Sabel, CF and Zeitlin, J, 'Learning from Difference: The New Architecture of Experimentalist Governance in the EU' (2008) 14 *European Law Journal* 271.
Salamon, LM, 'The New Governance and the Tools of Public Action: An Introduction' in LM Salamon (ed), *The Tools of Government: A Guide to the New Governance* (Oxford, Oxford University Press, 2002) 1.
Salazar, DJ and Alper, DK (eds), *Sustaining the Forests of the Pacific Coast: Forging Truces in the War in the Woods* (Vancouver, University of British Columbia Press, 2014).
Scheuerman, WE, *Between the Norm and the Exception* (Cambridge, Massachusetts Institute of Technology Press, 1994).
—— 'Carl Schmitt's Critique of Liberal Constitutionalism' (1996) 58 *The Review of Politics* 299.
—— 'The Economic State of Emergency' (2000) 21 *Cardozo Law Review* 1869.
—— 'Emergencies, Executive Power, and the Uncertain Future of US Presidential Democracy' (2012) 37 *Law & Social Inquiry* 743.
—— 'Survey Article: Emergency Powers and the Rule of Law After 9/11' (2006) 14 *Journal of Political Philosophy* 61.
Schmitt, C, *Political Theology*, G Schwab (trans) (Cambridge, MA, Massachusetts Institute of Technology Press 1985).
Scott, DN, 'Confronting Chronic Pollution: A Socio-legal Analysis of Risk and Precaution' (2008) 46 *Osgoode Hall Law Journal* 293.
—— 'When Precaution Points Two Ways: Confronting "West Nile Fever"' (2005) 20 *Canadian Journal of Law and Society* 27.
—— 'Situating Sarnia: "Unimagined Communities" in the New National Energy Debate' (2013) 25 *Journal of Environmental Law and Practice* 81.
Scott, J, 'Flexibility, "Proceduralization", and Environmental Governance in the EU' in G de Burca and J Scott (eds), *Constitutional Change in the EU: From Uniformity to Flexibility?* (Oxford, Hart Publishing, 2000) 259.
Seidenfeld, M, 'The Role of Politics in a Deliberative Model of the Administrative State' (2013) 81 *George Washington Law Review* 1397.
Shapiro, M, 'Administrative Law Unbounded: Reflections on Government and Governance' (2000) 8 *Indiana Journal of Global Legal Studies* 369.
Shelton, D, 'Developing Substantive Environmental Rights' (2010) 1 *Journal of Human Rights and the Environment* 89.

Shue, H, *Basic Rights* (Princeton, Princeton University Press, 1980).
Sossin, L, 'The McLachlin Court and the Promise of Procedural Justice' in DA Wright and AM Dodek (eds), *Public Law at the McLachlin Court: The First Decade* (Toronto, Irwin Law, 2011).
—— 'The Uneasy Relationship between Independence and Appointments in Canadian Administrative Law' in G Huscroft and Michael Taggart (eds), *Inside and Outside Canadian Administrative Law: Essays in Honour of David Mullan* (Toronto, University of Toronto Press, 2006) 50.
—— 'The Unfinished Project of *Roncarelli v Duplessis*: Justiciability, Discretion, and the Limits of the Rule of Law' (2010) 55 *McGill Law Journal* 661.
Stacey, J, 'The Environmental, Democratic and Rule-of-Law Implications of Harper's Environmental Assessment Legacy' (2016) 21 *Review of Constitutional Studies* 165.
—— 'The Environmental Emergency and the Legality of Discretion in Environmental Law' (2015) 52(3) *Osgoode Hall Law Journal* 983.
—— 'Preventive Justice, the Precautionary Principle and the Rule of Law' in T Tulich et al (eds), *Regulating Preventive Justice* (New York, Routledge, 2017) 23.
—— 'The Promise of the Rule of (Environmental) Law' (2016) 53(2) *Osgoode Hall Law Journal* 68.
—— 'The Rule-of-Law Underpinnings of Endangered Species Protection: *Minister of Fisheries and Oceans v David Suzuki Foundation*, 2012 FCA 40' (2014) 27 *Journal of Environmental Law and Practice* 57.
Stacey, J and Woolley, A, 'Can Pragmatism Function in Administrative Law?' (2016) 74 *Supreme Court Law Review* (2d) 211.
Steele, J, 'Participation and Deliberation in Environmental Law: Exploring a Problem-Solving Approach' (2001) 21 *Oxford Journal of Legal Studies* 415.
Stephenson, NL et al, 'Rate of Tree Carbon Accumulation Increases Continuously with Tree Size' (2014) 507 *Nature* 90.
Stewart, H, *Fundamental Justice: Section 7 of the Canadian Charter of Rights and Freedoms* (Toronto, Irwin Law, 2012).
Stewart, RB, 'The Reformation of American Administrative Law' (1975) *Harvard Law Review* 1667.
Stone, CD, 'Is There a Precautionary Principle?' (2001) 31 *Environmental Law Reporter* 10790.
Sunstein, CR, *Designing Democracy: What Constitutions Do* (Oxford, Oxford University Press, 2001).
—— *Laws of Fear: Beyond the Precautionary Principle* (Cambridge, Cambridge University Press, 2005).
—— 'On the Divergent American Reactions to Terrorism and Climate Change' (2007) 107 *Columbia Law Review* 503.
—— *Risk and Reason: Safety, Law, and the Environment* (Cambridge, Cambridge University Press, 2002).
—— 'Social and Economic Rights: Lessons from South Africa' (2000/2001) 11 *FORUM Constitutionnel* 123.
Swaigen, J and Woods, RE, 'A Substantive Right to Environmental Quality' in J Swaigen (ed), *Environmental Rights in Canada* (Toronto, Butterworths, 1981) 195.
Taggart, M, 'Proportionality, Deference, *Wednesbury*' (2008) *New Zealand Law Review* 423.

Taleb, NN, *The Black Swan*, 2nd edn (New York, Random House, 2010).

Talisse, RB, 'Deliberation' in D Estlund (ed), *The Oxford Handbook of Political Philosophy* (Oxford, Oxford University Press, 2012) 205.

Tarlock, AD, 'Is There a There There in Environmental Law' (2003) 19 *Journal of Land Use and Environmental Law* 213.

Teubner, G, 'Substantive and Reflexive Elements in Modern Law' (1983) 17 *Law and Society Review* 239.

Teubner, G and Beckers, A, 'Expanding Constitutionalism' (2013) 20 *Indiana Journal of Global Legal Studies* 523.

Theriault, S, 'The Food Security of the Inuit in Times of Change' (2011) 2 *Journal of Human Rights and the Environment* 136.

Tirone, S, Gallant, K and Sykes, K, 'Environmental Goals and Sustainable Prosperity Act and the People of the Province: EGSPA's Social Deficit' (2012) 35 *Dalhousie Law Journal* 71.

Tollefson, C, Gale, FP and Haley, D, *Setting the Standard: Certification, Governance and the Forest Stewardship Council* (Vancouver, University of British Columbia Press, 2008).

Tollefson, C and Thornback, J, 'Litigating the Precautionary Principle in Domestic Courts' (2008) 19 *Journal of Environmental Law and Practice* 33.

Tollefson, C, Zito, AR, Gale, FP, 'Symposium Overview: Conceptualizing New Governance Arrangements' (2012) 90 *Public Administration* 3.

Trubek, D and Trubek, L, 'New Governance and Legal Regulation: Complementarity, Rivalry, and Transformation' (2007) 13 *Columbia Journal of European Law* 539.

—— 'The World Turned Upside Down: Reflections on New Governance and the Transformation of Law' (2010) *Wisconsin Law Review* 719.

Tushnet, M, 'Emergencies and the Idea of Constitutionalism' in M Tushnet (ed), *The Constitution in Wartime* (Durham, Duke University Press, 2005) 39.

Underdal, A, 'Complexity and Challenges of Long-Term Environmental Governance' (2010) 20 *Global Environmental Change* 386.

Utzig, GF and Macdonald, DL, 'Citizens' Guide to Allowable Annual Cut Determinations' (BC Environmental Network Educational Foundation, 2000).

VanderZwaag, DL, 'The Precautionary Principle in Environmental Law and Policy: Elusive Rhetoric and First Embraces' (1998) 8 *Journal of Environmental Law and Practice* 355.

Varuhas, JNE, 'Against Unification' in H Wilberg and M Elliott (eds), *The Scope and Intensity of Substantive Review: Traversing Taggart's Rainbow* (Oxford, Hart Publishing, 2015) 91.

Viñuales, JE, 'The Rise and Fall of Sustainable Development' (2013) 22 *Review of European Community and International Environmental Law* 3.

Voigt, C, *Sustainable Development as a Principle of International Law* (Leiden, Martinus Nijhoff Publishers, 2009).

Waldron, J (ed) 'Is the Rule of Law an Essentially Contested Concept (in Florida)?' (2002) 21 *Law and Philosophy* 137.

—— *'Nonsense Upon Stilts': Bentham, Burke, and Marx on the Rights of Man* (London, Methuen, 1987).

Walter, E, 'From Civil Disobedience to Obedient Consumerism? Influences of Market-Based Activism and Eco-certification on Forest Governance' (2003) 41 *Osgoode Hall Law Journal* 531.

—— 'Decoding Codes of Practice: Approaches to Regulating the Ecological Impacts of Logging in British Columbia' (2005) 15 *Journal of Environmental Law and Practice* 143.

Walters, M, 'The Common Law Constitution in Canada: Return of *lex non scripta* as Fundamental Law' (2001) 51 *University of Toronto Law Journal* 91.

—— 'Dicey on Writing the Law of the Constitution' (2012) 32 *Oxford Journal of Legal Studies* 21.

—— 'Respecting Deference as Respect: Rights, Reasonableness and Proportionality in Canadian Administrative Law' in H Wilberg and M Elliott (eds), *The Scope and Intensity of Substantive Review: Traversing Taggart's Rainbow* (Oxford, Hart Publishing, 2015) 395.

Warren, ME and Pearse, H, *Designing Deliberative Democracy: The British Columbia Citizens' Assembly* (Cambridge, Cambridge University Press, 2008).

Whitaker, R, 'Keeping Up with the Neighbours? Canadian Responses to 9/11 in Historical and Comparative Context' (2003) 41 *Osgoode Hall Law Journal* 241.

Whitehead, RJ, Safranyik, L and Shore, TL, 'Preventative Management' in L Safranyik and B Wilson (eds), *Mountain Pine Beetle: A Synthesis of Biology, Management and Impacts on Lodgepole Pine* (Victoria, Pacific Forestry Centre, 2006) 173.

Whiteside, KH, *Precautionary Politics: Principle and Practice in Confronting Environmental Risk* (Cambridge, MA, Massachusetts Institute of Technology Press, 2006).

Wiersema, A, 'A Train without Tracks: Rethinking the Place of Law and Goals in Environmental and Natural Resources Law' (2008) 38 *Environmental Law* 1239.

Wilkinson, M, 'Three Conceptions of Law: Towards a Jurisprudence of Democratic Experimentalism' (2010) 2010 *Wisconsin Law Review* 673.

Williams, J, 'The Design of Performance-Based Natural Resource Regulation: Lessons from the BC Experience' (2005) 18 *Canadian Journal of Administrative Law and Practice* 61.

Willis, J, 'Three Approaches to Administrative Law: The Judicial, the Conceptual, and the Functional' (1935) 1 *University of Toronto Law Journal* 53.

Wilson, B, 'An Overview of the Mountain Pine Beetle Initiative' in TL Shore, JE Brooks and JE Stone (eds), *Mountain Pine Beetle Symposium: Challenges and Solutions* (Kelowna, Natural Resources Canada, 2003) 3.

Winfield, MS, 'Governance and the Environment in Canada From Regulatory Renaissance to "Smart Regulation"' (2007) 17 *Journal of Environmental Law and Practice* 69.

Wood, MC, '"You Can't Negotiate with a Beetle:" Environmental Law for a New Ecological Age' (2010) 50(1) *Natural Resources Journal* 167.

Wood, S, 'Environmental Management Systems and Public Authority in Canada: Rethinking Environmental Governance' (2002) 10 *Buffalo Environmental Law Journal* 129.

Wood, S, Tanner, G and Richardson, BJ, 'What Ever Happened to Canadian Environmental Law?' (2011) 37 *Ecology Law Quarter* 981.

Woolley, A, 'Legitimating Public Policy' (2008) 58 *University of Toronto Law Journal* 153.

World Commission on Environment and Development, *Our Common Future* (Oxford, Oxford University Press, 1987).

Wu, DWL, 'Embedding Environmental Rights in Section 7 of the Canadian Charter: Resolving the Tension between the Need for Precaution and the Need for Harm' (2014) 33 *National Journal of Constitutional Law* 191.

Wynne, B, 'May the Sheep Safely Graze? A Reflexive View of the Expert–Lay Knowledge Divide' in S Lash, B Szerszynski and B Wynne (eds), *Risk, Environment and Modernity: Towards a New Ecology* (London, SAGE Publications, 1998) 44.

—— 'Uncertainty and Environmental Learning' (1992) 2 *Global Environmental Change* 111.

Young, M, 'The Other Section 7' (2013) 62 *Supreme Court Law Review* (2d) 3.

—— 'The Right to Life, Liberty and Security of the Person' in P Oliver, P Macklem and N Des Rosier (eds), *Oxford Handbook of the Canadian Constitution* (Oxford Oxford University Press, 2017) 777.

—— 'Section 7 and the Politics of Social Justice' (2005) 38 *University of British Columbia Law Review* 539.

Zuckerman, I, 'One Law for War and Peace? Judicial Review and Emergency Powers between the Norm and the Exception' (2006) 13 *Constellations* 522.

Government Documents

Alberta Health Services, 'Cancer Incidence in Fort Chipewyan Follow-Up Report' (24 March 2014), www.albertahealthservices.ca/assets/healthinfo/poph/hi-poph-surv-cancer-overview-fort-chip-2014-03-24.pdf.

Berger, TR (Commissioner), 'Northern Frontier, Northern Homeland: The Report of the Mackenzie Valley Pipeline Inquiry, Volume 1' (Supply and Services Canada, 1977).

British Columbia Government, 'A Framework for Landscape Reserve Design in the Great Bear Rainforest' (4 July 2016), www.for.gov.bc.ca/tasb/slrp/lrmp/nanaimo/CLUDI/EBM_2016/GBR_LRD_Framework_Final_26july2016.pdf.

—— 'Great Bear Rainforest: Agreement Highlights', www.greatbearrainforest.gov.bc.ca/tile/gbr-agreement-highlights/.

British Columbia Legislative Assembly, *Official Reports of Debates (Hansard)*, 37th Parl, 2nd Sess, Vol 10 No 3 (6 Nov 2002).

British Columbia Ministry of Forests, 'Forest and Range Evaluation Program Logic Model' (2007), www.for.gov.bc.ca/ftp/hfp/external/!publish/frep/library/FREP_Logic_Model-oct2007.pdf.

—— 'Great Bear Rainforest Order' (January 2016) (BC Gaz I, Volume CLVI, No 4, 2016), www.for.gov.bc.ca/tasb/slrp/lrmp/nanaimo/CLUDI/GBR/Orders/GBR_LUO_Signed_29jan2016.pdf.

—— 'Timber Tenures in British Columbia: Managing Public Forests in the Public Interest' (June 2012), www.for.gov.bc.ca/ftp/hth/external/!publish/web/timber-tenures/timber-tenures-2006.pdf.

British Columbia Ministry of Forests and Range, 'Administrative Guide to Forest Stewardship Plans, Volume 1' (August 2009), www.for.gov.bc.ca/ftp/hth/external/!publish/Web/frpa-admin/agfsp/AGFSP-I-ver-2_1-final.pdf.

British Columbia Ministry of Forests, Lands and Natural Resources, 'A History of the Battle Against the Mountain Pine Beetle, 2000 to 2012' (2012), www.worldcat.org/title/history-of-the-battle-against-the-mountain-pine-beetle-2000-to-2012/oclc/812919832.

—— (Wildfire Management Branch), 'Discussion Paper: Proactive Wildfire Threat Reduction' (2014), docs.openinfo.gov.bc.ca/d63519414a_response_package_fnr-2014-00274.pdf.

Canadian Environmental Assessment Agency (CEAA), 'Backgrounder: Joint Review Panel for the Mackenzie Gas Project' (2005), www.ceaa.gc.ca/default.asp?lang=En&xml=99CDFBEE-2F6F-49BF-99C9-38AB1FF8C281.

Carr, J and McKenna, C (Ministers), 'Interim Measures for Pipeline Reviews' (Environment and Climate Change Canada and Natural Resources Canada Joint Backgrounder, January 2016), www.canada.ca/en/natural-resources-canada/news/2016/01/interim-measures-for-pipeline-reviews.html.

Commissioner of the Environment and Sustainable Development, '2011 December Report of the Commissioner of the Environment and Sustainable Development' (Government of Canada, 2011).

Council of the Federation, 'Canadian Energy Strategy' (2015).

Forest and Range Evaluation Program (FREP), '3 Year Strategic Plan: April 19, 2016' (British Columbia, 2016), www2.gov.bc.ca/assets/gov/farming-natural-resources-and-industry/forestry/frep/frep-docs/frep_3_year_strategic_plan_2016.pdf.

Forest Practices Board, 'Approval of Large Cutblocks to Control Mountain Pine Beetle in the Robson Valley', FPB/IRC/69 (British Columbia, 2002).

—— 'Balancing Community Needs and Pine Beetle Logging in the Robson Valley', FPB/IRC/78 (British Columbia, 2002).

—— 'Biodiversity Conservation During Salvage Logging in the Central Interior of BC', FPB/SR/35 (British Columbia, 2009).

—— 'Community Watersheds: From Objectives to Results on the Ground', FPB/SIR/40 (British Columbia, 2014).

—— 'A Decade in Review: Observations on Regulation of Forest and Range Practices in British Columbia', FPB/SR/46 (British Columbia, 2014).

—— 'The Effect of Mountain Pine Beetle Attack and Salvage Harvesting on Streamflows', FPB/SIR/16 (British Columbia, 2007).

—— 'Evaluating Mountain Pine Beetle Management in British Columbia', FPB/SR/20 (British Columbia, 2004).

—— 'Forest Stewardship Plans: Are They Meeting Expectations?' FPB/SIR/44 (British Columbia, 2015).

—— 'Monitoring Licensees' Compliance with Legislation', FPB/SIR/37 (British Columbia, 2013).

—— 'Nadina Beetle Treatments', FPB/IRC/99 (British Columbia, 2004).

—— 'Public Involvement in Forest Management Planning in BC', *Board Bulletin*, vol 15 (British Columbia, 2013).

—— 'A Review of the Early Forest Stewardship Plans Under FRPA', FPB/SR/28 (British Columbia, 2006).

—— 'Timber Harvesting in Beetle-Affected Areas', FPB/SR/44 (British Columbia, 2014).

Fulton, FJ (Commissioner), *Royal Commission of Inquiry on Timber and Forestry, 1909–1910* (Victoria, Government of British Columbia, 1910).

Health Canada, 'Wind Turbine Noise and Health Study: Summary of Results' (2014), www.hc-sc.gc.ca/ewh-semt/noise-bruit/turbine-eoliennes/summary-resume-eng.php.

Independent Electricity System Operator and Ontario Energy Board, 'Ontario Energy Report, October–December 2015: Electricity' (2015), www.ontarioenergyreport.ca/pdfs/5806_IESO_OntarioEnergyReportQ42016_Electricity_EN_FA.pdf.

Independent Expert Engineering Investigation and Review Panel, 'Report on Mount Polley Tailings Storage Facility Breach' (Government of British Columbia, 2015), www.mountpolleyreviewpanel.ca/final-report.

Intergovernmental Panel on Climate Change (IPCC), 'Climate Change 2014 Impacts, Adaption, and Vulnerability, A Summary for Policymakers' (2014) www.ipcc.ch/pdf/assessment-report/ar5/wg2/ar5_wgII_spm_en.pdf.

Major Projects Management Office (Canada), 'Interim Measures for Pipeline Reviews' (2017), mpmo.gc.ca/measures/254.

Nanwakolas Council, Coastal First Nations, and BC Ministry of Forests, Lands and Natural Resource Operations, 'Ecosystem Based Management on BC's Central and North Coast (Great Bear Rainforest): Implementation Update Report' (July 2012), coastfunds.ca/wp-content/uploads/2016/05/EBM_Implementation-Update_report_July-31_2012-1.pdf.

National Energy Board, '2014 Annual Report to Parliament' (Government of Canada, 2015).

National Energy Board (Gateway Panel), 'Considerations: Report of the Joint Review Panel for the Enbridge Northern Gateway Pipeline, Volume 2' (2013), publications.gc.ca/collections/collection_2014/one-neb/NE23-176-2013-2-eng.pdf.

National Round Table on the Environment and Economy and Public Policy Forum, 'Progress Through Process' (Government of Canada, 2012).

Natural Resources Canada, 'Responsible Resource Development' (2012), www.nrcan.gc.ca/media-room/backgrounders/2012/3269.

Pearse, PH (Commissioner), 'Timber Rights and Forest Policy in British Columbia' (Royal Commission on Forest Resources, 1976).

Priddle R (Chair), 'Report of the Public Review Panel on the Government of Canada Moratorium on Offshore Oil and Gas Activities in the Queen Charlotte Region of British Columbia' (Ministry of Natural Resources, 2004), www.nrcan.gc.ca/sites/www.nrcan.gc.ca/files/energy/pdf/eneene/sources/offext/pdf/prpcep-eng.pdf.

Privy Council Office of Canada, 'A Framework for the Application of Precaution in Science-Based Decision Making about Risk' (2003).

O'Connor, DR, 'Report of the Walkerton Inquiry' (Ontario Ministry of the Attorney General, 2002), www.archives.gov.on.ca/en/e_records/walkerton/index.html.

Oliver, J (Minister), 'An Open Letter from Natural Resources Minister Joe Oliver', *Globe and Mail* (9 January 2012), www.theglobeandmail.com/news/politics/an-open-letter-from-natural-resources-minister-joe-oliver/article4085663/.

Ontario Government, 'Source Protection' (2014, updated 2017), www.ontario.ca/environment-and-energy/source-protection.

Ontario Ministry of Energy, '2013 Long-Term Energy Plan' (2013), www.ontario.ca/document/2013-long-term-energy-plan.

Ontario Ministry of the Environment and Climate Change, 'Statement of Environmental Values' (no date), www.ebr.gov.on.ca/ERS-WEB-External/content/sev.jsp?pageName=sevList&subPageName=10001>.

Ontario Ministry of Natural Resources, 'Bats and Bat Habitats: Guidelines for Wind Power Projects' (July 2011), dr6j45jk9xcmk.cloudfront.net/documents/2719/stdprod-088155.pdf.

—— 'Bird and Bird Habitats: Guidelines for Wind Power Projects' (December 2011), dr6j45jk9xcmk.cloudfront.net/documents/2718/stdprod-071273.pdf.
Peel, AL (Chair), *The Future of Our Forests* (Victoria, Forest Resources Commission, 1991).
Public Safety Canada, 'Backgrounder: Security of Canada Information Sharing Act' (January 2015), www.canada.ca/en/news/archive/2015/01/security-canada-information-sharing-act.html.
Sloan, G (Commissioner), 'The Forest Resources of British Columbia' (Government of British Columbia, 1956).
Transportation Safety Board of Canada, 'Lac-Mégantic Runaway Train and Derailment Investigation Summary' (2014), www.tsb.gc.ca/eng/rapports-reports/rail/2013/r13d0054/r13d0054-r-es.asp.
Trudeau J, 'Minister of Fisheries, Oceans and the Canadian Coast Guard Mandate Letter', (November 2015), pm.gc.ca/eng/minister-fisheries-oceans-and-canadian-coast-guard-mandate-letter.
—— 'Prime Minister Justin Trudeau's Pipeline Announcement' (30 November 2016), pm.gc.ca/eng/news/2016/11/30/prime-minister-justin-trudeaus-pipeline-announcement.
United Nations Economic Commission for Europe and United Nations Environment Programme, 'Your Right to a Healthy Environment: A Simplified Guide to the Aarhus Convention on Access to Information, Public Participation in Decision-Making and Access to Justice in Environmental Matters' (July 2006), www.unece.org.
United States Environmental Protection Agency, 'Oil Cleanup Continues on Kalamazoo River', (June 2013), www.epa.gov/sites/production/files/2016-06/documents/enbridge-fs-20130624.pdf.
Yinka Dene Alliance, 'Save the Fraser Declaration' (May 2013), savethefraser.ca/Fraser-Declaration-May2013.pdf.
Yinka Dene Alliance and Save the Fraser, 'Save the Fraser Declaration: Solidarity Accord' (November 2013), savethefraser.ca/SolidarityAccord-nov2013.pdf.

Other References

'Blue Dot Campaign', David Suzuki Foundation, bluedot.ca.
Canadian Broadcasting Corporation (CBC), 'National Energy Board's Impartiality over Pipeline Decisions Questioned' (5 November 2014), www.cbc.ca/news/canada/new-brunswick/national-energy-board-s-impartiality-over-pipeline-decisions-questioned-1.2824507.
—— 'Study Suggests Link between Oilsands and Fort Chip Illnesses' (7 July 2014), www.cbc.ca/news/canada/edmonton/study-suggests-link-between-oilsands-and-fort-chip-illnesses-1.2698995.
Canadian Wind Energy Association, 'Wind Energy in Ontario' (2017), canwea.ca/wind-energy/ontario.
Commission for Environmental Cooperation. www.cec.org/.
Commissioner of the Environment and Sustainable Development Reports (Office of the Auditor General of Canada), www.oag-bvg.gc.ca/internet/English/parl_lp_e_901.html.

Dyer, C, 'Terror QC: More Will Quit Special Court', *Guardian* (20 December 2004), www.theguardian.com/politics/2004/dec/20/terrorism.humanrights.

Earth Charter Initiative, 'The Earth Charter', www.earthcharterinaction.org/content/pages/Read-the-Charter.html.

EcoJustice, 'Legal Backgrounder: The National Energy Board Act (1985)' (September 2012) www.ecojustice.ca/wp-content/uploads/2015/03/SEPT-2012_FINAL_NEBA-backgrounder.pdf.

Eliesen, M, 'View: Energy Executive Blasts Kind Morgan Review as "Fraudulent," Quits', *Tyee* (3 November 2014), thetyee.ca/Blogs/TheHook/2014/11/03/VIEW-energy-exec-blasts-Kinder-Morgan-quits.

Federation of British Columbia Naturalists, 'Memorandum of Fact and Law of the Applicant Federation of British Columbia Naturalists Carrying on Business as BC Nature' (*Gitxaala Nation et al v Canada (Attorney General & Minister of the Environment)*, 2016 FCA 187) (22 May 2015).

Forest Appeals Commission (British Columbia), www.fac.gov.bc.ca.

Forest Practices Board (British Columbia), www.bcfpb.ca.

Forest Stewardship Council, www.ic.fsc.org.

FSC-Watch, www.fsc-watch.com.

McCarthy, S, 'CSIS, RCMP Monitored Activist Groups before Northern Gateway Hearings', *Globe and Mail* (21 November 2013), www.theglobeandmail.com/report-on-business/industry-news/energy-and-resources/csis-rcmp-monitored-activists-for-risk-before-enbridge-hearings/article15555935/.

—— 'NEB to Assess Climate Issues in Energy East Pipeline Review', *Globe and Mail* (23 Aug 2017), beta.theglobeandmail.com/report-on-business/industry-news/energy-and-resources/energy-east-pipeline-review-topics-to-include-impact-of-emissions/article36069855/?ref=http://www.theglobeandmail.com.

McCulloch, M, Raynolds, M and Laurie, M, 'Life-Cycle Value Assessment of a Wind Turbine' (Pembina Institute, February 2000), www.pembina.org/reports/windlcva.pdf.

Morello, L and Climate Wire, 'Polar Ice Sheets Melting Faster than Predicted', *Scientific American* (March 2011), www.scientificamerican.com/article/polar-ice-sheets-melting-faster-than-predicted.

National Energy Board (NEB), www.neb-one.gc.ca.

Parfitt, B, 'Battling the Beetle: Taking Action to Restore British Columbia's Interior Forests' (Canadian Centre for Policy Alternatives, 2005).

Pembina Institute, 'Oil Sands Development and Climate Change: Implications for Canadians' (2006), www.pembina.org/reports/BC_oilgas06.pdf.

'PM Dumps Citizens' Assembly on Climate Change', *Australian* (7 October 2010), www.theaustralian.com.au/national-affairs/climate/pm-dumps-citizens-assembly-on-climate-change/story-e6frg6xf-1225935582575.

Pynn, L, 'Part Four: "It Looks Like Armageddon"', *Vancouver Sun* (10 September 2012), www.vancouversun.com/travel/Part+Four+looks+like+Armageddon/5814799/story.html.

—— 'Part One: In the Wake of a Plague', *Vancouver Sun* (10 September 2012), www.vancouversun.com/technology/Part+wake+plague/5800904/story.html.

Smith, M with Dobell, D, 'Place of Power: Lessons from the Great Bear Rainforest' (Tides Canada Foundation, 2010).

West Coast Environmental Law Association, 'Cutting up the Safety Net: Environmental Deregulation in British Columbia' (Vancouver, 2005).

Index